KNITTING FOR PLEASURE

KNITTING
FOR PLEASURE

MILDRED GRAVES RYAN

ILLUSTRATED BY MARTA CONE

DOUBLEDAY & COMPANY, INC., GARDEN CITY, NEW YORK

Book design: M. F. Gazze Nimeck
Title page and chapter ornament photo: E. A. Brozyna

Some material in this book has been previously published in *The Complete Encyclopedia of Stitchery* by Mildred Graves Ryan. Copyright © 1979 by Nelson Doubleday, Inc. Reprinted by permission.

Library of Congress Cataloging in Publication Data

Ryan, Mildred Graves, 1905–
Knitting for pleasure.

Includes index.
1. Knitting. I. Title.
TT820.R9 1983 746.9'2
ISBN 0-385-18510-3
Library of Congress Catalog Card Number 80–2870

Contents

Preface

To create something attractive brings a sense of pleasure and satisfaction. When the attractiveness of the individual is enhanced by the work, the enjoyment is increased. In order that no one may be denied this joy, this book has been written.

The appeal of knitting is wide-ranging. Through the ages, it has been a creative activity that has interested both men and women whether young or old, civilized or primitive, knowledgeable or ignorant, cultured or gauche. Persons of varying abilities, tastes, and interests can find enjoyment in knitting.

Because of this versatility, the material contained in this book presents information proceeding from the simple to the more complicated. For the beginner, it presents a step-by-step description in words and drawings of the basic procedures by which an interesting piece of knitting is made. It also offers suggestions for perfecting the skill, leading to more complicated and creative work.

The beginning chapters emphasize the need to understand the fundamentals. They lay the base for future work, whether one is an occasional or a constant knitter. They act as a reference for selecting designs and supplies, interpreting the specialized language, and manipulating yarn and needles in a graceful, steady manner.

Special concentration is placed on the two basic stitches. Interesting ways to combine them are mentioned with ideas for projects to create. One realizes that one can knit for a lifetime without feeling the need to progress beyond this stage.

For those who find greater satisfaction in solving problems and developing individuality, suggestions are offered. Fancy stitch patterns, design details, and hints on fitting are mentioned. A catalog of fashions with accompanying directions helps to make the information become a reality. The designs are diversified so there is something for everyone to knit and use.

Without the assistance and encouragement of friends and associates, it would have been impossible to prepare this book. I am also indebted to the many persons who supplied information concerning various types of yarns and supplies, and to those companies who granted permission to reproduce photographs and directions in this book.—M.G.R.

KNITTING FOR PLEASURE

Getting Started Right

Beginning to knit is an adventure with its ups and downs. At first you feel so clumsy. Hands and needles do not work in unison. Synchronization is a problem. But do not despair. Just keep trying. Soon fingers will move gracefully as the needles click in harmony. It is at this point that knitting becomes a pleasure.

To ensure this feeling, it is wise to start carefully. Perfect each procedure before trying another. You may think such a precaution is needless and plunge onward too soon. Please don't. It leads to mistakes and uneven knitting. Developing a good knitting technique is a must.

As you progress, you will realize that in some instances there is more than one way of achieving certain results. If you are wise, you will try each technique. In this way, you can decide which method you prefer.

BEGIN WITH THE YARN

Knitting seems easier if the yarn is wound in a ball. If your yarn is not in this form, take time to rewind it. This can be done in several ways. One method is mentioned here.

When converting a skein to a ball, ask someone to help you. It is easier to work with the opened skein slipped over another person's hands than over the back of a chair. Be careful not to stretch the yarn.

Winding a Ball

When using this method, the end of yarn with which you knit is on the outside of the ball. Begin by winding the yarn loosely around your fingers about a dozen times. Slip the loops from your fingers. Lay them in your left hand parallel to your fingers. This allows you to cross them as you continue to wrap the yarn around the fingers. Slip your fingers from under the yarn at intervals, turning the ball as it increases in size. Keeping your fingers under the yarn as you wind prevents the yarn from being stretched. Try to produce a perfectly round ball.

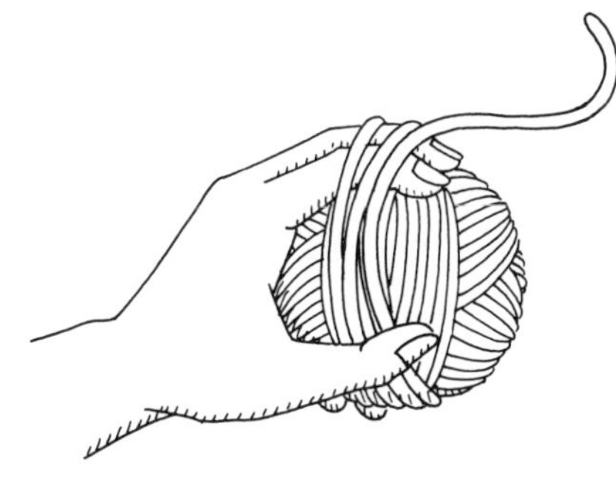

CASTING ON STITCHES

Now you are ready to knit. The first step in the procedure is to put the required number of stitches on a needle. For a first attempt, cast on about 20 stitches for a practice sample. This can be done in several ways. Two of them are described here.

Starting with a Slip Loop or Knot

To make the loop, hold the yarn between your thumb and first finger. Bring the ball end over the one between your fingers, forming a small circle. With a knitting needle, draw the yarn from the ball through the circle, forming a loop. Pull the ends of the yarn in opposite directions to decrease the size of the loop. This makes it fit the needle closely. You have made your first stitch.

The distance the loop is placed from the end of the yarn will depend on which method you are using for casting on stitches. Sometimes the slip knot is placed close to the end, and at other times some distance from it.

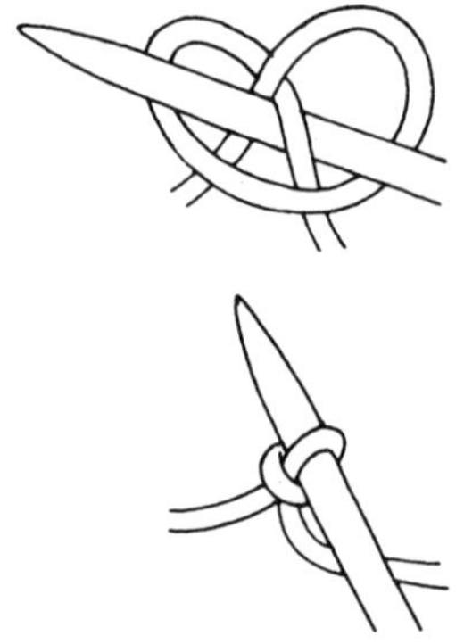

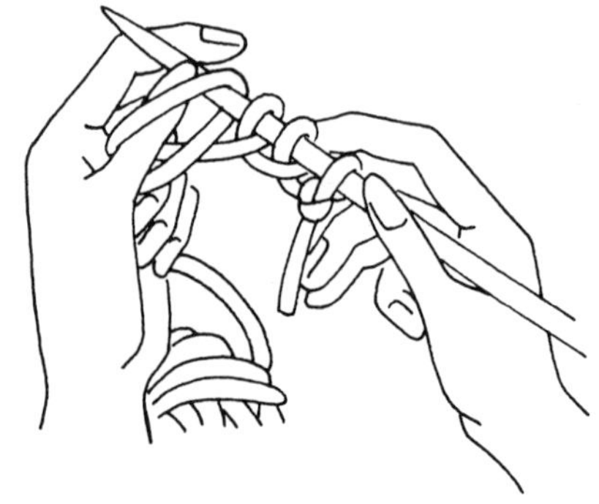

Casting On—Method 1

This is the easiest way to cast on stitches, but the stretchy, openwork finish does not offer the best results. The work is done with one needle and one end of yarn.

Start with a slip knot. Place it close to the end of the yarn and on the needle, which you hold in your right hand. Wrap the yarn around the thumb of your left hand, from right to left, so the yarn passes under and then over the thumb.

Insert the needle through the loop so it passes upward under the thumb. Slip your thumb from the loop, leaving the loop on the needle. Continue this procedure until the required number of stitches are on the needle. Keep the stitches close together by gently pulling the yarn after making each loop.

Casting On—Method 2

This manner of casting on stitches is referred to as knitting on stitches, which seems to describe the procedure accurately. Just as in knitting you need two needles and one end of yarn, as you do in casting on stitches this way. This method is used not only to begin a piece of knitting, but also when it is necessary to cast on stitches in the middle of a piece of knitting when you do not have a free end of yarn to use.

To start the procedure, make a slip knot close to the end of the yarn. Pass the needle in your left hand through the loop. Follow by inserting the needle in your right hand into the loop, but under the left-hand needle. Pass the yarn under and over the right-hand needle (A).

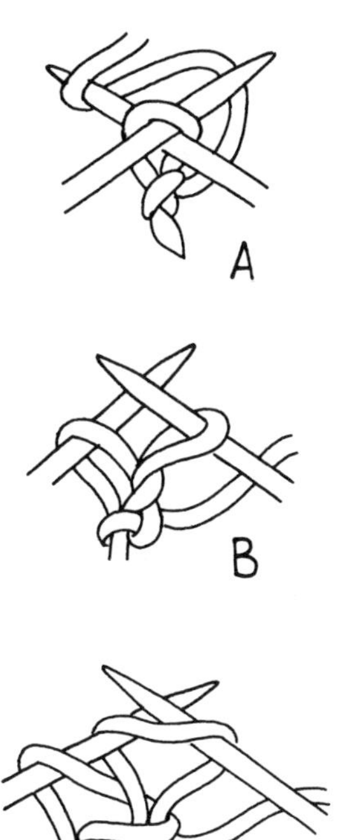

Draw the yarn through the loop. Be careful not to pull the loop off the needle as you do this. It should remain on the left-hand needle (B).

Now it is time to transfer the new loop (or stitch) from the right-hand needle to the left-hand one. As you do this, twist the stitch as you put it on the left-hand needle, keeping the right-hand needle on top of the left-hand one (C).

When the stitch is in place, remove the right-hand needle from the on-top position, then slip it under the left-hand needle and through the stitch. You are ready to knit the next stitch. Continue in this way until the required number of stitches have been cast on.

YOU'RE NOW READY TO KNIT

With the cast-on stitches in place, the actual knitting can start. You should not have any problem except finding a comfortable way to hold your needles and yarn so that you knit with an even tension. This is most important. Try the suggestions mentioned here. Then make your own decision.

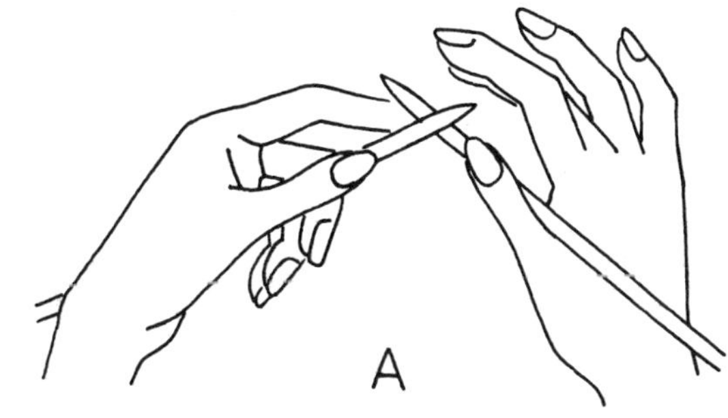

Holding the Needles

There are two possibilities for holding the needle in the right hand. The first way allows you to position the needle in your hand as if it were a pencil, between the thumb and first finger (A). For the other method, place the hand above the needle (B).

Whichever way you select for holding the right-hand needle, the left hand is placed above the needle, which is held between the thumb and first finger, as shown in both A and B.

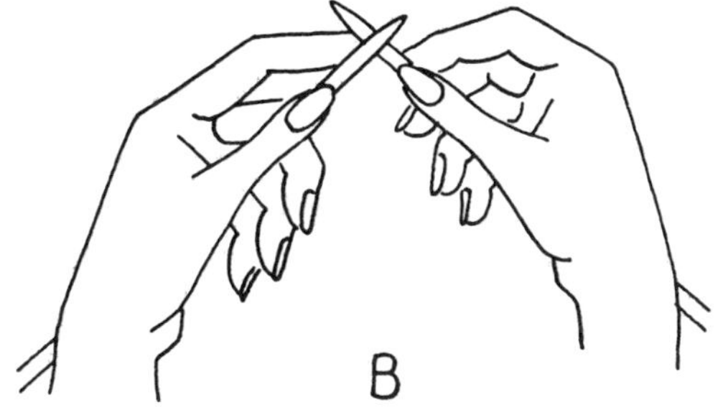

Positioning the Yarn

The position for holding the yarn also varies. Again, it is ease and comfort that influence the method you select. Always keep in mind that the tension on the yarn should allow an even flow. If this does not happen, the finished work will have an irregular, unattractive look.

You can hold the yarn in either the right or the left hand. When the yarn is held in the right hand, the technique is referred to as the *English method;* when in the left hand, as the *Continental method.* Holding the yarn in the left hand makes it easy for the left-hander to knit following the directions for a right-handed knitter.

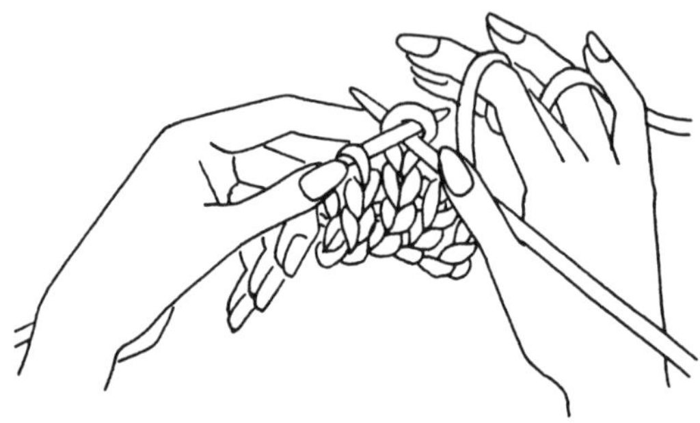

Yarn in the Right Hand (English Method). Thread the yarn over the first finger, under the middle one, and over the middle joint of the ring finger. Your first finger moves the yarn around the needle in your right hand to make a stitch, as the middle and ring fingers regulate the flow of yarn. Remember, the stitch should not be too tight or too loose. Also be sure to hold the yarn loose enough so it will not be stretched. As you practice, you will learn to adjust your fingers so that the yarn moves smoothly through them.

Yarn in the Left Hand (Continental Method). For this method, wrap the yarn twice around the first finger, as shown in the accompanying drawing. Control the yarn by holding it lightly against the palm with your little finger. The tension on the yarn is maintained by the first finger, which moves downward to form each stitch.

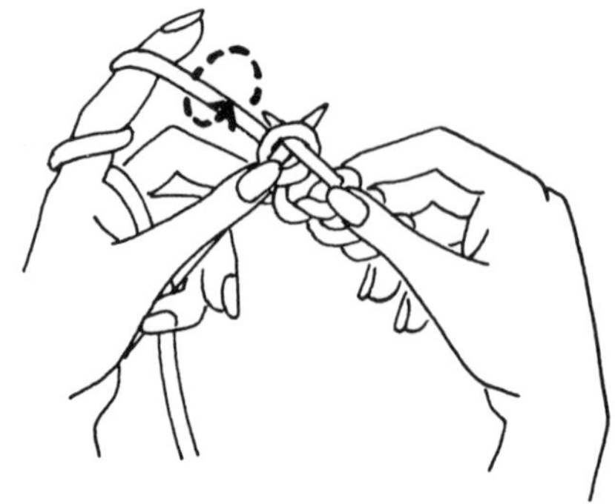

In order to make a stitch, insert the right-hand needle through the loop on the left-hand needle from front to back. Maneuver the needle around the yarn in order to draw the yarn through the loop. Unless you are left-handed, this method may seem to require more coordination of the fingers than when the yarn is held in the right hand.

Making a Knit Stitch—English Method

This is one of the two basic stitches and the first one for you to try. Fortunately, it is the easiest to make.

After you have cast on the required number of stitches, put the needle with the cast-on stitches in your left hand. Hold the needle near the tip between the thumb and first finger. Pick up the empty needle and strands of yarn with your right hand. Insert this needle in the first loop (or stitch) on the left-hand needle. Do this from the front, passing under the left-hand needle (A). Keep your hands close together with the yarn in back of the work. Notice that the tips of the two needles seem to rest on the first finger of the left hand.

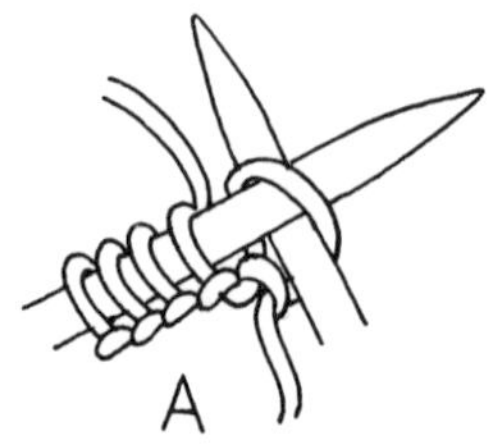

To make the stitch, wrap the yarn under and over the top of the right-hand needle, moving from right to left to right (B). Draw the yarn through the loop, making a new stitch on the right-hand needle (C). Be careful to pull through the working thread only. If you are not careful, you may pull through part of the stitch. If this occurs, you may find yourself with an extra stitch or a hole.

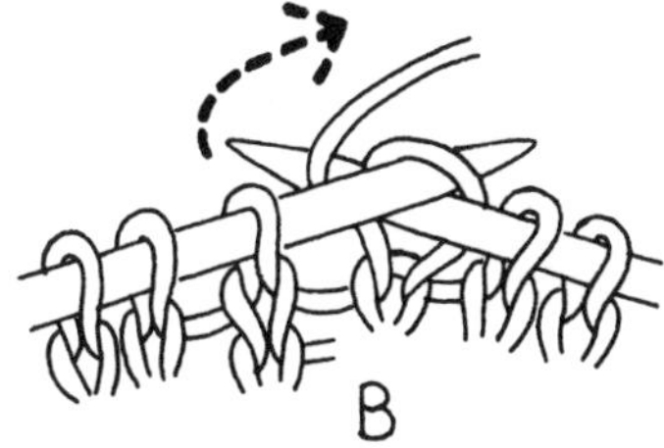

Slip the old stitch from the left-hand needle (D). You have made your first knit stitch and are ready to make another one.

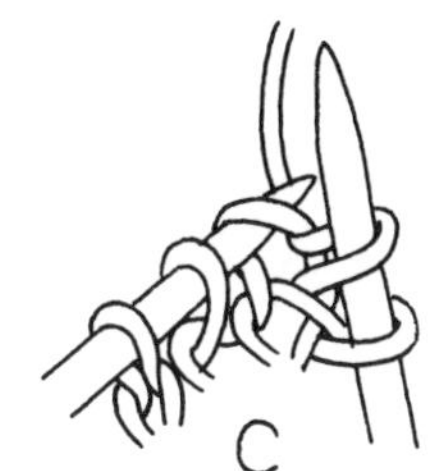

To do that, insert the needle in the stitch on the left-hand needle. Repeat the process you used for making the first stitch. It is best if the stitch you are working on is near the top of your needle. This keeps the work from stretching. Adjust the placement of your stitches continually to maintain this position.

Proceed in this way until all of the stitches have been removed from the left-hand needle. Check to be sure that the stitches do not twist incorrectly.

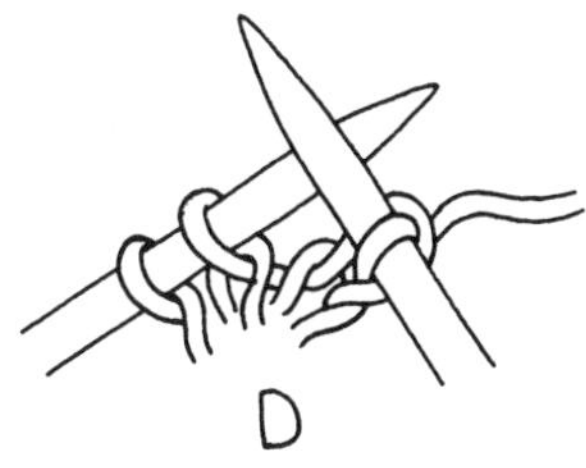

For the second row, transfer the needle with the stitches to your left hand, turning the work around. Insert the empty needle in the first stitch, ready to make a new stitch.

There are two ways to handle the knitting of this stitch. It can be knitted or simply slipped from the left needle to the right one. Knitting the first stitch makes a firm finish. Slipping the first stitch creates a chain stitch finish, which is often used when edges are to be joined or the stitches picked up. If you slip the stitch from the left needle to the right one, pass the yarn to the back of your work between the two needles. Remember, if you decide to knit the stitch, to keep the yarn in back.

After you form the first stitch, continue knitting as for the first row. When you complete the row, notice the raised ridge of stitches you have made. They are called garter stitches.

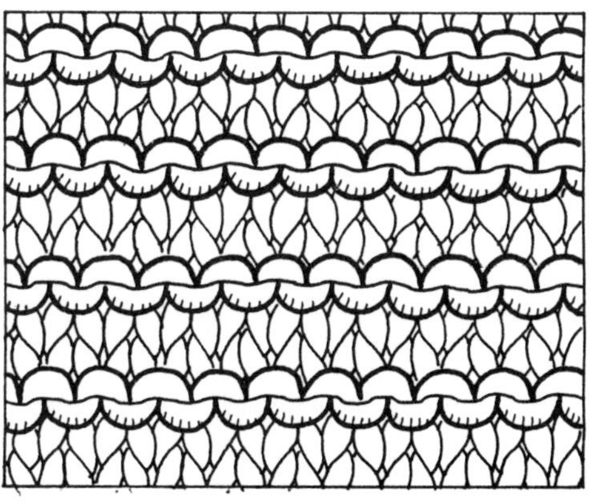

Garter Stitch. The garter stitch is often referred to as *plain knitting*. The stitches appear the same on both sides, making a reversible knitted piece.

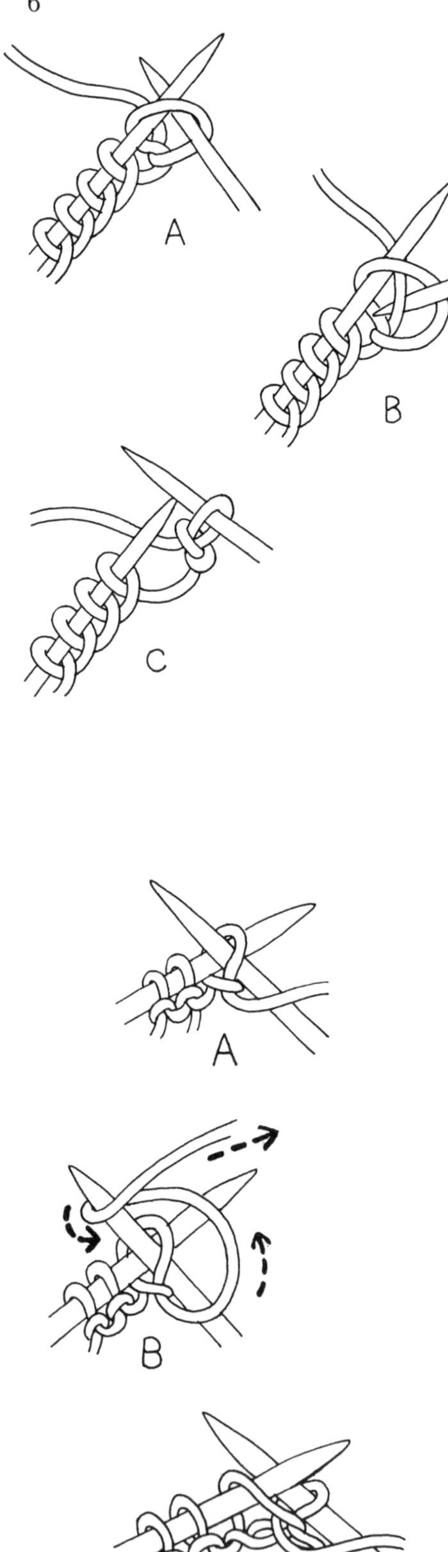

Making a Knit Stitch—Continental Method

This method for forming the knit stitch can be used by both right-handed and left-handed knitters. Begin by inserting the point of the right-hand needle into the front of the loop on the left-hand needle, moving the needle from left to right. Pass the point of the right-hand needle to the right of the yarn that comes from the first finger of the left hand. Then maneuver the point of the needle toward the back and behind the yarn (A).

In preparation for drawing the yarn through the loop, move the first finger of the left hand back so that the yarn lies taut over the needle. Bring the point of the right-hand needle forward and through the stitch on the left needle (B). As you do this, the yarn is pulled through the loop. Slip the stitch off the left-hand needle (C), making one knit stitch. Continue in this way until the row is completed.

For the second row, transfer the needle with the stitches to your left hand, turning the work around. Insert the empty needle into the first stitch. Slip or knit it. Then continue knitting as for the first row. When you have finished, you will have made a row of garter stitches.

Making a Purl Stitch—English Method

Once you have mastered the knit stitch, it is time for you to learn to purl. It is the second basic stitch. Although the knit stitch can be used alone, the purl stitch never can be. It must always be combined with the knit stitch. By doing this in different ways, a variety of pattern stitches can be developed.

To make a purl stitch, hold the needles in the usual manner. There are, however, certain differences in the placement of the yarn and the right-hand needle. Bring the yarn in front of your work instead of in back, as for the knit stitch. Put the right-hand needle in front of the left-hand needle, not in back of it.

Begin by inserting the empty needle, which is in your right hand, in the first stitch, passing it through the front of the stitch from right to left (A). Bring the yarn, which is in front of the needle, over, under, and over the right-hand needle (B). Draw the right-hand needle backward, carrying the yarn through the stitch. Let the needle slide under the left-hand needle. Slip the old stitch off the left-hand needle, completing a purl stitch (C). Continue to make all purl stitches this way.

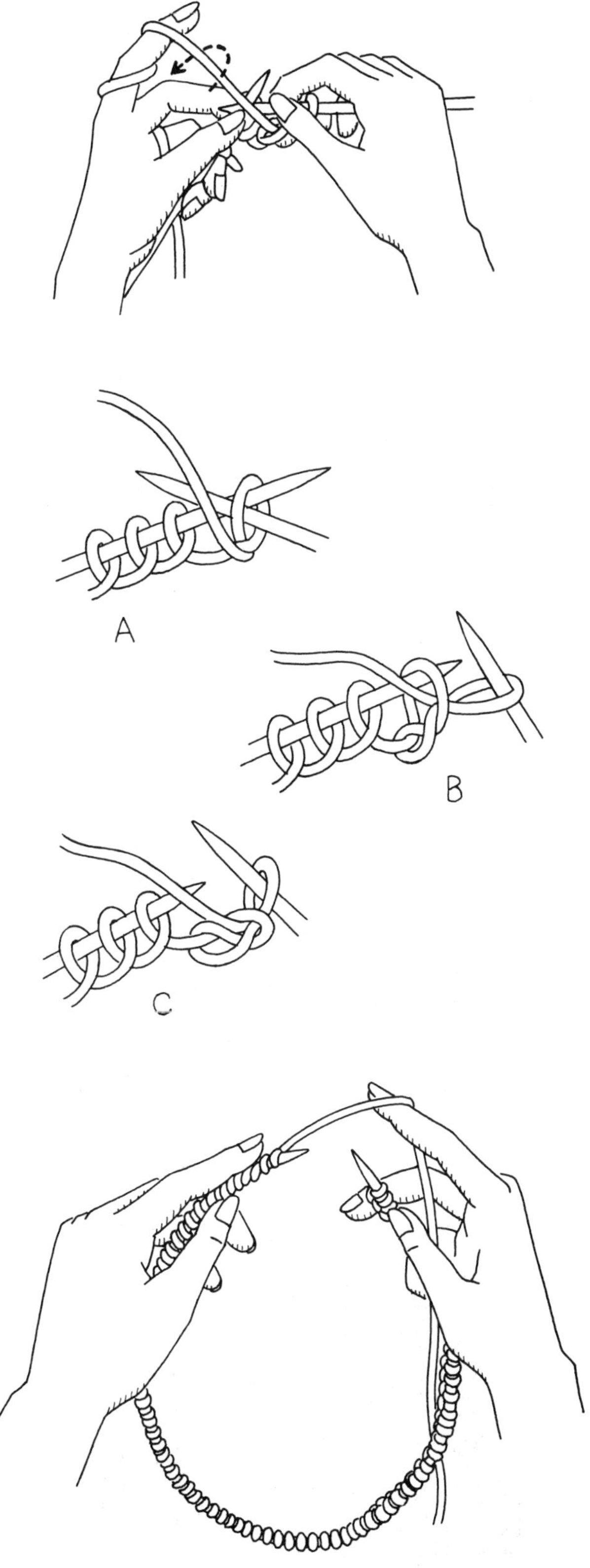

Making a Purl Stitch—Continental Method

Hold the yarn and needles (top, right) in the same position as for the knit stitch. With the yarn in front of the work, put the point of the right-hand needle through the front of the stitch from right to left and under the yarn (A). Notice that the yarn is to the left of the stitch. Twist the needle around the yarn, passing the point of the needle up and over the yarn, then downward from right to left in back of the yarn. Hold the strand of yarn on the needle with your left thumb.

Bring the right-hand needle point back through the loop on the left needle, with the right-hand needle passing under the point of the left-hand needle (B). Slip the loop off the left-hand needle, completing one purl stitch (C). Continue in this way until the row of stitches has been completed.

Flat Knitting on a Circular Needle. Sometimes it is easier to knit a large flat piece on a circular needle than it is on straight needles. Instead of working in the round, knit back and forth as you would on straight needles.

Hold the needle so the tip that holds the first cast-on stitch is in your right hand, and the other end with the last cast-on stitch is in your left hand. Insert the right-hand tip into that last stitch. Begin to knit in the usual way. Continue to the beginning point.

Instead of continuing as you usually do when knitting on a circular needle, turn the needle so the wrong side of the work is toward you. Be sure to do this at the end of each row as you continue to knit.

COMBINING KNIT AND PURL STITCHES

Once you have learned to make these two stitches, you can combine them for many different looks. Some people find them so interesting that they never try other techniques.

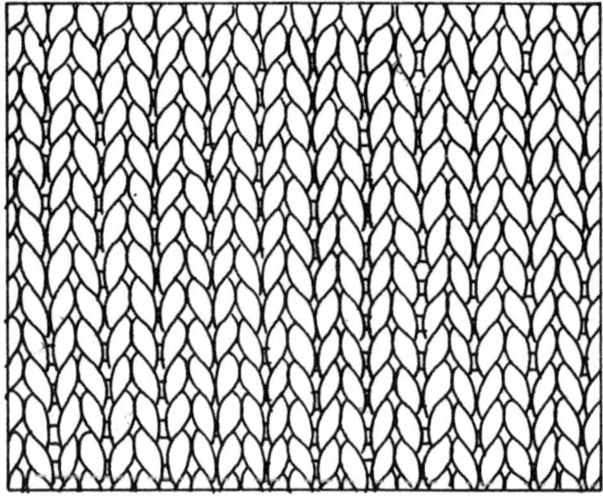

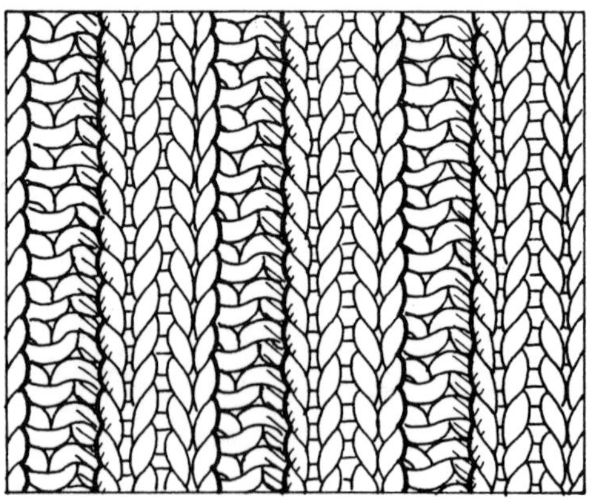

Stockinette Stitch—Straight Needle. This stitch (top) creates a smooth surface of vertical rows of chain-like stitches on one side and raised horizontal ridges on the other. It is made by knitting a row of knit stitches and then a row of purl stitches.

After knitting a row of knit stitches, insert the empty needle, in the right hand, into the first stitch on the left-hand needle. Move it through the front of the stitch from right to left. Slide the stitch to the right-hand needle. Then carry the yarn to the front of the work so you can begin the purling.

Put the right-hand needle into the next stitch on the left-hand needle. Remember to pass it through the front of the stitch from right to left.

Continue purling until you have made a row of stitches. At the end of the row, switch the needles again.

In order to obtain the stockinette effect, you must begin to work alternating rows of knit and purl stitches. The third row is knitted; the fourth, purled. Follow this alternating procedure for the required number of rows.

One thing to remember is that when the smooth surface of the stockinette stitch is toward you, knit the stitches. When the bumpy surface of the stockinette stitches, which appears as horizontal rows of garter stitches, is toward you, purl the stitches.

Reverse Stockinette Stitch. The purled side of the stockinette stitch (center), which is usually considered the wrong side, can be used as the right side. When the knitting is employed this way, it is referred to as the *reverse stockinette stitch*. The effect resembles a smaller version of garter stitches placed close together. The fabric seems to have a pebbly surface.

Ribbing. This is another way to combine knit and purl stitches (left). By alternating a certain number of knit stitches with a certain number of purl stitches, a series of vertical ridges can be made. Probably the most commonly used combination is knit 2 stitches and purl 2 stitches, although others such as knit 1, purl 1, or knit 3, purl 3, are frequently seen.

After deciding which sequence you want to use, knit the required number of stitches in the usual way. Then bring the yarn to the front of the needle in order to purl. Purl the necessary number of stitches and return the yarn to the back of the work. Repeat the knit and purl sequence of stitches until the required number of ribs have been made.

In making the next row, remember that the stitches you knit in the first row will be purled in the second, and the purled stitches will be knitted. In other words, when the stitches with the smooth surface are toward you, knit the stitches, but when the stitches with the bumpy surface is toward you, purl the stitches.

ENDING THE KNITTING

There is always a time when the knitting must end. The procedure for doing this is called *binding off* or *casting off*. The technique is used not only for finishing your work, but also for shaping various parts of a garment, such as an armhole and a neckline, or for creating some design detail, such as a buttonhole.

Usually this technique is done on the wrong side of the work. Watch carefully that you do not make the stitches too tight; there is a tendency to do this. Work the stitches loosely enough so that the finished edge will have the necessary amount of stretch.

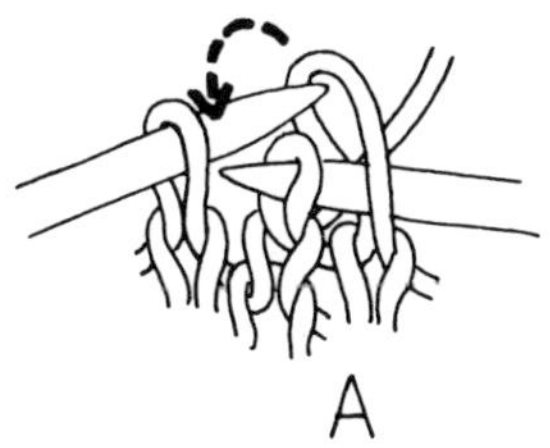

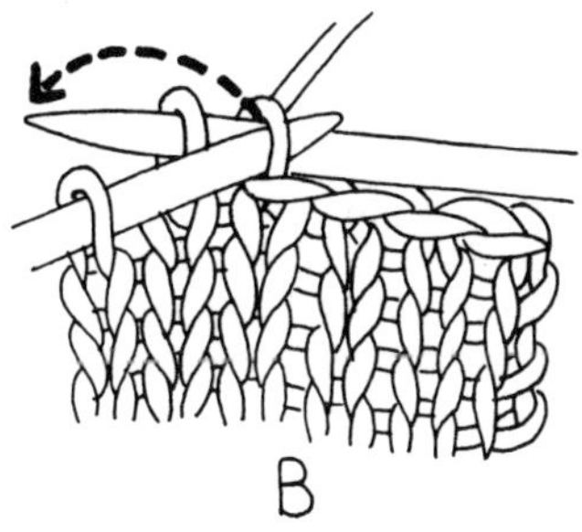

Binding Off on the Knit Side

Slip or knit loosely the first stitch to be removed from the left-hand needle to the right-hand one. Knit the second stitch loosely. Two stitches are now on the right-hand needle, and you can start reducing the number of stitches.

To do this, slip the left-hand needle through the left side of the first stitch on the right-hand needle. Raise the stitch slightly. Pass it over the second stitch and the tip of the right-hand needle (A). Drop the stitch from the needle. This leaves one stitch on the needle.

Repeat the process by knitting the next stitch loosely. Bring the second stitch over the third and the tip of the needle (B).

Continue this procedure until only one stitch remains on the needle. Cut the yarn about 3 inches (7.5 cm) from the stitch. Pass the end through the remaining stitch. Tighten the stitch by pulling the end of the yarn. If you wish, you can weave the end of the yarn into the knitting.

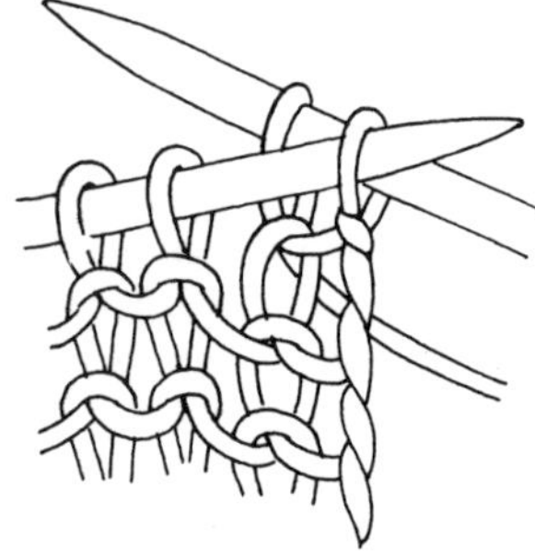

Binding Off on the Purl Side

Follow the same general procedure. Begin by purling two stitches. Carry the yarn to the back of the work. Then, working as for the knit side, insert the left-hand needle through the left side of the first stitch on the right-hand needle. Pass the first stitch over the second and the tip of the needle. Continue as for the knit side, passing the second stitch over the third, and the third over the fourth. Remember to bring the yarn to the back after each new stitch has been purled.

Binding Off Ribbing

Work the correct procedure for the knit stitches and then the purl stitches, alternating in the correct sequence. This permits the ribbing to retain the close-ribbed appearance. If you do not bind off this way, the edge of the ribbing will open up in a fluted fashion.

Binding Off Two Pieces Together

Sometimes you may want to join two pieces of work by binding them off together. To do this, be sure the two pieces have the same number of stitches.

With each part on its needle, hold the two together with the left hand. The right sides should be together, with the points of the needles pointing toward the right.

Insert the right-hand needle into the front of the first stitch on both needles and knit a stitch. Repeat the procedure for the second stitches. Then slip the first stitch over the second one, as in the general binding-off procedure. Continue in this way until all of the stitches are removed from the needle.

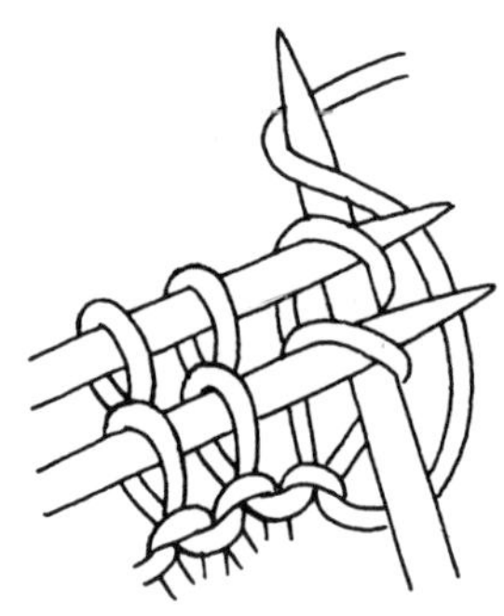

WORKING IN THE ROUND

Some articles are constructed in a tubular form. There are two ways to produce this seamless type of fabric: you can use a circular needle or a set of double-pointed needles. The method you employ usually depends on the size of the item you are producing. The circular needle works well for a big article. It accommodates a large number of stitches and is comfortable to use. Also, it allows the weight of the project to rest in your lap, making it less tiring to knit. The double-pointed needles seem more convenient for knitting smaller items such as socks and mittens.

One thing to be careful about when using a circular needle is to select one in the correct length. The stitches should lie easily on the needle. They should not be crowded, nor should they be stretched. Generally the needle should be about 2 inches (5 cm) shorter than the circumference of the item you are making. Since circular needles are available in lengths of 16, 24, 29, and 36 inches (40.5, 61, 73.5, 91.5 cm), the smallest tubular piece you should knit on this type of needle would be 18 inches (46 cm).

The techniques for knitting are similar whichever type of needle you choose. However, there are a few differences, which are mentioned here.

Casting On the Stitches

The methods employed for flat knitting can also be used when working in the round. Whichever method you choose, check the placement of the stitches carefully. They have a tendency to twist on the needle. Knitting a twist into the work is a disaster. There is nothing to do but rip.

Circular Needle. Both methods can be used when knitting with this type of needle. If you like method 1, work with only one end of the needle, but if method 2 is your favorite, knit with both ends. Keep the finished edge of the stitches inside and the looped edge on the outside. This precaution helps to keep the stitches from twisting. When you have cast on the required number of stitches, lay the needle on a flat surface. Check again to see that the cast-on edge is in the correct position. When you are certain that each stitch is properly placed, insert the right-hand point into the first stitch on the left-hand portion of the needle and begin to knit.

Double-pointed Needles and Method 2. In case method 2 is your favorite way of casting on stitches, follow these directions when working in the round. Knit on 1/3 of the required number of stitches.

Then cast on an extra stitch, but leave it on the right-hand needle. Transfer the needle to your left hand, allowing the first needle to dangle. Pick up another needle in your right hand. Cast on 1/3 of the necessary number of stitches. Knit an extra stitch, but leave it on the right-hand needle.

Transfer the needle to your left hand. Continue casting on the remaining 1/3 of the stitches with the fourth needle in the right hand. You may find this procedure awkward because of the swinging needles. Watch carefully so that none of the stitches slip off the needles.

After you have cast on the required number of stitches, lay the needles on the table to form a triangle. The first needle you used should form the left side of the triangle. Be sure that the stitches are not twisted on the needle. The finished edge should be on the inside, with the loop edge on the outside.

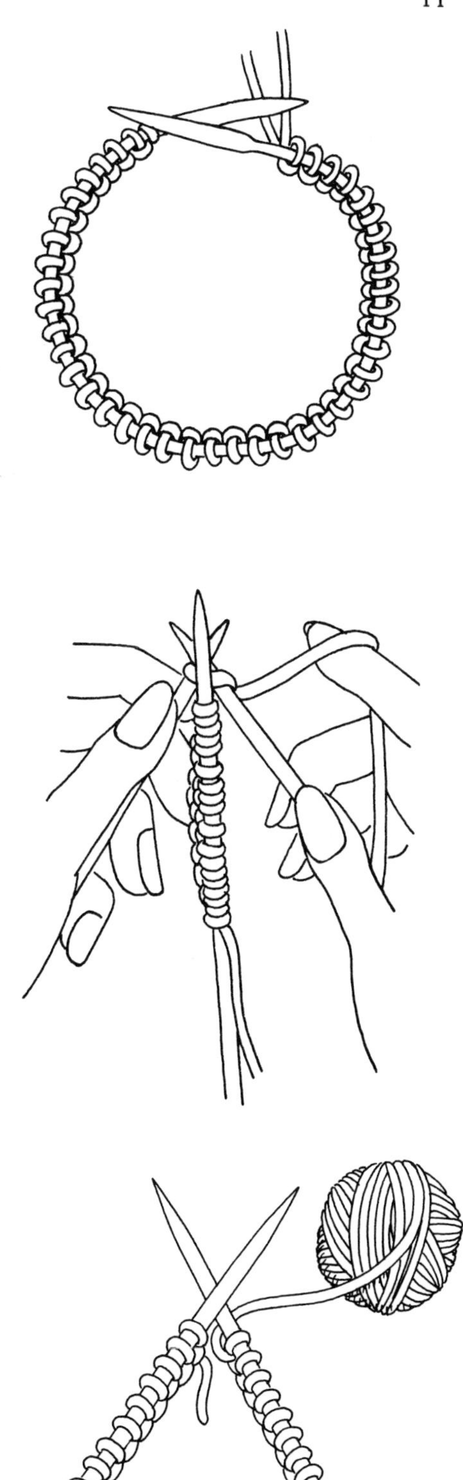

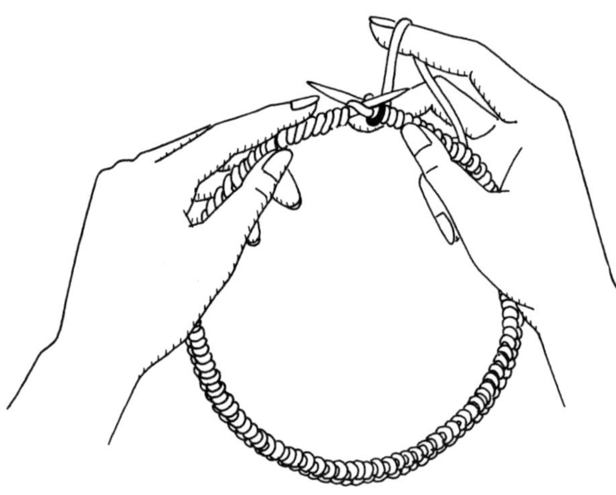

Knitting with a Circular Needle

After casting on the correct number of stitches, check them carefully to be sure that none are twisted. Run your finger along the lower edge. Each stitch should lie flat and face the center of the circle. Slip a ring marker over the point of the needle in your right hand to mark the end of the row. The ball of yarn should be attached to the last stitch.

Pick up the needle so the tip with the first cast-on stitch is in your left hand and the tip with the last stitch in your right hand. Insert the right-hand tip into the first stitch. Pull the yarn firmly as you knit this stitch—you want to eliminate the possibility of leaving a gap between the stitches here.

Knit all the stitches to the marker, working on the far side of the circle instead of the part closer to you. The wrong side of the piece should be on the outside and the right side on the inside. If you are working in stockinette stitch, knit the stitches instead of purling.

At the end of the first round, check for twisted stitches. Be sure that there are none. If you find one, ravel out the stitches—it is the only way to correct the error. With the stitches in the correct position, slip the marker onto the other tip of the needle. This is done before the first stitch of each round. With the stitches in the correct position, begin the second round. Continue knitting in this manner for the required number of rounds.

Notice that, when knitting with a circular needle, the work proceeds in the same direction, round and round. And you may be surprised that the results appear different. Instead of making a garter stitch when the second row is completed, you have a stockinette stitch. (In flat knitting, the stockinette stitch is made with a row of knit stitches followed by a row of purl stitches.)

Knitting with Double-pointed Needles

After the stitches are in place, arrange the three needles in the form of a triangle. Be sure the lower edge of each stitch faces inward and that there are no twisted stitches or twists between the needles. Slip a ring marker over the needle following the last stitch.

Pick up the needle with the first cast-on stitch with the left hand. Insert the fourth needle, which is free of stitches, into the first stitch and knit it. Hold the yarn firmly as you knit this stitch in order to close the gap between the needles. Always do this when knitting the first stitch on

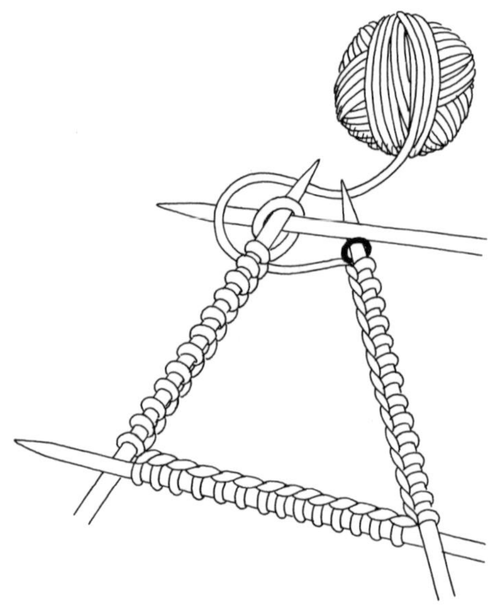

each needle. Work so that the two needles you are knitting with are on top of the other two needles. Hold the item so that you are knitting with the needles that are away from you instead of those close to you. Be sure that the right side of the work is on the inside of the tube.

When all the stitches have been knitted off the first needle, shift needles. Transfer the empty needle to your right hand and pick up the second needle with your left hand. Insert the needle into the first stitch on the second needle and continue to knit all the stitches on this needle. Repeat the process on the third needle until the marker is reached. This indicates that you have worked the stitches on the three needles, making one round.

Slip the marker onto the needle holding the last stitch you have knitted and then begin the next round. Always slip the marker from one needle to the next to mark the start of each new round until the item is completed.

Although almost any stitch pattern can be knitted in the round, an adjustment in the sequence of rows is required. This is because the right side always faces you. For instance, when knitting the stockinette stitch, all of the rows are knitted, but for the garter stitch, one row is knitted and the other purled.

KNITTING LEFT-HANDED

Knitting is a two-handed activity. Both hands share the responsibility almost equally for making a stitch. Because of this, it is not difficult for a left-handed person to knit in the regular fashion. In fact, the Continental (or German) method for holding the yarn lends itself equally well to the hand manipulation of the right-handed or the left-handed person. Maintaining a right-to-left direction in knitting is better than trying to knit from left to right.

Try These Tips

If you continue to have problems in learning to knit, experiment with these suggestions. One of them may provide the correct help.

Ask a friend to sit in front of a long mirror while you sit in back of her. Watch what she does with her hands and her yarn. In the mirror, the motions she makes will appear left-handed to you. Working with your own needles and yarn, duplicate what she does. Proceed slowly so you develop a rhythmic procession of motions.

Sometimes sitting opposite a right-handed knitter can also be helpful. Repeat the motions by using the hand directly opposite the one your friend uses. For instance, your left hand would be opposite the right hand of the right-handed knitter.

Another way to attack this problem is to convert the instructions written for the right-handed knitter. This means substituting "right hand" for "left hand" and "right-handed" for "left-handed" and vice versa when following directions.

Doing this, however, can create problems unless you are very careful. For instance, if you are making a cardigan, the buttonholes that are normally on the right-hand side would be on the left. This would necessitate rewriting the directions for the sweater to button in the correct direction.

The same consideration must be given to the making of sleeves if the right and left sides differ in shaping. You know how strange your sleeves will look if you try to put the right-hand sleeve in the left-hand armhole.

Also, when working with stitch patterns that produce a diagonal effect, remember the movement of the design line will run in the opposite direction. And if the directions include a "slip 1, knit 1, pass slip stitch over (sl 1, K 1, psso)," remember the slant will be to the right, and a "knit 2 together (K 2 tog)" will also slant to the right.

Know Your Yarn

Some people receive pleasure from the feel and sight of yarn. You may be one of them. Today yarns seem more beautiful than ever. Colors span the rainbow. Textures are wide-ranging. Mounds of fluffy, looped, twisted, velvety, or bulky yarns greet you. No longer do you have to use just the plain and smooth—now you can experiment with the unusual to create fascinating effects.

This profusion in looks, however, can cause problems. Unless you understand how the distinguishing features react, you may be disappointed in the results. Sometimes the yarn that looks so beautiful in the ball appears most unattractive when used for the wrong design.

Of course, it is always wise to follow the suggestions for yarn accompanying the directions you are using. Experts have made the selection for you. The day may arrive, however, when the store does not have the yarn you need or the color you want. It is at such times that an understanding of yarn is helpful. The yarn and the design are so dependent on each other that you cannot think of one without the other. The more you know about yarn, the more you will enjoy your knitting.

CHECKING THE FIBER CONTENT

As you read the label on the yarn, notice that the fiber content is listed. For instance, it may read "virgin wool" or perhaps "76% cotton/16% acrylic/8% polyester." The fibers and the proportions in which they are mixed bring significant characteristics to the yarn. Understanding what they are makes it easier to select the right yarn.

Yarns are usually made of animal and synthetic fibers, singly or in combination. Recently other natural fibers—cotton, linen, and silk—are being used for yarns. Although wool yarns are usually thought to produce the most beautiful results, synthetic yarns are becoming increasingly popular.

Wool. The wool from sheep is versatile, having many outstanding characteristics. Manufacturers have tried to copy these natural properties in synthetics, but have never been able to achieve perfect results.

Pure wool is soft and warm, some softer than others. It can be dyed in lovely colors and spun in several weights. Because the yarn is strong and elastic, it creates a durable, long-wearing yarn that can be reused from time to time. It even seems to resist fire better than other fibers. Perhaps you have observed that wool seems to absorb moisture without feeling clammy. In these days of energy concern, it is well to remember that this yarn seems to maintain a more even temperature than other fibers. All of these attributes make wool yarns very special to work with.

Other Animal Fibers. Often yarns in this classification are thought of as wool, but this term properly describes only the fleece of sheep. Yarns may be made from the hair of other animals. Generally they are soft and attractive, spun in various weights from light to very thick. The yarns are usually less resilient than wool and can be more expensive. Among these are angora, alpaca, cashmere, and mohair yarns.

A lovely look can be produced by working with a specially prepared cordlike silk yarn. The satiny sheen and soft silkiness create a feeling of luxury.

Other Natural Fibers. Cotton and linen, which are vegetable fibers, are being used more often for knitting yarns. Sometimes they are used singly to create a distinctive yarn; sometimes each is combined with other fibers. For instance, a predominately cotton yarn might have small amounts of acrylic and polyester added to it. The yarns often have an interesting crinkled surface.

Cotton yarn is soft and less elastic than wool. It is available in various weights, often appearing as a cord. Cotton yarns are most appropriate for warm weather fashions.

Linen yarn has the crispness of linen fabrics. Because of the cool property of the fiber, it can be used most effectively for lightweight sweaters.

Man-made. This type of yarn seems to increase in variety continually. New developments bring constant change. If you check your labels, you will find a variety of names listed, sometimes in combination. Acrylic, Dacron, nylon, Orlon, polyester, rayon, vinyon, and viscose are among the synthetics mentioned. Sometimes they are combined with natural fibers to produce different effects. Some are designed for easy care and hard wear, and may be nonallergenic. This property is a lifesaver for those who cannot tolerate wool. Machine washability provides another asset.

Of this grouping, the acrylics seem to be the most popular. The yarn seems to have the warmth and versatility of wool. Because of its spongy nature, it is sometimes difficult to block the knitting so that it lies flat. But its machine washability and dryability are assets many knitters insist on.

Rayon ribbon creates a different knitted look. The silk-like ribbon is soft, with a delicate sheen, and ⅝ inch (1.6 cm) wide. If you work with needles in the larger sizes, such as no. 13, a lovely effect results.

STUDYING THE CONSTRUCTION

Variations in the yarn derive not only from the fiber content but also from the construction. By varying the procedure, different effects are produced.

Counting the Ply

This term is sometimes referred to as fold and, mistakenly, is often thought to identify the weight and thickness of the yarn. It really doesn't. *Ply* simply refers to the number of spun threads that are twisted to make a strand of yarn. Two, three, or four strands can be employed, leading to the designation 2-ply, 3-ply, or 4-ply.

It may surprise you that lightweight

yarns can be made of three or four threads, whereas a heavy one can consist of only two. Or you may find both a lightweight and a heavyweight yarn made of the same number of plies. Although the ply does not influence the weight or the thickness of the yarn, it can contribute to the strength. A 4-ply yarn can be tougher than a 2-ply.

Distinguishing the Weights

Yarns are made in several different weights. Actually, this designation indicates the thickness of the yarn, ranging from the very fine to the heavy.

Lightweight yarn can be smooth or fuzzy or have an unusual texture. It works equally as well in making a lacy shawl or a closely knit fabric-like material on fine needles. Baby wear, bed jackets, and sweaters are other articles frequently made of lightweight yarn.

Medium-weight yarn can be employed for a wide variety of articles. Everything that does not have a sheer, filmy look or a coarse one can be made with this weight of yarn. Dresses, suits, jackets, sweaters, and accessories work up nicely in it.

Heavyweight yarn is especially suitable for outdoor wear because of its warmth. Fashions that require a bulky look, such as Aran-style garments, hats, suits, and sweaters, can be made of this type of yarn.

Super-weight yarn is a really bulky yarn, often 2-ply. Two loose, thick strands of spun woolen yarn are twisted together to form a heavy strand.

Sports-weight yarn is an in-between weight. When you want to make an article that should be heavier than you could construct using a medium-weight yarn, but a little lighter than that made with a 4-ply worsted, try this type. It is available in 2, 3, or 4 plies and in a wide range of colors and textures.

Recognizing the Textural Qualities

Probably one of the nicest things about yarns is the pleasure you can receive from just touching and seeing them. The soft squashiness of some, the frothy sheerness of others, and the array of beautiful colors can all contribute to a pleasing experience.

Usually you think of yarn as being smooth and plain more often than textured. By creating a surface interest, knitting can be given a completely different look. The twisting and uneven outline creates various effects. It should be remembered, however, that yarns with textural interest such as nubbiness or fluffiness should not be selected if a fancy stitch pattern is to be knitted. They are not compatible. Use a plain stitch for yarns with great interest. If, however, the yarn is smooth, experiment with more elaborate stitch patterns until just the right effect is obtained.

Some of the textural differences appear as nubs and loops, producing a three-dimensional effect. Nubs may be spun at equal distances, often in a contrasting color. Sometimes thick spots of cotton are placed in the yarn for a slubbed effect. Then, for a change in look, there are the fluffy yarns that seem so airy and fragile. Thin ones appear so delicate in contrast to thick, big, loose strands of yarn. There are also those that feel stiff and wiry.

When using nubby and knotty yarns, check carefully as you knit for mistakes. They are difficult to see, and it is so annoying to discover an error later. Also, it is difficult to correct rows when working with knotty yarn. You will find it easier to check the size of the piece by using a tape measure than by counting rows.

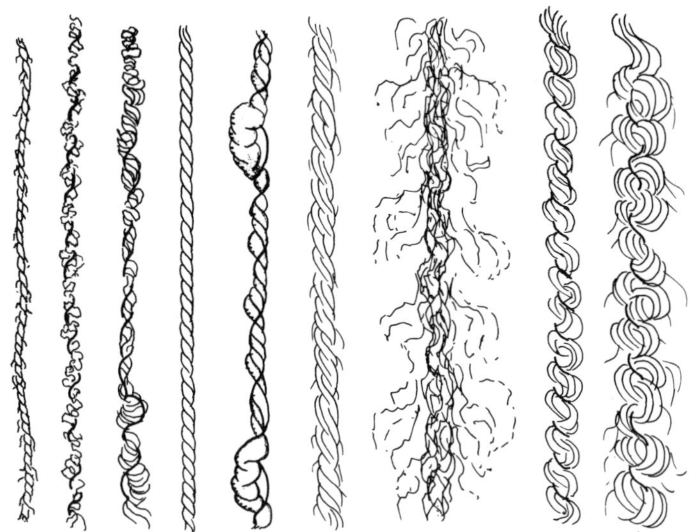

SMART SHOPPING

The test of how much you know about yarn will come when you have to decide which to use. Unless you feel very sure of yourself, it is better to select the yarn suggested for a chosen design. The designer and manufacturer have carefully determined which yarn is best for the look they wish to create. Any change in the type and size of the yarn may result in a disappointing piece of knitting.

Buying at a Reliable Store

Shopping in a reputable shop offers a sense of security. Usually yarns from good manufacturers are available. Judging quality is made easier. Also, in this type of store you will find knowledgeable clerks. They can provide invaluable guidance.

Another advantage is a policy allowing returns. It is so important that you buy sufficient yarn at one time to complete the article that you may buy more than is needed. To be able to return the surplus yarn is a valuable service.

When buying yarn, always check the label to be sure that you are purchasing the same color and that the dye lot number is identical. Colors can change from one dye lot to another.

Checking Quality

Price usually indicates quality—the higher the price, the better the quality. There are, however, various factors that determine quality. The fiber, the color, and the ability of the yarn to resist fading, felting, pilling, and rubbing will influence the quality and the price.

Washing makes some yarns shrink, stretch, fade, or become coarse and rough. Sometimes chemically treated yarns, which produce a "shrink-proof" or "shrink-resistant" product, stretch when laundered unless they are knitted with firm tension.

Even the color influences the price. It costs more to produce gentle, subtle hues than it does loud, jarring ones.

Although no article is better than the yarn from which it is knitted, varying requirements control the need for top quality. Judging when less than the best can be used needs careful consideration in these days of high prices. Estimating how long you can use an item and how long it takes to make it will give you some idea of how much you should spend for the yarn. For instance, a fad item that you can make quickly does not demand the same high quality as a classic design that takes hours and hours to knit. Often the less expensive yarns are sturdy and can be used effectively for many types of articles.

You will also find that good wool yarn can be reused. When an article has outworn its usefulness, it can be ripped apart and the yarn used again.

Considering Appropriateness

It has always been a matter for discussion whether a home sewer should select pattern or fabric first. The same question may confront the knitter. It seems, however, that in knitting the design is chosen before the yarn. Of course it is possible to chose the wrong design for the purpose for which it is to be used. In such a case, the yarn may not provide the look or give the service that you expect. This is always disappointing.

It is also frustrating to make something for yourself that looks pretty in the hand but dreadful when you wear it. Too often the design of the yarn is not considered in connection with the individual. But it is just as important for you to do this as it is, when sewing, to select a flattering pattern and fabric. The yarn, the design, and the stitch pattern should be right for each other as well as for you.

Remember that, because yarns have various characteristics, there is a difference in the way they can be handled. Some may be used for fancy pattern stitches, whereas others should be used only for simple stitches. For instance, a fluffy yarn looks great in a garter stitch but destroys the look of a lacy pattern. Soft yarns are excellent for a baby's sweater but a disaster for a man's.

Certain items require yarns with special characteristics. For example, when you are knitting a bathing suit, the yarn should be the type you can knit on small needles so the suit will not stretch when you are in the water. Also a guarantee that the color is fast in sun and water is a must.

If you are combining yarns, be sure to use the same type. Yarns work up differently and respond differently to blocking. You do not want your knitting spoiled because it seems to shrink in one place and stretch in another.

Thinking About Care

To some knitters "easy to care for" is of the upmost importance. Usually the label on the yarn explains how to take care of the yarn when it has been made into an article. Some labels give more information than others. Generally the label will state whether the yarn should be dry-cleaned, hand-washed, machine-washed, or machine-dried. Watch for those words. It is best to follow the listed instructions.

3

Work with the Correct Tools

Knitting is one craft that requires few tools. In fact, only knitting needles are needed. But they are available in such a variety of sizes that you must be careful to select the one that is just right for the yarn you are using and the item you are making. Knitters usually own a wide range of needles so they always have the correct pair at their fingertips.

Although they are not a must, there are some gadgets that simplify the knitting process. It is usually wise to try them and then determine the ones you would like to use.

SELECTING THE RIGHT NEEDLES

Knitting needles are made in different types, materials, sizes, and lengths. Knowing about each of the variations will help you become a better knitter. The yarn and needles depend on each other so closely that it is impossible to create the correct look if they are not in harmony.

In selecting your needles for a specific project, you will of course be guided by the directions you are using. The size and type of the needle to be used will be mentioned.

Types of Needle

There are two types of needle: straight and circular. The straight needles can be single- or double-pointed. Most of your knitting will probably be done on single-pointed straight needles.

Single-pointed Straight Needle. This type has one tapered end, forming a point. The opposite end has a permanently attached knob that keeps the stitches from falling off the needle. Usually the needle is marked with a size designation. The needles are sold in a set of two.

Knitting on straight needles produces a flat piece of work. You knit back and forth to form rows of stitches, turning at the end of each row.

In selecting a needle, be sure to check the tip carefully. It is the portion of the needle that first comes in contact with the yarn. If it is not just right, it may split or snag the yarn. The tip should not be too pointed or sharp, but instead have a very slight roundness so you do not feel pricked when it touches you. In turn, the point

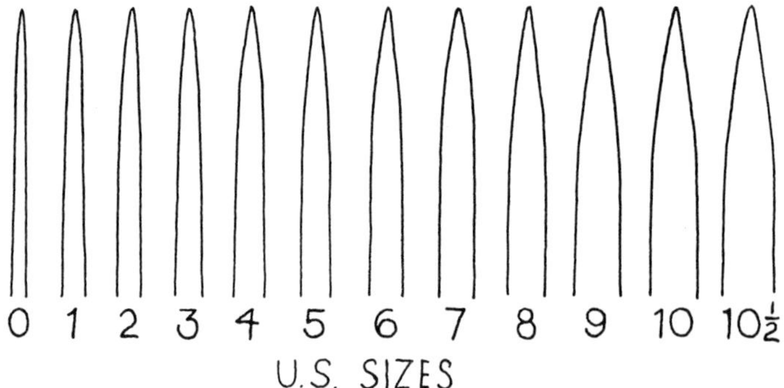

should not be so curved that it splits the yarn when inserted in a stitch. You should be able to slip the needle into the loop and draw the new stitch onto the needle without any trouble.

The point should taper gradually and evenly to the shaft. This makes it possible to construct each stitch so the loops are of uniform size and the work is even. Also be certain that the entire needle is smooth. Rough spots will snag the yarn, creating problems.

Be sure to take good care of your needles. Store them flat, with ends protected. Some people feel that rubbing the needles occasionally with waxed paper will keep them smooth.

Double-pointed Needle. As the name implies, this type of needle has two points. Both ends are tapered to a point. They are usually sold in a set of four.

Double-pointed needles are available in a variety of sizes and lengths. They are used for knitting in the round to make a tubular piece. In fact, they are sometimes called sock needles. No doubt you have seen mittens, socks, and neck ribbings being made with this type.

Circular Needle. This is a rather recent invention. It simplifies the making of a tubular item such as a skirt without seams. A circular needle also makes it easier to make a raglan sweater where the knitting begins at the neckline or a sweater with a circular yoke.

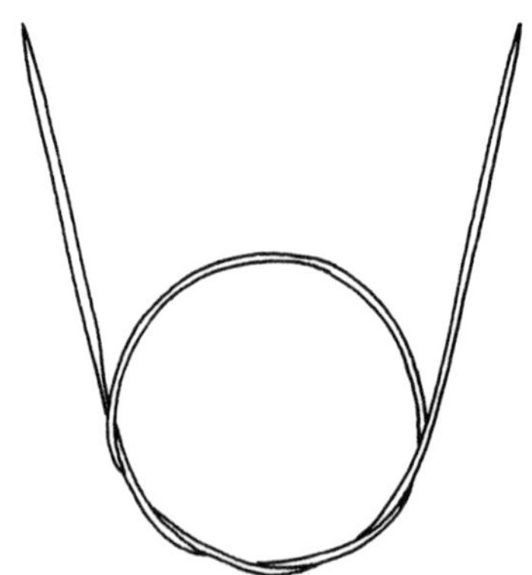

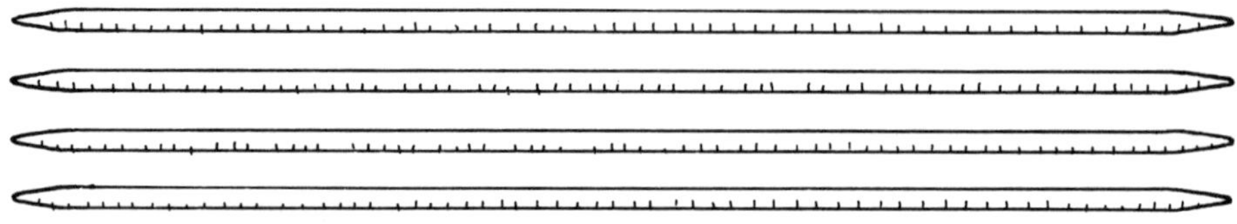

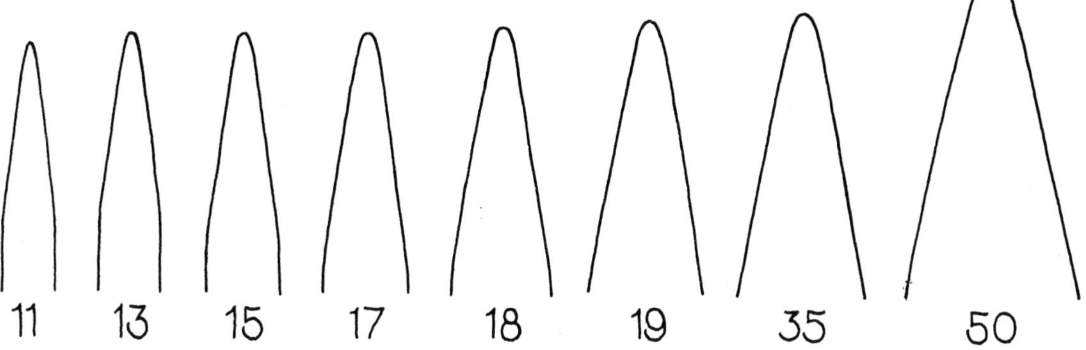

The needle can be used for flat work by working back and forth. This offers a solution to the knitting of large pieces with many stitches on straight needles that are too short to accommodate the stitches.

In selecting a circular needle, be sure the tips and the center portion are smoothly joined. A rough spot will snag the yarn, making the work more difficult and the finished product less attractive. Usually the needle consists of two aluminum or nylon tips forming two firm sections connected by a flexible nylon cord.

Materials

Over the years, the materials from which knitting needles are made have changed. Probably the first needles were made of wood or bone, but today aluminum and plastic seem to be favored.

Aluminum Needles. These are usually light in weight and quite rigid. If you find one that seems flexible, be sure to bend it slightly to see if it returns immediately to a straight line. It should.

Plastic Needles. These are flexible, especially in the smaller sizes. They are made in many different colors. Some people think the knitting is looser when made with plastic needles.

Steel Needles. These may be difficult to find, since other materials have been successfully substituted for the metal except in the smallest sizes. In these small sizes they are stiff enough to keep their shape and at the same time flexible enough to make very fine stitches.

Wood Needles. They are usually found only in the larger sizes. Be sure that they are smooth and that the points are tapered properly.

Size

The diameter and the length should be considered when selecting knitting needles. The directions you are using will be helpful, but be sure to note which type of sizing is being used. This is especially important if you are following directions found in a book or magazine published in a foreign country.

Diameter. This dimension is indicated by three numbering systems: U.S. Standard, or American; English; and Continental Metric. The chart (page 22) and the drawings shown above will indicate some of the differences in sizing. You will notice that in American sizing the larger numbers indicate the larger sizes.

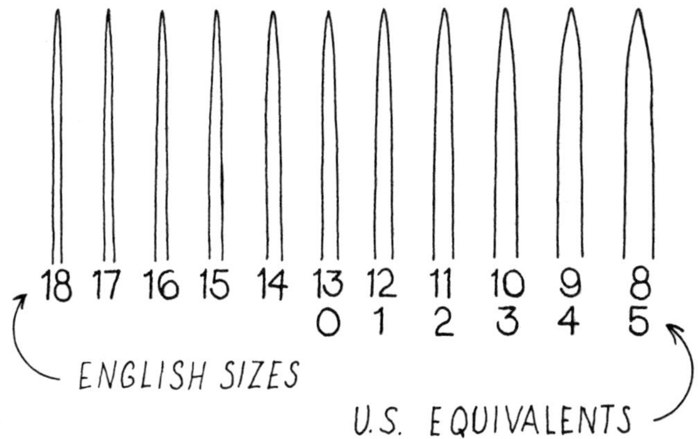

KNITTING NEEDLES — DIAMETER

American U.S. Standard	Diameter MM	English	Continental Metric
		18	
		17	
		16	
000		15	
00		14	2
0	2.1	13	2¼
1	2.4	12	2½
2	2.8	11	3
3	3.2	10	3¼
4	3.5	9	3½
5	3.8	8	4
6	4.2	7	4½
7	4.6	6	5
8	5.0	5	5½
9	5.3	4	6
10	5.8	3	6½
10½	6.6	2	7
11	8.0	1	7½
13	9.2	00	8½
15	10.2	000	9
17	12.7		
18	14.3		
19	16.0		
35	19.0		
50	25.4		

Length. Careful consideration should be given the length of the *straight needles* you use. They are available in different lengths. Usually the chosen length depends on the article being constructed. If only a few stitches are required, then a short needle seems more convenient, saving the longer type for the larger item.

Crowding stitches on the needle makes it difficult to watch the stitch pattern as it develops. There is also the possibility that you will find a certain length more comfortable to use than another. The length of your arm and type of chair you sit in to knit will influence your choice.

When selecting a **circular needle,** be sure to note the circumference of the article you are making. Considering the number of stitches you need and how many stitches you will knit to the inch will help you determine how long the needle should be. Usually a length at least 2 inches (5 cm) less than the circumference of the work is a good guide to follow.

Not every style of needle is made in all lengths and sizes. The material, type, and purpose for which the needles are to be used influence the sizing.

NEEDLE SIZES — LENGTH AND MATERIALS

Type	Aluminum		Plastic		Wood		Nylon		Aluminum Tip with Nylon Cord	
	Length	Size	Length	Size	Length	Size	Length	Size	Length	Size
Single-pointed	10″	0-15	10″	1-15						
	14″	0-19	14″	1-50	14″	11-15				
Double-pointed	7″	0-8	7″	0-8						
	10″	0-15	10″	0-15						
Circular	16″	0-12½					16″	3-10½	16″	0-10½
	24″	0-10½					24″	1-10½	24″	0-10½
	29″	0-15					29″	1-15	24″	0-15
	36″	8-15					36″	5-15	36″	9-15

Suitability

The size of the needle you select has a definite effect on the look of the knitting. Because of this, it is most important that the needle and yarn be appropriate both for each other and for the article being made. The ideal needle size for the yarn should show off the beauty and texture of the yarn and still keep the work firm enough to hold its shape.

If the needles are too large for the yarn, the knitting will be loose and will not have any body. This allows the knitting to stretch. It is difficult to return the article to its original size and shape, even with blocking.

Knitting on needles too small will produce the opposite results. The knitting will become too firm. It will seem stiff, with too much body.

Jiffy knitting has become popular. The speed and ease with which an article can be made is amazing. Sometimes special needles are needed for this type of knitting. They are available in much larger sizes, such as 17, 19, 35, and 50. In diameter, they range from ½ to 1 inch (1.3 to 2.5 cm).

KNITTING AIDS AVAILABLE

Although yarn and needles are the two items necessary for knitting, there are a few gadgets that you may find helpful. They include counters, holders, and markers, as well as some that are usually thought of in connection with crocheting and sewing.

Bobbin. This type of yarn holder makes the work easier when knitting with multicolors, as for Argyle and Fair Isle patterns. The bobbin is available in two sizes—one for fine yarn, the other for thick.

Select one that is light in weight and can hold the yarn firmly in place. Also be sure the yarn is not crowded on the bobbin.

Counters. These are small devices that keep a record of stitches and rows, increases and decreases, when knitting.

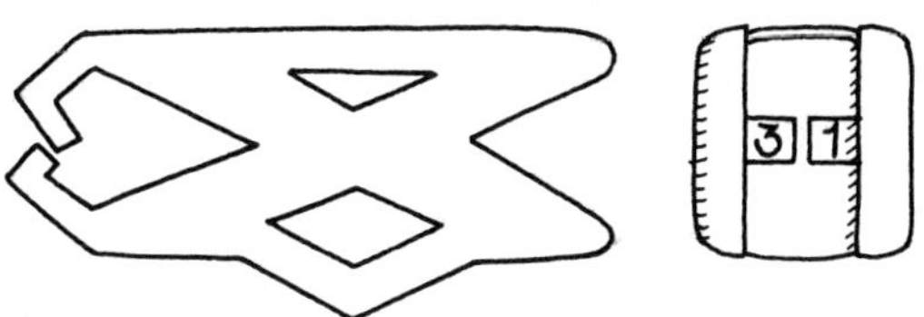

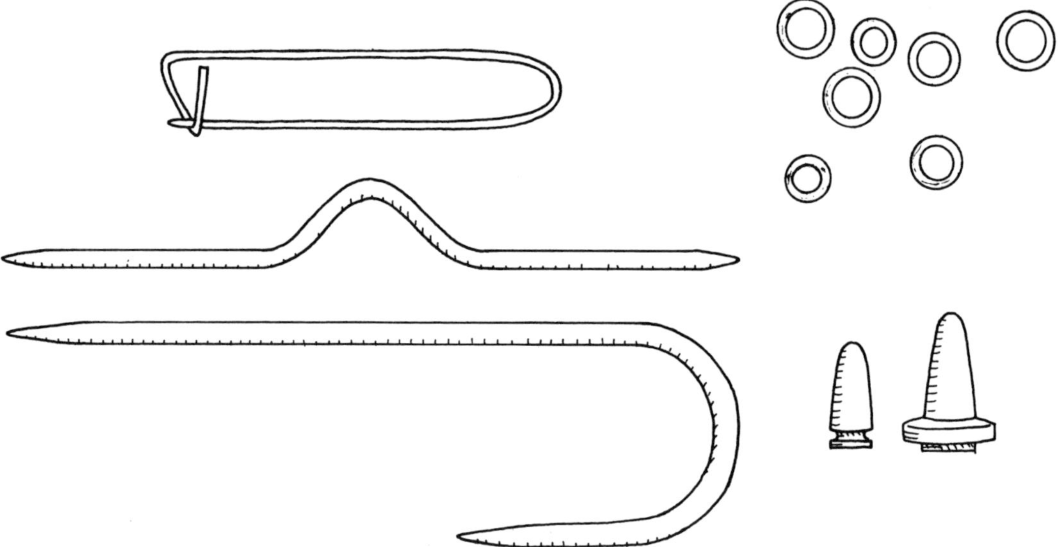

They are made in different styles and save you the trouble of counting. By keeping the counter on the needle and setting it to the number of the row being made, you can eliminate confusion and mistakes and make knitting less time-consuming.

Gauge. A *card* for checking needle sizes is handy to have. The better ones are made of metal or plastic—holes in cardboard often increase in size after use. The needle should slip through easily. If it does not, the size of the needle may be larger than you thought.

There is also a *counter* or *ruler* that allows you to determine the number of stitches and rows to the inch. Different types are available. In case you cannot find a gauge, try making one. Use a 4-inch (10 cm) cardboard square, and cut a 2-inch (5 cm) square in the center. Mark dimensions on the side.

Holders. Stitch holders are available in two types: one for holding stitches that are to be worked later, and another to hold stitches in cable knitting. You will find them sized for knitting with regular as well as bulky yarn. Try to select one as close in size as possible to that of the needle you are using.

The first type resembles a safety pin. It keeps one section from raveling while another section is being knitted. The holder is available in different lengths from 1¾ inches to 10 inches (4.5 to 25.5 cm).

Cable stitch needles or holders look like a small double-pointed needle with a U-shaped head in the center or a U-shaped hook.

Markers. Colored plastic rings make good markers. They are used to indicate separate sections, places where a pattern begins and ends or where increases and decreases are made. The rings are available in various sizes and in two types —regular and open-coil.

Point Protector. This gadget is made of rubber. It slips over the end of the needle, not only protecting the knitter, but also keeping the knitting from slipping off the needle. They are made in various sizes—small, medium, and large.

OTHER EQUIPMENT

There will be times when you will need tools that you usually think of as crocheting or sewing equipment. Hooks, needles, scissors, and tape measure are in this group.

Crochet Hooks. Perhaps you do not

realize what an important part a crochet hook plays in knitting. You will use it to finish edges, join seams, or add a decorative trim. While one does not like to think about dropped stitches, they do happen. A crochet hook makes the picking up of the stitches much easier to accomplish.

Just one hook is not enough. You will probably need several. The one you use will depend on the knitting. The stitch gauge of the crocheting should be comparable to that of the knitting on which you are working. Select a hook that is about the same thickness as the knitting needles you are using. Crochet hooks come in a wide variety of sizes and materials.

Aluminum hooks are made in sizes B to K in a 6-inch (15 cm) length.

Bone hooks are available in sizes 1 to 6, which are comparable to sizes B to G.

Plastic hooks are made in sizes D to J and in a 5½-inch (14 cm) length.

Steel hooks range in size from large, 00, to very fine, 14, in a 5-inch (12.5 cm) length.

Wooden hooks are large and long, 9 or 10 inches (23 or 25.5 cm) in length.

In selecting a crochet hook, check the hook carefully. It should not be too sharply notched or pointed, to avoid the possibility of hurting your fingers and damaging the yarn.

Needles. They perform many important functions. You will use a needle for making seams, grafting, and working the Duplicate Stitch, among others. For such tasks, your needle should have a blunt point and a large eye. A tapestry needle works well. Sometimes a crewel needle may be employed for finishing touches. Whichever type you select, be sure that the eye is large enough for the yarn to pass through easily.

Needle Threader. Sometimes it may seem almost impossible to thread the needle with heavy yarn. When this happens, try a little gadget made especially for this purpose.

Scissors. You will need a pair for clipping yarn. The points should be sharp, so keep the scissors in a case.

Tape Measure. This is a must. You will use it constantly in checking the size of the item you are making. Because accurate measurements are so important, select a good tape, one that will not stretch or shrink. By keeping it with your knitting equipment instead of your sewing tools, you will be sure to use the same one when making an article.

You may find in some instances that a 6-inch (15 cm) plastic ruler will be easier to use than a tape measure.

CHOOSING A CONTAINER

Naturally you will want to keep all of your knitting tools in one place. There are many ways to do this. Knitting bags and boxes may be purchased in a wide variety of sizes, shapes, and materials. Most people find a knitting bag is handier to use. It is often inconvenient to find something at the bottom of a box without dumping out the contents.

In selecting a bag, try to find one that is easy to carry and at the same time large enough to hold the type of knitting you do. If you knit only small pieces, then of course you will not need as large a bag as if you were knitting a bulky sweater. Also remember that folding your work is better than jamming it into the bag.

Plan on using a small case or envelope for holding the small equipment. Leaving everything loose in the bottom of the bag will not only damage the tools but also create a frustrating situation when you are trying to find a specific item. Keeping needles in the packaging you bought them in will make them easier to identify. Winding a circular needle loosely and storing it flat will keep it in good condition.

How to Understand the Directions

Knitting directions can seem confusing. There are so many new words and phrases to understand—it is almost like learning a new language! Actually, knitting does seem to have a language of its own, which every knitter should learn. Unless you do, transforming yarn into an article, using two needles, will be difficult.

Instructions for making a knitted article are usually written with abbreviations. This conserves space on the printed page, but does make the directions more difficult to follow. To make them even more difficult to remember, the abbreviations vary from author to author, and from country to country. For that reason, always study the listing of abbreviations before you actually begin your work. Then read the directions for the item you are making. If they contain unfamiliar abbreviations and procedures, be sure to check them carefully. This avoids mistakes. If you think you will need to refer to them later, mark the pages on which the abbreviations are listed for quick reference. Unusual abbreviations and directions often need frequent checking in order to avoid mistakes, which are time-consuming and a nuisance to correct.

On the following pages, the most commonly used abbreviations and terms are mentioned. You will probably notice that in many instances the first letter of the word becomes the abbreviation.

ABBREVIATIONS

alt	alternate
atst	at the same time
B	back
BC	back cross
beg	beginning
CC	contrasting color
ch	chain
cn	cable needle or cable holder
cont	continue
cr 2	cross 2. Knit into 2nd st on left needle, then 1st st
cross 2 L	knit into back of 2nd st, then into front of 1st st in usual way. Let both sts drop off needle together
cross 2 R	purl into front of 2nd st, then into front of 1st st in usual way
dec	decrease
dec L	decrease left
dec R	decrease right
dp or dpn	double-pointed needle
FC	front cross
foll	following
g or gr	gram

g.st	garter stitch
in(s)	inch(es)
incl	inclusive
inc	increase
inc L	increase to the left
inc R	increase to the right
K	Knit
Kb	knit into back of stitch
KIB	knit through st below next st
LH	left-hand needle
lp(s)	loop(s)
M 1	make 1 stitch
MC	main color
o	work no rows or no stitches
pat(s)	pattern(s)
pnso or p.n.s.o.	pass or pull next stitch over
psso or p.s.s.o.	pass or pull slipped stitch over
pu 1	pick up 1 stitch
P	purl
Pb	purl into back of stitch
rem	remaining
rep	repeat
* or **	repeat directions in same order following asterisk
* * or ( )	repeat directions found between asterisks or parentheses
RH	right-hand needle
rnd	round
rs	right side
sc	single crochet
SKP	slip 1, knit 1, pass slip stitch(es) over knit(s)
sl, s	slip
sp	single-pointed
sps	spaces
ssk	slip, slip knit
st(s)	stitch(es)
st st	stocking or stockinette stitch
tbl	through back of loops
tog	together
tw	twist
ws	wrong side
wl (y) fwd	wool (yarn) forward
wl (y) bk	wool (yarn) back
wrn = yon	wool around needle = yarn over needle
yb or wyib	yarn to back of work
yf or wyif	yarn to front of work
yo or yon	yarn over needle

TERMS

The basic terms used in knitting are listed here in dictionary form, to make it easier for you to refer to them. In some instances you will find the technique described in more detail in other sections of the book when it is actually being used in the construction of a stitch pattern or an article.

Attaching Yarn. When it is necessary to fasten two strands of yarn together, it should be done in such a way as to produce a strong and inconspicuous joining (below). Whenever possible, it is best to attach the new piece with a knot at the beginning of a row. When the work is finished, weave each end separately into the knitting or seam.

Binding Off. To finish a piece of knitting, the stitches must be secured by a special process. This procedure is called binding off. It is described more fully in Chapter 1.

Blocking. In order to give a professional look to a piece of knitting, it is pinned to a padded surface and steam-pressed.

Casting Off. This is a term used instead of *binding off*. The procedure is the same.

Casting On. Putting stitches on a knitting needle is known as casting on. It can be done in various ways, which are described in Chapter 1.

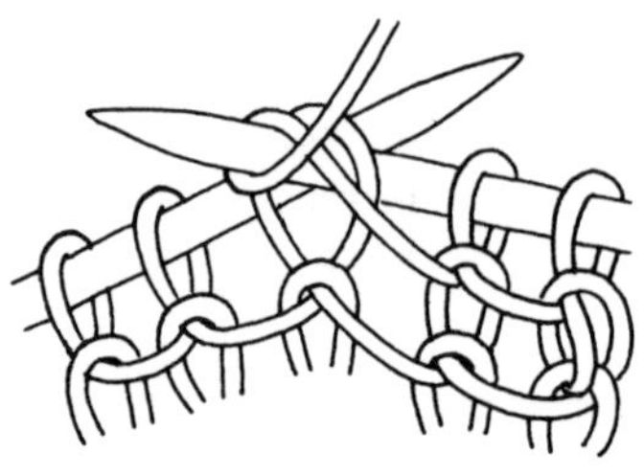

Cross Purl

Changing Colors. Sometimes a design requires two or more colors. To shift from one color to another, twist the two colors together at the joining (above). Carry the unused yarn loosely across the knitting on the wrong side. Pick up the new color from under the one that is to be dropped. Doing it this way prevents holes from appearing.

Cross Knit. This is a variation of plain knitting, sometimes referred to as Italian or Twist Stitch. Instead of working into the front of the stitch, place the needle into the back. The row of purl stitches is made in the regular way.

Cross Knit

Cross Purl. A variation of purling is created by this technique. Instead of inserting the needle into the front of the stitch, put it into the back. Plain knitting is used for the knit row.

Decreasing. This term refers to reducing the number of stitches in order to shape a knitted piece. It can be done in several ways.

For Method 1, knit two stitches together, instead of knitting one in the usual manner. It is done on a knit row.

Place the right-hand needle through the front of the second stitch and then through the first one. Make a regular knit stitch, drawing the yarn through both stitches. Slip the two stitches off the needle as one, decreasing the number of stitches by one.

To decrease in purling, purl two stitches together in a purl row.

This method can also be used for knitting more than two stitches together.

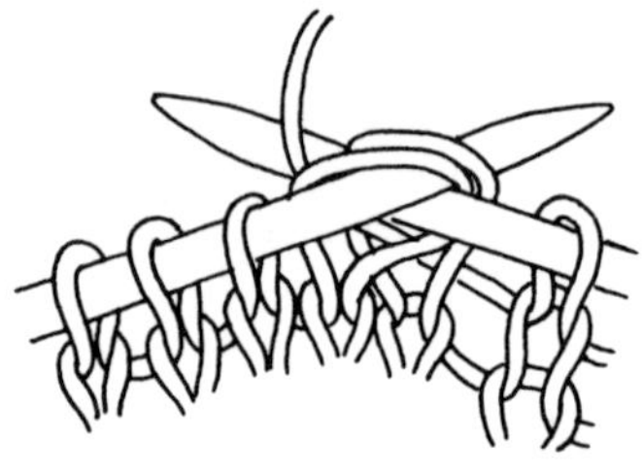

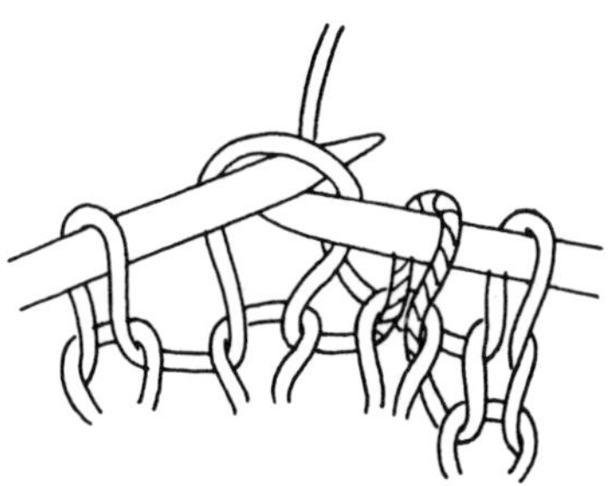

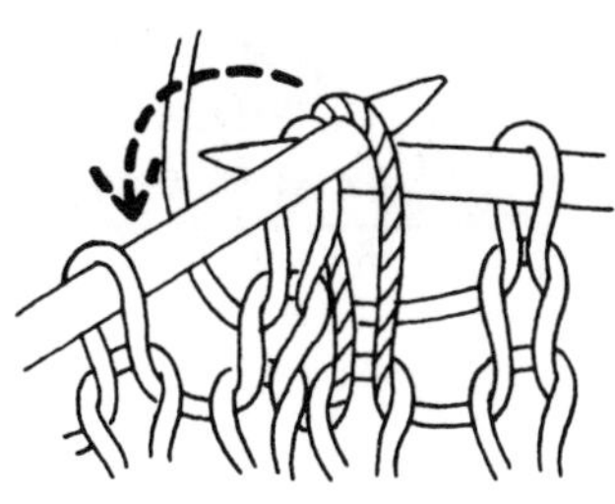

For Method 2 (top left, right), use a slip stitch. Slip one stitch from the left-hand needle to the right-hand one without knitting. Knit the next stitch.

Using the left-hand needle, bring the slipped stitch over the knitted one and off the tip of the right-hand needle.

The abbreviation seen in directions for this way of decreasing is *psso*.

Double Throw. Directions for creating an openwork effect often use this term. Insert the needle into the stitch as for knitting or purling. Wind the yarn around the needle as many times as required. Pull all the loops through the stitch.

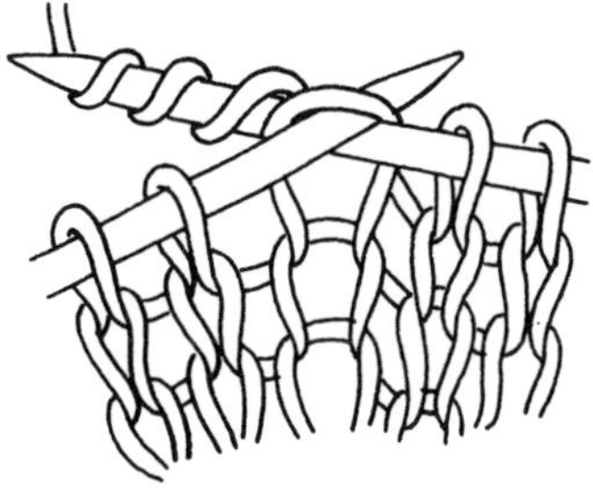

Dropped Stitches. Unless you are careful, a stitch may drop off the needle accidentally. When this happens, do not panic. Just pick up the dropped stitch and return it to the needle.

For the best results, use a crochet hook. Insert the hook in the dropped stitch. Pull the horizontal strand of yarn of the row above through the loop. Continue working upward until the row of stitches on the needle is reached. Slip the picked-up stitch onto the needle. Be careful not to twist it.

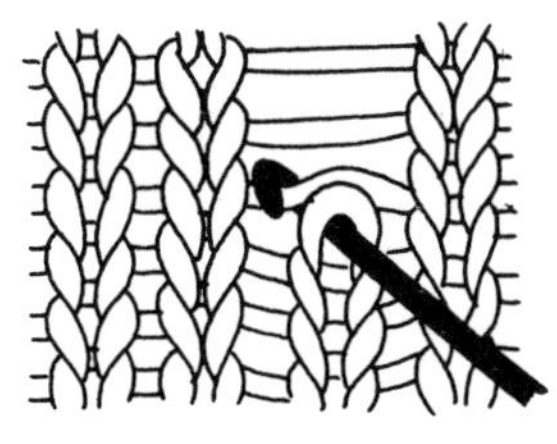

When working with the *stockinette stitch,* it is best to pick up the dropped stitch with the smooth or right side of the knitting toward you.

For the *garter stitch,* turn the work first to one side and then to the other so that the stitch design will be kept.

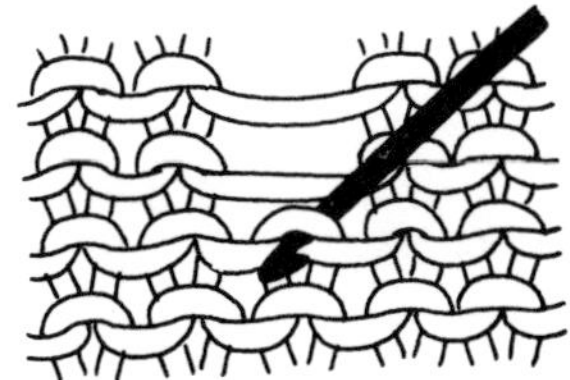

Duplicate Stitch. This is a form of embroidery. Yarn is worked over a knitted stitch, tracing the outline of the stitch.

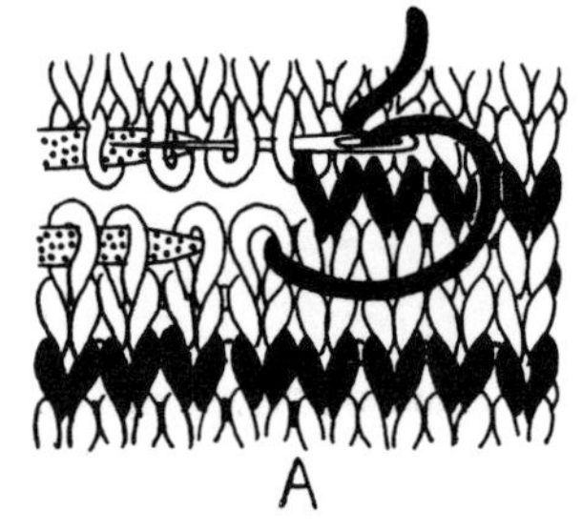

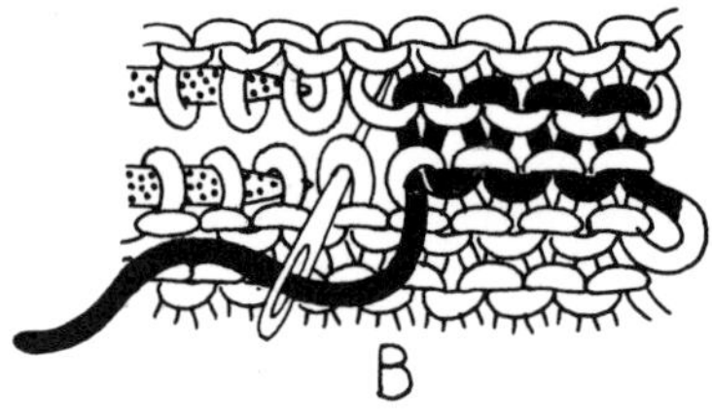

Grafting. This term refers to a method of joining two knitted sections horizontally with invisible results. Work with a blunt embroidery needle and matching yarn. Lay the pieces flat on a table so that the loops are opposite each other. Withdraw the knitting needles, loop by loop, as the blunt needle passes through the stitches, duplicating a knitted stitch (A) and a purled stitch (B).

Except for the first and last stitch in a row, the needle enters each loop twice. Be sure to keep the tension even between the new grafted stitches and the other ones.

Increasing—Knit. Sometimes a stitch pattern or technique requires adding a stitch. To do this, first knit into the front of the stitch in the regular way, but do not remove the old stitch from the left-hand needle (A). Instead, move the right-hand needle under the left one. Knit into the back of same stitch to produce the extra stitch (B). Slip the old stitch off the left-hand needle (C), leaving two stitches on the right-hand needle instead of one.

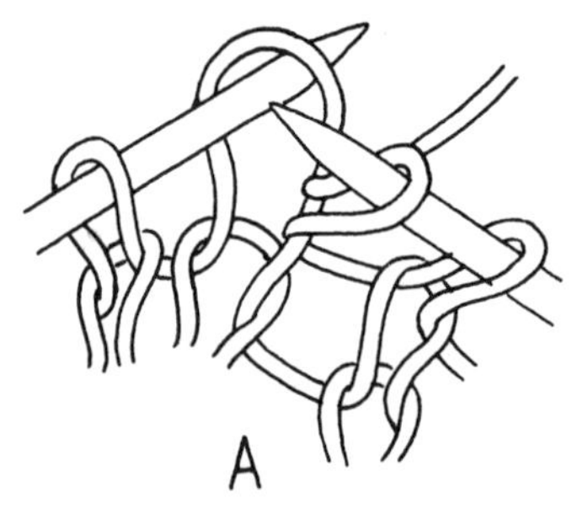

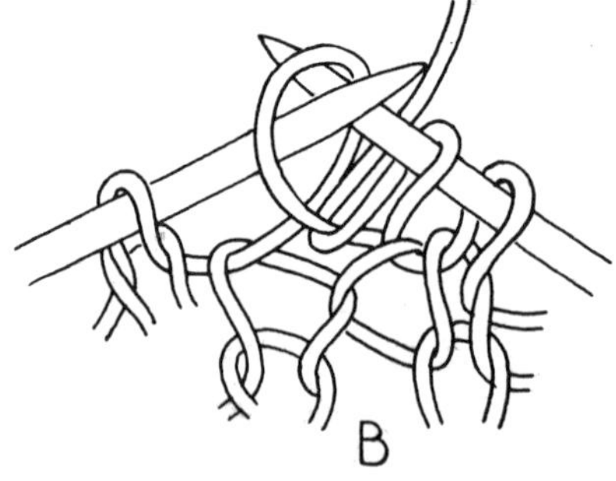

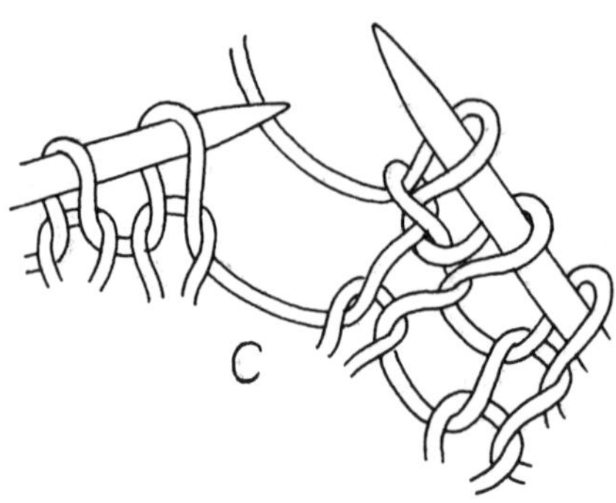

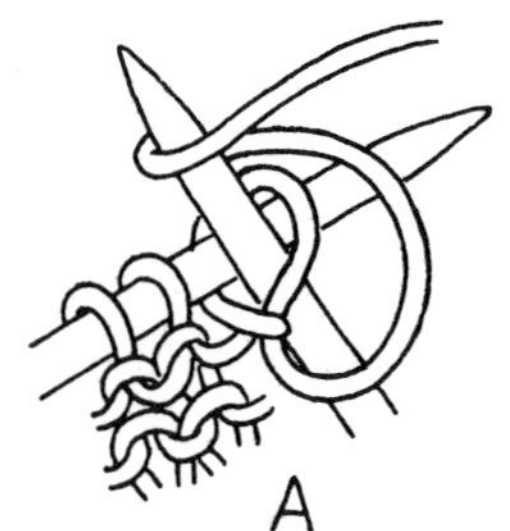

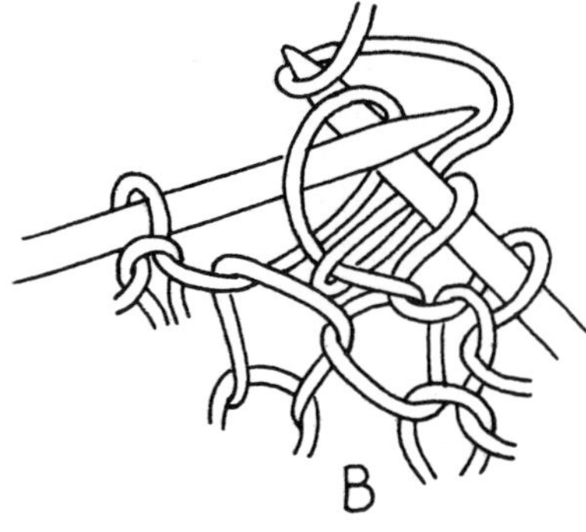

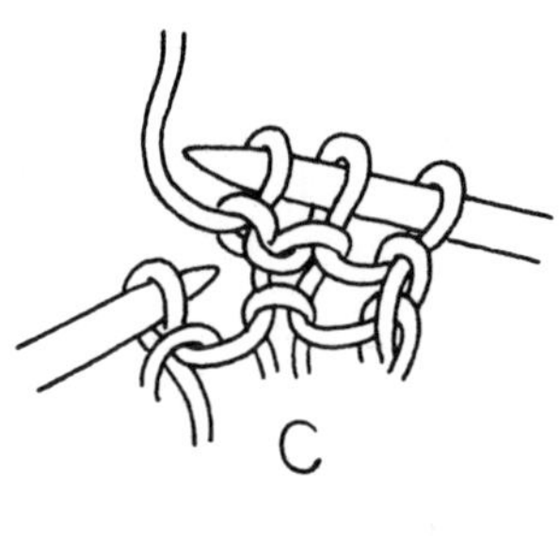

Increasing—Purl. To increase when purling, first purl into the front of the stitch in the regular way, but do not remove the stitch from the needle (A). Instead, make the extra stitch by purling into the back of the same stitch (B). Slip the old stitch off the left-hand needle, leaving two stitches on the right-hand needle instead of one (C).

Knit in Back. When the directions mention knitting in back or knitting through the back of the stitch, the needle is slipped into the back of the stitch instead of the front. The right-hand needle moves from right to left under the needle in the left hand and to the back of it. The needle is then inserted in the stitch, moving in the same direction, and the stitch knitted in the usual manner.

Knit the Row Below. This technique is sometimes used to produce a ribbed effect without purling a stitch. Instead of knitting into the stitch on the needle, insert the needle into the stitch of the row below, dropping the stitch down one row. When the wrong side is checked, two loops appear instead of the usual one. This procedure should never be used for the first or last stitch of a row.

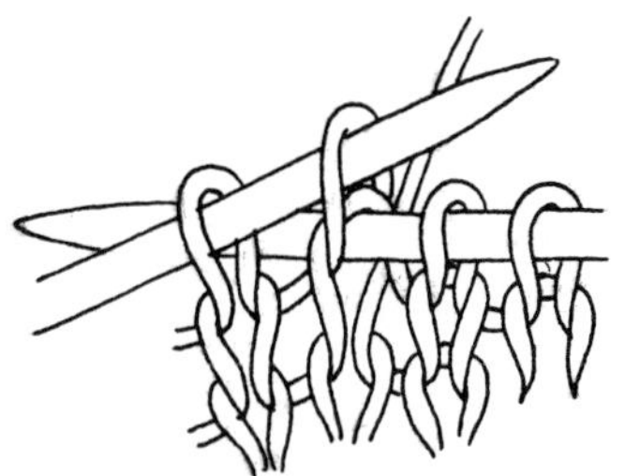

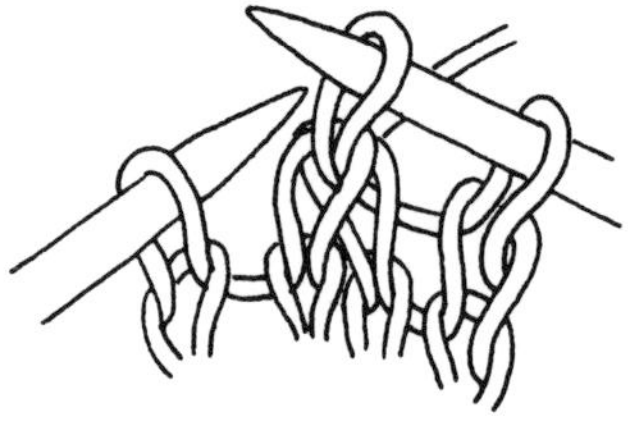

Knit Two Together. Sometimes it is necessary to knit two stitches together. When the directions mention this term, slip the needle through two stitches instead of one and knit in the usual way. One stitch has been made from two. The two stitches can be seen grouped together under the needle.

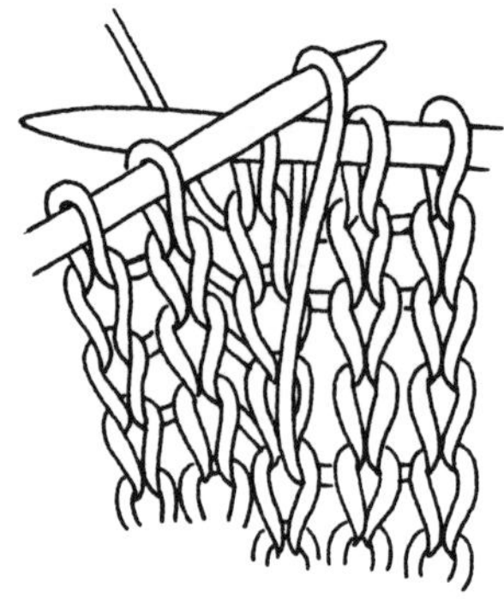

Knitting a Loop from Below. In order to create a decorative effect, this procedure is included in some directions. The stitch in which the right-hand needle is to be inserted will be indicated. Knit through this stitch. Pull up the loop until it reaches the working row of knitting. The loop may be slipped over the next stitch to be made or worked in a way designated in the directions.

Knitwise. When this term appears in knitting directions, it indicates that the procedure is to be done as though it is to be knitted.

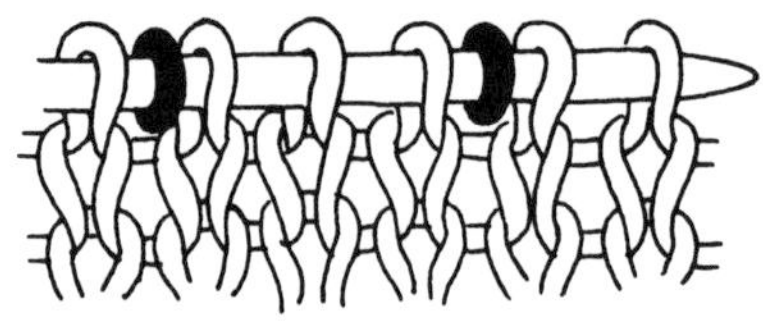

Mark the Place. In order to avoid mistakes, it is helpful to place a marker at a point where a special technique is to be worked, such as a decrease or increase. The marker can be a tiny ring made especially for this purpose, or a piece of yarn can be used.

First, place the marker on the right-hand needle at the designated spot. Slip it from one needle to the other as the work progresses.

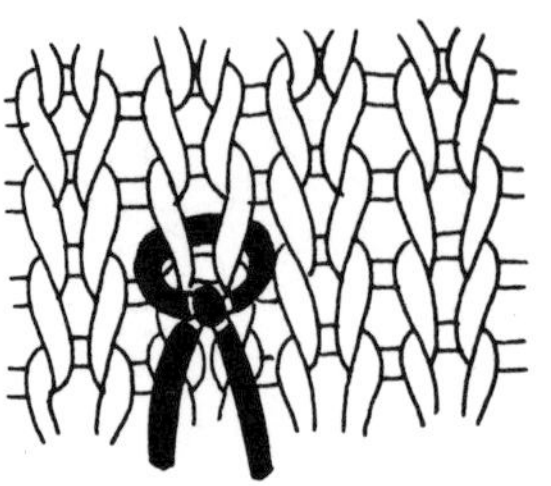

If you use yarn, select one in a contrasting color. Use a slip loop to hold the yarn in place. Leave ends of about 2 inches (5 cm) in length.

Multiple Of. This is a term often seen when a pattern stitch is being made that requires a definite number of stitches. When the instructions read "multiple of," it indicates that the number of foundation stitches to be made must be divisible by the stated number. For instance, a multiple of 5 would mean 10, 15, or 20 stitches would be needed.

If the directions read "multiple of 5 plus 3," then 3 stitches would be added to the total number, making it necessary to use 13, 18, or 23 stitches.

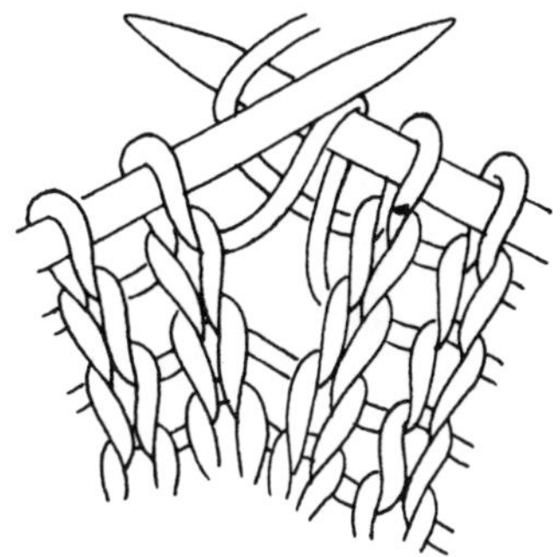

Pick Up One Stitch. (Top) This term indicates a type of yarn over. It produces a slightly smaller space in the work.

Put the tip of the right-hand needle under the yarn stretching between the two needles. Make a knit or purl stitch under this yarn. It is used as a stitch.

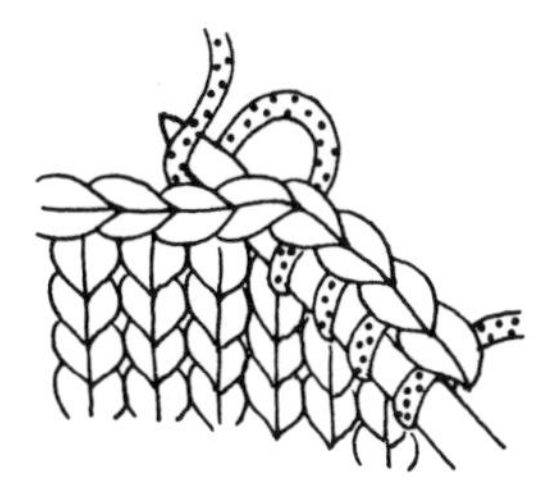

Picking Up Stitches. When one part of an article is to be knit onto another one, such as a band added to a neckline or a sleeve to the armhole of a sweater, this technique is used. Picking up may be done with a knitting needle or a crochet hook. If a knitting needle is used, the stitch is placed directly on the needle. If a crochet hook is used, however, the loop must be transferred from the crochet hook to the knitting needle.

Work from right to left with the right side of the knitting toward you. Hold the needle and the yarn in the right hand, the knitting in the left.

Insert the needle in the first stitch of the first row below the edge. Bring the yarn around the needle. Draw it through, forming a loop or stitch on the right-hand needle. Repeat this procedure until the required number of stitches have been picked up.

Pull or Pass Next Stitch Over. This term indicates a way to decrease a stitch while purling. Sometimes it is referred to as *purl reverse.*

Begin by purling the first stitch of the decrease. Return it to the left-hand needle.

Insert the right-hand needle in the next stitch to the left of the one returned to the left-hand needle. Draw it over the purled stitch. Then return the original purled stitch to the right-hand needle.

Purling in Back of Stitch. These directions may seem confusing unless you follow the drawing. Instead of inserting the right-hand needle into the stitch in front of the left-hand needle, put it through the back of the stitch and at the same time move the right-hand needle in front of the left-hand one. Then place the yarn around the needle and finish the purl stitch.

Purlwise. When this term appears in knitting directions, it indicates that the procedure is to be done as though it is to be purled.

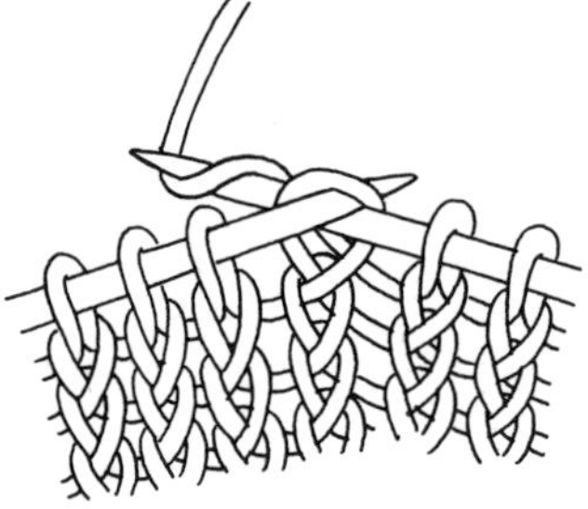

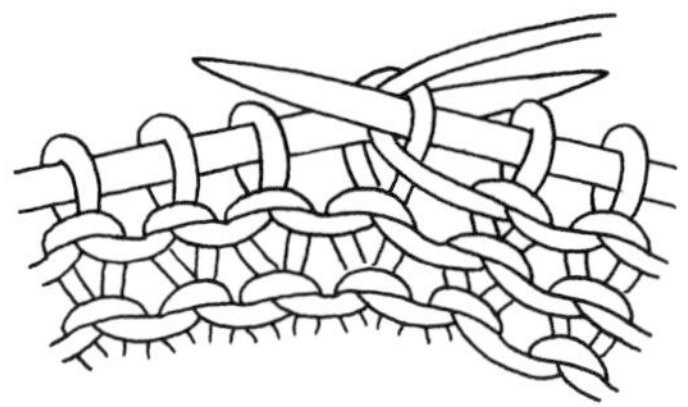

Reverse the Stitch. (Above) By reversing the position of the yarn when knitting and purling for the stockinette stitch, a slightly different effect can be created. It is referred to as the Plaited Stockinette Stitch and seems to have a little more elasticity.

The stitches are worked from the front as usual. The position of the yarn is reversed, however, with the yarn put over the needle on the knit row and under the needle on the purl row.

Sometimes the wrong side of the stockinette stitch is called a Reverse Stitch.

Ridge. A ridge is made by knitting two rows of knit stitches, once across in one direction and then once back.

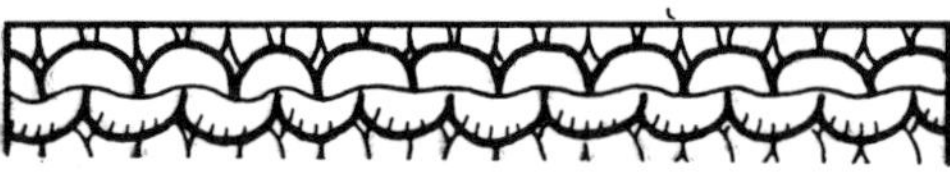

Ripping Back. (Below) No one likes to rip, but there are times that it must be done. Mistakes do happen. They should be detected as soon as possible to simplify the ripping process.

If the error appears on the row being worked, do not take the knitting off the needles. Begin by returning the stitches to the left-hand needle, retracting the stitches that were made after the mistake. Do this by inserting the left-hand needle into the loop or stitch through which the yarn is passing. Slip the right-hand needle out of the last stitch that was made, leaving one less stitch on this needle. Continue this technique until the point of the mistake is reached. This procedure keeps the stitches from becoming twisted. It can be used for both knit and purl stitches.

If the mistake is not discovered until the knitting has been turned and another row worked on, the knitting should be ripped back in the same way, row by row. Some persons find this tedious and prefer to remove the work from the needle and ravel out the stitches in order to make the correction. When this is done, the stitches may become twisted unless the task is carefully undertaken. To avoid twisting, ravel the last row, stitch by stitch, placing each stitch on a fine needle as it is ripped. The stitches can then be knitted onto the regular needle.

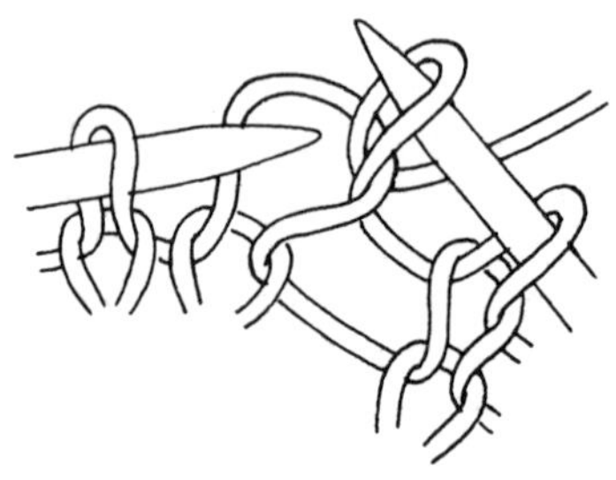

Ripping—Putting Stitches on Needle. Sometimes it is necessary to ravel out some of the knitting in order to make a correction. As the stitches are put back on the needle, be sure to keep them from twisting. Insert the needle from front to back through each loop, for both the knit side and the purl side, as shown in the accompanying drawing. When you resume knitting, put the needle in your left hand.

Row. A row is made when the knitting proceeds once across the needle.

Slip a Stitch. This term indicates that a stitch is to be passed from the left-hand needle to the right-hand one without knitting. This is sometimes done at the beginning of a row. When following directions for a stitch pattern, however, it may be necessary to slip a stitch some distance from the end.

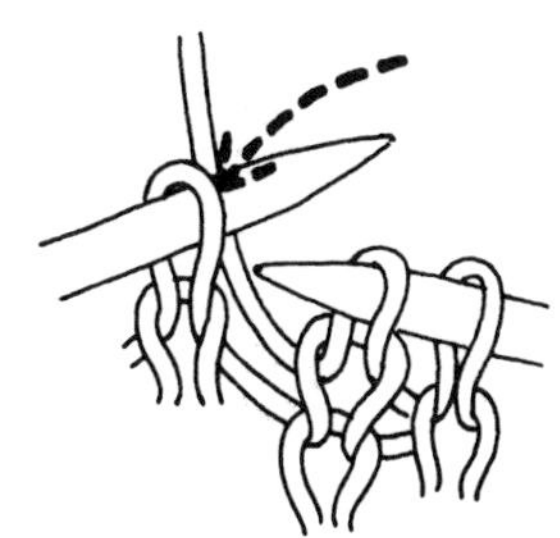

Usually a stitch is slipped purlwise from the left-hand needle to the right-hand one by inserting the right-hand needle into the front of the stitch. Then transfer the stitch without knitting or purling it. Keep the yarn in back of the work.

Slip Loop. Sometimes this term is used instead of *slip knot.* Directions for making it are found in Chapter 1.

Slip, Slip Knit. In directions for decreasing the number of stitches, this term is sometimes found. Slip, one at a time, the first and second stitches knitwise from the left-hand needle to the right-hand one. Insert the point of the left-hand needle into the front of these stitches, moving from left to right. With the needles in this position, knit the stitches together.

Twisted Stitches. Twisted stitches should be avoided. They upset the regularity of the work, producing a flaw. If the stitches are being made correctly, the yarn passes over the needle always in the same direction and with the stitches lined up evenly on the needle. The part of the loop or stitch that is in front of the needle should be closer to the point (A). If it is not (B), then the stitch is twisted and needs to be turned on the needle. Learn to recognize twisted stitches quickly so that stitches that have fallen off the needle or have been ripped off can be returned to the needle in their proper position.

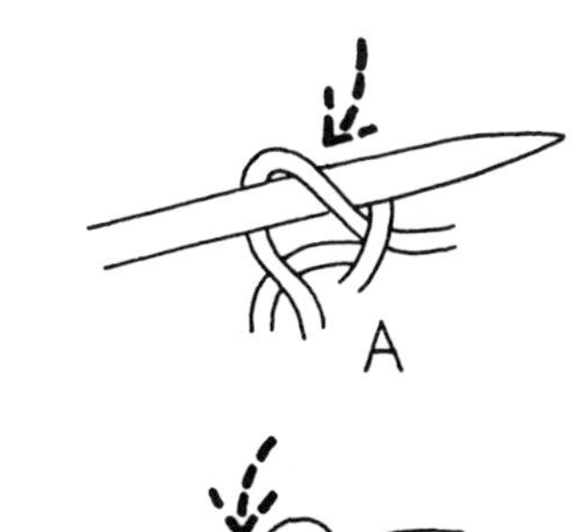

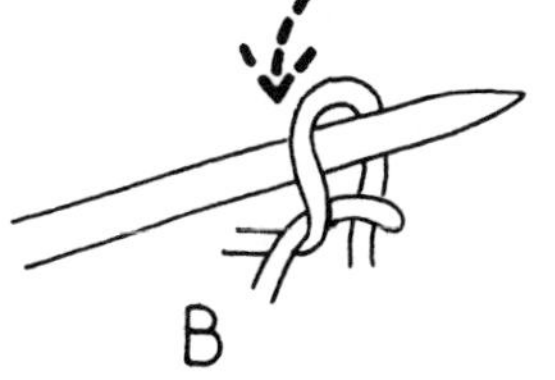

Winding Yarn. Putting yarn into ball form is known as winding. There are several ways of doing this. They are mentioned in Chapter 1.

Work Even. This term means to continue knitting the pattern as previously done, using the same number of stitches without decreases or increases.

Working In Ends. Exposed ends of yarn and knots should be avoided. Yarn tied at the edge can be finished by working the threads up and down along the edge.

If it is necessary to join two pieces of yarn with a knot in the middle of a row, the knot can be eliminated when the article is completed. Untie the knot, which should be on the wrong side of the work. Slip the left-hand yarn into the back of several stitches to the right, the right-hand end in the stitches to the left. When carefully interlocked, they will be invisible. If the ends are too long, they should be clipped.

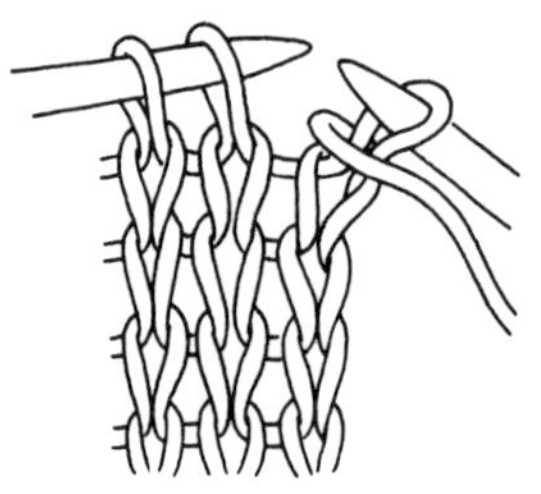

Yarn Forward. Sometimes this term is used instead of the words *yarn in front.*

Yarn in Front. It is sometimes necessary to bring the yarn from the back of the work to the front. To do this, slip the yarn between the two needles. In this position, the knitting can continue.

Yarn Over. The way this procedure is done depends on whether it is worked in a knit row or a purl row. But in each case a loop is formed on the right-hand needle, adding an extra stitch.

Before a knit stitch, bring the yarn to the front of the work and place it under and over the right-hand needle (A). Then knit the stitch. When the next row is knitted, the stitch will appear as in B.

Before a purl stitch, wrap the yarn completely around the right-hand needle. Then purl the stitch (C).

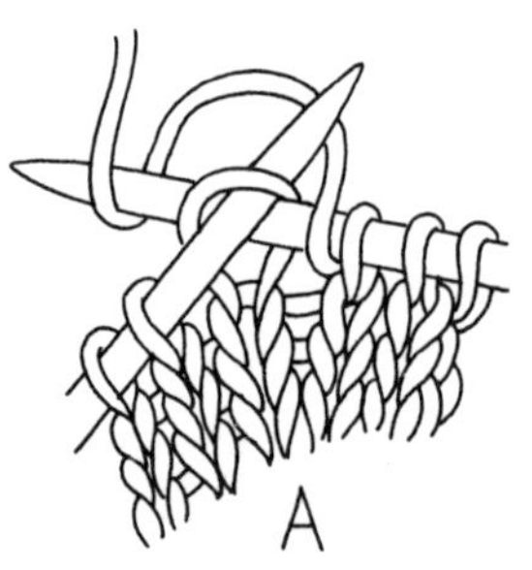
A

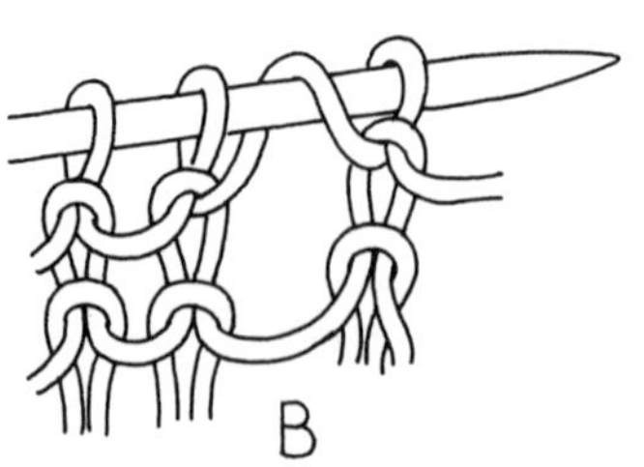
B

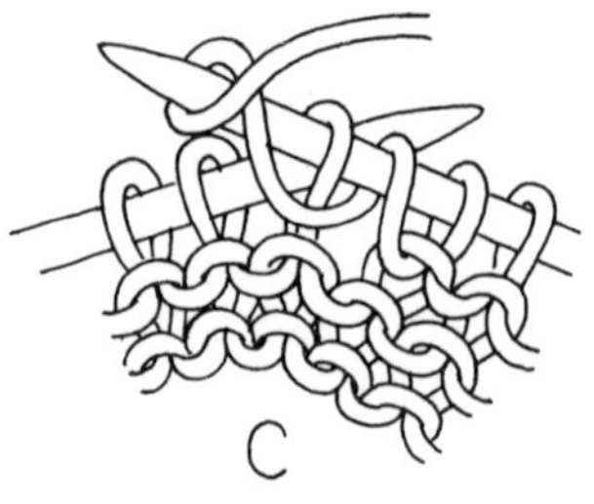
C

How to Choose a Project

After learning to knit and purl, you are ready to make something interesting. In fact, you may attempt this as you try different techniques. Some people find practicing boring unless they are constructing an item.

So that your first knitting experience is pleasant, select the project carefully. Be sure it is easy to knit. Choosing too difficult a project can have frustrating results. As you become more accomplished, your knitting can become more complicated. But at all stages it should be attractive and fun to make.

JUDGING FOR SIMPLICITY

Learning to recognize the easy-to-make is a must. Look for a design using the garter stitch that requires no shaping. Keep it small. Having few stitches on the needle makes the rows seem to flash by. The article grows as if by magic.

Although large needles speed up the process, medium-sized ones are easier to handle. Also, when working with a small number of stitches, try short needles. They are less awkward to use.

Smooth, pliable yarn of a medium weight will also make the process less difficult. Be sure to choose a color you like. It makes watching the stitches more pleasant. You will also find that when there is a color contrast between the needle and the yarn, it is simpler to keep track of the stitches.

ANALYZING PERSONAL CHARACTERISTICS

This is a part of picking a project that is often neglected. Designs and yarns are not always selected for their becoming effect, yet they should be. They have the power to make you look more attractive. You can appear shorter or taller, smaller or larger, slimmer or more rounded, by the correct use of lines, colors, and textures. They can even make an area seem smaller and, at the same time, add fullness to another. Attention can be drawn to an asset as a liability is camouflaged. Creating these illusions depends on how well you can select your pattern and yarn.

Before you decide which design to use, look at yourself. Do not take the examination lightly. See yourself as a candid camera does. Too often we look at ourselves through rose-colored glasses. Please don't. Be as critical of yourself as you would be of someone else. Consider your assets as well as your liabilities. Take

note of your size, your shape, and your coloring. Notice whether you stand erect or whether you have a tendency to slump. If you do, you probably have round shoulders, a hollow chest, a prominent abdomen, and a sway back.

As you make this analysis, also note whether your body seems to be in good proportion. Is the length of your waist too short or too long for your height? Do your hips seem to protrude too far in the rear? You should remember that, because of their clinging quality, knits can, unless carefully chosen, emphasize unattractive characteristics.

Because color plays such an important part in creating a flattering effect, be sure to note the facial tones, especially of your skin. All skins, whether dark or light, include red and yellow tones. Some people have a predominance of red in their skin, whereas others have a predominance of yellow. Often it is forgotten that when red and yellow are combined, orange is the result. Orange can be lightened to give a creamy skin tone, or darkened to a deep rich brown. Your skin may be light in tone, or it may be a darker shade. If you enjoy sunbathing, your skin tones may fluctuate between light and dark.

Remembering Likes and Dislikes

During one's lifetime, one develops clothing likes and dislikes that are probably related to personality traits. Before selecting a design, consider this facet of dressing in a general way. Do you prefer fussy clothes to tailored ones, dainty to tweedy, sporty to dressy, frilly to plain, classic to high-styled, demure to sophisticated, dramatic to understated? Do you like your colors bright and dazzling or pale and subdued? Do you like yarns that are fine or coarse, soft or rough, limp or stiff? Will it be a classic sweater in a subdued color or one with blocks of wild hues? A cashmere cardigan or a bulky fisherman? A simple V neck or a draped cowl? This probing could go on and on. Continue until you have the answers. Intense emotional reactions can be encouraged by the use of the wrong line, color, and texture. It is important that you avoid this.

SELECTING THE RIGHT PATTERN FOR YOU

One aspect of selecting the right project is the fun of using optical illusion. As if by magic, new looks can be created with flattering effects. It has always seemed strange that a woman will spend so much money and time trying to reduce the size of her figure by dieting and exercise when she could to some extent change her apparent size by employing the tricks of optical illusion. Although your eyes usually tell the truth, there are times when lines, colors, and textures deceive you.

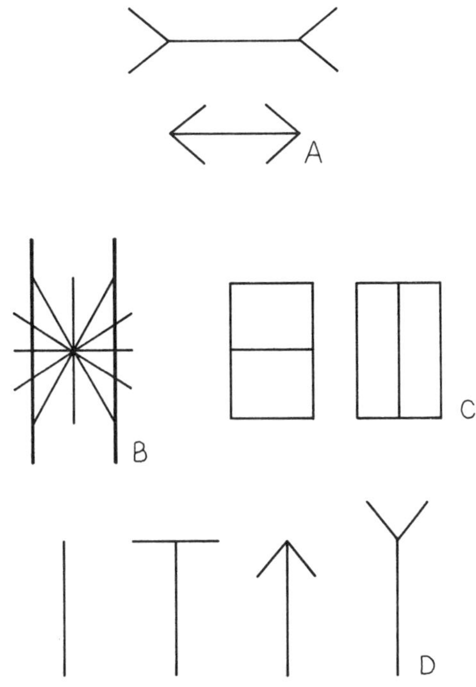

Tricks with Lines

If you cannot quite believe this, study the lines and shapes here. No doubt you have seen them before. In diagram A, notice how much shorter the lower line appears than the upper, yet both of the lines are the same length. If this example does not convince you, look at the heavy lines in diagram B. They seem to bulge, yet the lines are really straight.

Then, if you are still skeptical, observe the rectangles in C. They surely do not appear the same although they actually are. The vertical line makes the rectangle seem much narrower and taller than the horizontal line does.

When you learn to use optical illusion correctly, it becomes pure magic. You can make yourself seem larger or smaller, taller or shorter, thinner or stouter by employing the tricks of optical illusion—and this applies to the face as well as the figure.

In order to use this magic device, you should understand how the eye reacts to line. The eye follows the direction the line takes. For instance, in diagram D there are four lines of the same length, but notice how different the lengths appear. In the first, the eye moves upward and continues to do just that because there is no other line to stop it. But in the second, the eye meets an oppositional line, forcing it to stop and move horizontally instead of vertically. This makes the line seem shorter. However, in the third line, when the eye meets the oppositional line, the eye turns downward, and of course the line seems shorter. But in the fourth line, when the eye contacts the oppositional lines, it continues upward, making the line appear taller.

By using these tricks, you can keep the eye moving upward if you wish to appear taller and in turn thinner, and downward if you want to seem shorter and more rounded. Notice how the design lines of the hats and sweater dresses on the pages following influence the size of the figure just as they did in the diagrams.

Tricks with Space

Although the eye is influenced by the direction a line takes, it is also affected by the way a space is divided. Remember how the vertical and horizontal lines changed the appearance of the rectangles.

Notice how this type of illusion affects the appearance of the fashion figures (A). It is easy to see that the sweater and skirt makes the figure appear much shorter than the sweater dress with long center closing does.

Many interesting optical illusions can be achieved by dividing large spaces into smaller areas. But remember the proportion of the spaces to each other will affect the illusion that results. Observe the rectangles (B) and how the width of the panel appears to affect the size of the rectangle. When the two parallel lines forming the panel are close enough together so the eye has a path in which to move upward, both the rectangle and figure appear taller and narrower. But when the lines are placed far apart, the eye has a tendency to move from one side of the panel to the other. You can see that this makes the object seem wider and of course shorter. You should remember this trick of optical illusion not only when selecting the design of a sweater, but also when wearing the cardigan. Leaving it open so a narrow panel is formed will make you seem thinner, but if you let it fly open so a wide panel results, you will increase your apparent size a great deal.

Although it is commonly believed that vertical lines make an object appear taller and in turn thinner, and that horizontal lines have a widening effect, there are times when the reverse is true. It is because of this that you should always ask yourself how your eyes perceive an object. To look taller, the eye must continue to move upward. As you look at diagram C, on the following page, notice how much narrower and higher the block of horizontal lines appears than the one made of vertical lines. When the spaces between the lines are proportioned so that the eye moves quickly from one line to the next one without stopping, the spacing is more important than the

direction the lines are taking. In this instance, spaces between the horizontal lines create a vertical illusion. Because of this, be sure to analyze a striped design to see which way the eye will move.

Look Up or Across

Before you begin to apply these tricks of optical illusion, you should decide whether you need to keep the eye moving upward or crosswise. Once you have made this decision, begin to experiment. Some suggestions are mentioned here to help you create a becoming illusion.

Looking Taller. To produce the correct effect isn't always easy when working with knitted articles. So often the knitted item is a sweater, which has a tendency to make one look larger and in turn shorter. Remember, however, that straight lines moving in a vertical direction usually create a lengthening and slimming effect. A cardigan sweater worn slightly open; a collarless neckline with a V line; long, tight sleeves; a straight skirt; a tight-fitting turtle neckline—all will make you appear taller and thinner. Certain stitch patterns, such as a cable, can keep the eye moving upward when correctly placed.

Your face and neck can also be made to seem more slender by the use of vertical illusions. A V neckline, a narrow collar that forms a V shape, and a collar worn open at the throat and high at the back of the neck will keep the eye moving upward. Notice that the apparent shape of the face seems to change as the shape of the neckline varies. Even the manner of draping a cowl has its altering effect.

Accessories can contribute to creating a vertical illusion. A long, narrow scarf and a hat with an upturned brim or tilt can be used to carry the eye upward.

Looking Shorter. The eye likes to move in a horizontal fashion. When the eye is allowed to do this, the figure appears shorter and slightly more rounded. A two-piece effect, such as a sweater and skirt, or a sweater worn wide open will

produce this illusion. Wide sleeves and those with cuffs that end at the bustline or hipline will draw the eye across the figure, seeming to add breadth to these areas. A high round collar and a bulky cowl will add apparent roundness. Short capes and jackets create the same effect.

A hat with a turned-down brim and a short, wide scarf draped across the shoulders will seem to shorten the figure.

Stitch patterns, such as a series of cable, may carry the eye across the figure. Designs in which curved lines are dominant will also do this.

Promoting an Asset

Although the eye usually follows the direction a line takes, you should remember that the eye is attracted to the more dominant line. Notice, in the accompanying diagram, how your eye focuses its attention on the longer or more emphatic line in each drawing. This makes it possible for you to attract the eye to any part of your costume. By using this trick carefully, you can camouflage figure problems and at the same time call attention to an attractive feature. A draped cowl, an interesting yoke, or a dashing scarf can draw attention to a pretty face. With the eyes focused on the face, out-of-proportion hips may be unnoticed.

Choosing a Pleasing Color

Nearly everyone finds it difficult to use color so the effect is pleasing. It is so easy to use too much or the wrong kind. It is usually only by practice that you can develop a good color sense.

Creating Illusions. One of the first things to remember is that color allows you to produce illusions that change the apparent appearance of a person or object. For instance, you can look larger or smaller or feel warmer or cooler depending on the color you wear. Warm or advancing colors, such as red and yellow, will make you appear larger, whereas a cool or receding color, such as blue, will make you seem smaller.

The intensity of a color should also be considered. Bright colors have the power to make you appear larger, whereas quiet, grayed hues seem to make the figure fade into the background, thus appearing smaller. This is the reason why a bright blue sweater will make you look larger than one made of a soft, medium blue.

The value of a color, too, will influence the apparent size of an object. Dark colors will seem to decrease the size; light colors, to increase it. Have you ever observed how much larger your feet look in white shoes than they do in black ones?

Another way of using color to create interesting illusions is to divide the design into parts by employing different hues. Of course, you have to be careful when you use colors in this way if you are trying to achieve a tall, slender look. For instance, a sweater of one color and a skirt of another will make the figure look shorter than the same design in one color. Also, the introduction of a contrasting hue in an accessory, such as a scarf or hat, will tend to make the figure appear shorter unless you remember to employ the art principles, so that the eye moves from one to the other in an upward motion.

If you decide to introduce contrasting hues or values in your costume, remember that the larger the area to be covered, the more subdued the color should be, and the smaller the space, the stronger the contrast can be. A slender person with a lovely figure will look exceedingly good in a bright sweater, whereas a plump person will appear huge in the same brilliant hue. Therefore, if you love bright colors and do not have a good figure, it is better to limit their use to a small space, such as a scarf or hat. But if you want to introduce a contrasting color in several accessories, then the value and intensity of the color should be subdued.

Another interesting color note that can be employed to great advantage is the power of a light color to attract and hold the attention of the eye. This makes it possible for you to introduce a light color to play up a good feature so that a figure irregularity may remain unnoticed. For instance, if you have hips that are out of proportion, you should not call attention to them by putting a white band on the lower edge of a dark sweater. Instead, introduce the light touch at the neckline so that the eye is attracted to the face.

Selecting a Flattering Texture

Texture is often overlooked when choosing a becoming design. It shouldn't be. Although you may choose the lines

and colors that are perfect for you, the effect can be destroyed unless the correct texture is used. In knitting, both the yarn and the stitch pattern contribute to the textured effect. Some yarns are soft and seem to cling to the figure, whereas others are stiff and bulky, standing away from the body. A cable stitch, with its rounded design pattern, can make the figure seem larger than a ribbed one with its straight lines. Because of these differences, it is important for you to give some thought to these distinguishing traits and the effect they have on the figure.

Although bulky and heavy textures conceal the outline of the figure, they increase the size of the wearer, depending on the weight of the yarn. You will find light- or moderate-weight yarn more flattering to the average figure. Yarns of the heavier type, however, can be used by the tall, well-proportioned athletic figure, but they should be avoided by the tiny and the plump.

Yarns that form a smooth surface when knitted will minimize the figure, whereas those that are fluffy and definitely textured will make the figure seem more rounded.

Dull textures seem to make the silhouette of the figure seem indistinct. This is important to remember if your figure is not well proportioned.

Shiny textures, such as found in glittering yarns, have a tendency to increase the size of the figure. They also seem to highlight the silhouette. It is better to refrain from using them unless you have a perfect figure.

Lacy pattern stitches do not seem to have any effect on the apparent size of the figure. However, the outline of the figure is revealed. This makes it possible for anyone to see how fat or how thin you are. Unless you have a lovely figure, it would be better to avoid transparent textures.

When selecting a stitch pattern, be sure to consider its effect on the figure. Designs of moderate size and interest, and those with an indefinite allover pattern, with the lines and colors blended, can be flattering. Be sure that there is a distinct vertical motion in the design in case you want to appear taller. Usually, patterned textures make the figure seem larger than plain ones.

Watching the Fashions

Before you select a knitting project to wear, study the fashion trends. Browse through magazines, study advertisements, window-shop, and do not forget to check what ready-to-wear is showing. No doubt you will notice that there are extremes in styles—fads that go out of fashion quickly. You will soon realize that there are exclusive models from name designers. Although the price of these designs is probably prohibitive, check the group carefully. Usually it provides ideas, foretelling the fashions of tomorrow. Because knitting is time-consuming, you want to be sure that the project you make will still be in style when you finish it. Of course, the perennial favorites—the conservative classic styles—are an excellent choice.

No doubt you will find that certain fashions will be unbecoming. Do not feel you have to wear them. You will be much wiser to dress in style and look attractive than to dress in fashion and appear unattractive. Learn to adapt fashion to fit your needs. Select the lines, colors, and textures that are right for you, creating the image you want to portray.

6

Combine the Basics

Although you could knit forever using the plain knitting stitches, it is fascinating to see how many looks can be produced by combining them. On the next few pages you will find some of these combinations. Garter and stockinette stitches are arranged to form a variety of geometric designs. They add a textural quality that promotes plain knitting into the realm of the interesting.

One of the things to remember when working with these stitch patterns is that they will probably be most effective when worked in a solid color. Variegated colors may detract from the definite outline of the designs. Also, a change of color for a striped effect may produce an unexpected "wrong side" look to the stitches that are purled on the right side.

Before using one of the pattern stitches, knit a sample, so that you can study the resulting effect. Usually these patterns can be substituted when the directions call for the garter or stockinette stitches. Perhaps you will think of some other ways to combine knits and purls.

As you study the directions, you will notice that they are written without abbreviations in order to make the knitting easier to do. It enables you to concentrate on the stitch construction and not on trying to remember the meaning of the abbreviations.

All Fools' Welt Pattern

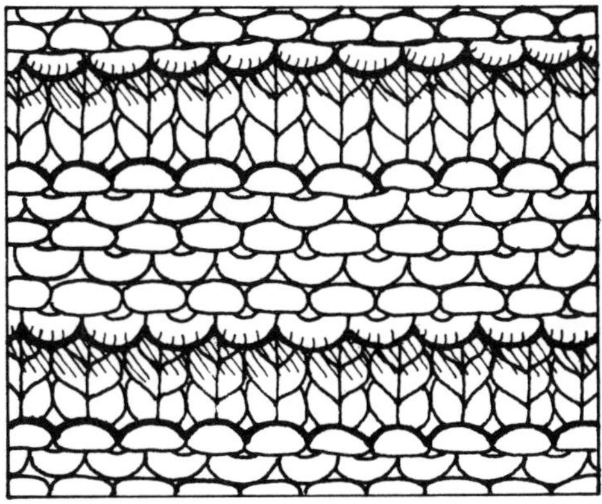

This is an easy-to-make stitch pattern with a striped effect. It is interesting to note that it has many names, such as Dispute, Puzzle, and Wager Welt.

For the **beginning row**, cast on as many stitches as required.
For the **first row,** knit.
For the **second row,** purl.
For the **third row,** knit.
For the **fourth row,** knit.
For the **fifth row,** knit.
For the **sixth row,** knit.
For the **seventh row,** knit.
For the **eighth row,** knit.
Repeat the **eight rows** as many times as required.

Escalator Pattern

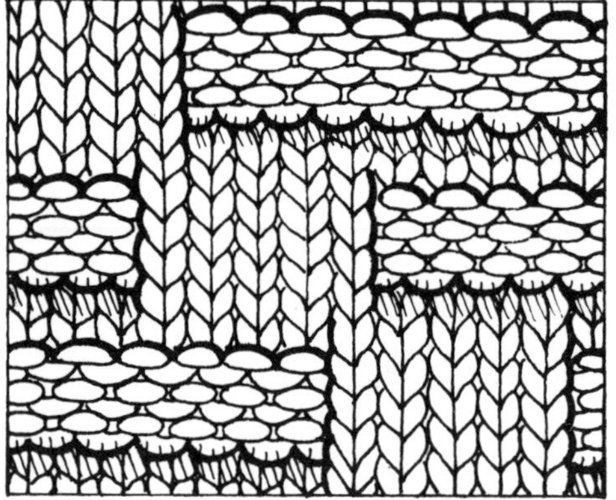

The step formation of purl-stitch bands produces a diagonal movement to this stitch pattern.

For the **beginning row,** cast on a multiple of 32 stitches.
For the **first row,** repeat the following procedure. * Knit 5. Purl 11. *
For the **second row,** repeat the following procedure. * Knit 11. Purl 5. *
For the **third row,** repeat the first row.
For the **fourth row,** purl.
For the **fifth row,** knit.
For the **sixth row,** purl.
For the **seventh row,** purl 4. Repeat the following procedure. * Knit 5. Purl 11. * End with knit 5, purl 7.
For the **eighth row,** knit 7. Repeat the following procedure. * Purl 5. Knit 11. * End with purl 5, knit 4.
For the **ninth row,** repeat the seventh row.
For the **tenth row,** purl.
For the **eleventh row,** knit.
For the **twelfth row,** purl.
For the **thirteenth row,** purl 8. Repeat the following procedure. * Knit 5. Purl 11. * End with knit 5, purl 3.
For the **fourteenth row,** knit 3. Repeat the following procedure. * Purl 5. Knit 11. * End with purl 5, knit 8.
For the **fifteenth row,** repeat the thirteenth row.
For the **sixteenth row,** purl.
For the **seventeenth row,** knit.
For the **eighteenth row,** purl.
For the **nineteenth row,** knit 1, purl 11. Repeat the following procedure. * Knit 5. Purl 11. * End with knit 4.
For the **twentieth row,** purl 4. Repeat the following procedure. * Knit 11. Purl 5. * End with knit 11, purl 1.
For the **twenty-first row,** repeat the nineteenth row.
For the **twenty-second row,** purl.
For the **twenty-third row,** knit.
For the **twenty-fourth row,** purl.
Repeat the **first through twenty-fourth rows** as many times as required.

Square Pattern

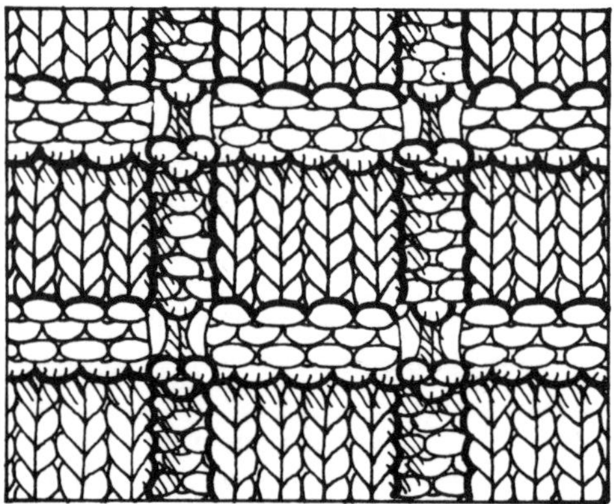

This stitch pattern is frequently used for Swedish designs.

For the **beginning row,** cast on a multiple of 6 stitches plus 2.
For the **first row,** knit 2. Repeat the following procedure. * Purl 4. Knit 2. *
For the **second row,** purl 2. Repeat the following procedure. * Knit 4. Purl 2. *
For the **third row,** repeat the second row.
For the **fourth row,** repeat the first row.
For the **fifth row,** repeat the second row.
For the **sixth row,** repeat the first row.
For the **seventh row,** repeat the second row.
For the **eighth row,** repeat the first row.
Repeat the **first through eighth rows** as many times as required.

Block Pattern

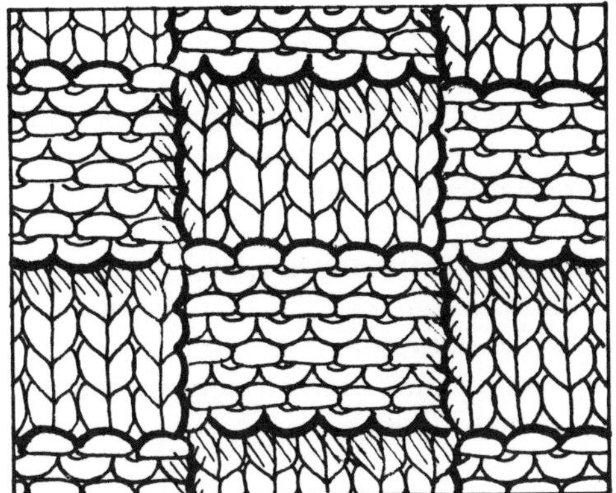

Dice Pattern is the name that is sometimes given this pattern. The easy-to-make check design can be varied in size if different numbers of knit and purl stitches are combined.

For the **beginning row,** cast on a multiple of 10 stitches plus 5.
For the **first row,** knit 5. Repeat the following procedure. * Purl 5. Knit 5. *
For the **second row,** purl 5. Repeat the following procedure. * Knit 5. Purl 5. *
For the **third row,** repeat the first row.
For the **fourth row,** repeat the second row.
For the **fifth row,** repeat the first row.
For the **sixth row,** repeat the first row.
For the **seventh row,** repeat the second row.
For the **eighth row,** repeat the first row.
For the **ninth row,** repeat the second row.
For the **tenth row,** knit 5. Repeat the following procedure. * Purl 5. Knit 5. *
Repeat the **first through tenth rows** as required.

A variation of this pattern can be made by arranging the stitches to appear as oblong blocks.

For the **beginning row,** cast on a multiple of 10 stitches plus 5.
For the **first row,** knit.
For the **second row,** knit 5. Repeat the following procedure. * Purl 5. Knit 5. *
For the **third row,** repeat the first row.
For the **fourth row,** repeat the second row.
For the **fifth row,** repeat the first row.
For the **sixth row,** repeat the second row.
For the **seventh row,** repeat the first row.
For the **eighth row,** purl 5. Repeat the following procedure. * Knit 5. Purl 5. *
For the **ninth row,** repeat the first row.
For the **tenth row,** repeat the eighth row.
For the **eleventh row,** repeat the first row.
For the **twelfth row,** repeat the eighth row.
Repeat the **first through twelfth rows** as many times as required.

Basket Weave Pattern

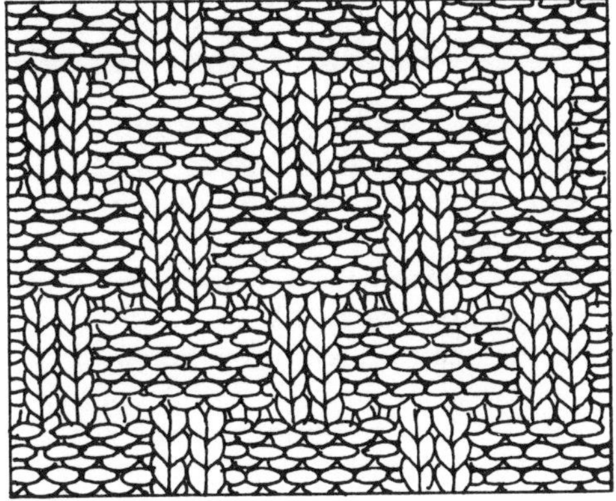

This is a well-known English pattern that is simple to make. The combination of stitches can vary to produce different effects.

For the **beginning row,** cast on a multiple of 8 stitches.
For the **first row,** knit 1. Purl across row. End with knit 1.
For the **second row,** knit 1. Purl 2. Repeat the following procedure. * Knit 2. Purl 6. * End with knit 2, purl 2, knit 1.
For the **third row,** knit 3. Repeat the following procedure. * Purl 2. Knit 6. * End with purl 2, knit 3.
For the **fourth row,** repeat the second row.
For the **fifth row,** repeat the first row.
For the **sixth row,** knit 1. Repeat the following procedure. * Purl 6. Knit 2. * End with purl 6, knit 1.
For the **seventh row,** knit 7. Purl 2. Repeat the following procedure. * Knit 6. Purl 2. * End with knit 7.
For the **eighth row,** repeat the sixth row.
Repeat the **first through eighth rows** as many times as required.

Double Basket Pattern

An interesting arrangement of ribs and stripes produces a checkerboard effect. It seems to create a wavy effect when left unpressed.

For the **beginning row,** cast on a multiple of 18 stitches plus 10.

For the **first row,** repeat the following procedure. * Knit 11. Purl 2. Knit 2. Purl 2. Knit 1. * End with knit 10.

For the **second row,** purl 1, knit 8, purl 1. Repeat the following procedure. * Purl 1. Knit 2. Purl 2. Knit 2. Purl 2. Knit 8. Purl 1. *

For the **third row,** repeat the following procedure. * Knit 1. Purl 8. Knit 2. Purl 2. Knit 2. Purl 2. Knit 1. * End with knit 1, purl 8, and knit 1.

For the **fourth row,** purl 10. Repeat the following procedure. * Purl 1. Knit 2. Purl 2. Knit 2. Purl 11. *

For the **fifth row,** repeat the first row.

For the **sixth row,** repeat the second row.

For the **seventh row,** repeat the third row.

For the **eighth row,** repeat the fourth row.

For the **ninth row,** knit.

For the **tenth row,** purl 2. Knit 2. Purl 2. Knit 2. Purl 2. Repeat the following procedure. * Purl 10, knit 2. Purl 2. Knit 2. Purl 2. *

For the **eleventh row,** repeat the following procedure. * Knit 2. Purl 2. Knit 2. Purl 2. Knit 2. Purl 8. * End with knit 2. Purl 2. Knit 2. Purl 2. Knit 2.

For the **twelfth row,** purl 2. Knit 2. Purl 2. Knit 2. Purl 2. Repeat the following procedure. * Knit 8. Purl 2. Knit 2. Purl 2. Knit 2. Purl 2. *

For the **thirteenth row,** repeat the following procedure. * Knit 2. Purl 2. Knit 2. Purl 2. Knit 10. * End with knit 2. Purl 2. Knit 2. Purl 2. Knit 2.

For the **fourteenth row,** repeat the tenth row.

For the **fifteenth row,** repeat the eleventh row.

For the **sixteenth row,** repeat the twelfth row.

For the **seventeenth row,** repeat the thirteenth row.

For the **eighteenth row,** purl.

Repeat the **first through eighteenth rows** as many times as required.

Lozenge Pattern

Triangular shapes forming squares give an interesting look to this old Italian stitch pattern.

For the **beginning row,** cast on a multiple of 5 stitches.

For the **first row,** repeat the following procedure. * Purl 1. Knit 4. *

For the **second row,** repeat the following procedure. * Purl 3. Knit 2. *

For the **third row,** repeat the second row.

For the **fourth row,** repeat the following procedure. * Purl 1. Knit 4. *

For the **fifth row,** repeat the fourth row.

For the **sixth row,** repeat the following procedure. * Knit 2. Purl 3. *

For the **seventh row,** repeat the sixth row.

For the **eighth row,** repeat the following procedure. * Knit 4. Purl 1. *

Repeat the **first through eighth rows** as many times as required.

Arabic Cross Pattern

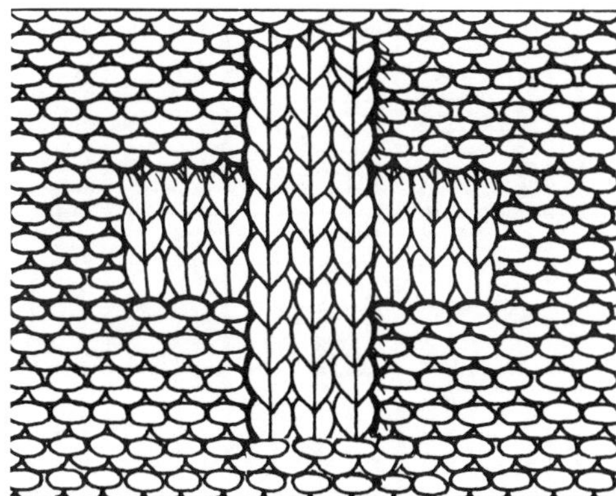

This design resembles those found in very old pieces of knitting.

For the **beginning row,** cast on a multiple of 12 stitches plus 1.

For the **first row,** purl.

For the **second row,** knit.

For the **third row,** purl 5. Repeat the following procedure. * Knit 3 stitches through back loop. Purl 9. * End the last repeat by purling 5 stitches instead of 9.

For the **fourth row,** knit 5. Repeat the following procedure. * Purl 3. Knit 9. * End the last repeat by knitting 5 stitches instead of 9.

For the **fifth row,** repeat the third row.

For the **sixth row,** repeat the fourth row.

For the **seventh row,** purl 2. Repeat the following procedure. * Knit 9 stitches through back loop. Purl 3. * End the last repeat by purling 2 stitches instead of 3.

For the **eighth row,** knit 2. Repeat the following procedure. * Purl 9. Knit 3. * End the last repeat by knitting 2 stitches instead of 3.

For the **ninth row,** repeat the seventh row.

For the **tenth row,** repeat the eighth row.

For the **eleventh row,** repeat the third row.

For the **twelfth row,** repeat the fourth row.

For the **thirteenth row,** repeat the third row.

For the **fourteenth row,** repeat the fourth row.

For the **fifteenth row,** purl.

For the **sixteenth row,** knit.

Repeat the **first through sixteenth rows** as many times as required.

Harris Tweed Stitch

This arrangement of knit and purl stitches gives an interesting raised and somewhat checked effect.

For the **beginning row,** cast on a multiple of 4 stitches.

For the **first row,** repeat the following procedure. * Knit 2. Purl 2. *

For the **second row,** repeat the first row.

For the **third row,** knit.

For the **fourth row,** purl.

For the **fifth row,** repeat the first row.

For the **sixth row,** repeat the first row.

For the **seventh row,** purl.

For the **eighth row,** knit.

Repeat the **first through eighth rows** as many times as required.

Diamond Pattern

This is another stitch pattern that creates a reversible knitted fabric, although the design does not appear quite the same on both sides.

For the **beginning row,** cast on a multiple of 15 stitches.

For the **first row,** repeat the following procedure. * Knit 1. Purl 13. Knit 1. *

For the **second row,** repeat the following procedure. * Purl 2. Knit 11. Purl 2. *

For the **third row,** repeat the following procedure. * Knit 3. Purl 9. Knit 3. *

For the **fourth row,** repeat the following procedure. * Purl 4. Knit 7. Purl 4. *

For the **fifth row,** repeat the following procedure. * Knit 5. Purl 5. Knit 5. *

For the **sixth row,** repeat the following procedure. * Knit 1. Purl 5. Knit 3. Purl 5. Knit 1. *

For the **seventh row,** repeat the following procedure. * Purl 2. Knit 5. Purl 1. Knit 5. Purl 2. *

For the **eighth row,** repeat the following procedure. * Knit 3. Purl 9. Knit 3. *

For the **ninth row,** repeat the seventh row.

For the **tenth row,** repeat the sixth row.

For the **eleventh row,** repeat the fifth row.

For the **twelfth row,** repeat the fourth row.

For the **thirteenth row,** repeat the third row.

For the **fourteenth row,** repeat the second row.

Repeat the **first through fourteenth rows** as many times as required.

Tulip Pattern

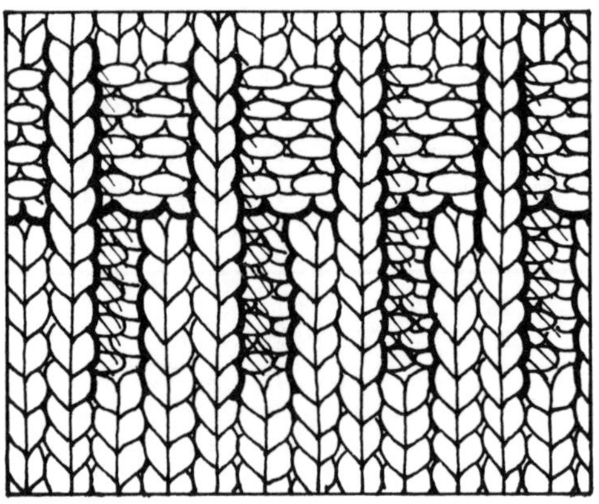

This is another stitch pattern with a French origin. The stitch arrangement creates an unusual textural effect.

For the **beginning row,** cast on a multiple of 3 stitches.

For the **first row,** repeat the following procedure. * Knit 1 in back. Knit 2. *

For the **second row,** repeat the following procedure. * Purl 2. Purl 1 in back. *

For the **third row,** repeat the first row.

For the **fourth row,** repeat the second row.

For the **fifth row,** repeat the following procedure. * Knit 1 in back. Purl 1. Knit 1 in back. *

For the **sixth row,** repeat the following procedure. * Purl 1 in back. Knit 1. Purl 1 in back. *

For the **seventh row,** repeat the fifth row.

For the **eighth row,** repeat the sixth row.

For the **ninth row,** repeat the following procedure. * Purl 2. Knit 1 in back. *

For the **tenth row,** repeat the following procedure. * Purl 1 in back. Knit 2. *

For the **eleventh row,** repeat the ninth row.

For the **twelfth row,** repeat the tenth row.

Repeat the **first through twelfth rows** as many times as required.

Zigzag Garter Stitch

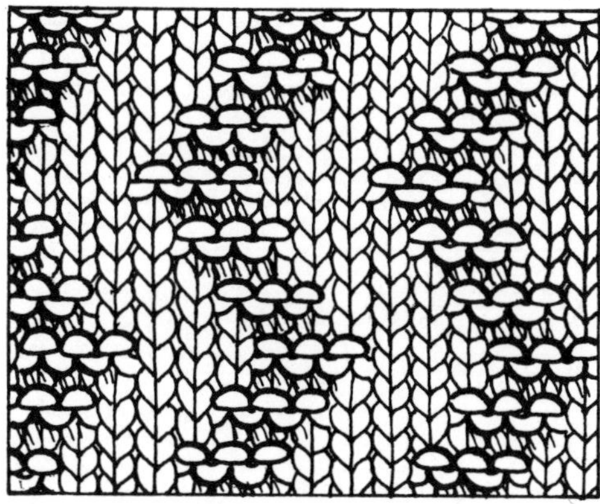

Working in this design pattern gives simple knit and purl stitches an interesting look.

For the **beginning row,** cast on a multiple of 6 stitches plus 2.

For the **first row,** knit 1. Purl across row to last stitch. Knit 1.

For the **second row,** knit 1. Repeat the following procedure. * Knit 3. Purl 3. * Knit 1.

For the **third row,** repeat the first row.

For the **fourth row,** knit 1, purl 1. Repeat the following procedure. * Knit 3. Purl 3. * End with knit 3, purl 2, knit 1.

For the **fifth row,** repeat the first row.

For the **sixth row,** knit 1, purl 2. Repeat the following procedure. * Knit 3. Purl 3. * End with knit 3, purl 1, knit 1.

For the **seventh row,** repeat the first row.

For the **eighth row,** knit 1. Repeat the following procedure. * Purl 3. Knit 3. * End with knit 1.

For the **ninth row,** repeat the first row.

For the **tenth row,** knit 1, purl 2. Repeat the following procedure. * Knit 3. Purl 3. * End with knit 3, purl 1, knit 1.

For the **eleventh row,** repeat the first row.

For the **twelfth row,** knit 1, purl 1. Repeat the following procedure. * Knit 3. Purl 3. * End with knit 3, purl 2, knit 1.

Repeat the **first through twelfth rows** as many times as required.

Diagonal Rib Pattern

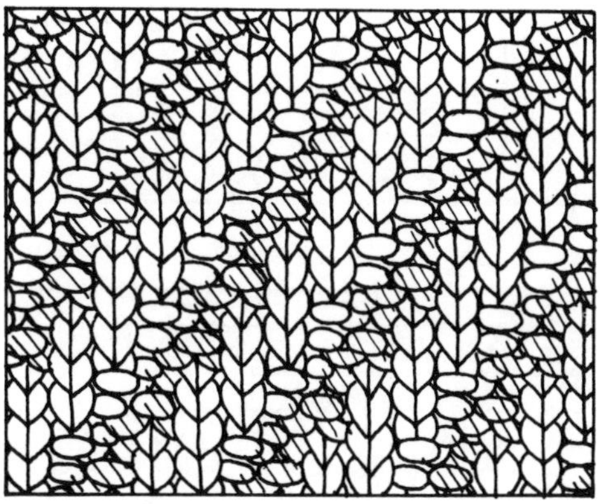

A subtle diagonal effect is achieved by using this arrangement of stitches.

For the **beginning row,** cast on a multiple of 4 stitches.

For the **first row,** repeat the following procedure. * Knit 2. Purl 2. *

For the **second row,** knit the purl stitches and purl the knit stitches of the previous row.

For the **third row,** repeat the following procedure. * Knit 1. Purl 2. Knit 1. *

For the **fourth row,** repeat the second row.

For the **fifth row,** repeat the following procedure. * Purl 2. Knit 2. *

For the **sixth row,** repeat the second row.

For the **seventh row,** repeat the following procedure. * Purl 1. Knit 2. Purl 1. *

Repeat the **second through seventh rows** as many times as required.

Broken Diagonal Rib Pattern

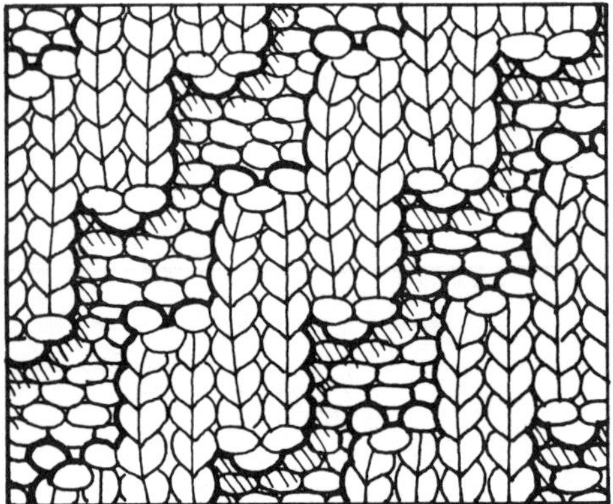

This stitch pattern creates a step effect as bands of ribbing are placed side by side.

For the **beginning row,** cast on a multiple of 8 stitches.

For the **first through fourth rows,** repeat the following procedure. * Purl 4. Knit 4. *

For the **fifth row,** knit 2. Repeat the following procedure. * Purl 4. Knit 2. *

For the **sixth row,** purl 2. Repeat the following procedure. * Knit 4. Purl 2. *

For the **seventh row,** repeat the fifth row.

For the **eighth row,** repeat the sixth row.

For the **ninth through twelfth rows,** repeat the following procedure. * Knit 4. Purl 4. *

For the **thirteenth row,** repeat the sixth row.

For the **fourteenth row,** repeat the fifth row.

For the **fifteenth row,** repeat the thirteenth row.

For the **sixteenth row,** repeat the fourteenth row.

Repeat the **first through sixteenth rows** as many times as required.

Mistake Stitch Ribbing

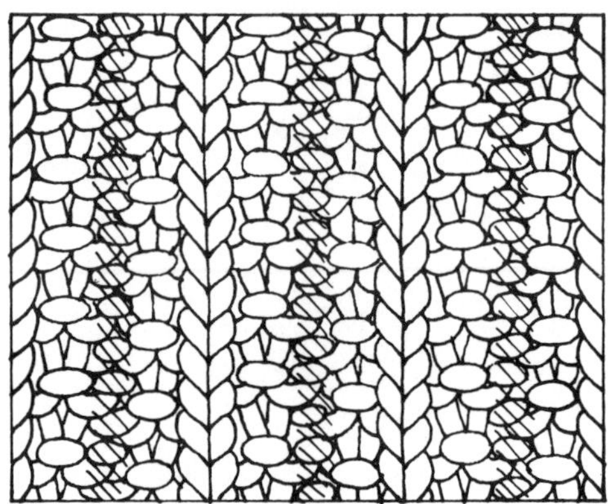

This unusual arrangement of stitches provides a bold ribbing pattern.

For the **beginning row,** cast on a multiple of 4 stitches plus 3.

For the **first row,** repeat the following procedure. * Knit 2. Purl 2. * End with knit 2, purl 1.

Repeat the **first row** as many times as required.

Chevron Pattern

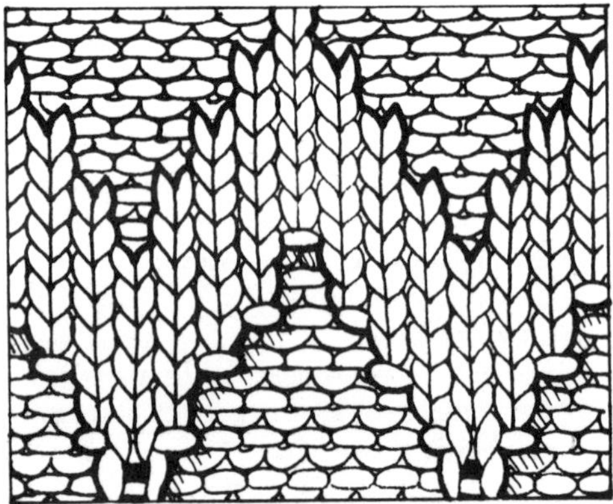

This zigzag design is interesting in that the knitting appears the same on both sides. However, the effect of the stitches is reversed.

For the **beginning row,** cast on a multiple of 8 stitches plus 1.

For the **first row,** knit 1. Repeat the following procedure. * Purl 7. Knit 1. *

For the **second row,** purl 1. Repeat the following procedure. * Knit 7. Purl 1. *

For the **third row,** knit 2. Repeat the following procedure. * Purl 5. Knit 3. * End row with purl 5, knit 2.
For the **fourth row,** purl 2. Repeat the following procedure. * Knit 5. Purl 3. * End row with knit 5, purl 2.
For the **fifth row,** knit 3. Repeat the following procedure. * Purl 3. Knit 5. * End row with purl 3, knit 3.
For the **sixth row,** purl 3. Repeat the following procedure. * Knit 3. Purl 5. * End row with knit 3, purl 3.
For the **seventh row,** knit 4. Repeat the following procedure. * Purl 1. Knit 7. * End row with purl 1, knit 4.
For the **eighth row,** purl 4. Repeat the following procedure. * Knit 1. Purl 7. * End the row with knit 1, purl 4.
For the **ninth row,** repeat the second row.
For the **tenth row,** repeat the first row.
For the **eleventh row,** repeat the fourth row.
For the **twelfth row,** repeat the third row.
For the **thirteenth row,** repeat the sixth row.
For the **fourteenth row,** repeat the fifth row.
For the **fifteenth row,** repeat the eighth row.
For the **sixteenth row,** repeat the seventh row.
Repeat the **first through sixteenth rows** as many times as required.

Pinnacle Crepe Pattern

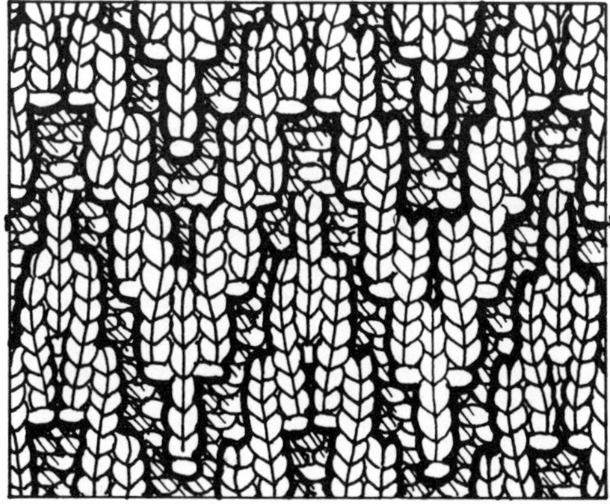

This easy-to-make pattern results in a lovely textural effect with an interesting design that seems to close up in twisted fashion when left unpressed.

For the **beginning row,** cast on a multiple of 18 stitches.
For the **first row,** repeat the following procedure. * Knit 1. Then purl 2 and knit 2 twice. Purl 1. Follow with knit 2 and purl 2 twice. *
For the **second row,** repeat the following procedure. * Knit 2 and purl 2 twice. Then knit 1. Follow with purl 2 and knit 2 twice. Purl 1. *
For the **third row,** repeat the first row.
For the **fourth row,** repeat the second row.
For the **fifth row,** repeat the following procedure. * Purl 2 and knit 2 twice. Then purl 3. Knit 2. Purl 2. Knit 2. Purl 1. *
For the **sixth row,** repeat the following procedure. * Knit 1. Purl 2. Knit 2. Purl 2. Knit 3. Then purl 2 and knit 2 twice. *
For the **seventh row,** repeat the fifth row.
For the **eighth row,** repeat the sixth row.
For the **ninth row,** repeat the following procedure. * Purl 1. Then knit 2 and purl 2 twice. Knit 1. Follow with purl 2 and knit 2 twice. *
For the **tenth row,** repeat the following procedure. * Purl 2 and knit 2 twice. Then purl 1. Follow by knit 2 and purl 2 twice. Knit 1. *
For the **eleventh row,** repeat the ninth row.
For the **twelfth row,** repeat the tenth row.
For the **thirteenth row,** repeat the following procedure. * Knit 2 and purl 2 twice. Knit 3. Purl 2. Knit 2. Purl 2. Knit 1. *
For the **fourteenth row,** repeat the following procedure. * Purl 1. Knit 2. Purl 2. Knit 2. Purl 3. Then knit 2 and purl 2 twice. *
For the **fifteenth row,** repeat the thirteenth row.
For the **sixteenth row,** repeat the fourteenth row.
Repeat the **first through sixteenth rows** as many times as required.

Sand Stitch

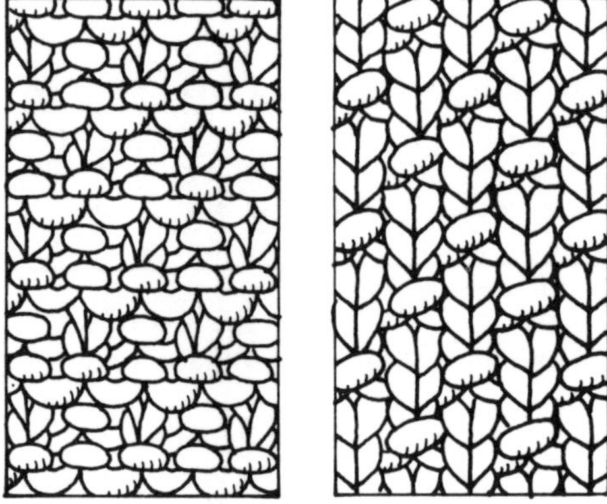

This stitch pattern creates a reversible fabric but with different textural effects. The reverse side is sometimes referred to as Dot or Spot Stitch.

For the **beginning row,** cast on a multiple of 2 stitches.

For the **first row,** knit.

For the **second row,** repeat the following procedure. * Knit 1. Purl 1. *

For the **third row,** knit.

For the **fourth row,** repeat the following procedure. * Purl 1. Knit 1. *

Repeat the **first through fourth rows** as many times as required.

Seed Stitch

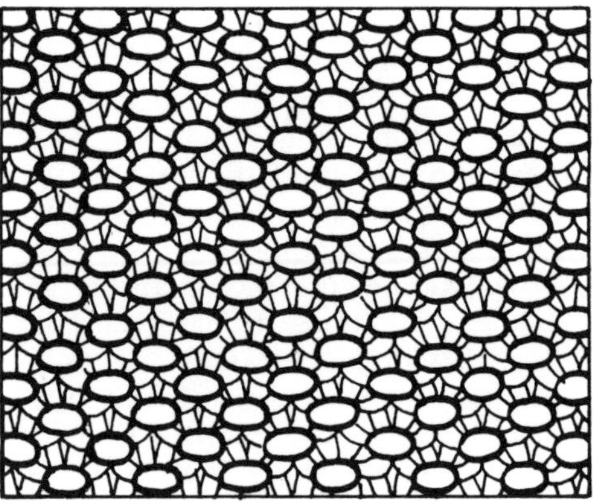

This stitch pattern creates the same pebbled effect on both sides and makes a fabric that lies flat. It is sometimes called Moss or Rice Stitch.

For the **beginning row,** cast on a multiple of 2 stitches.

For the **first row,** repeat the following procedure. * Knit 1. Purl 1. *

For the **second row,** repeat the following procedure. * Purl 1. Knit 1. *

Repeat the **first and second rows** as many times as required.

Seed Block Pattern

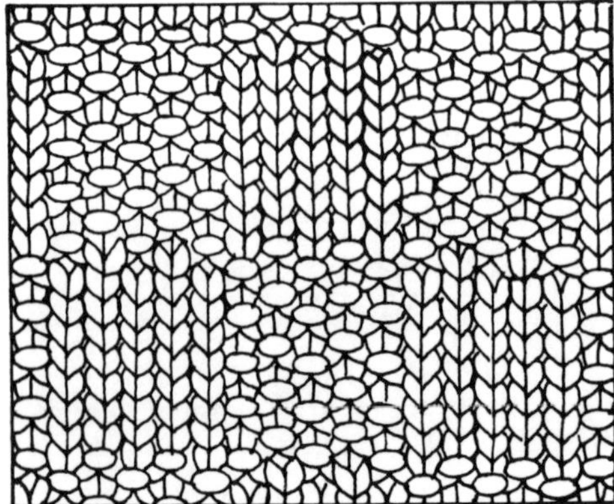

Interesting designs may be made by using Seed Stitch. Here it is used for a checkerboard effect.

For the **beginning row,** cast on a multiple of 10 stitches plus 2.

For the **first row,** knit 1. Repeat the following procedure. * Purl 1. Knit 1. Purl 1. Knit 1. Purl 6. * End with knit 1.

For the **second row,** knit 1. Repeat the following procedure. * Knit 5. Purl 1. Knit 1. Purl 1. Knit 1. Purl 1. * End with knit 1.
For the **third row,** repeat the first row.
For the **fourth row,** repeat the second row.
For the **fifth row,** repeat the first row.
For the **sixth row,** repeat the second row.
For the **seventh row,** repeat the first row.
For the **eighth row,** repeat the second row.
For the **ninth row,** knit 1. Repeat the following procedure. * Purl 6. Knit 1. Purl 1. Knit 1. Purl 1. * End with knit 1.
For the **tenth row,** knit 1. Repeat the following procedure. * Purl 1. Knit 1. Purl 1. Knit 1. Purl 1. Knit 5. * End with knit 1.
For the **eleventh row,** repeat the ninth row.
For the **twelfth row,** repeat the tenth row.
For the **thirteenth row,** repeat the ninth row.
For the **fourteenth row,** repeat the tenth row.
For the **fifteenth row,** repeat the ninth row.
For the **sixteenth row,** repeat the tenth row.
Repeat the **tenth through sixteenth rows** as many times as required.

Chevron Seed Pattern

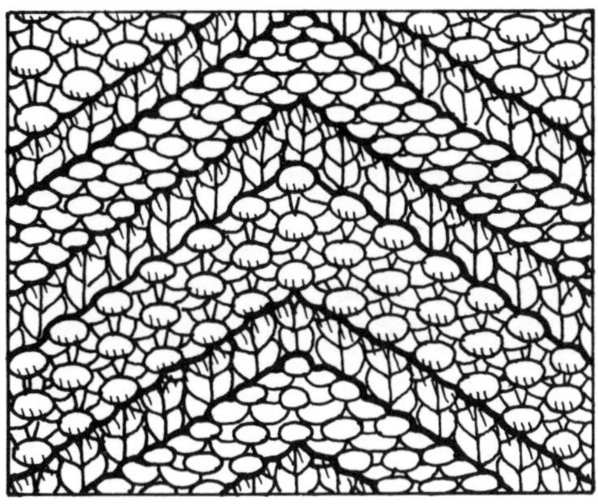

Working seed stitches in zigzag fashion creates this pattern with an interesting textural quality.
For the **beginning row,** cast on 22 stitches plus 1.
For the **first row,** knit 1. Repeat the following procedure. * Purl 3. Then knit 1 and purl 1 twice. Knit 1. Purl 5. Knit 1. Then purl 1 and knit 1 twice. Purl 3. Knit 1. *
For the **second row,** purl 1. Repeat the following procedure. * Purl 1. Knit 3. Then purl 1 and knit 1 twice. Purl 1. Knit 3. Purl 1. Then knit 1 and purl 1 twice. Knit 3. Purl 2. *
For the **third row,** knit 1. Repeat the following procedure. * Knit 2. Purl 3. Then knit 1 and purl 1 five times. Knit 1. Purl 3. Knit 3. *
For the **fourth row,** knit 1. Repeat the following procedure. * Purl 3. Knit 3. Then purl 1 and knit 1 four times. Purl 1. Knit 3. Purl 3. Knit 1. *
For the **fifth row,** purl 1. Repeat the following procedure. * Purl 1. Knit 3. Purl 3. Then knit 1 and purl 1 three times. Knit 1. Purl 3. Knit 3. Purl 2. *
For the **sixth row,** knit 1. Repeat the following procedure. * Knit 2. Purl 3. Knit 3. Then purl 1 and knit 1 twice. Purl 1. Knit 3. Purl 3. Knit 3. *
For the **seventh row,** knit 1. Repeat the following procedure. * Purl 3. Knit 3. Purl 3. Knit 1. Purl 1. Knit 1. Purl 3. Knit 3. Purl 3. Knit 1. *
For the **eighth row,** knit 1. Repeat the following procedure. * Purl 1. Knit 3,

purl 3 and knit 3 twice. Purl 1. Knit. 1. *

For the **ninth row,** knit 1. Repeat the following procedure. * Purl 1. Knit 1. Purl 3. Knit 3. Purl 5. Knit 3. Purl 3. Knit 1. Purl 1. Knit 1. *

For the **tenth row,** knit 1. Repeat the following procedure. * Purl 1. Knit 1. Purl 1. Then knit 3 and purl 3 twice. Knit 3. Then purl 1 and knit 1 twice. *

For the **eleventh row,** knit 1. Repeat the following procedure. * Purl 1 and knit 1 twice. Purl 3. Knit 3. Purl 1. Knit 3. Purl 3. Then knit 1 and purl 1 twice. Knit 1. *

For the **twelfth row,** knit 1. Repeat the following procedure. * Purl 1 and knit 1 twice. Purl 1. Knit 3. Purl 5. Knit 3. Then purl 1 and knit 1 three times. *

For the **thirteenth row,** purl 1. Repeat the following procedure. * Purl 1 and knit 1 three times. Purl 3. Knit 3. Purl 3. Then knit 1 and purl 1 twice. Knit 1. Purl 2. *

For the **fourteenth row,** knit 1. Repeat the following procedure. * Knit 2. Then purl 1 and knit 1 twice. Follow by purling 1 and knitting 3 twice; purl 1 and knit 1 three times. Knit 2. *

Repeat the **first through fourteenth rows** as many times as required.

Diamond Brocade Pattern

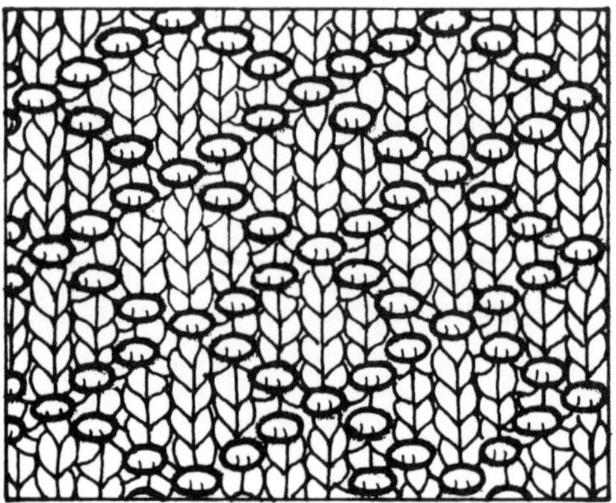

The delicate diamond outline of this well-known old pattern is a favorite. Sometimes it is called the Single Diamond Pattern. It lends itself to variations.

For the **beginning row,** cast on a multiple of 6 stitches plus 1.

For the **first row,** knit 3. Repeat the following procedure. * Purl 1. Knit 5. * End with purl 1, knit 3.

For the **second row,** purl 2. Repeat the following procedure. * Knit 1. Purl 1. Knit 1. Purl 3. * End with knit 1, purl 1, knit 1, purl 2.

For the **third row,** repeat the following procedure. * Knit 1. Purl 1. Knit 3. Purl 1. * End with knit 1.

For the **fourth row,** repeat the following procedure. * Knit 1. Purl 5. * End with knit 1.

For the **fifth row,** repeat the third row.

For the **sixth row,** repeat the second row.

Repeat the **first through sixth rows** as many times as required.

7 Add a Technique

Although many attractive items can be made by just combining knit and purl stitches in the usual manner, many more can be created by manipulating the yarn, needles, and stitches in different ways. Each technique produces a special effect, varying from the firm and sturdy to the lacy and fragile. In order to become familiar with the procedures, you should make a swatch to practice each movement. Directions will be easier to understand after studying the information presented here.

SLIP A STITCH

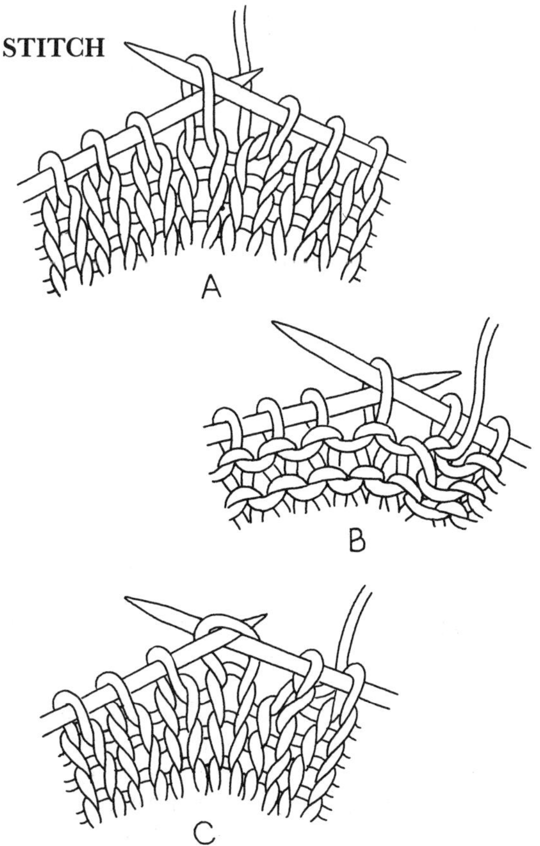

This technique is one of the easiest and quickest to do and, at the same time, one of the most effective. A stitch is passed from the left-hand to the right-hand needle without knitting. The procedure can be employed in various ways to move the stitch in different directions—vertically, horizontally, and diagonally—over the surface of the knitting. Because the slipped stitches draw the other stitches together, the resulting fabric is usually firm and compact.

In slipping a stitch, the loop is lengthened to make it more than one row high. A vertical loop appears on one side; a loose horizontal ridge on the other. It is best to work with the yarn relaxed. Never stretch it taut. Unless otherwise mentioned in the directions, the stitch is slipped purlwise.

To **slip purlwise in a knit row,** keep yarn in back. Insert the right-hand needle into the front of the stitch on the left-hand needle (A).

To **slip purlwise in a purl row,** work in

the same manner except that the yarn is in front of the work (B).

To **slip knitwise in a knit row,** insert needle into front of stitch, holding yarn in back (C).

To **slip knitwise in a purl row,** keep yarn in front. Insert needle into front of stitch from left to right (D).

There are many slip-stitch patterns including the Close, Heel, and Waffle Brioche stitches. Directions for two of them are given here. Notice how different the surface texture appears.

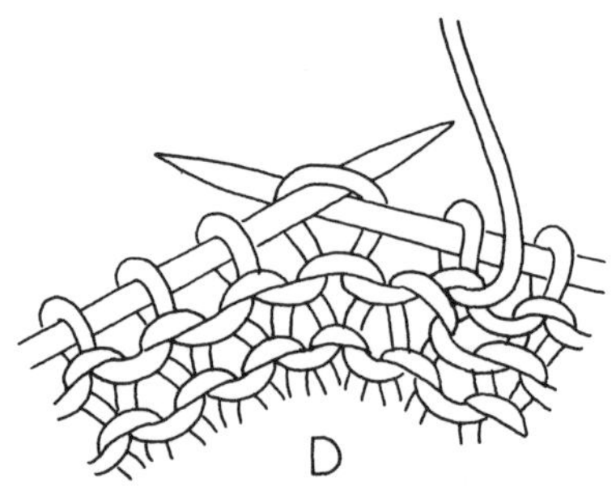

Heel Stitch

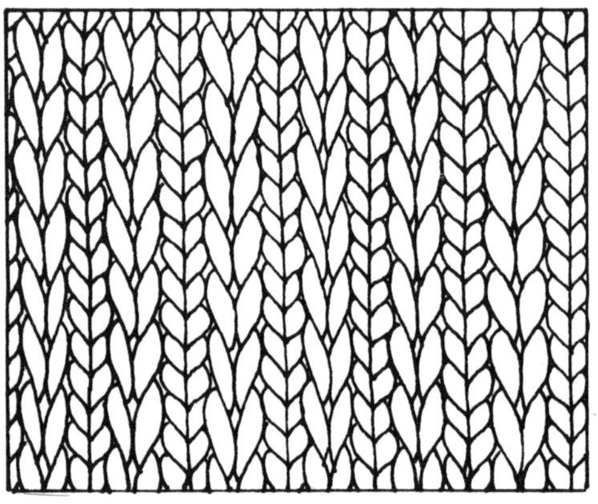

This stitch pattern creates a solid, sturdy fabric with a striped effect.

For the **beginning row,** cast on an uneven number of stitches.

For the **first row,** purl.

For the **second row,** knit 1. Repeat the following procedure. * Slip 1 with yarn in back. Knit 1. *

Repeat the **first and second rows** as many times as required.

Close Stitch

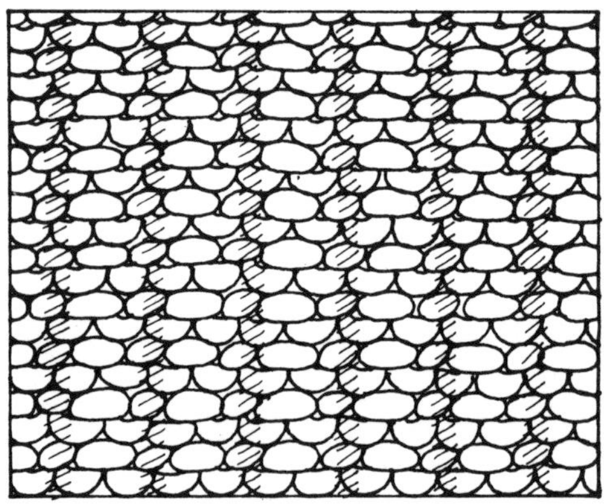

This variation of the Heel Stitch produces a ribbed effect in an interesting texture.

For the **beginning row,** cast on an odd number of stitches.

For the **first row,** knit.

For the **second row,** knit 1. Repeat the following procedure. * Slip 1 with yarn in back. Knit 1. *

Repeat the **first and second rows** as many times as required.

YARN FORWARD AND BACK

Sometimes the yarn is moved forward and backward as the stitch pattern progresses. When the directions suggest that the yarn should be brought "forward" or the stitch worked with the yarn "in front," bring the yarn from the back of the work to the front, passing it between the needles. When it needs to be returned to the back, repeat the process, moving the yarn backward between the needles.

When making the Woven Check Pattern, this technique is combined with a slip stitch to create a textured fabric that appears quite different from the two in which the yarn remained in the back.

Woven Check Pattern

A feeling of woven fabric results when the stitches are worked this way.

For the **beginning row,** cast on an uneven number of stitches.

For the **first row,** knit 1. Repeat the following procedure. * Yarn forward. Slip 1. Yarn back. Knit 1. *

For the **second row,** purl 2. Repeat the following procedure. * Yarn back. Slip 1. Yarn forward. Purl 1. *

Repeat the **first and second rows** as many times as required.

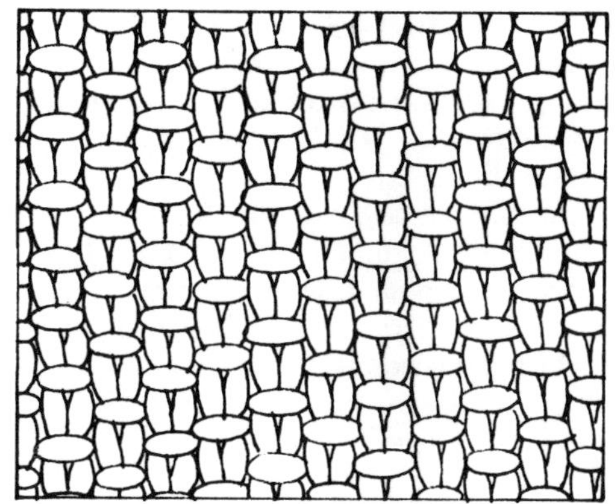

YARN OVER

This technique, which is easy to do, produces amazing results. Laces, eyelets, as well as some firmer-textured stitch patterns, require a yarn over. Variations in design are many, but each one will have a series of openings, forming a design.

In making a yarn over, an extra stitch is placed on the needle between two stitches. This is done by putting the yarn over the top of the right-hand needle before making the next stitch. On the return row, the yarn over is worked as a separate stitch.

Because the yarn over is actually an increase, this gain must be removed sometime. This can be done in several ways, such as knitting two stitches together.

The actual way to handle the yarn depends on the type of stitch that appears before and after the yarn over, and whether it is being made when working a stockinette or garter stitch.

Knit 1, Yarn Over, Knit 1. When the directions indicate that this sequence of stitches is to be followed when working in stockinette stitch, proceed this way. Knit a stitch with the yarn in back. Then bring the yarn forward between and under the needles in a purl stitch position. Carry the yarn over the top of the needle. Insert the needle in the stitch, and knit it in the usual manner (A).

Knit 1, Yarn Over, Purl 1. Begin by knitting one stitch. Then bring the yarn forward between the needles. Carry the yarn up and over the right-hand needle, then down and under, encircling the needle to bring it back to a purling position in front of the needle. Then purl a stitch (B).

Purl 1, Yarn Over, Purl 1. Purl the first stitch. Bring the yarn up and over the right-hand needle, then down and under the needle, returning it to its original position ready to purl the next stitch (C).

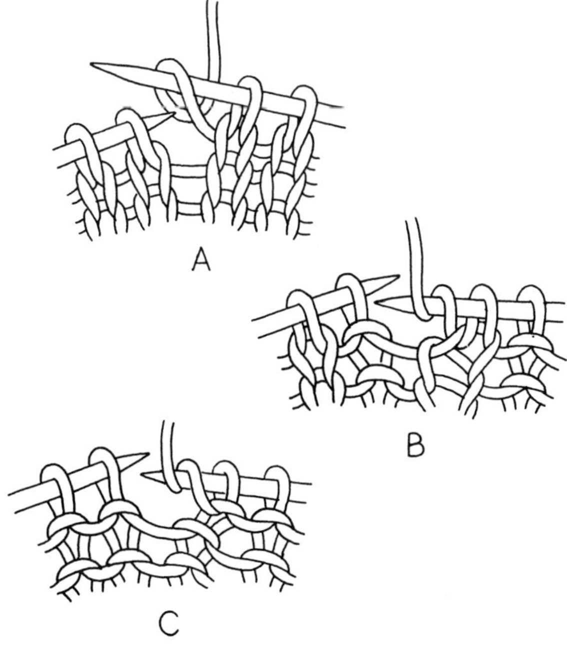

Purl 1, Yarn Over, Knit 1. Purl the first stitch. With yarn in this position, carry yarn over the top of the right-hand needle from front to back in position to knit a stitch (D).

In case you are working in garter stitch and the directions read, **Knit 1, Yarn Over, Knit 1,** work this way. Knit a stitch, bring yarn forward over the right-hand needle, then under and back (E).

Purl 1, Yarn Over, Purl 1. Purl the first stitch. Carry the yarn back under the right-hand needle. Then bring the yarn forward, passing over the needle (F).

As you read knitting directions, you will notice that this technique is used for many pattern stitches. One of the prettiest is the Fuchsia Pattern. Try it to practice this procedure. You will be surprised how easy it is to do.

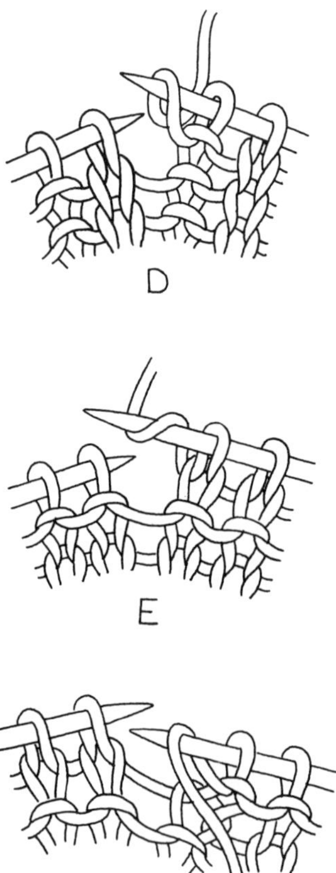

Fuchsia Pattern

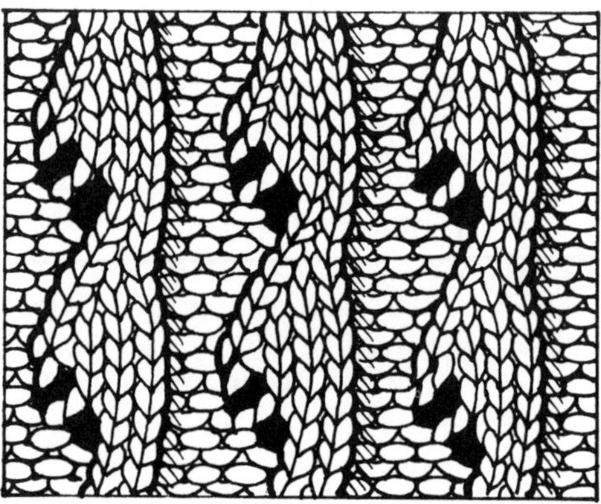

This motif creates a raised striped effect with an interesting use of eyelets and is a traditional German stitch pattern.

For the **beginning row,** cast on a multiple of 6 stitches.

For the **first row,** repeat the following procedure. * Purl 2. Knit 2. Yarn over. Purl 2. *

For the **second row,** repeat the following procedure. * Knit 2. Purl 3. Knit 2. *

For the **third row,** repeat the following procedure. * Purl 2. Knit 3. Yarn over. Purl 2. *

For the **fourth row,** repeat the following procedure. * Knit 2. Purl 4. Knit 2. *

For the **fifth row,** repeat the following procedure. * Purl 2. Knit 4. Yarn over. Purl 2. *

For the **sixth row,** repeat the following procedure. * Knit 2. Purl 5. Knit 2. *

For the **seventh row,** repeat the following procedure. * Purl 2. Knit 3. Knit 2 together. Purl 2. *

For the **eighth row,** repeat the fourth row.

For the **ninth row,** repeat the following procedure. * Purl 2. Knit 2. Knit 2 together. Purl 2. *

For the **tenth row,** repeat the second row.

For the **eleventh row,** repeat the following procedure. * Purl 2. Knit 1. Knit 2 together. Purl 2. *

For the **twelfth row,** repeat the following procedure. * Knit 2. Purl 2. Knit 2. *

Repeat the **first through twelfth rows** as many times as required.

KNIT TOGETHER

In making the Fuchsia Pattern, you were asked to knit two stitches together. This direction is frequently found when making yarn-over stitch patterns in order to decrease a stitch that has been added. The technique can be used on knit and purl stitches, and in the front and back of the stitches.

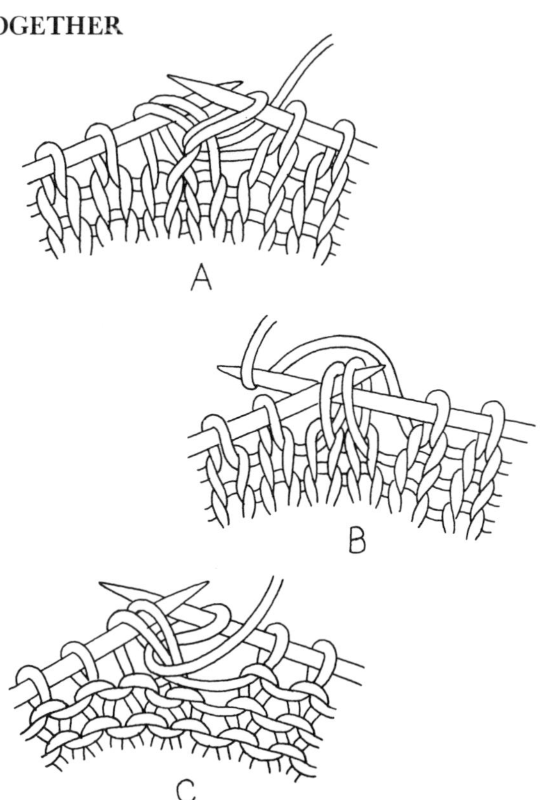

Knit Two Together. This technique is usually worked on a knit row. The right-hand needle enters two stitches through the front; knit them together in the regular manner (A).

Knit Two Together Through the Back. Slip the right-hand needle into the two loops in back of the left-hand needle. Knit a stitch in the usual manner (B).

Purl Two Together. Insert the right-hand needle through the front of both stitches on the left-hand needle. Purl in the usual way (C).

Purl Two Together Through the Back. Insert the right-hand needle through the back of both stitches on the left-hand needle. Purl (D).

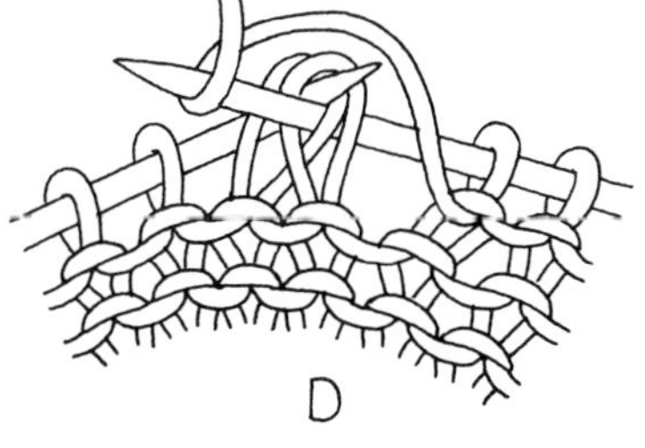

PASS SLIP STITCH OVER

Another technique that is frequently used when making yarn-over patterns is this one. It is another way of decreasing the number of stitches.

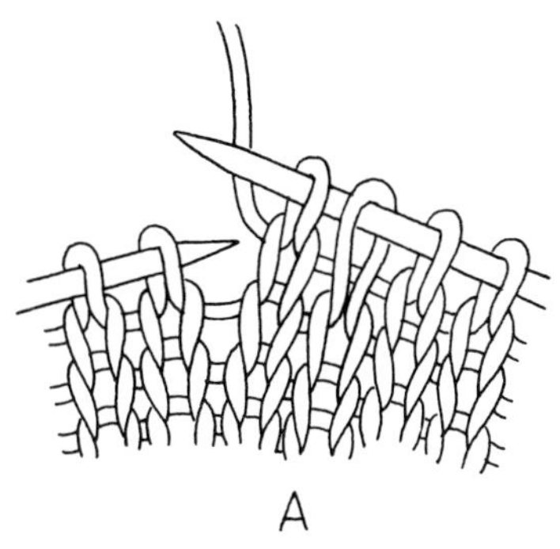

Usually the directions will read: **slip 1 stitch, knit 1, and pass slip stitch over,** (sl 1, K 1, psso). Actually what you are doing is binding off the slipped stitch. After passing a stitch from the left-hand needle to the right-hand needle without knitting it, knit one stitch in the usual way (A). Then pick up the slipped stitch with the left-hand needle (B) and bring it over the knitted stitch, allowing it to slip off the tip of the needle.

In case the directions ask you to perform this technique on a purl row, slip the stitch knitwise. Then purl the next stitch (C). Insert the left-hand needle into the front of the slipped stitch. Bring it over the slipped stitch (D).

One of the patterns that uses this technique is the Dewdrop. In the eight rows that are required to create the design, you will be given several chances to try to perform this procedure skillfully.

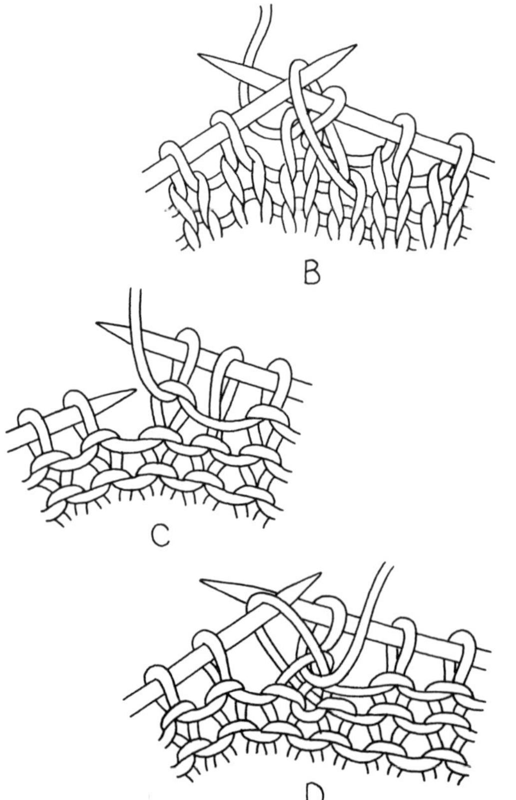

Dewdrop Pattern

This dainty openwork pattern is of English origin. Instead of curling, as so many knitted designs do, this one remains flat.

For the **beginning row,** cast on a multiple of 6 stitches plus 1.

For the **first row,** knit 2. Repeat the following procedure. * Purl 3. Knit 3. * End row with purl 3, knit 2.

For the **second row,** purl 2. Repeat the following procedure. * Knit 3. Purl 3. * End row with knit 3, purl 2.

For the **third row,** repeat the first row.

For the **fourth row,** knit 2. Repeat the following procedure. * Put yarn over. Then slip 1, knit 2 together, and pass slip stitch over. Yarn over. Knit 3. * End with yarn over, slip 1, knit 2 together, and pass slip stitch over. Yarn over. Knit 2.

For the **fifth row,** repeat the second row.

For the **sixth row,** repeat the first row.

For the **seventh row,** repeat the second row.

For the **eighth row,** knit 2 together. Repeat the following procedure. * Yarn over. Knit 3. Yarn over. Then slip 1, knit 2 together, and pass slip stitch over. * End with yarn over. Knit 3. Yarn over. Then slip 1, knit 1, and pass slip stitch over.

Repeat the **first through eighth rows** as many times as required.

KNIT IN FRONT, KNIT IN BACK

When you find words in the directions such as above, you know you are making some kind of twisted stitch. Changing the position of the needles and yarn produces a braided effect.

Twisted Knit Stitch. To make this stitch, insert the right-hand needle in the back of the stitch. Bring the yarn under the needle and knit the stitch in the regular manner. Purl the return row. **Cross Knit** is another term used for this technique (**A**).

Twisted Purl Stitch. Insert the right-hand needle through the back of the stitch. Then put the yarn over the needle in the usual way and purl the stitch. Knit the return row. **Cross Purl** is another term used for this technique (**B**).

By changing the position of the yarn, a slightly different effect is created. It is called a Plaited Stitch and sometimes is referred to as Reverse Stitch.

Plaited Knit Stitch. Insert the right-hand needle in the front of the stitch as for a regular knit stitch. Then, instead of bringing the yarn under the needle, put it over the needle to knit the new stitch (**C**).

Plaited Purl Stitch. Insert the right-hand needle in the stitch as for a regular purl stitch. Then, instead of putting the yarn over the needle, bring it under the needle to purl the new stitch (**D**).

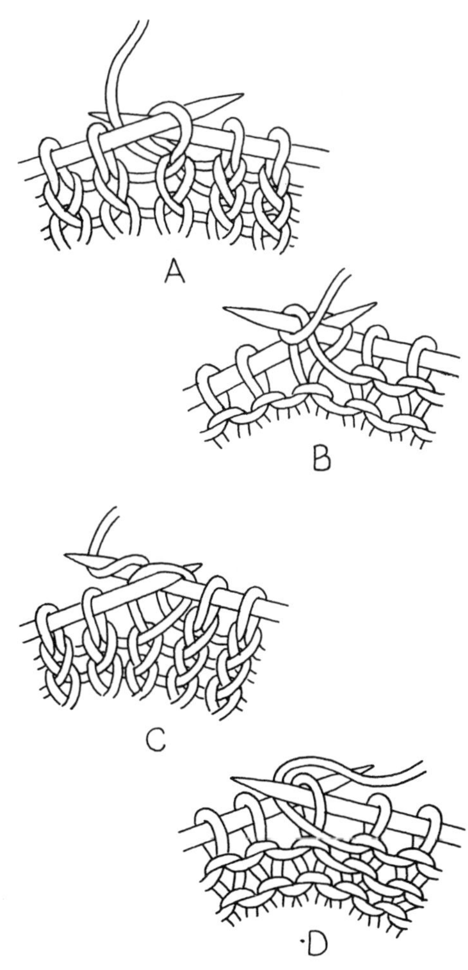

Twisted Rib Pattern

This is a simple variation of the usual knit-1, purl-1 type of ribbing.

For the **beginning row,** cast on a multiple of 2.

For the **first row,** repeat the following procedure. * Knit 1 with needle in back. Purl 1. *

For the **second row,** repeat the following procedure. * Knit the purl stitches and purl the knit stitches of the previous row. * Remember to work into the back of each knit stitch.

Repeat the **first and second rows** as many times as required.

Another interesting textured effect can be produced by knitting in front and back of the same stitch. The technique creates puffy dots on the surface of the fabric. They can vary in size depending on the number of times the procedure is worked into a stitch.

The knot is produced by knitting several times into the same stitch and then slipping all of the extra loops over the first stitch. In the beginning, you may find it awkward to knit in this fashion, but gradually you will be able to manipulate the stitches easily. In working the pattern, the spacing of the knots and the number can be changed for the desired effect.

One of the knotted stitches that uses this technique is the Popcorn Stitch. To make the decorative feature, knit in the front and back of a loop twice. Then slip the second (A), third, and fourth stitches over the first loop, making one knot (B). One way to make this stitch pattern is given here.

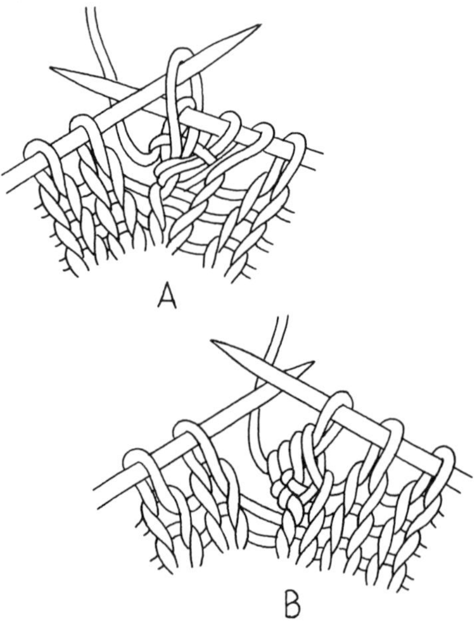

Popcorn Stitch

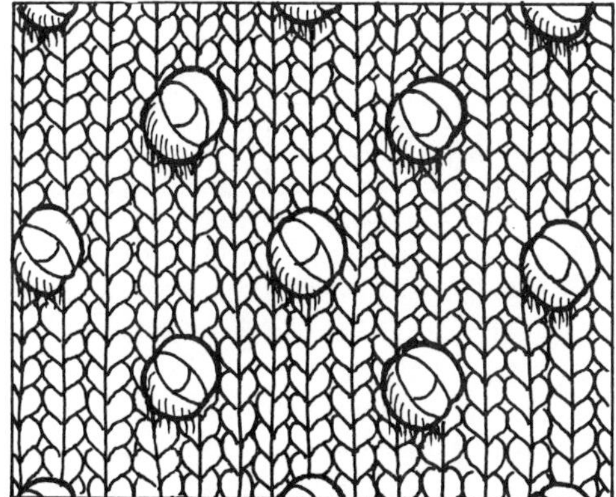

In making this stitch pattern, you will notice that the knots are staggered. This is accomplished by alternating their placement in the rows in which they are knitted.

For the **beginning row,** cast on a multiple of 6 stitches plus 3.
For the **first row,** knit.
For the **second row,** purl.
For the **third row,** knit 1. Repeat the following procedure to make a popcorn knot. * Knit in front and back of the next stitch twice. Then slip the second, third, and fourth stitches over the first. Knit 5. * End by making another popcorn and knitting 1 stitch.
For the **fourth row,** purl.
For the **fifth row,** knit.
For the **sixth row,** purl.
For the **seventh row,** knit 4. Repeat the following procedure. * Knit in front and in back of next stitch twice. Then slip the second, third, and fourth stitches over the first. Knit 5. * End by making another popcorn and knitting 4 stitches.
For the **eighth row,** purl.
For the **ninth row,** knit.
For the **tenth row,** purl.
For the **eleventh row,** repeat row 3.
Repeat the **fourth through tenth rows** as many times as required.

Remember that a purl, knit, purl sequence of rows is placed between each design row, and that the placement of the knots alternates in the design rows.

A larger knot called a bobble can be made by changing the technique slightly. Instead of just knitting in the front and back of a stitch, the work is turned and the stitches that have just been made are purled (A). The knitting is returned to its original position and the stitches knitted. Then the second, third, and fourth stitches are slipped over the first stitch, completing the bobble (B).

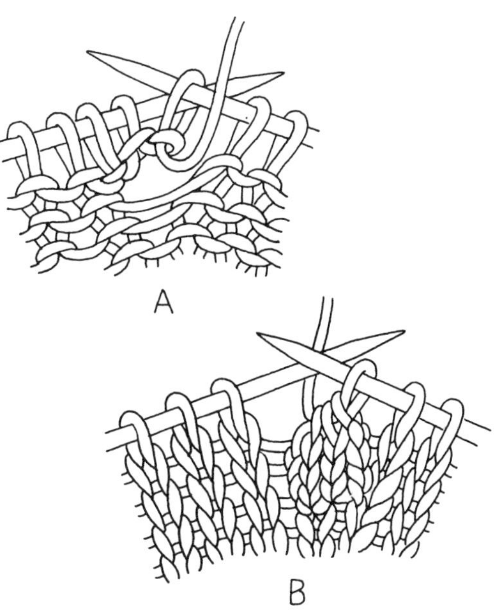

Bobble Stitch

Puffy mounds dot the surface when this pattern stitch is used. They can be arranged singly, as shown here, or grouped together to create motifs.

For the **beginning row,** cast on a multiple of 6 stitches plus 5.

For the **first five rows,** knit.

For the **sixth row,** knit 5. Repeat the following procedure. * To make 6 bobble stitches, do this 3 times in the next stitch—yarn over and knit 1. Turn work around and slip 1 stitch. Purl 5 across the 6 bobble stitches. Turn again and slip 1 stitch. Knit 5. Turn again and purl 2 stitches together 3 times. Turn again and slip 1 stitch, knit 2 together, pass slip stitch over. This sequence of stitches completes the bobble. Knit 5. *

For the **seventh row,** knit 5. Repeat the following procedure. * Purl 1 stitch through its back loop. Knit 5. *

For the **eighth through eleventh rows,** knit.

For the **twelfth row,** knit 8. Repeat the following procedure. * Knit bobble in next stitch as in the sixth row. Knit 5. * End with knit 3.

Repeat the **first through twelfth rows** as required.

CROSS RIGHT, CROSS LEFT

Although these words may not appear in the directions you are using, they do indicate the direction of the stitches as they lean to the right or left. Sometimes the stitches are referred to as Twist Stitches.

Many interesting twist stitch patterns are created by this technique. The procedure is always the same. A stitch is skipped. Then the next stitch is knitted and left on the needle. Follow by knitting the skipped stitch and dropping both stitches from the needle.

The direction of the twist depends on whether the stitches are knitted in the front or the back of the loop. If you knit into the front of the loop, the stitch turns to the right, but if you knit into the back, the stitch will pull to the left. For these directions, two stitches are needed.

Knit a Cross Right. Skip the first stitch on the left-hand needle. Start the knitting with the second stitch in the regular manner, inserting the right-hand needle into the front of the loop (A). As you do this, the needle passes over the skipped stitch and under the left-hand needle. After completing this stitch, allow it to remain on the needle as you insert the needle in the skipped stitch (B). Knit this stitch. Then drop both stitches from the left-hand needle. You will find this maneuver easier to execute if you work with a looser than usual tension on the yarn.

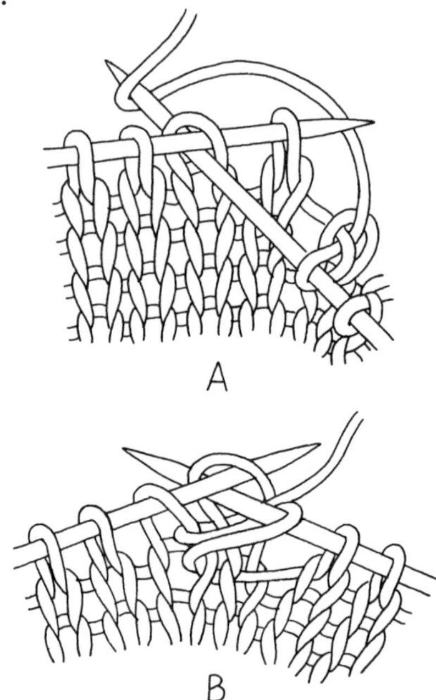

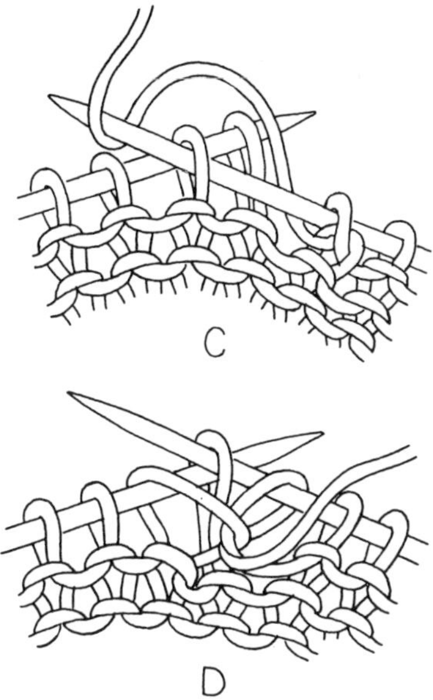

Purl a Cross Right. Insert the right-hand needle into the second stitch on the left-hand needle, ignoring the first stitch. Purl this stitch (C). Do not drop it off the needle. Instead purl the skipped stitch (D) and allow both stitches to slip from the needle.

Knit a Cross Left. Skip the first stitch on the left-hand needle. Knit into the back of the next stitch (E). Leave it on the needle. Then insert the right-hand needle into the back of the skipped stitch and knit it (F). Slip both stitches from the needle together.

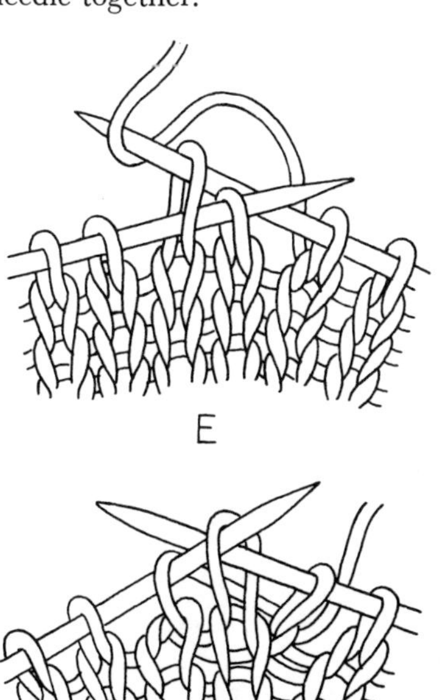

Purl a Cross Left. Skip the first stitch on the left-hand needle. Purl into the front of the next stitch (G). Bring it over the skipped stitch and off the needle. Then purl into the front of the skipped stitch (H) and slip it off the left-hand needle.

It is possible to work with three stitches instead of two. To do this, you follow this sequence. Begin with the third stitch, follow with the first, and end with the second.

The Diamond Lattice Pattern on the next page is one of the twist stitch patterns that require this technique.

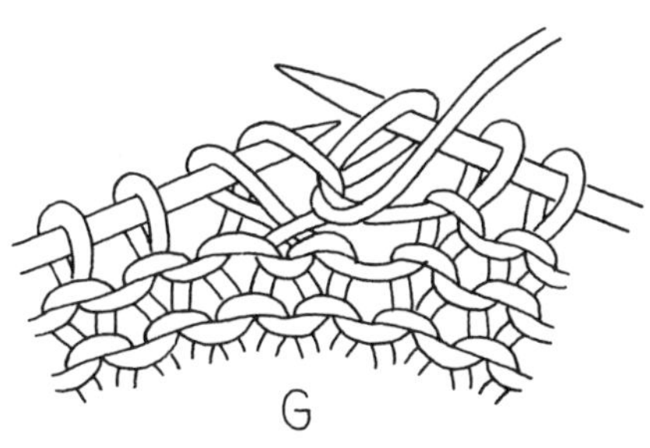

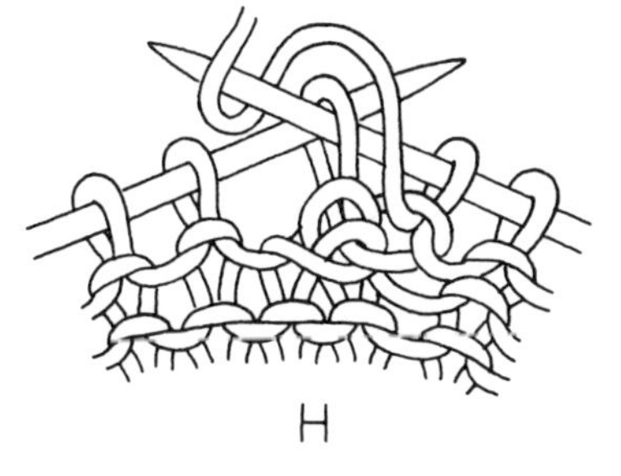

Diamond Lattice Pattern

Crossed stitches create this raised diamond design, which has an elastic quality.

For the **beginning row,** cast on a multiple of 6 stitches plus 2.

For the **first row,** knit 3. Repeat the following procedure. * Cross right by inserting the right-hand needle into the front of the second stitch on the left-hand needle. Knit but do not slip stitch off the needle. Knit into the front of the first stitch on the needle. Slip both stitches off the needle together. Knit 4. * End row by knitting 3.

For the **second row,** purl.

For the **third row,** repeat the following procedure. * Knit 2. Cross right by inserting the right-hand needle into the front of the second stitch on the left-hand needle. Knit but do not remove stitch from needle. Knit into the front of the first stitch on the needle. Slip both stitches off the needle together. Then cross left by inserting right-hand needle into the back of the second stitch on the left-hand needle. Knit but do not remove stitch from the needle. Bring the right-hand needle with the stitch on it to the front of the work. Knit the first, or skipped, stitch from the front. Slip both stitches off the needle together. * End row with knit 2.

For the **fourth row,** purl.

For the **fifth row,** knit 1. Repeat the following procedure. * Cross right as described in first row. Knit 2. Cross left as described in third row. * End row with knit 1.

For the **sixth row,** purl.

For the **seventh row,** repeat the following procedure. * Cross right as described in first row. Knit 4. * End row with a cross right.

For the **eighth row,** purl.

For the **ninth row,** knit 1. Repeat the following procedure. * Cross left as described in third row. Knit 2. Cross right as described in first row. * End with knit 1.

For the **tenth row,** purl.

For the **eleventh row,** repeat the following procedure. * Knit 2. Cross left as described in the third row. Cross right as described in the first row. * End with knit 2.

For the **twelfth row,** purl.

Repeat the **first through twelfth rows** as many times as required.

Cable Stitch

A Cable Stitch pattern is made by crossing a group of stitches to the left and right, passing either in front or back of a second group of stitches. The technique creates a ropelike design or cable. Although this stitch pattern appears complicated, it can be made quite easily. It just requires a bit of practice.

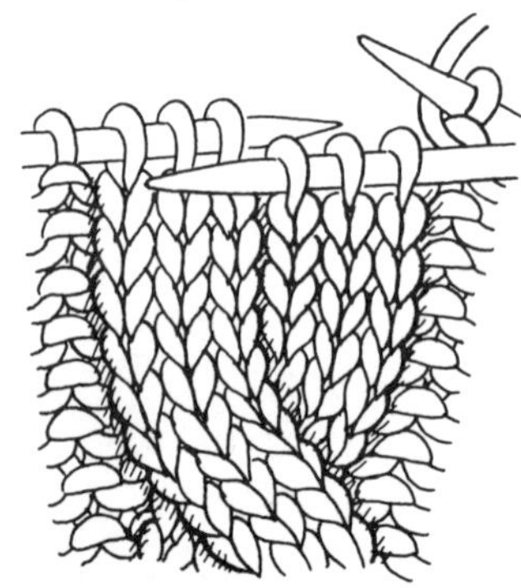

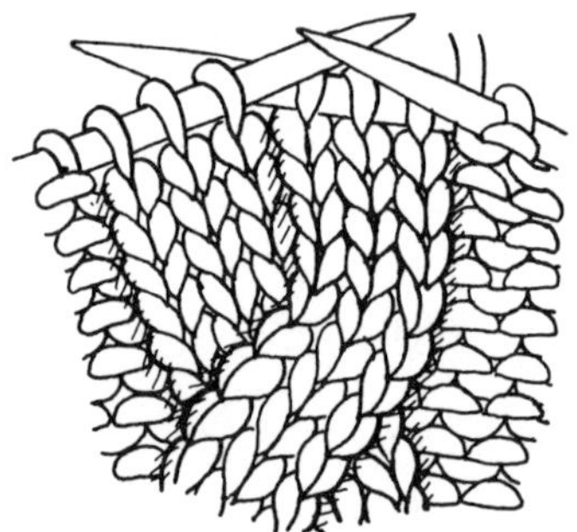

The cable is made by crossing one group of stitches either in front or in back of a second group of stitches. The size and shape of the cable can vary. The change in the numbers of stitches and rows will create different effects.

The cable or twisted pattern is created on one row of stitches at the desired place in the design. Of course, the directions will indicate whether the stitches will cross to the right or left.

In making the cable, knit to the place where the design is to start. Note how many stitches are being used for the cable. If the cable twists from left to right, place the first half of these stitches onto a cable needle or a double-pointed needle. Keep this needle in back of your knitting as you knit the second half of the cable stitches (A). Then knit the skipped stitches that are on the cable needle (B).

If the cable is twisting from right to left, the stitches on the cable needle are held in front of the work instead of in back as you knit the second half of the cable stitches (C). To complete the cable, knit the skipped stitches on the cable needle (D).

After maneuvering the stitches in this way, continue to knit the row in the regular manner. Usually a stockinette stitch is used for the cable, with purl stitches forming the background. The contrast seems to give prominence to the design.

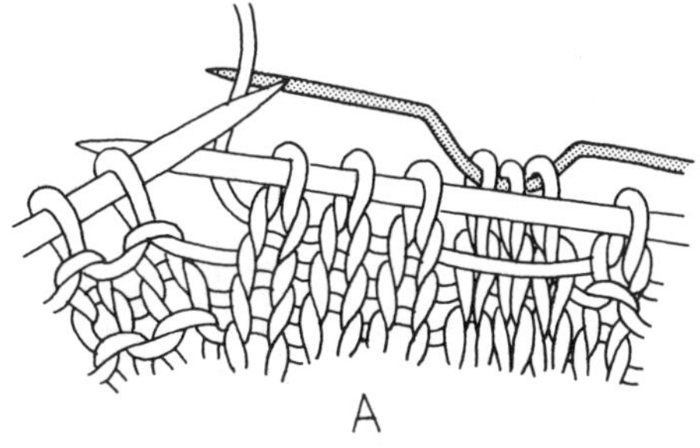

A

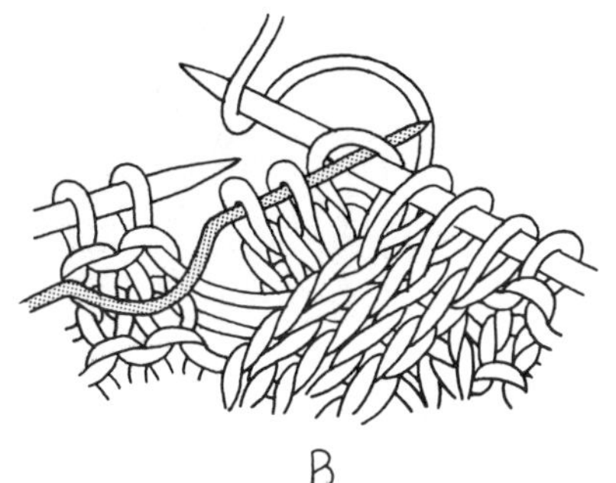

B

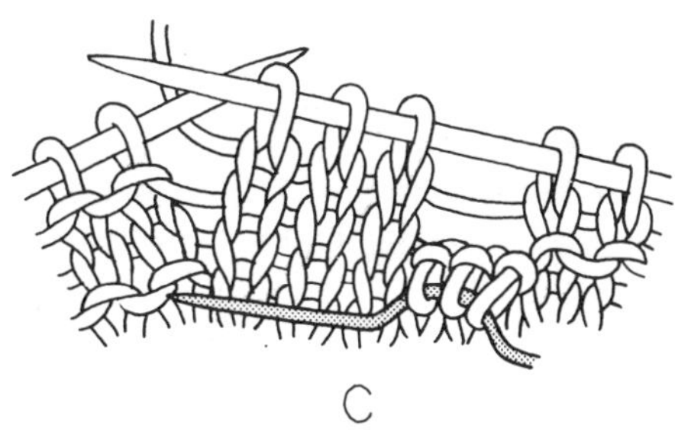

C

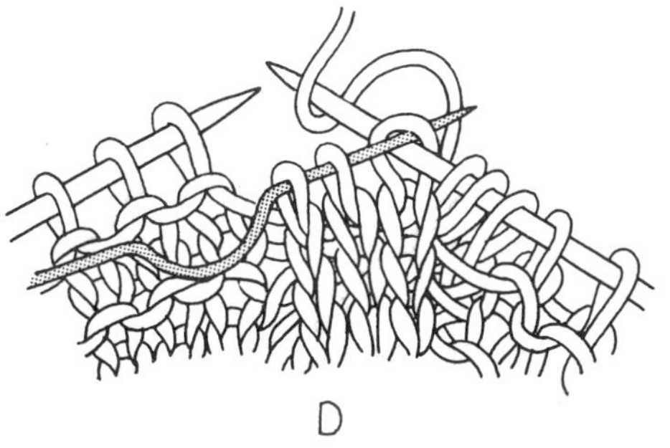

D

There are many types of cable patterns, as well as variations of the basic stitch pattern, which is shown here.

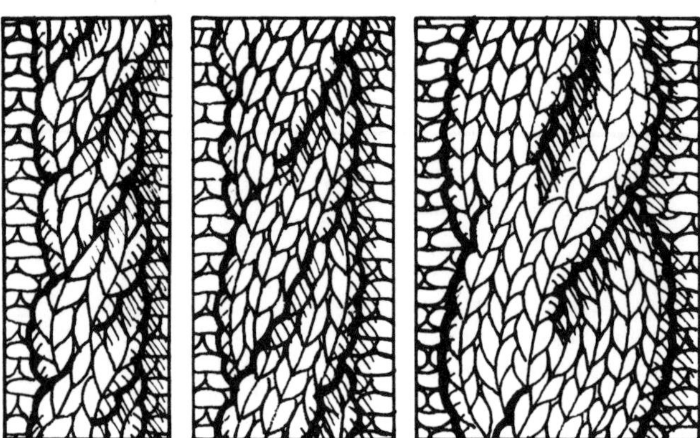

Cable Stitch Pattern—Four-stitch

For the **beginning row**, cast on 12 stitches for cable.
For the **first row**, knit 4. Purl 4. Knit 4.
For the **second row**, purl 4. Knit 4. Purl 4.
For the **third row**, repeat first row.
For the **fourth row**, purl 4. Slip next 2 stitches onto a double-pointed needle. Leave in back. Knit 2. Then knit the 2 stitches on the double-pointed needle. Purl 4.
Repeat the **first through fourth rows** as many times as required.

Cable Stitch Pattern—Six-stitch

For the **beginning row**, cast on 10 stitches for cable.
For the **first row**, knit 2. Purl 6. Knit 2.
For the **second row**, purl 2. Knit 6. Purl 2.
For the **third row**, repeat the first row.
For the **fourth row**, purl 2. Slip the next 3 stitches onto a double-pointed needle. Leave in back. Knit 3. Then knit the 3 stitches on the double-pointed needle. Purl 2.
For the **fifth row**, repeat the first row.
For the **sixth row**, repeat the second row.
Repeat the **first through sixth rows** as many times as required.

Cable Stitch Pattern—Eight-stitch

For the **beginning row**, cast on 12 stitches for cable.
For the **first row**, knit 2. Purl 8. Knit 2.
For the **second row**, purl 2. Knit 8. Purl 2.
For the **third row**, repeat the first row.
For the **fourth row**, purl 2. Slip the next 4 stitches onto a double-pointed needle. Leave needle in back. Knit 4. Then knit the 4 stitches on the double-pointed needle. Purl 2.
For the **fifth row**, repeat the first row.
For the **sixth row**, repeat the second row.
For the **seventh row**, repeat the first row.
For the **eighth row**, repeat the second row.
For the **ninth row**, repeat the first row.
For the **tenth row**, repeat the second row.
Repeat the **first through tenth rows** as many times as required.

KNIT IN ROW BELOW

This technique produces an elongated stitch. Sometimes it is referred to as a Double Stitch. When the directions mention that you "knit one in the row below," insert the right-hand needle in the loop below the next stitch on the left-hand needle. Put the yarn around the needle in order to knit a stitch. Draw the loop through the stitch. Slip both stitches off the needle. Draw the stitch upward gently to lengthen it. Because this technique is always worked between regular stitches, a ribbed effect is created. The Double Brioche Stitch is a stitch pattern that uses this technique.

Double Brioche Stitch

This pattern is sometimes referred to as Three-dimensional Honeycomb. It is a versatile one, creating different looks when the weight of the yarn and size of the needles are varied.

For the **beginning row,** cast on an even number of stitches.

For the **first row,** knit.

For the **second row,** repeat the following procedure. * Knit 1. To knit the next stitch, insert the needle in the center of stitch in row below and knit through both loops. * End by knitting 2 stitches.

For the **third row,** knit.

For the **fourth row,** knit 1. Repeat the following procedure. * Knit 1. To knit the next stitch, insert the needle in the center of stitch in row below and knit through both loops. * End by knitting 1 stitch.

Repeat the **first through fourth rows** as many times as required.

KNIT A LOOP FROM BELOW

This technique gives the knitted surface a decorative touch. An elongated loop is made by inserting the needle in a stitch several rows below the row being made. After knitting the stitch at the designated place, pull up the yarn gently so the loop will lie flat on the knitted surface (A). More than one loop can be knitted into the same stitch (B).

A stitch pattern that uses this technique is the Lazy Daisy Stitch. You will notice that the surface becomes dotted with tiny eyelets at the base of each motif.

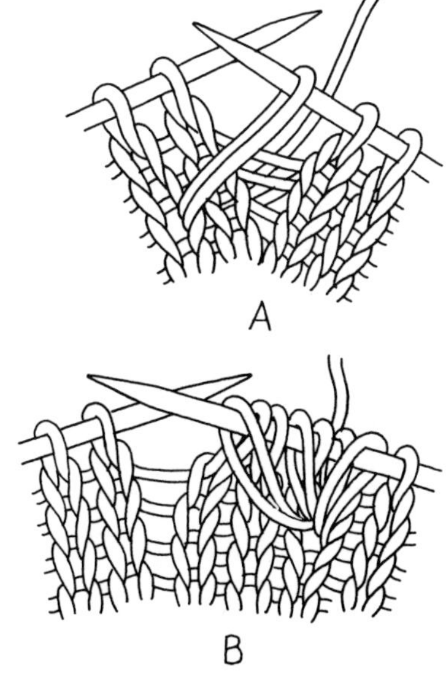

Lazy Daisy Stitch

Looped stitches add an embroidered look to an otherwise plain surface.

For the **beginning row,** cast on a multiple of 10 stitches plus 5.

For the **first row,** purl.

For the **second row,** knit.

For the **third row,** purl.

For the **fourth row,** knit.

For the **fifth row,** purl.

For the **sixth row,** knit 5. Repeat the following procedure. * Insert needle into a stitch 5 rows below the third stitch from the tip of the left-hand needle, and pull up a loop. Knit 5. Insert the needle in the same stitch, pulling up a second loop. Knit 5. *

For the **seventh row,** purl 4. Repeat the following procedure. * Purl 2 together in back. Purl 5. Purl 2 together. Purl 3. * End with purl 4.

For the **eighth row,** knit 7. Repeat the following procedure. * Insert needle in the same stitch below in which loops were made in the sixth row, and pull up a loop. Place it on the left-hand needle. Knit through back of loop and front of next stitch together. Knit 9. * End row with knit 7.

For the **ninth row,** purl.

For the **tenth row,** knit.

For the **eleventh row,** purl.

For the **twelfth row,** knit.

For the **thirteenth row,** purl.

For the **fourteenth row,** knit 10. Repeat the following procedure. * Insert needle into a stitch 5 rows below the third stitch from the tip of the left-hand needle, and pull up a loop. Knit 5. Insert the needle in the same stitch, pulling up a second loop. Knit 5. * End row with knit 10.

For the **fifteenth row,** purl 9. Repeat the following procedure. * Purl 2 together in back. Purl 5. Purl 2 together in back. Purl 3. * End with purl 9.

For the **sixteenth row,** knit 12. Repeat the following procedure. * Insert needle in the same stitch below in which loops were made in the fourteenth row, and pull up a loop. Place it on the left-hand needle. Knit through back of loop and front of next stitch together. Knit 9. * End row with knit 12.

For the **seventeenth row,** purl.

Repeat the **second through seventeenth rows** as many times as required.

CARRY YARN ACROSS

Strands of yarn loosely crossing the surface of the knitted fabric can create an attractive effect. By anchoring the strands in the center, a design can create various impressions such as a bowknot or butterfly.

After slipping a certain number of stitches, the working yarn is carried behind the slipped stitches so that the knitting can be resumed (A).

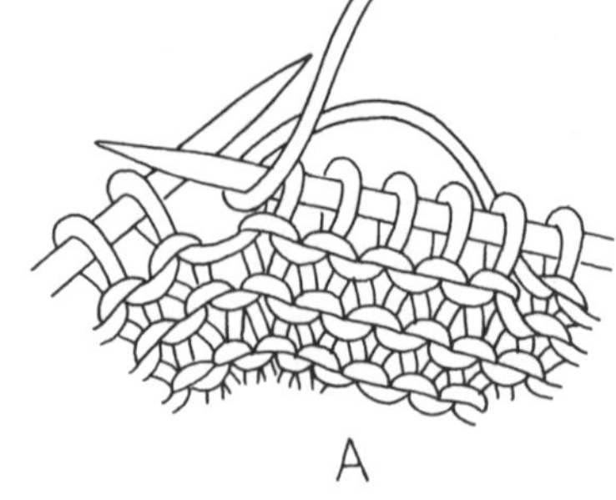

A

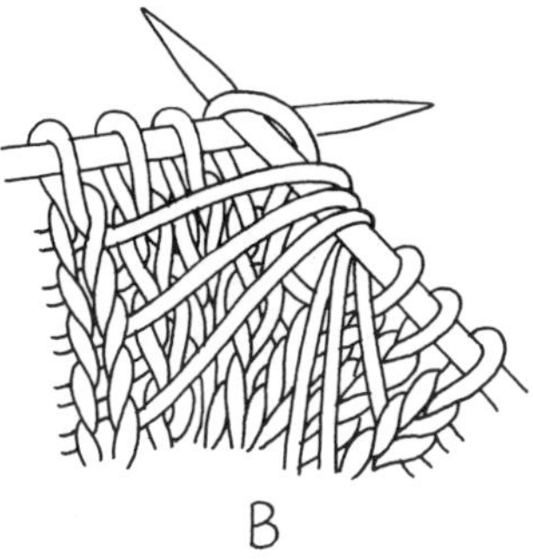

After several rows are knitted in which the slipped stitches have been made, the needle picks up the loose strands and knits a stitch (B). This procedure gathers and holds the strands together, forming a design. Of course, the directions you are following will indicate where the stitch should be taken.

Butterfly Pattern

This is a pattern in which slip stitches create the design motif. In fact, this stitch is sometimes called Butterfly Slip Stitch.

For the **beginning row,** cast on a multiple of 10 stitches plus 4.

For the **first row,** knit 2. Repeat the following procedure. * Bring yarn forward. Slip 5. Take yarn back. Knit 5. * End the row with yarn forward. Slip 5. Yarn forward. Slip 5. Yarn back. Knit 2.

For the **second row,** purl.

For the **third row,** repeat the first row.

For the **fourth row,** purl.

For the **fifth row,** repeat the first row.

For the **sixth row,** purl.

For the **seventh row,** repeat the first row.

For the **eighth row,** purl.

For the **ninth row,** repeat the first row.

For the **tenth row,** purl 4. Repeat the following procedure. * For the next stitch, which falls in the middle of the 5 slipped stitches, insert the right-hand needle upward through the 5 loose strands of yarn. Transfer them to the left-hand needle. Purl this stitch together with the 5 loose strands. Purl 9 stitches. * End row by purling 4 stitches.

For the **eleventh row,** knit 7. Repeat the following procedure. * Yarn forward. Slip 5. Yarn back. Knit five. * End row yarn forward, slip 5. Yarn back. Knit 7.

For the **twelfth row,** purl.

For the **thirteenth row,** repeat the eleventh row.

For the **fourteenth row,** purl.

For the **fifteenth row,** repeat the eleventh row.

For the **sixteenth row,** purl.

For the **seventeenth row,** repeat the eleventh row.

For the **eighteenth row,** purl.

For the **nineteenth row,** repeat the eleventh row.

For the **twentieth row,** purl 9. Repeat the following procedure. * For the next stitch, which falls in the middle of the 5 slipped stitches, insert the right-hand needle upward through the 5 loose strands of yarn. Transfer them to the left-hand needle. Purl this stitch together with the 5 loose strands. Purl 9. *

Repeat the **first through twentieth rows** as many times as required.

WRAP YARN AROUND

Double Throw is another term indicating this technique. It is a way of making elongated stitches. The yarn is wrapped several times around the needle instead of just once. The directions will indicate the correct number. It produces a lacy openwork band which might be described as an insertion between two solid areas.

After inserting the needle into the stitch, wrap the yarn around the needle a certain number of times. Draw all loops through the stitch. Then on the next row, the extra loops will drop off the needle as you work the stitch.

An example of this technique is found in the directions for making the Drop Stitch.

Drop Stitch

Openwork bands dominate this stitch pattern. It is easy and quick to do.

For the **beginning row,** cast on the desired number of stitches.

For the **first row,** insert the needle in the first stitch. Wind the yarn around the needle 3 times before completing the knit stitch. Continue knitting in this way across the row.

For the **second row,** purl, letting the extra 3 loops drop.

Knit and purl the required number of rows before repeating the **first and second rows.**

Repeat the preceding procedure for as many rows as required.

CHANGE COLOR

Introducing a second color adds an interesting design detail to knitting. It can be done in several ways. The method to select depends on its appropriateness to the pattern.

For horizontal stripes, and some allover designs, the color change is made at the beginning of the row. This is the easiest method to use. The new colored yarn is tied to the one being used as if you were joining two ends of yarn, below. Slide the knot close to the needle. The unused strand of yarn is carried up the side of the piece, row to row. The edge will be neater if you drop the strand you have been using on the right side of the work and pick up the new yarn behind it, on the wrong side. This procedure twists the strands together along the edge. Usually the change of color is made at the beginning of a knit row.

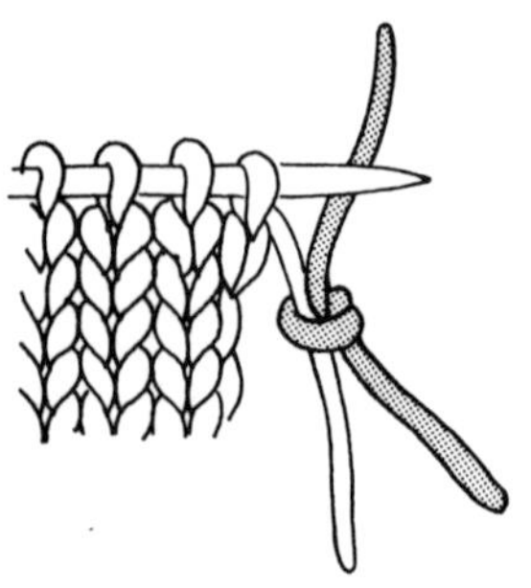

For wide vertical stripes, bands, and large areas in which colors are changed mid-row, a ball of yarn is needed for each color. When the point is reached to introduce the new color, the working yarn is dropped, falling over the new one, which is picked up from underneath it. This allows the two yarns to be twisted together, preventing a gap in the knitting, top of next page.

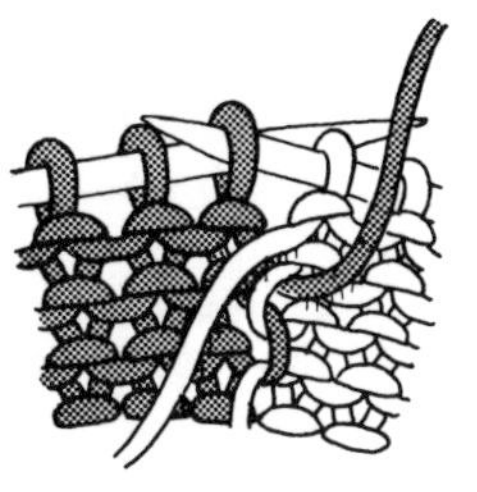

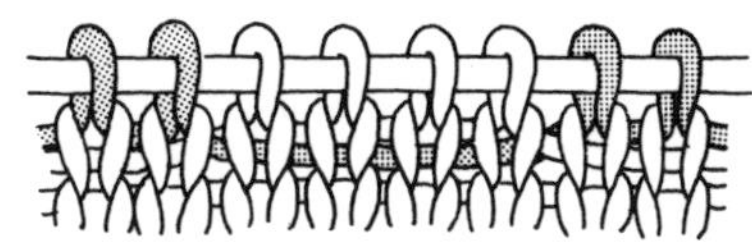

For pattern designs in which two colors are changed at frequent intervals, the yarn that is not being used is carried across the back of the work. This can be done in two ways, depending on the distance between the changes.

Stranding. For short spans of no more than five stitches, strands of yarn can be carried loosely across the back of the work. This procedure is referred to as stranding.

The stitches can be made by controlling the two yarns with one hand in the usual manner, picking up and dropping the required yarn at designated intervals. However, some persons feel that it is better to use two hands with the first color in the right hand and handled as in the English method, and the second color in the left hand as in the Continental style. They think this way is quicker and that the tension is more evenly distributed. You can try both methods and decide which one provides the best results.

In working this way, the two strands of yarn are used in alternating fashion, depending on the design. A strand of yarn is placed over the first finger of the left hand in the Continental manner. When that color is to be used, the needle in the right hand picks it up and pulls it through the first loop on the left-hand needle (A). At the same time, the right hand controls the stranding yarn. When the knitting is done with the right hand, the left hand controls the loose strands (B).

For purling, the work progresses in the same way. When purling with the right hand, the left hand controls the loose strand (C), but when the purl stitches are made with the left hand, the right hand controls the stranding (D).

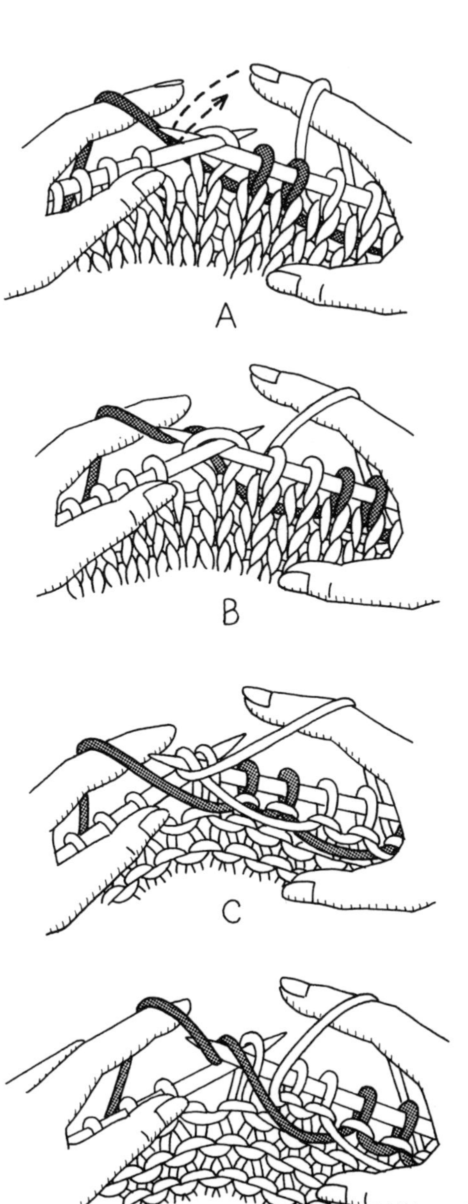

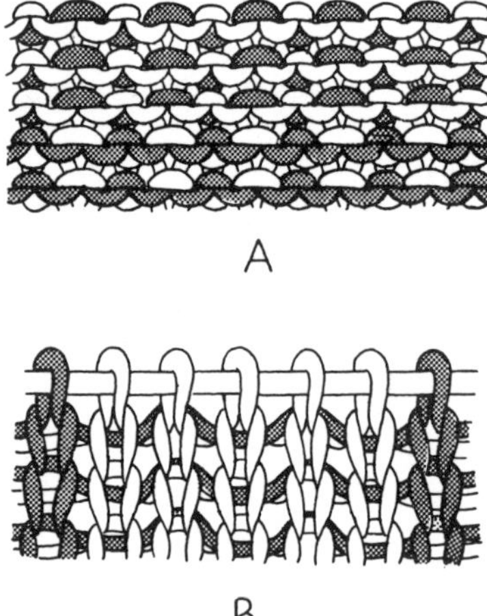

To weave the right-hand yarn above a knit stitch, hold yarn away from the knitting with the first finger on right hand. Then use left-hand yarn to knit a stitch (A).

To weave right-hand yarn below a knit stitch, start by bringing the right-hand and left-hand yarns into position as in (B). Then take the right-hand yarn back around and under the right-hand needle. As you do this, draw the left-hand stitch through the loops (C).

To weave left-hand yarn above a knit stitch, place it over the right-hand needle (D). Then knit a stitch with the right-hand yarn.

Weaving. When the design requires that more than five stitches be made between color changes, it is better to lace the out-of-use yarn into the back of the fabric (A). This method is referred to as weaving. The technique is similar to stranding. However, there are no loose strands on the back of the fabric to be snagged. Instead, the yarn is worked alternately above and below each stitch, resulting in a thick, sturdy material (B).

Again, this technique can be executed using one or two hands. Working with two hands, which is generally considered the easier one to do, requires practice until a rhythm is developed. Remembering when to weave one of the yarns above or below a stitch may be confusing. Studying the drawings shown here may be helpful. Always keep one color in the right hand, and the other in the left.

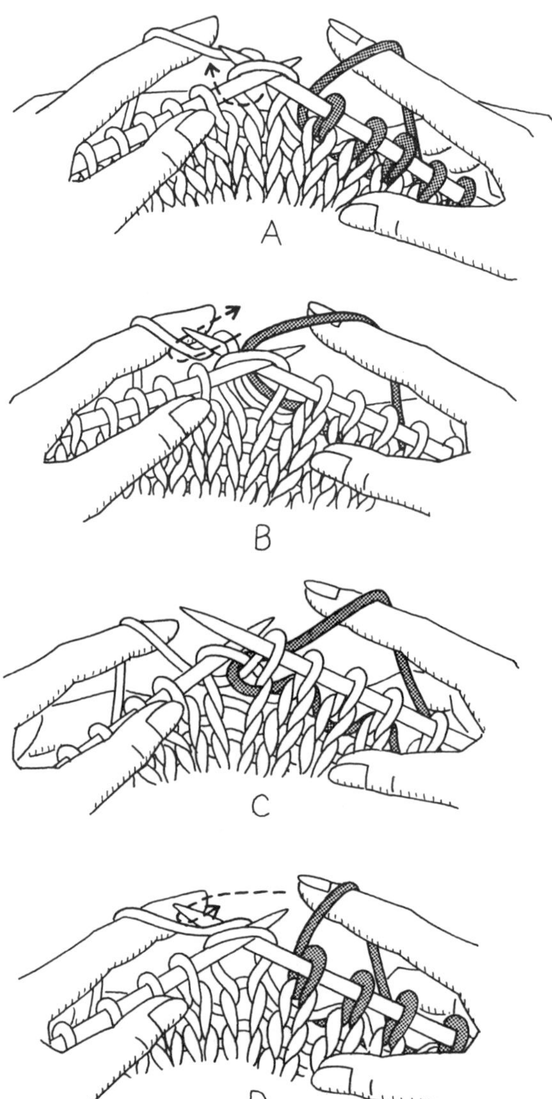

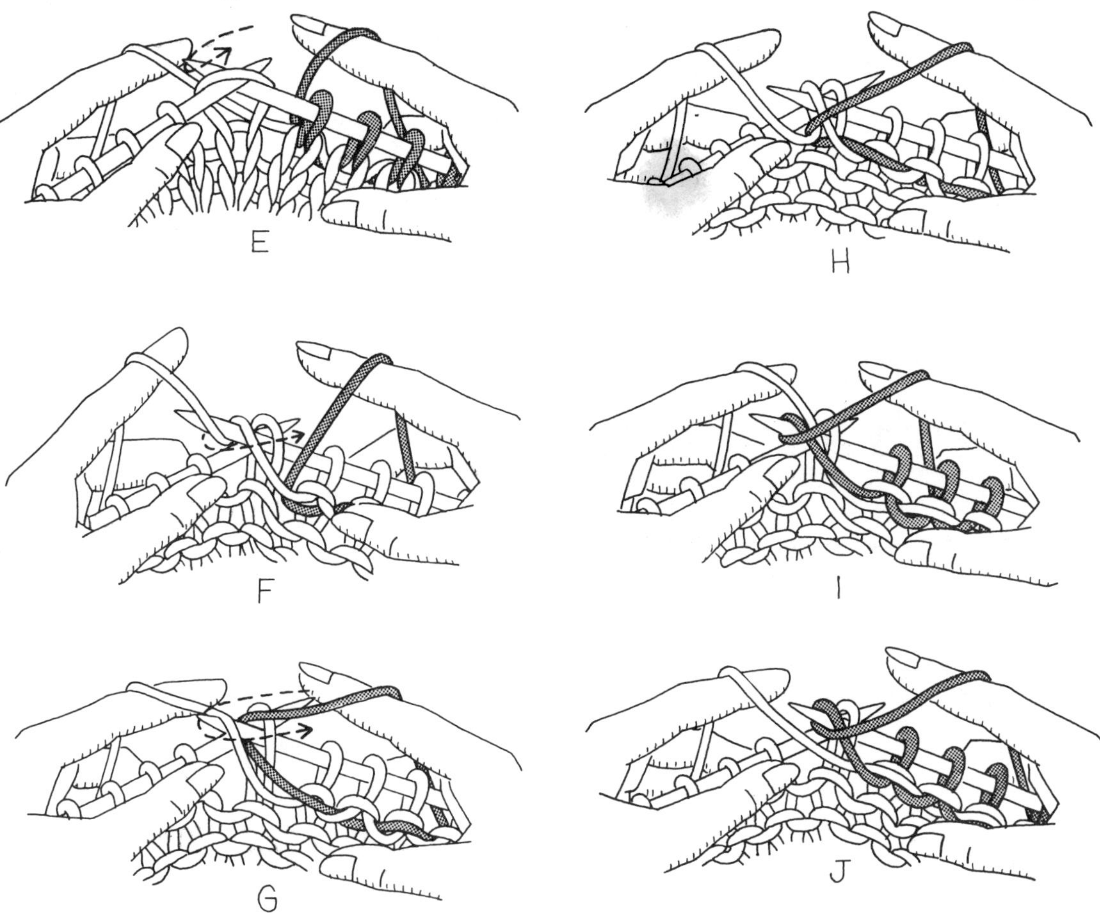

To weave left-hand yarn below a knit stitch, hold the yarn away from the work with the first finger on left hand (E). Then knit a stitch with the right-hand yarn.

To weave right-hand yarn above a purl stitch, draw the strand up with first finger on right hand (F). Then make a purl stitch with the left-hand yarn.

To weave right-hand yarn below a purl stitch requires two movements of the yarn. Begin as if to purl with the right-hand yarn. Follow as if to purl with the left-hand yarn (G). Then bring the right-hand yarn around and under the stitch made with the left-hand yarn (H). Finish by drawing the purl stitch through the loop.

To weave left-hand yarn above a purl stitch, carry the yarn over the right-hand needle (I). Then purl a stitch with the right-hand yarn.

To weave left-hand yarn below a purl stitch, hold the left-hand yarn taut with the first finger of the left hand as you purl a stitch with the right-hand yarn (J).

There are innumerable ways of combining two or more colors. By using the basic stitches and colorful yarns, stripes, checks, plaids, and various motifs can be created. A classic sweater can be given a new look by employing this simple technique.

One way to do this is by using the stitch pattern shown here. Two colors are used to produce a realistic brick-type design. The stitch is most effective when it is worked in a light and a dark color. Use the dark for the bricks; the light for the mortar.

Brick Pattern

Two colors can be used to create a realistic brick-type design. This stitch is most effective when it is worked in a light and a dark color. Use the dark for the bricks, light for the mortar.

For the **beginning row,** cast on a multiple of 4 stitches plus 3, using the light color.

For the **first row,** knit, using the lighter color.

For the **second row,** repeat the first row.

For the **third row,** change to the darker color. Knit 1. Repeat the following procedure. * Slip 1 stitch with yarn in back. Knit 3. * For the last 2 stitches, slip 1 and knit 1.

For the **fourth row,** use the darker color. Purl 1. Repeat the following procedure. * Slip 1 stitch with yarn in front. Purl 3. * For the last 2 stitches, slip 1 and purl 1.

For the **fifth row,** change to the lighter color. Knit.

For the **sixth row,** repeat the fifth row.

For the **seventh row,** change to the darker color. Knit 3. Repeat the following procedure. * Slip 1 with yarn in back. Knit 3. *

For the **eighth row,** continue to use the darker color. Repeat the following procedure. * Slip 1 with yarn in front. Purl 3. *

Repeat the **first through eighth rows** as many times as required.

KNIT DOUBLE

This is an interesting form of tubular knitting. Two layers are knit at the same time using one strand of yarn. The work is done in rows. The stockinette stitch can be used for both sides, or a pattern stitch can be introduced to present a more textured look to the surface.

Tubular Knitting Stitch Pattern

For the **beginning row,** cast on a multiple of 2 stitches.

For the **first row,** repeat the following procedure across the row. * Bring yarn to front of work. Slip first stitch as if to purl. Return yarn to back. Knit 1. * Alternating the position of the yarn and treatment of the stitches produces the double fabric.

For the **second row,** repeat the first row.

Continue repeating the **first row** as many times as necessary.

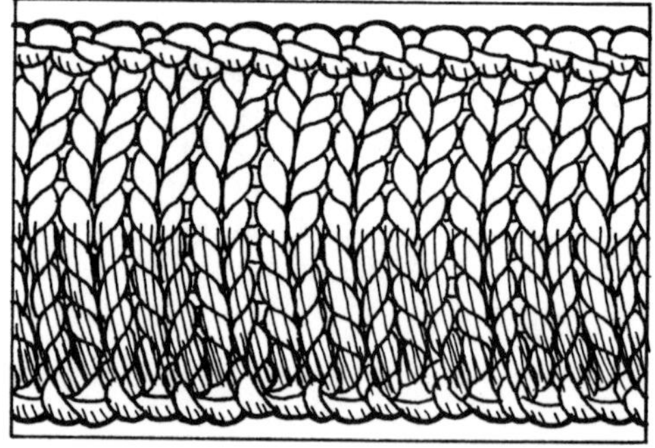

KNIT BIAS

Garter stitches are given a new dimension when worked this way. The bias effect creates an interesting look.

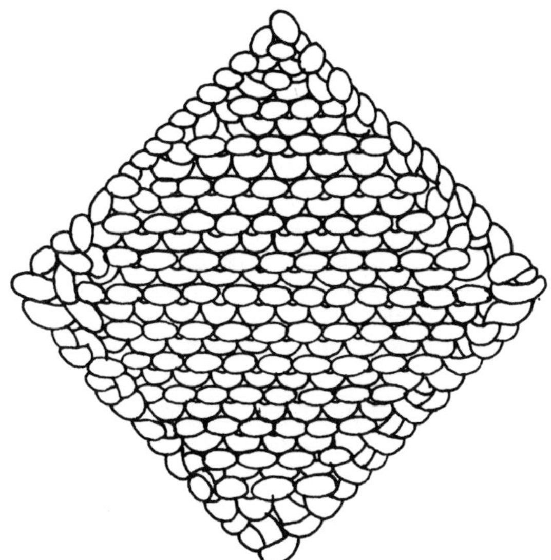

Bias Garter Stitch

For the **beginning row,** cast on 3 stitches.

For the **first row,** knit 1. Put yarn over from back to front, returning to the back between the needles. Knit 1. Yarn over again. Knit 1.

For the **second row,** knit 5.

For the **third row,** knit 1. Yarn over as in first row. Knit 3. Yarn over. Knit 1.

For the **fourth row,** knit 7.

For the **fifth row,** knit 1. Yarn over as in first row. Knit 5. Yarn over. Knit 1.

For the **sixth row,** knit 9.

Follow the above procedure, increasing the number of stitches, until the required size is reached. Note that each increase follows the first stitch and precedes the last one.

To taper the remaining half of the square, make the decrease on the odd-numbered rows.

For the **odd-numbered rows,** knit 1. Then slip 1, knit 1, and pass slip stitch over. Knit across to last 3 stitches. Then knit 2 together. Knit 1.

For the **even-numbered rows,** knit.

8

How to Vary the Stitch Pattern

Hundreds of stitch patterns can be created by combining the two basic knitting stitches—knit and purl. Many of them date back to the earliest days of knitting and vary from heavy bulky designs to cobwebby sheers. As knitting spread from country to country, the stitch patterns assumed a national feeling. Directions were handed down from generation to generation and adapted to fit the requirements of the knitter. A few of these stitch patterns are mentioned here. You will find it interesting to identify the distinguishing characteristics.

Some of the stitch patterns are more difficult to make than others, but do not be afraid to experiment. Knit a sample before using it for an article. This makes it possible for you to judge the effect of your handiwork.

TRY SOMETHING EASY

In case you have just been working with the basic techniques in making garter and stockinette stitches, you will find it wiser to select an easy-to-make stitch pattern when advancing to more complicated techniques. This does not mean that the stitch pattern has to look plain. Instead, it may appear lacy and difficult to knit. Some stitch patterns in this classification are shown here.

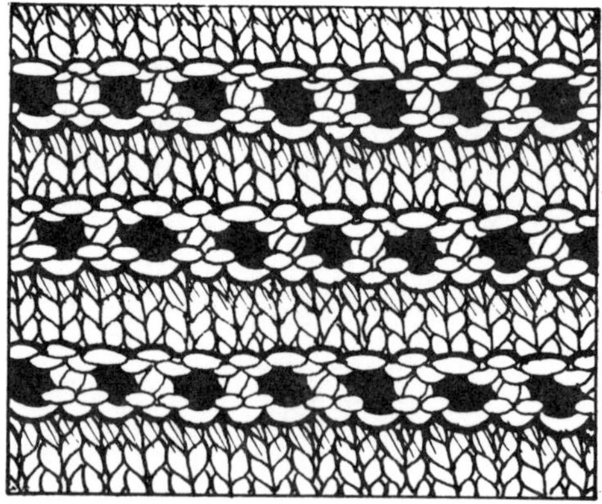

Ribbon Eyelet Pattern

Rows of eyelets seem to give a ridged effect to this stitch pattern.

For the **beginning row,** cast on an odd number of stitches.

For the **first row,** knit.

For the **second row,** purl.

For the **third row,** knit.

For the **fourth row,** knit.

For the **fifth row,** repeat the following procedure. * Knit 2 together. Yarn over. * End with knit 1.

For the **sixth row,** knit.

Repeat the **first through sixth rows** as many times as required.

Cat's Eye Pattern

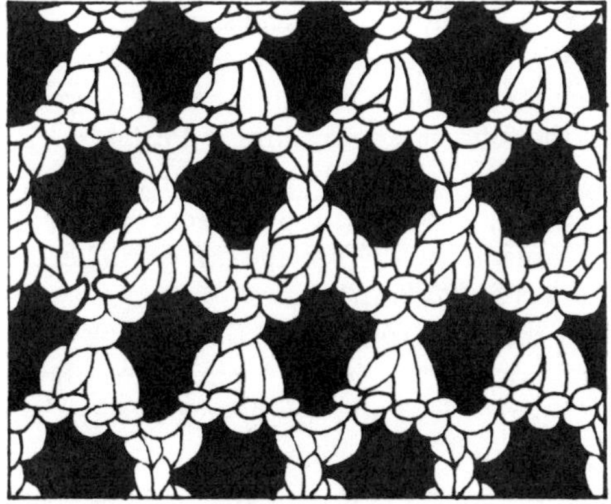

This is a Shetland allover lace pattern that is easy to make. By varying the weight of the yarn and size of the needle, the size of the meshes can be changed.

For the **beginning row,** cast on a multiple of 4 stitches.

For the **first row,** purl 2. Repeat the following procedure. * Put yarn around needle to make 1 stitch. Purl 4 together. * End with purl 2.

For the **second row,** knit 2. Repeat the following procedure. * Knit 1. Then knit 1, purl 1, and knit 1 into the stitch that was made in the first row. * End with knit 2.

For the **third row,** knit.

Repeat the **first through third rows** as many times as required.

Lace Feather Faggot Pattern

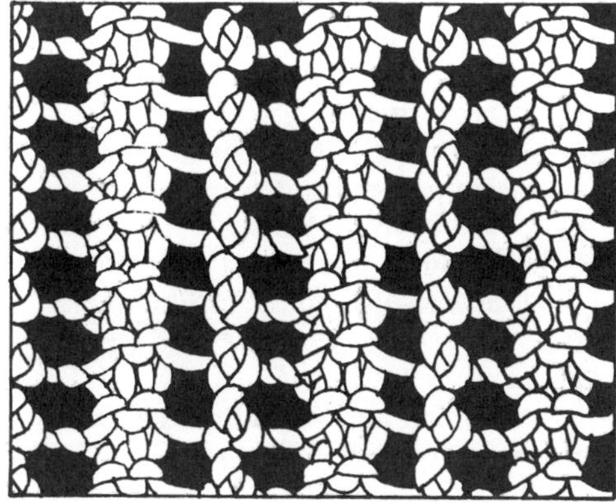

This arrangement of stitches gives a feeling of a lacy insertion.

For the **beginning row,** cast on a multiple of 4 stitches.

For the **first row,** repeat the following procedure. * Knit 1. Yarn over. Purl 2 together. Knit 1. *

Repeat the **first row** as many times as required.

Old Shale Pattern

This pattern is sometimes known as the Feather and Fan Stitch and is among the well-known Shetland lace designs.

For the **beginning row,** cast on a multiple of 18 stitches.

For the **first row,** knit.

For the **second row,** purl.

For the **third row,** repeat the following procedure. * Knit 2 together 3 times. Then put yarn over and knit 1, 6 times. Knit 2 together 3 times. *

For the **fourth row,** knit.

Repeat the **first through fourth rows** as many times as required.

Crochet-knit Traveling Eyelet Pattern

This is a lovely old Italian pattern. It creates a dainty, lacy look.

For the **beginning row,** cast on a multiple of 6 stitches plus 8.

For the **first row,** knit 1. Put yarn over. Then slip 1, knit 1, pass slip stitch over. Knit 2. Repeat the following procedure. * Knit 2 together. Yarn over. Then slip 1, knit 1, and pass slip stitch over. Knit 2. * At the last 3 stitches, knit 2 stitches together. Put yarn over. Knit 1.

For the **second row,** knit 1, purl 1. Repeat the following procedure. * Purl 4. Purl into the front and back of the next stitch, which was the yarn-over of previous row. * For the last 6 stitches, purl 5 and knit 1.

For the **third row,** knit 2. Repeat the following procedure. * Knit 2 together. Yarn over. Then slip 1, knit 1, and pass slip stitch over. Knit 2. *

For the **fourth row,** knit 1, purl 2. Repeat the following procedure. * Purl into the front and back of the next stitch. Purl 4. * For the last 4 stitches, purl into the front and back of the next stitch. Purl 2. Knit 1.

Repeat the **first through fourth rows** as many times as required.

THINKING ABOUT TEXTURE

Some stitch patterns produce a fabriclike texture with surface interest. They can vary in weight from light to heavy, depending on the technique and yarn you use. As for the surface, the looks are many. It can be flat or raised, smooth or rough. Some have a three-dimensional effect with the stitches forming a design that may move in various directions. Study the stitch patterns on the next few pages; you will be surprised how they vary in appearance.

Fabric Stitch

There is a feeling of homespun to this solid and sturdy stitch pattern, which creates a lovely textured quality.

For the **beginning row,** cast on an uneven number of stitches.

For the **first row,** knit 1. Repeat the following procedure. * Slip 1 stitch with yarn in front. Knit 1. *

For the **second row,** knit 1. Purl 1. Repeat the following procedure. * Slip 1 with the yarn in back. Purl 1. * End with knit 1.

Repeat the **first and second rows** as many times as required.

Tunisian Stitch

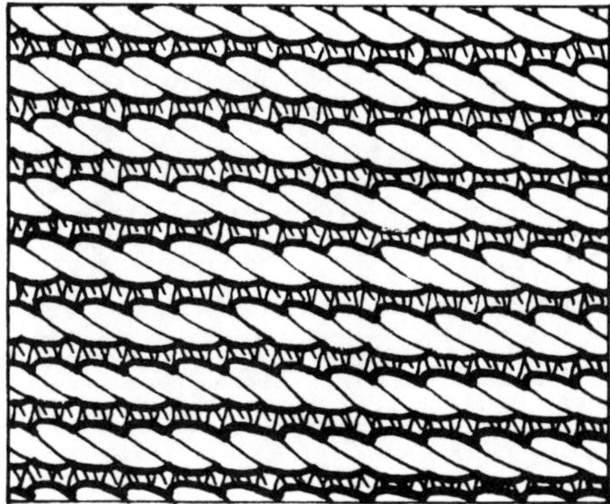

This stitch pattern creates a look similar to the Afghan Stitch found in crocheting. It produces a sturdy fabric.

For the **beginning row,** cast on the required number of stitches.

For the **first row,** slip 1 stitch. Then bring yarn forward between the needles. Slip the next stitch. Wrap yarn around needle, leaving yarn in front. Slip the next stitch. Continue this way across row. End the row with a yarn-over. Hold it in position with left thumb as needle is turned.

For the **second row,** knit 2 together through the back across the row. Do this by putting the needle through the back of the last yarn-over stitch and the last slipped stitch and knit them together. Continue this way, knitting each stitch with the correct yarn-over stitch.

Repeat the **first and second rows** as many times as required.

Herringbone Pattern

A realistic adaptation of a woven herringbone fabric is produced with this stitch arrangement.

For the **beginning row,** cast on a multiple of 7 stitches plus 1.

For the **first row,** purl.

For the **second row,** repeat the following procedure. * Knit 2 together. Knit 2. Make a 1-stitch increase by inserting tip of right-hand needle downward in back of left-hand needle through the top of the purl stitch below the next stitch, and knit. Then knit the stitch above this. Knit 2. * End row with knit 1.

Repeat **first and second rows** as many times as required.

Diagonal Stitch

The stitches are worked so that a diagonal striped effect is produced. It can be used for an allover effect as well as for bands and panels.

For the **beginning row,** cast on a multiple of 2 stitches.

For the **first row,** purl.

For the **second row,** repeat the following procedure. * Knit 2 together. Leave them on the left-hand needle. Then insert the right-hand needle between these 2 stitches and knit the first stitch again. Follow by slipping both stitches from the needle at the same time. *

For the **third row,** purl.

For the **fourth row,** knit 1. Repeat the following procedure. * Knit 2 together. Leave them on the left-hand needle. Then insert the right-hand needle between these 2 stitches and knit the first stitch again. Follow by slipping both stitches from the needle at the same time. * End row with knit 1.

Repeat the **first through fourth rows** as many times as required.

Scattered Oats Pattern

The alternating direction of small looped stitches gives the surface an embroidered look.

For the **beginning row,** cast on a multiple of 4 stitches plus 1.

For the **first row,** repeat the following procedure. * Knit 2. Slip 1 purlwise. Knit 1. * End with knit 1.

For the **second row,** purl 1. Repeat the following procedure. * Purl 1. Slip 1 purlwise. Purl 2. *

For the **third row,** repeat the following procedure. * Slip 2 stitches onto a double-pointed needle, leaving needle in back. Knit the slip stitch that was slipped in the second row. Knit the 2 stitches on the double-pointed needle. Knit 1. * End with knit 1.

For the **fourth row,** purl.

For the **fifth row,** repeat the first row.

For the **sixth row,** repeat the second row.

For the **seventh row,** knit 1. Repeat the following procedure. * Knit 1. Place the slip stitch of the previous row on a double-pointed needle and leave in front. Knit 2. Knit the stitch from the double-pointed needle. *

Repeat the **first through seventh rows** as many times as required.

Pretty Separates
Page 216

COURTESY OF BERNAT YARN & CRAFT CORP.

COURTESY OF COATS & CLARK INC.

Shawl and Sacque
Page 219

Lacy Baby Set
Page 221

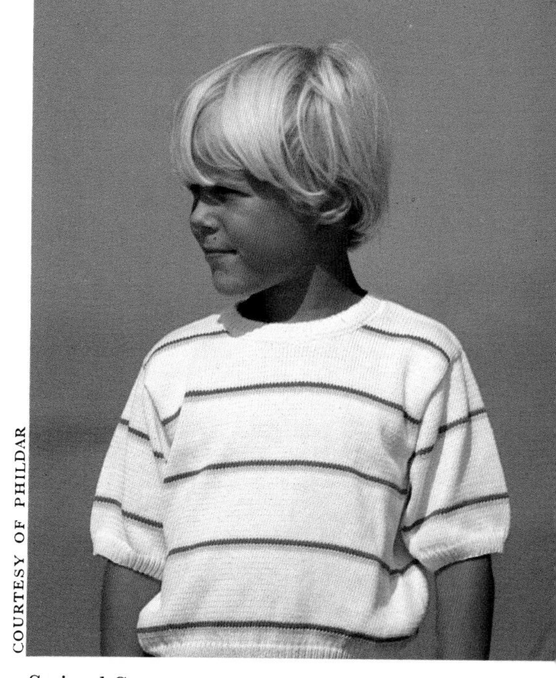

COURTESY OF PHILDAR

Striped Sweater
Page 224

Striped Cable Sweater
Page 223

COURTESY OF BERNAT YARN & CRAFT CORP.

His and Her Sweater
Page 226

Embossed Check Pattern

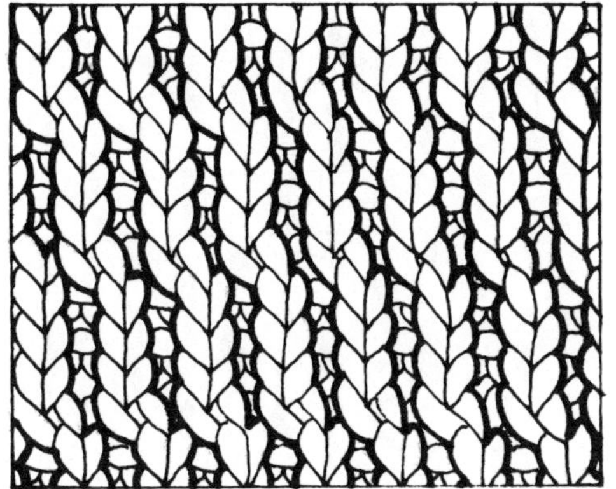

The raised and twisted effect of this Italian pattern gives a smart textural quality to the surface.

For the **beginning row,** cast on an uneven number of stitches.

For the **first row,** knit each stitch through the back.

For the **second row,** repeat the following procedure. * Knit 1. Purl 1 in back. * End with knit 1.

For the **third row,** repeat the following procedure. * Purl 1. Knit 1 in back. * End with purl 1.

For the **fourth row,** repeat the second row.

For the **fifth row,** knit each stitch through the back.

For the **sixth row,** repeat the following procedure. * Purl 1 in back. Knit 1. * End with purl 1 in back.

For the **seventh row,** repeat the following procedure. * Knit 1 in back. Purl 1. * End with knit 1 in back.

For the **eighth row,** repeat the sixth row.

Repeat the **first through eighth rows** as many times as required.

Peppercorn Stitch

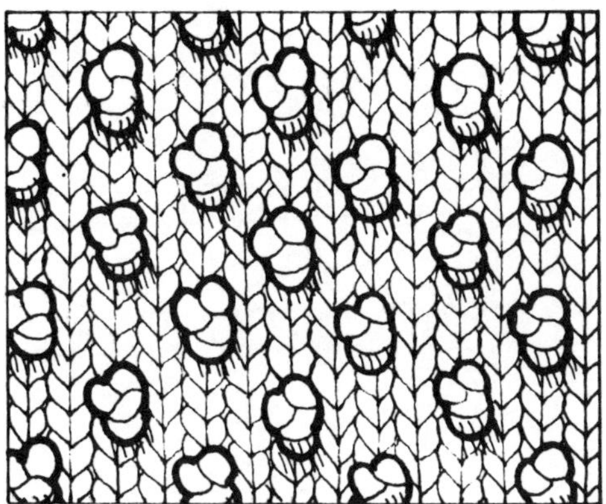

A pebbly, textural quality is given this stitch pattern for an interesting 3-dimensional effect.

For the **beginning row,** cast on a multiple of 4 stitches plus 3.

For the **first row,** purl.

For the **second row,** knit 3. Repeat the following procedure. * Knit next stitch. Then slide this stitch onto the left-hand needle without removing the right-hand needle, and with the left-hand needle in the front of the stitch. With the needles in this position, knit 3 times into the back. Knit 3. *

For the **third row,** purl.

For the **fourth row,** knit 1. Repeat the following procedure. * Knit next stitch. Then slide this stitch onto the left-hand needle without removing the right-hand needle, and with the left-hand needle in the front of the stitch. With the needles in this position, knit 3 times into the back. Knit 3. * End with knit 1.

Repeat the **first through fourth rows** as many times as required.

Waffle Stitch

This is another stitch that has an interesting textural quality.

For the **beginning row,** cast on a multiple of 2 stitches.

For the **first row,** repeat the following procedure. * Knit 1 in back. Purl 1. *

For the **second row,** repeat the following procedure. * Purl 1 in back. Knit 1. *

Repeat the **first and second rows** as many times as required.

Waffle Brioche Pattern

This stitch pattern seems to give a soft honeycomb effect.

For the **beginning row,** cast on a multiple of 3 stitches plus 2.

For the **first row,** knit 1. Repeat the following procedure. * Put yarn over. Slip 1 knitwise with yarn in back. Insert needle into the back of 2 stitches and knit them together. * End with knit 1.

For the **second row,** knit 3. Repeat the following procedure. * Slip 1 knitwise with yarn in back. Knit 2. * End with slip 1 knitwise with yarn in back. Knit 1. Notice that the slipped stitches are the yarn-overs of the previous row.

For the **third row,** knit 1. Repeat the following procedure. * Knit 2 together by inserting needle through back of loops. Yarn over. Slip 1 knitwise with yarn in back. * End with knit 1.

For the **fourth row,** knit 2. Repeat the following procedure. * Slip 1 knitwise with yarn in back. Knit 2. * Notice that the slipped stitches are the yarn-overs of the third row.

Repeat the **first through fourth rows** as many times as required.

Diamond Quilting Pattern

Diagonally placed loops give this English pattern a soft but definite line.

For the **beginning row,** cast on 6 stitches plus 4.

For the **first row,** purl.

For the **second row,** knit 4. Repeat the following procedure. * Knit the next 2 stitches, wrapping yarn twice around needle. Knit 4. *

For the **third row,** purl 4. Repeat the following procedure. * With yarn in front, slip next 2 stitches purlwise, dropping the extra wrapped stitches. Purl 4. *

For the **fourth row,** knit 4. Repeat the following procedure. * With yarn in back, slip next 2 stitches purlwise. Knit 4. *

For the **fifth row,** purl 4. Repeat the following procedure. * With yarn in front, slip next 2 stitches purlwise. Purl 4. *

For the **sixth row,** knit 2. Repeat the following procedure. * Skip next 2 stitches. Knit the next stitch, inserting needle through front. Leave on needle. Then knit the first and second stitches on left needle. Drop the third stitch from needle. Slip the next stitch onto a double-pointed needle and leave in front. Knit 2. Knit the stitch from the double-pointed needle. * End with knit 2.

For the **seventh row,** purl.

For the **eighth row,** knit 2. Then knit 1, wrapping yarn twice around needle. Knit 4. Repeat the following procedure. * Knit next 2 stitches, wrapping yarn around twice. Knit 4. * End with knit 1, wrapping yarn around twice. Knit 2.

For the **ninth row,** purl 2. With yarn in front, slip 1 stitch, dropping the wrapped stitches. Purl 4. Repeat the following procedure. * With yarn in front, slip 2 stitches, dropping the wrapped stitches. Purl 4. * End with yarn in front. Slip 1 stitch, dropping the wrapped stitches. Purl 2.

For the **tenth row,** knit 2. Slip next stitch purlwise with yarn in back. Repeat the following procedure. * Knit 4. With yarn in back, slip next 2 stitches purlwise. * End with knit 4. Then, with yarn in back, slip next stitch purlwise. Knit 2.

For the **eleventh row,** purl 2. With yarn in front, slip 1 stitch purlwise. Repeat the following procedure. * Purl 4. With yarn in front, slip next 2 stitches. * End with purl 4. With yarn in front, slip 1 stitch. Purl 2.

For the **twelfth row,** knit 2. Repeat the following procedure. * Slip next stitch onto a double-pointed needle, leaving it in front. Knit 2. Knit the stitch from the double-pointed needle. Skip next 2 stitches. Knit next stitch, inserting needle in front of stitch. Leave on needle. Knit first and second stitches on left-hand needle. Drop third stitch from needle. * End with knit 2.

Repeat the **first through twelfth rows** as many times as required.

Lattice Stitch

This grouping of stitches creates a bold design pattern that gives a basket weave effect.

For the **beginning row**, cast on a multiple of 6 stitches.

For the **first row**, repeat the following procedure. * Knit 4. Purl 2. *

For the **second row**, knit the purl stitches and purl the knit stitches of previous row.

For the **third row**, repeat the following procedure. * Slip 2 stitches onto a double-pointed needle. Leave at back. Knit 2. Knit the 2 stitches on the double-pointed needle. Purl 2. *

For the **fourth row**, repeat the second row.

For the **fifth row**, purl 2. Repeat the following procedure. * Knit 2. Slip 2 onto a double-pointed needle. Leave in back. Knit 2. Purl the 2 stitches on the double-pointed needle. * End with knit 4.

For the **sixth row**, repeat the second row.

For the **seventh row**, repeat the following procedure. * Purl 2. Slip 2 onto a double-pointed needle. Leave in front. Knit 2. Knit the 2 stitches from the double-pointed needle. *

For the **eighth row**, repeat the second row.

For the **ninth row**, knit 4. Repeat the following procedure. * Slip 2 onto a double-pointed needle. Leave in front. Purl 2. Knit the 2 stitches from the double-pointed needle. Knit 2. * End with purl 2.

Repeat the **second through ninth rows** as many times as required.

Bowknot Pattern

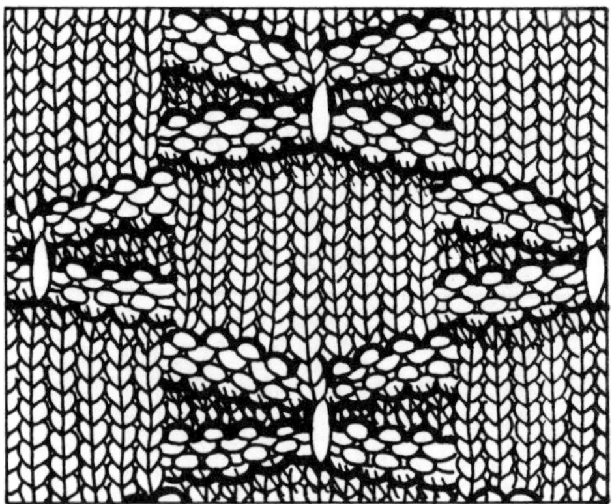

Graceful bows, worked in a block-type design, can produce a dainty effect when knitted in a lightweight yarn.

For the **beginning row**, cast on a multiple of 18 stitches plus 9.

For the **first row**, knit 9. Repeat the following procedure. * Purl 9. Knit 9. *

For the **second row**, purl 9. Repeat the following procedure. * Knit 9. Purl 9. *

For the **third row**, knit.

For the **fourth row**, purl.

For the **fifth row**, knit.

For the **sixth row**, purl.

For the **seventh row**, repeat first row.

For the **eighth row**, repeat second row.

For the **ninth row**, knit 13. Repeat the following procedure. * Insert needle into the front of the next stitch, 9 rows below. Draw up a loop. Slip the loop onto the left-hand needle. Knit the loop and the next stitch together. Knit 17 stitches. * End last repeat with 13 knit stitches.

For the **tenth row**, purl.

For the **eleventh row**, purl 9. Repeat the following procedure. * Knit 9. Purl 9. *

For the **twelfth row**, knit 9. Repeat the following procedure. * Purl 9. Knit 9. *

For the **thirteenth row**, knit.

For the **fourteenth row**, purl.

For the **fifteenth row**, knit.

For the **sixteenth row**, purl.

For the **seventeenth row**, repeat the eleventh row.

For the **eighteenth row**, repeat the twelfth row.

For the **nineteenth row**, knit 4. Repeat the following procedure. * Working in the ninth row below, pull up a loop. Knit it together with next stitch, as in the ninth row. Knit 17 stitches. * End with 4 knit stitches.

For the **twentieth row,** purl.

Repeat the **first through twentieth rows** as required.

Bell and Rope Pattern

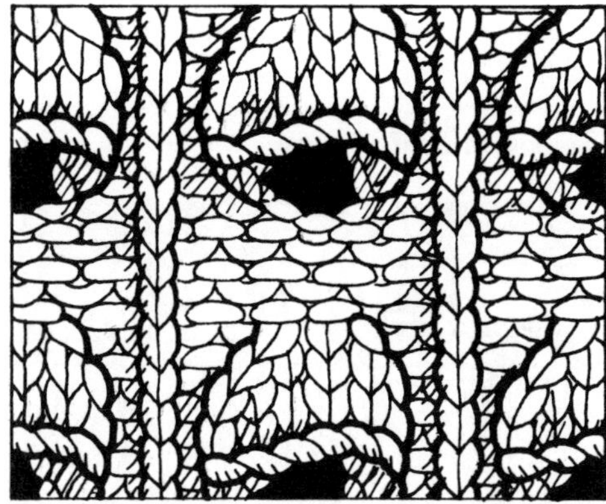

This arrangement of stitches gives the effect of swinging bells.

For the **beginning row,** cast on a multiple of 5 stitches.

For the **first row,** purl 2. Repeat the following procedure. * Knit 1 stitch through the back. Purl 4. * End with knit 1 stitch through the back, purl 2.

For the **second row,** knit 2, purl 1 stitch through the back. Repeat the following procedure. * Knit 4. Purl 1 stitch through the back. * End with knit 2.

For the **third row,** purl 2. Repeat the following procedure. * Knit 1 stitch through the back. Purl 2. Cast on 8 stitches for the bell. Purl 2. * End with knit 1 stitch through the back, purl 2.

For the **fourth row,** knit 2. Purl 1 stitch through the back. Repeat the following procedure. * Knit 2. Purl 8 for the bell. Knit 2. Purl 1 stitch through the back. * End with knit 2.

For the **fifth row,** purl 2. Repeat the following procedure. * Knit 1 stitch through the back. Purl 2. Knit 8 for the bell. Purl 2. * End with knit 1 stitch through the back, purl 2.

For the **sixth row,** repeat the fourth row.

For the **seventh row,** purl 2. Repeat the following procedure. * Knit 1 stitch through the back. Purl 2. In making the bell, slip 1 stitch, knit 1 stitch. Pass slip stitch over knit stitch. Knit 4. Knit 2 together. Then purl 2. * End with knit 1 stitch through the back, and purl 2.

For the **eighth row,** knit 2, purl 1 stitch through the back. Repeat the following procedure. * Knit 2. For the bell, purl 2 together, purl 2, purl 1 decrease in reverse by purling 1 stitch. Return it to the left needle. Insert right needle through the stitch beyond and, lifting it over the stitch just purled, slide it off the needle. Then knit 2. Purl 1 stitch through the back. * End with knit 2.

For the **ninth row,** purl 2. Repeat the following procedure. * Knit 1 stitch through the back. Purl 2. For the bell, slip 1, knit 1, pass slip stitch over knit stitch, knit 2 together. Then purl 2. * End with knit 1 stitch through the back, purl 2.

For the **tenth row,** knit 2. Purl 1 stitch through the back. Repeat the following procedure. * Knit 1. For the top of the bell, knit 2 together, and then knit another 2 together. Knit 1. Purl 1 stitch through the back. * End with knit 2.

Repeat the **first through tenth rows** as many times as required.

Raised Diamond Pattern

An interesting 3-dimensional effect results when this design pattern is used.

For the **beginning row,** cast on a multiple of 7 stitches.

For the **first row,** knit.

For the **second row,** purl.

For the **third row,** knit.

For the **fourth row,** purl 3. Knit 1. Purl 3.

For the **fifth row,** knit 3. Then purl the next stitch, first into the front, then into the back, and finally into the front again. Knit 3.

For the **sixth row,** purl 3. Knit 3. Purl 3.

For the **seventh row,** knit 3. Then purl into the front and back of next stitch. Purl 1. Then purl into front and back of next stitch. Knit 3.

For the **eighth row,** purl 3. Knit 5. Purl 3.

For the **ninth row,** knit 3. Purl into the front and back of next stitch. Purl 3. Again purl into the front and back of next stitch. Knit 3.

For the **tenth row,** purl 3. Knit 7. Purl 3.

For the **eleventh row,** knit 3. Purl into the front and back of the next stitch. Purl 5. Then purl into front and back of the next stitch. Knit 3.

For the **twelfth row,** purl 3. Knit 9. Purl 3.

For the **thirteenth row,** knit 3. Purl 2 together. Purl 5. Purl 2 together in back. Knit 3.

For the **fourteenth row,** purl 3. Knit 7. Purl 3.

For the **fifteenth row,** knit 3. Purl 2 together. Purl 3. Purl 2 together in back. Knit 3.

For the **sixteenth row,** purl 3. Knit 5. Purl 3.

For the **seventeenth row,** knit 3. Purl 2 together. Purl 1. Purl 2 together in back. Knit 3.

For the **eighteenth row,** purl 3. Knit 3. Purl 3.

For the **nineteenth row,** knit 3. Purl 3 together. Knit 3.

For the **twentieth row,** purl 3. Knit 1. Purl 3.

Repeat the **first through twentieth rows** as many times as required.

Embossed Leaf Pattern

The leaves give a 3-dimensional effect to this beautiful old German pattern.

For the **beginning row,** cast on a multiple of 8 stitches plus 7.

For the **first row,** purl 7. Repeat the following procedure. * Knit 1. Purl 7. *

For the **second row,** knit 7. Repeat the following procedure. * Purl 1. Knit 7. *

For the **third row,** purl 7. Repeat the following procedure. * Insert needle between the stitch just knitted and the next, picking up the connecting thread. Then knit into the back of it, making 1 stitch. Knit 1. Again insert the needle between the stitch just knitted and the next, picking up the connecting thread. Then knit into the back of it, making 1 stitch. Purl 7. *

For the **fourth row,** knit 7. Repeat the following procedure. * Purl 3. Knit 7. *

For the **fifth row,** purl 7. Repeat the following procedure. * Knit 1 and put yarn over twice. Knit 1. Purl 7. *

For the **sixth row,** knit 7. Repeat the following procedure. * Purl 5. Knit 7. *

For the **seventh row,** purl 7. Repeat the following procedure. * Knit 2. Yarn over. Knit 1. Yarn over. Knit 2. Purl 7. *

For the **eighth row,** knit 7. Repeat the following procedure. * Purl 7. Knit 7. *

For the **ninth row,** purl 7. Repeat the following procedure. * Knit 2. Then slip 2 knitwise, knit 1, and pass the 2 slip stitches over. Knit 2. Purl 7. *

For the **tenth row,** repeat the sixth row.

For the **eleventh row,** purl 7. Repeat the following procedure. * Knit 1. Then slip 2 knitwise, knit 1, and pass the 2 slip stitches over. Knit 1. Purl 7. *

For the **twelfth row,** repeat the fourth row.

For the **thirteenth row,** purl 7. Repeat the following procedure. * Slip 2 knitwise, knit 1, and pass the 2 slip stitches over. Purl 7. *

For the **fourteenth row,** repeat the second row.

For the **fifteenth row,** purl 3. Repeat the following procedure. * Knit 1. Purl 7. * End with knit 1, purl 3.

For the **sixteenth row,** knit 3. Repeat the following procedure. * Purl 1. Knit 7. * End with purl 1, knit 3.

For the **seventeenth row,** purl 3. Repeat the following procedure. * Insert needle between the stitch just knitted and the next, picking up the connecting thread. Then knit into the back of it, making 1 stitch. Knit 1. Make another stitch. Purl 7. * End by making 1 stitch. Knit 1. Make another stitch. Purl 3.

For the **eighteenth row,** knit 3. Repeat the following procedure. * Purl 3. Knit 7. * End with purl 3, knit 3.

For the **nineteenth row,** purl 3. Repeat the following procedure. * Knit 1 and yarn over twice. Knit 1. Purl 7. * End with knit 1 and yarn over twice. Knit 1. Purl 3.

For the **twentieth row,** knit 3. Repeat the following procedure. * Purl 5. Knit 7. * End with purl 5 and knit 3.

For the **twenty-first row,** purl 3. Repeat the following procedure. * Knit 2. Yarn over. Knit 1. Yarn over. Knit 2. Purl 7. * End with knit 2. Yarn over. Knit 1. Yarn over. Knit 2. Purl 3.

For the **twenty-second row,** knit 3. Repeat the following procedure. * Purl 7. Knit 7. * End with purl 7, knit 3.

For the **twenty-third row,** purl 3. Repeat the following procedure. * Knit 2. Then slip 2 knitwise, knit 1, and pass the 2 slip stitches over. Knit 2. Purl 7. * End with knit 2. Then slip 2 knitwise, knit 1, and pass the 2 slip stitches over. Knit 2. Purl 3.

For the **twenty-fourth row,** repeat the twentieth row.

For the **twenty-fifth row,** purl 3. Repeat the following procedure. * Knit 1. Then slip 2 knitwise, knit 1, and pass the 2 slip stitches over. Knit 1. Purl 7. * End with knit 1. Then slip 2 knitwise, knit 1, and pass the 2 slip stitches over. Knit 1. Purl 3.

For the **twenty-sixth row,** repeat the eighteenth row.

For the **twenty-seventh row,** purl 3. Repeat the following procedure. * Slip 2 knitwise, knit 1, and pass the 2 slip stitches over. Purl 7. * End with slip 2 knitwise, knit 1, and pass the 2 slip stitches over. Purl 3.

For the **twenty-eighth row,** repeat the sixteenth row.

Repeat the **first through twenty-eighth rows** as many times as required.

HOW TO CREATE A NOVELTY RIBBING

Ribbing is one of the basics of knitting. Every knitter knows how to knit two, purl two, but few realize how many novelty ribbings there are. In fact, substituting one of the ribbings shown here for the classic one is rare. Why don't you consider it?

In choosing a rib pattern, be sure to make a test swatch. Some ribbings are more resilient than others. Make certain that the one you have chosen is not too loose for the purpose for which it is to be used. Also remember that a ribbing can be used for a design detail other than a banding at the lower edge of a sweater. In fact, a sweater made completely of ribbing can be most effective.

Suggestions for a variety of ribbings are found on the following pages. Notice that some are more decorative than others.

Cross Cord Rib Pattern

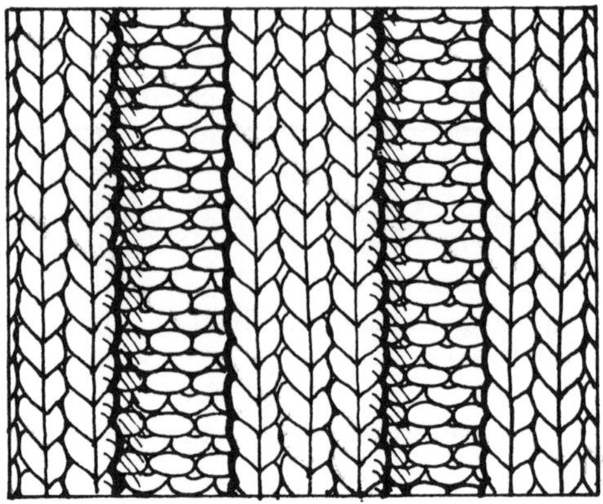

This is another old Italian pattern that has an interesting textural quality.

For the **beginning row,** cast on a multiple of 6 stitches plus 3.

For the **first row,** repeat the following procedure. * Knit 3 stitches in back. Purl 3. * End row by knitting 3 stitches in back.

For the **second row,** purl 3 in back. Repeat the following procedure. * Knit 3. Purl 3 in back. *

Repeat the **first and second rows** as many times as required.

Lace Rib Pattern

An interesting arrangement of stitches give the look of linked chains with an eyelet center.

For the **beginning row,** cast on a multiple of 5 stitches plus 2.
For the **first row,** knit 2. Repeat the following procedure. * Purl 3. Knit 2. *
For the **second row,** purl 2. Repeat the following procedure. * Knit 1. Yarn over. Then slip 1, knit 1, and pass slip stitch over. Purl 2. *
For the **third row,** repeat the first row.
For the **fourth row,** purl 2. Repeat the following procedure. * Knit 2 together. Yarn over. Knit 1. Purl 2. *
Repeat the **first through fourth rows** as many times as required.

Corded Rib Pattern

A smart textural quality is the dominant feature of this old Italian pattern.
For the **beginning row,** cast on a multiple of 4 stitches plus 2.
For the **first row,** knit 1. Repeat the following procedure. * Slip 1, knit 1, and pass slip stitch over. Then make 1 stitch by picking up the connecting yarn that runs between the stitch just worked and the next stitch, and knit in back of this stitch. Then purl 2. * Knit 1.
Repeat the **first row** as many times as required.

Herringbone Rib Pattern

When this stitch pattern is left unpressed, the diagonal lines in the rib produce a herringbone effect.
For the **beginning row,** cast on 9 stitches plus 3.
For the **first row,** repeat the following procedure. * Purl 3. Knit 2 together, but do not slip from left-hand needle. Knit the first of these 2 stitches again, slip both stitches off needle. Do this 2 more times. * End with purl 3.
For the **second row,** repeat the following procedure. * Knit 3, purl 6. * End with knit 3.
For the **third row,** repeat the following procedure. * Purl 3, knit 1. Knit 2 together, but do not slip from left-hand needle. Knit the first stitch again, slip both stitches off needle. Do this once more. Knit 1. * End with purl 3.
For the **fourth row,** repeat the second row.
Repeat **first through fourth rows** as required.

Wheat Ear Rib Pattern

An interesting textural look is created by working ribs in this fashion.

For the **beginning row,** cast on a multiple of 5 stitches plus 2.

For the **first row,** repeat the following procedure. * Purl 3. Put right-hand needle between the first and second stitches on the left-hand needle, moving from the back to the front. Knit the second stitch. Then knit the first stitch and slide both stitches together from the needle. * End with purl 2.

For the **second row,** repeat the following procedure. * Knit 3. Skip the next stitch, purling the second stitch. Then purl the skipped stitch. Slide both stitches together off the needle. * End with knit 2.

Repeat the **first and second rows** as many times as required.

Cross Stitch Rib Pattern

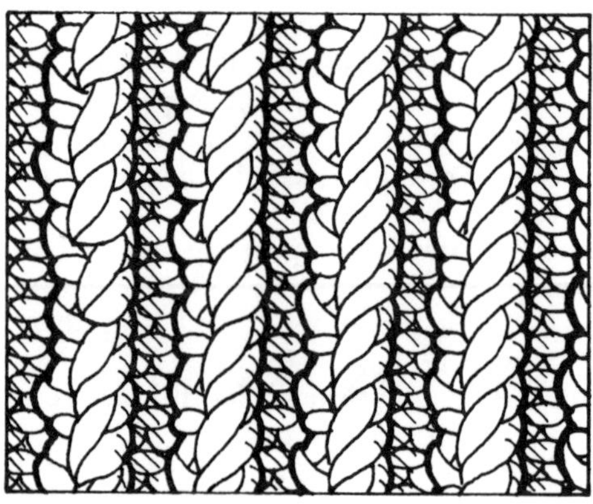

Plain ribbing can be given a different look when it is twisted on both sides of the knitting.

For the **beginning row,** cast on a multiple of 3 stitches plus 1.

For the **first row,** purl 1. Repeat the following procedure. * Knit in back of second stitch. Leave it on the left-hand needle. Then knit in front of the first stitch, and slip both off together. Purl 1. *

For the **second row,** knit 1. Repeat the following procedure. * Purl 2. Knit 1. *

Repeat the **first and second rows** as many times as required.

Braided Rib Pattern

Ribbing can be given a new look by using this stitch pattern.

For the **beginning row,** cast on a multiple of 5 stitches plus 2.

For the **first row,** purl 2. Repeat the following procedure. * Insert needle between first and second stitches on the left-hand needle, moving from back to front. Then knit the second stitch. Follow by knitting the first stitch. Slip both stitches from needle at the same time. Knit 1. Purl 2. *

For the **second row,** knit 2. Repeat the following procedure. * Purl the second stitch before purling the first stitch. Slip both stitches from needle together. Purl 1. Knit 2. *

Repeat the **first and second rows** as many times as required.

Imitation Embroidery Pattern

This interesting ribbed effect is dotted with tiny bells and eyelets.

For the **beginning row,** cast on a multiple of 6 stitches plus 3.

For the **first row,** knit 1. Purl 2. Knit 3. Repeat the following procedure. * Purl 3. Knit 3. * End with purl 2, knit 1.

For the **second row,** knit 3. Repeat the following procedure. * Purl 3. Knit 3. *

For the **third row,** knit 1, purl 2. Repeat the following procedure. * Put yarn over right-hand needle. Knit 3 together. Yarn over. Purl 3. * Then end by putting yarn over. Knit 3 together. Yarn over. Purl 2. Knit 1.

For the **fourth row,** repeat the second row.

Repeat the **first through fourth rows** as many times as required.

MIXING COLORS

Simple stitch patterns can become exciting through the use of colors. Although we are surrounded by lovely color arrangements in nature, it seems difficult to use color wisely and well. Often color is employed in such a profusion that the results seem tasteless. Instead, color should be used with a subtle touch so that the design seems alive and interesting, but as a harmonious blend.

Before choosing a color combination, study the fashion looks of the moment. Arrange yarns of various colors so you can observe their effect on each other. It is the perfect blending that you want to train your eye to detect. Some stitch patterns to test your color sense are mentioned on the following pages.

Basket Pattern

Stripes of garter stitches can be given added interest by introducing a slip stitch and a second color. The pattern is also effective when worked in 1 color.

For the **beginning row,** cast on a multiple of 4 stitches plus 3. Use 1 or 2 colors. If using 2 colors—A and B—follow these directions. Cast on with color A.

For the **first row,** purl.

For the **second row,** attach color B. Knit 3. Repeat the following procedure. * Slip 1 stitch with yarn in back. Knit 3. *

For the **third row,** continue with B, knit 3. Repeat the following procedure. * Slip 1 stitch with yarn in front. Knit 3. *

For the **fourth row,** repeat the second row.

For the **fifth row,** repeat the third row.

For the **sixth row,** change to color A and knit.

For the **seventh row,** purl, continuing with A.

Repeat the **second through seventh rows** as required.

Bicolor Diagonal Stripe Pattern

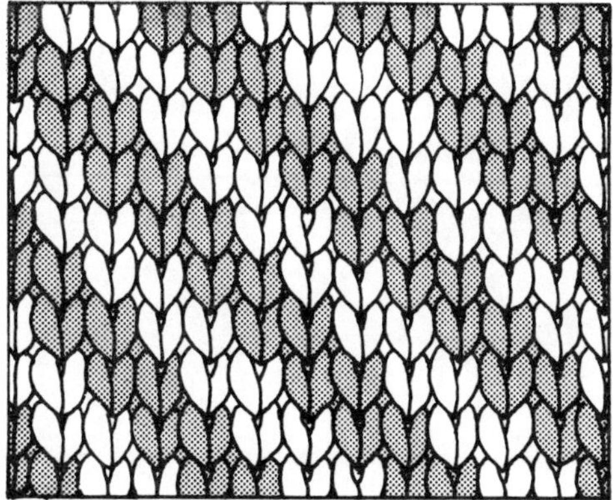

Introducing a second color adds interest to a design, especially when it is worked in a diagonal direction.

For the **beginning row,** cast on a multiple of 4 stitches, using the darker color.

For the **first row,** purl.

For the **second row,** work with the lighter color. Knit 1. Repeat the following procedure. * Slip 2 with yarn in back. Knit 2. * End row with slip 2, knit 1.

For the **third row,** continue to use lighter color. Knit 1. Repeat the following procedure. * Slip 1 with yarn in front. Purl 3. * End with slip 1, purl 1, knit 1.

For the **fourth row,** use darker color. Knit 1. Slip 1 with yarn in back. Repeat the following procedure. * Knit 2. Slip 2 with yarn in back. * End with knit 2.

For the **fifth row,** continue with darker color. Knit 1. Purl 1. Repeat the following procedure. * Slip 1 with yarn in front. Purl 3. * End by slipping 1 stitch and knitting 1.

For the **sixth row,** work with lighter color. Knit 1. Repeat the following procedure. * Knit 2. Slip 2 with yarn in back. * End with knit 3.

For the **seventh row,** continue with lighter color. Knit 1. Purl 2. Repeat the following procedure. * Slip 1 with yarn in front. Purl 3. * End with knit 1.

For the **eighth row,** change to darker color. Repeat the following procedure. * Knit 2. Slip 2 with yarn in back. * End with knit 2. Slip 1. Knit 1.

For the **ninth row,** continue to use darker color. Knit 1. Repeat the following procedure. * Purl 3. Slip 1 stitch with yarn in front. * End by purling 2 and knitting 1.

Repeat the **second through ninth rows** as many times as required.

Honeycomb Tweed Pattern

By using 2 colors, this French pattern is given a solid, tweedy look.

For the **beginning row,** cast on an uneven number of stitches, using the lighter color.

For the **first row,** use the lighter color. Repeat the following procedure. * Knit 1. Slip 1 purlwise. * End with knit 1.

For the **second row,** continue to use lighter color. Purl.

For the **third row,** change to darker color. Knit 2. Repeat the following procedure. * Slip 1 purl stitch. Knit 1. * End with knit 1.

For the **fourth row,** continue with the darker color. Purl.

Repeat the **first through fourth rows** as many times as required.

Corn-on-the-cob Stitch

Using yarns in 2 colors gives this design pattern a dotted look. Although the colors are worked in stripes, they do not create the usual effect.

For the **beginning row,** cast on a multiple of 2 stitches. Use 2 colors, light and dark.

For the **first row**, knit, using the lighter yarn.

For the **second row,** use the darker yarn. Repeat the following procedure. * Knit 1. Slip 1. * End with knit 1.

For the **third row,** use the darker yarn. Repeat the following procedure. * Bring yarn forward. Slip 1. Put yarn back. Knit 1. * Be sure to slip the light stitches and knit the dark ones, bringing the yarn forward before each slip stitch and back after each.

For the **fourth row,** use the lighter yarn. Repeat the following procedure. * Slip 1. Knit 1 into back of stitch. * Be sure to knit the light stitches into the back of the stitch and slip the dark stitches, keeping yarn in the back.

For the **fifth row,** use the lighter yarn. Repeat the following procedure. * Knit 1. Bring yarn forward. Slip 1. Take yarn to back. * Be sure to knit the light stitches and slip the dark ones, with the yarn brought forward before a slip stitch and back afterward.

Repeat the **second through fifth** rows as many times as required.

Star Stitch

Although this stitch pattern could be made of a single color, the design is more effective when 2 are used.

For the **beginning row,** cast on a multiple of 4 stitches plus 1, using the darker color.

For the **first row,** purl.

For the **second row,** change to the lighter color. Knit 1. Repeat the following procedure. * Slip 1 with yarn in back. Insert needle under the connecting thread between the stitch just slipped and the next one, and knit 1. Slip 1 with yarn in back. Knit 1. Then pass the first slipped stitch over 3 stitches. Knit 1. *

For the **third row,** purl.

For the **fourth row,** use the darker yarn. Knit 3. Repeat the following procedure. * Slip 1 with yarn in back. Insert needle under the connecting thread between the stitch just slipped and the next one, and knit 1. Slip 1 with yarn in back. Knit 1. Then pass the first slipped stitch over 3 stitches. Knit 1. * End with knit 2.

For the **fifth row,** purl.

Repeat the **second through fifth rows** as many times as required.

Hexagon Pattern

This pattern is most effective when worked in 2 colors—dark and light.

For the **beginning row,** cast on eight stitches plus 6, using the darker yarn.

For the **first row,** knit.

For the **second row,** also knit.

For the **third row,** work with the lighter color. Knit 2. Repeat the following procedure. * Slip 2 with yarn in back. Knit 6. * End by slipping 2 stitches and knitting 2.

For the **fourth row,** purl 2. Repeat the following procedure. * Slip 2 with yarn in front. Purl 6. * End by slipping 2 stitches and purling 2.

For the **fifth row,** repeat the third row.

For the **sixth row,** repeat the fourth row.

For the **seventh row,** repeat the third row.

For the **eighth row,** repeat the fourth row.

For the **ninth row,** change to the darker color. Knit.

For the **tenth, eleventh, and twelfth rows,** knit.

For the **thirteenth row,** change to the lighter color. Knit 6. Repeat the following procedure. * Slip 2 with yarn in back. Knit 6. *

For the **fourteenth row,** purl 6. Repeat the following procedure. * Slip 2 with yarn in front. Purl 6. *

For the **fifteenth row,** repeat the thirteenth row.

For the **sixteenth row,** repeat the fourteenth row.

For the **seventeenth row,** repeat the thirteenth row.

For the **eighteenth row,** repeat the fourteenth row.

For the **nineteenth and twentieth rows,** change to darker color. Knit.

Repeat the **first through twentieth rows** as many times as required.

Blister Check Pattern

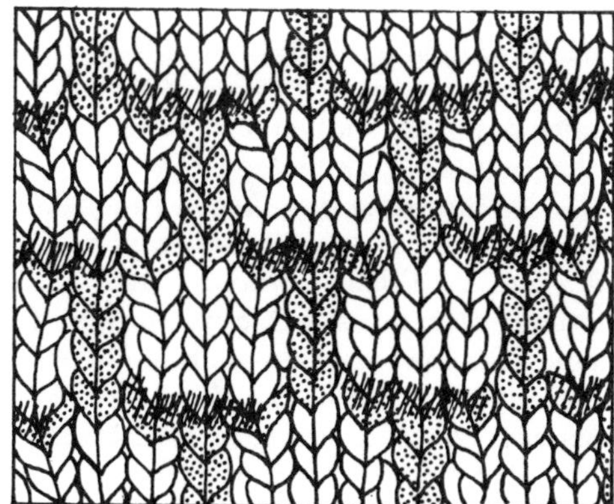

This pattern is sometimes referred to as Coin Stitch. The stitches produce a raised coin-shaped dot. This stitch pattern is most effective when 2 contrasting colors are used—A and B.

For the **beginning row,** cast on a multiple of 4 stitches plus 1, using color A.

For the **first row,** knit, with color A.

For the **second row,** purl, continuing to use color A.

For the **third row,** knit with color B.

For the **fourth row,** purl with color B.

For the **fifth row,** repeat the third row.

For the **sixth row,** repeat the fourth row.

For the **seventh row,** use color A. Knit 2. Repeat the following procedure. * Drop next stitch off needle carefully. Unravel 4 rows down. Pick up color A stitch from the second row below. Insert needle into this stitch and under the 4 connecting threads of color B. Knit, catching the 4 loose strands in back of the stitch. Knit 3. * End with 2 knit stitches.

For the **eighth row,** purl with color A.

For the **ninth row,** knit with color B.

For the **tenth row,** purl with color B.

For the **eleventh row,** knit with color B.

For the **twelfth row,** purl with color B.

For the **thirteenth row,** use color A. Knit 4. Repeat the following procedure. * Drop next stitch. Unravel 4 rows down. Pick up the color A stitch from 5 rows below, in the same way as in the seventh row. Knit 3. * End by knitting 1.

Repeat the **second through thirteenth rows** as many times as required.

Colors can also be arranged to form more definite geometric patterns. Stripes can be dramatic, with either the right or wrong side being used effectively.

Dividing an area into shapes, producing in some instances a patchwork pattern, adds interest. Triangles, squares, and rectangles can be used. A quilt block or a fabric print may provide inspiration.

More intricate geometric designs form a jacquard type of knitting. Small shapes and lines are used to create an allover effect producing a striped feeling. This allows for an interesting use of several colors.

When just 2 colors are used, the knitting is referred to as Fair Isle. A true Fair Isle pattern is marked with an adaptation of the Armada Cross forming a striped motif, moving horizontally. The stockinette stitch produces the best background for this intermingling of shape and color.

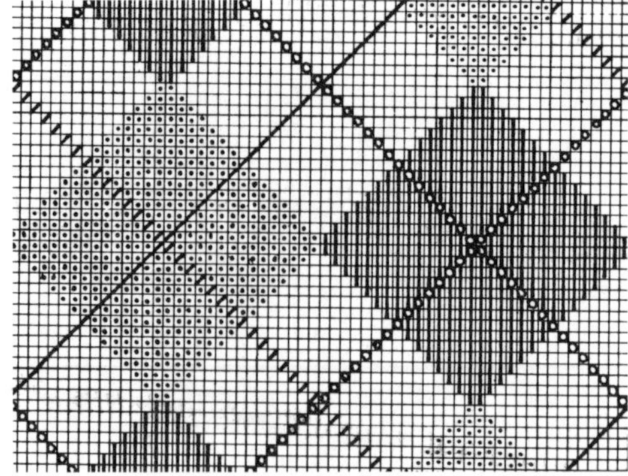

One of the most distinctive design patterns is the Argyle, an adaptation of a Scottish clan tartan. Diamond-shape blocks in different colors are crossed by lines for a plaid effect. Usually each color is wound on a separate bobbin. Change in color can easily be made by following a chart such as the one shown here. It is important that the colors be twisted together as the change is made so that no unsightly spaces appear in the finished work. The knit material should be smooth and even. The work is knitted flat, using a knit row followed by a purl row.

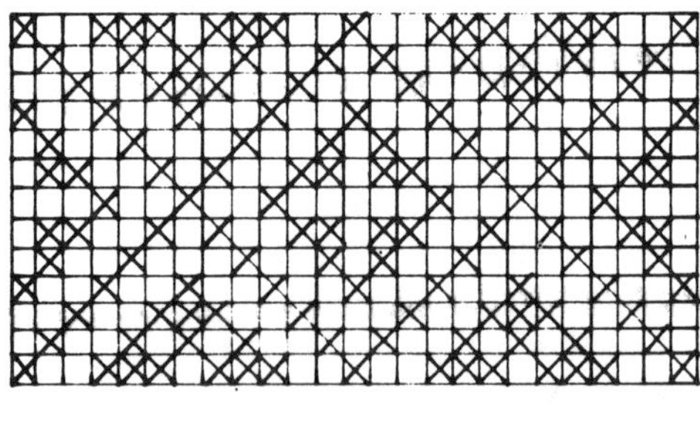

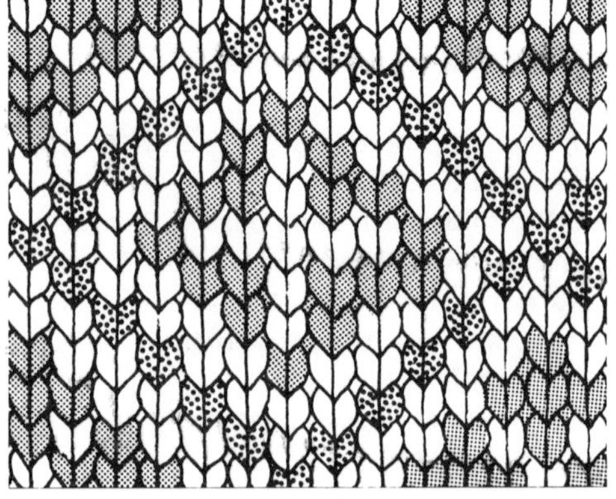

DECORATING WITH CABLES

A cable can create a beautiful effect. The motif seems to stand away from the background producing an embossed look. A plain sweater can suddenly look important through the introduction of a cabled panel. When the cables are arranged correctly, they give a slenderizing effect to the design. Some of the many cable patterns are shown here.

Mock Cable Pattern

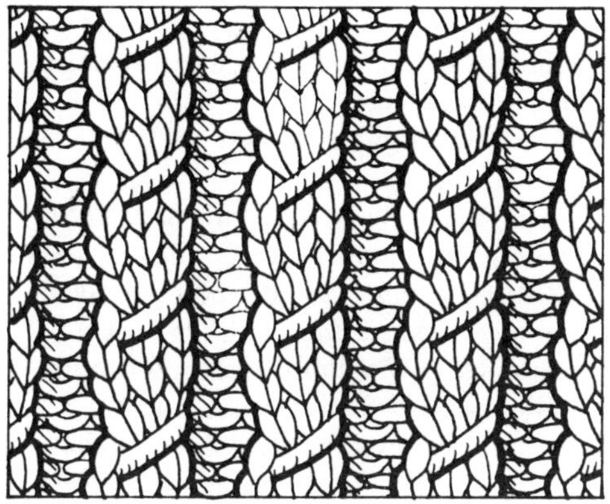

This type of knitting creates a flatter version of a cable pattern.

For the **beginning row,** cast on a multiple of 8 stitches.

For the **first row,** repeat the following procedure. * Purl 5. Knit 3. *

For the **second row,** repeat the following procedure. * Purl 3. Knit 5. *

For the **third row,** repeat the following procedure. * Purl 5. Slip 1. Knit 2. Wrap yarn around needle to make 1 stitch. Then pass the slip stitch over the 2 stitches that were knitted and the 1 that was made. *

For the **fourth row,** repeat the second row.

Repeat the **first through fourth rows** as many times as required.

Miniature Cable Pattern

This is a dainty version of the Cable Pattern. Only 2 stitches are used to form the design.

For the **beginning row,** cast on a multiple of 4 stitches plus 2.

For the **first row,** knit 2. Repeat the following procedure. * Purl 2. Knit 2. *

For the **second row,** purl 2. Repeat the following procedure. * Knit 2. Purl 2. *

For the **third row,** repeat the first row.

For the **fourth row,** purl 2. Repeat the following procedure. * Knit 2 together but do not remove the needle. Insert right-hand needle between the 2 stitches just knitted together. Knit the first again. Then slip both stitches from needle together. Purl 2. *

Repeat the **first through fourth rows** as many times as required.

Chain Cable Pattern

A chainlike wavy effect is created by this cable stitch. Sometimes it is called Double Ribbon Stitch.

For the **beginning row**, cast on 12 stitches for the cable motif.

For the **first row**, knit 2. Purl 8. Knit 2.

For the **second row**, purl 2. Slip next 2 stitches onto a double-pointed needle and leave in back. Knit 2. Then knit the 2 stitches on the double-pointed needle. Slip next 2 stitches onto a double-pointed needle and leave in front. Knit 2. Then knit the 2 stitches on the double-pointed needle. Purl 2.

For the **third row**, repeat the first row.

For the **fourth row**, purl 2. Knit 8. Purl 2.

For the **fifth row**, repeat the first row.

For the **sixth row**, purl 2. Slip next 2 stitches onto a double-pointed needle and leave in front. Knit 2. Then knit the 2 stitches on the double-pointed needle. Slip next 2 stitches onto a double-pointed needle and leave in back. Knit 2. Then knit the 2 stitches on the double-pointed needle. Purl 2.

For the **seventh row**, repeat the first row.

For the **eighth row**, repeat the fourth row.

Repeat the **first through eighth rows** as many times as required.

Horseshoe Cable Pattern

Sometimes this cable pattern is called Double Cable. One design motif seems to melt into the next.

For the **beginning row**, cast on 12 stitches for the cable motif.

For the **first row**, knit 2. Purl 8. Knit 2.

For the **second row**, purl 2. Slip the next 2 stitches onto a double-pointed needle. Leave in back. Knit 2. Then knit the 2 stitches on the double-pointed needle. Slip the next 2 stitches onto a double-pointed needle. Leave in front. Knit 2. Then knit the 2 stitches on the double-pointed needle. Purl 2.

For the **third row**, repeat the first row.

For the **fourth row**, purl 2. Knit 8. Purl 2.

For the **fifth row**, repeat the first row.

For the **sixth row**, repeat the fourth row.

For the **seventh row**, repeat the first row.

For the **eighth row**, repeat the fourth row.

Repeat the **first through eighth rows** as many times as required.

Clustered Cable Pattern

Small blocks of cables create a checkerboard effect. It is a German pattern and sometimes called Checked Cable.

For the **beginning cable,** cast on a multiple of 12 stitches plus 6.

For the **first row,** purl 6. Repeat the following procedure. * Knit 6. Purl 6. *

For the **second row,** knit 6. Repeat the following procedure. * Purl 6. Knit 6. *

For the **third row,** repeat the first row.

For the **fourth row,** repeat the second row.

For the **fifth row,** purl 6. Repeat the following procedure. * Slip next 3 stitches onto a double-pointed needle. Leave in back. Knit 3. Then knit the 3 stitches on the double-pointed needle. Purl 6. *

For the **sixth row,** knit 6. Repeat the following procedure. * Purl 6. Knit 6. *

For the **seventh row,** purl 6. Repeat the following procedure. * Knit 6. Purl 6. *

For the **eighth row,** knit 6. Repeat the following procedure. * Purl 6. Knit 6. *

For the **ninth row,** knit 6. Repeat the following procedure. * Purl 6. Knit 6. *

For the **tenth row,** purl 6. Repeat the following procedure. * Knit 6. Purl 6. *

For the **eleventh row,** repeat the ninth row.

For the **twelfth row,** repeat the tenth row.

For the **thirteenth row,** repeat the following procedure. * Slip 3 stitches onto a double-pointed needle. Leave in back. Knit 3. Knit the 3 stitches on the double-pointed needle. Purl 6. * End by slipping 3 stitches onto a double-pointed needle. Leave in back. Knit 3. Knit the 3 stitches on the double-pointed needle.

For the **fourteenth row,** purl 6. Repeat the following procedure. * Knit 6. Purl 6. *

For the **fifteenth row,** knit 6. Repeat the following procedure. * Purl 6. Knit 6. *

For the **sixteenth row,** purl 6. Repeat the following procedure. * Knit 6. Purl 6. *

Repeat the **first through sixteenth rows** as many times as required.

Plait Cable Pattern

This form of cable knitting creates a braided effect that seems to give a smart look and is not complicated to make.

For the **beginning row,** cast on 13 stitches for the cable motif.

For the **first row,** purl 2. Knit 9. Purl 2.

For the **second row,** knit 2. Purl 9. Knit 2.

For the **third row,** purl 2. Slip the next 3 stitches onto a double-pointed needle. Leave in front. Knit 3. Then knit the 3 stitches from the double-pointed needle. Knit 3. Purl 2.

For the **fourth row,** repeat the second row.

For the **fifth row,** repeat the first row.

For the **sixth row,** repeat the second row.

For the **seventh row,** purl 2. Knit 3. Slip next 3 stitches onto a double-pointed needle. Leave in back. Knit 3. Knit the 3 stitches from the double-pointed needle. Purl 2.

For the **eighth row,** repeat the second row.

Repeat the **first through eighth rows** as many times as required.

Gull Stitch

The raised effect of this stitch pattern makes a lovely panel motif, which is frequently used for Aran-type knitting.

For the **beginning row,** cast on 10 stitches to make 1 rib or panel.

For the **first row,** knit 2. Purl 6. Knit 2.

For the **second row,** purl 2. Knit 2. With yarn in back, slip 2. Knit 2. Purl 2.

For the **third row,** knit 2. Purl 2. With yarn in front, slip 2. Purl 2. Knit 2.

For the **fourth row,** purl 2. Slip next 2 stitches onto a double-pointed needle. Leave in back. Knit 1. Then knit the 2 stitches on the double-pointed needle. Slip next stitch onto the double-pointed needle. Leave in front. Knit 2. Then knit 1 from the double-pointed needle. Purl 2.

Repeat the **first through fourth rows** as many times as required.

Acorn Pattern

A bulky raised quality results when this old English pattern is used to create an allover effect.

For the **beginning row,** cast on a multiple of 10 stitches plus 2.

For the **first row,** knit 1, purl 3, knit 4. Repeat the following procedure. * Purl 6. Knit 4. * End with purl 3, knit 1.

For the **second row,** knit 4, purl 4. Repeat the following procedure. * Knit 6, purl 4. * End with knit 4.

For the **third row,** knit 1, purl 1. Repeat the following procedure. * Slip next 2 stitches onto a double-pointed needle. Leave in back. Knit 2. Purl the 2 stitches on double-pointed needle, making a back cross. Insert needle under thread connecting 2 stitches of previous row. Knit 1 and purl 1. Then slip next 2 stitches onto double-pointed needle and leave in front. Purl 2. Knit 2 from double-pointed needle for front cross. Purl 2. * End by purling 1, knitting 1.

For the **fourth row,** knit 2. Repeat the following procedure. * Purl 2. Knit 2. *

For the **fifth row,** knit 1, purl 1. Repeat the following procedure. * Knit 2. Purl 2. * End row with knit 2, purl 1, and knit 1.

For the **sixth row,** repeat fourth row.

For the **seventh row,** knit 2. Repeat the following procedure. * Slip 1 stitch. Knit 1. Pass slip stitch over. Purl 6. Knit 2 together. Knit 2. *

For the **eighth row,** knit 1. Purl 2. Knit 6. Repeat the following procedure. * Purl

4. Knit 6. * End row with purl 2, knit 1.

For the **ninth row,** knit 1. Insert needle under thread connecting 2 stitches of previous row and knit it. Repeat the following procedure. * For front cross, leave double-pointed needle in front of work. Purl 2. For back cross, leave double-pointed needle in back. Knit 1 and purl 1 into connecting thread of previous row. * End front cross. Purl 2. For back cross, leave needle in back. Knit once into connecting thread of previous row. Knit 1.

For the **tenth row,** knit 1, purl 1. Repeat the following procedure. * Knit 2. Purl 2. * End row with knit 2, purl 1, knit 1.

For the **eleventh row,** knit 2. Repeat the following procedure. * Purl 2. Knit 2. *

For the **twelfth row,** repeat tenth row.

For the **thirteenth row,** knit 1, purl 3. Repeat the following procedure. * Knit 2 together. Knit 2. Slip 1. Knit 1. Pass slip stitch over. Purl 6. * End row with knit 2 together. Knit 2. Slip 1. Knit 1. Pass slip stitch over. Purl 3. Knit 1.

Repeat the **second through thirteenth rows** as many times as required.

Wavy Rib Pattern

The slight change in line direction gives a curving effect to this broken diagonal.

For the **beginning row,** cast on a multiple of 6 stitches.

For the **first row,** repeat the following procedure. * Purl 4. Knit 2. *

For the **second row,** repeat the following procedure. * Purl 2. Knit 4. *

For the **third row,** repeat the first row.

For the **fourth row,** repeat the second row.

For the **fifth row,** repeat the first row.

For the **sixth row,** repeat the second row.

For the **seventh row,** repeat the following procedure. * Purl 2. Slip 2 onto a double-pointed needle. Leave in back. Knit 2. Purl the 2 from the double-pointed needle. *

For the **eighth row,** repeat the following procedure. * Knit 2. Purl 2. Knit 2. *

For the **ninth row,** repeat the following procedure. * Purl 2. Knit 2. Purl 2. *

For the **tenth row,** repeat the eighth row.

For the **eleventh row,** repeat the ninth row.

For the **twelfth row,** repeat the eighth row.

For the **thirteenth row,** repeat the following procedure. * Slip 2 onto a double-pointed needle and leave in back. Knit 2. Purl the 2 from the double-pointed needle. Purl 2. *

For the **fourteenth row,** repeat the following procedure. * Knit 4. Purl 2. *

For the **fifteenth row,** repeat the following procedure. * Knit 2. Purl 4. *

For the **sixteenth row,** repeat the fourteenth row.

For the **seventeenth row,** repeat the fifteenth row.

For the **eighteenth row,** repeat the fourteenth row.

Repeat the **second through eighteenth rows** as many times as required.

Basket Cable Pattern

This stitch produces a bulky look that can be effective when worked in panels.

For the **beginning row,** cast on a multiple of 8 stitches plus 4.

For the **first row,** knit 2. Then purl to the last 2 stitches. Knit these.

For the **second row,** knit.

For the **third row,** knit 2. Purl to the last 2 stitches. Knit these.

For the **fourth row,** knit.

For the **fifth row,** knit 2. Purl to the last 2 stitches. Knit these.

For the **sixth row,** knit 2. Repeat the following procedure. * Slip the next 4 stitches onto a double-pointed needle. Hold it in back. Knit 4. Then knit the 4 stitches on the double-pointed needle. * End with knit 2.

For the **seventh row,** knit 2. Purl to the last 2 stitches. Then knit these.

For the **eighth row,** knit.

For the **ninth row,** repeat seventh row.

For the **tenth row,** knit.

For the **eleventh row,** repeat seventh row.

For the **twelfth row,** knit 6. Repeat the following procedure. * Slip the next 4 stitches onto a double pointed needle. Hold it in front. Knit 4. Then knit the 4 stitches on the double-pointed needle. * End by knitting 6.

Repeat the **first through twelfth rows** as many times as required.

Lace Cable Pattern

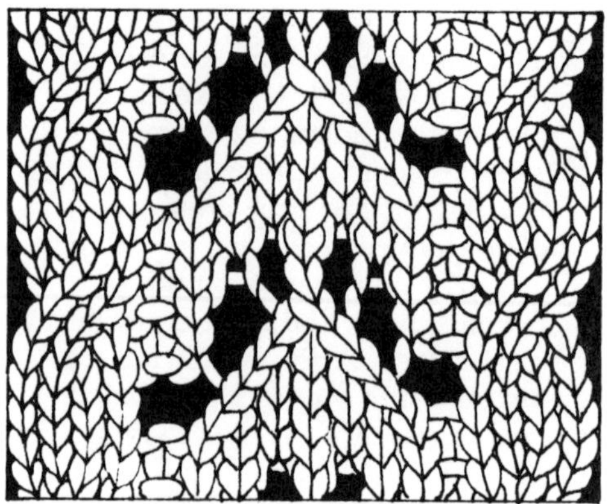

This attractive arrangement of stitches is found among Norwegian patterns.

For the **beginning row,** cast on 19 stitches plus 2.

For the **first row,** repeat the following procedure. * Purl 2. Knit 4 in back. Knit 1. Yarn over. Knit 2 together through back of stitch. Knit 3. Knit 2 together. Yarn over. Knit 1. Knit 4 in back. * End with purl 2.

For the **second row,** repeat the following procedure. * Knit 2. Purl 4 in back. Knit 1. Purl 7. Knit 1. Purl 4 in back. * End with knit 2.

For the **third row,** repeat the following procedure. * Purl 2. Knit 4 in back. Knit 2. Yarn over. Knit 2 together through back of stitch. Knit 1. Knit 2 together. Yarn over. Knit 2. Knit 4 in back. * End with purl 2.

For the **fourth row,** repeat the second row.

For the **fifth row,** repeat the following procedure. * Purl 2. Knit in back of 4 cable stitches. Knit 3. Yarn over. Then slip 1, knit 2 together, and pass slip stitch over. Yarn over. Knit 3. Knit in back of 4 cable stitches. * End with purl 2.

For the **sixth row,** repeat the second row.

For the **seventh row,** repeat the following procedure. * Purl 2. Knit in back of 4 stitches. Knit 9. Knit in back of 4 stitches. * End with purl 2.

For the **eighth row,** repeat the second row.

Repeat **first through eighth rows** as required.

Slipped Cable Pattern

A new twist is given this cable pattern through the use of a slipped stitch.

For the **beginning row,** cast on a multiple of 6 stitches plus 2, and purl a starting row.

For the **first row,** purl 2. Repeat the following procedure. * Skip 1 stitch. Insert right-hand needle from front to back into next stitch and knit the stitch. Do not drop stitch from left-hand needle. Then insert right-hand needle into back loop of skipped stitch and knit the stitch. Drop both stitches from left-hand needle. Skip 1 stitch. Insert right-hand needle into back loop of next stitch and knit the stitch. Do not drop stitch from left-hand needle. Insert right-hand needle into front loop of skipped stitch and knit the stitch. Drop both stitches from left-hand needle. Purl 2. *

For the **second row,** knit 2. Repeat the following procedure. * Purl 4. Knit 2. *

For the **third row,** purl 2. Repeat the following procedure. * Knit 4. Purl 2. *

For the **fourth row,** repeat the second row.

Repeat the **first through fourth rows** as many times as required.

WORKING IN TWO SIZES

Changing the size of the needles while knitting can produce varying effects. Notice how different the ones shown here appear.

Threaded Cross Stitch

This stitch pattern creates a diagonal direction to the design but adds small crossing stitches for added interest. Needles of 2 sizes are used for this type of knitting. One needle should be about 4 sizes larger than the other one.

For the **beginning row,** cast on a multiple of 2 stitches, using the larger needle.

For the **first row,** knit, using the smaller needle.

For the **second row,** purl with the larger needle.

For the **third row,** use the smaller needle. Repeat the following procedure. * Insert point of right-hand needle through first stitch as if to purl. Knit the second stitch, leaving it on the left-hand needle. Then knit the first stitch through the back loop. Slide both stitches together from the left-hand needle. *

For the **fourth row,** purl, using the larger needle.

For the **fifth row,** use the smaller needle. Knit 1. Repeat the following procedure. * Insert the needle through the second stitch as if to purl. Knit the next stitch, leaving it on the left-hand needle. Knit the previous, or second, stitch through the back loop, as previously done. Slide both stitches together from the left-hand needle. * End by knitting 1.

Repeat the **second through fifth rows** as many times as required.

Grecian Plait Stitch

This stitch pattern develops an interesting textural quality, with a small braided effect dotted with open spaces. Work with needles in 2 sizes—one about 4 sizes larger than the other.

For the **beginning row,** cast on a multiple of 2 stitches using larger needle.

For the **first row,** use the smaller needle. Knit.

For the **second row,** use the larger needle. Purl.

For the **third row,** continue with smaller needle. Insert needle in second stitch, lifting it over the first and then knitting it. Then knit the first stitch. Continue this way across row, lifting the even-numbered stitches over the uneven ones before knitting each. End row with knit 1.

For the **fourth row,** return to larger needle. Purl.

Repeat the **third and fourth rows** as many times as required.

Gathered Stitch

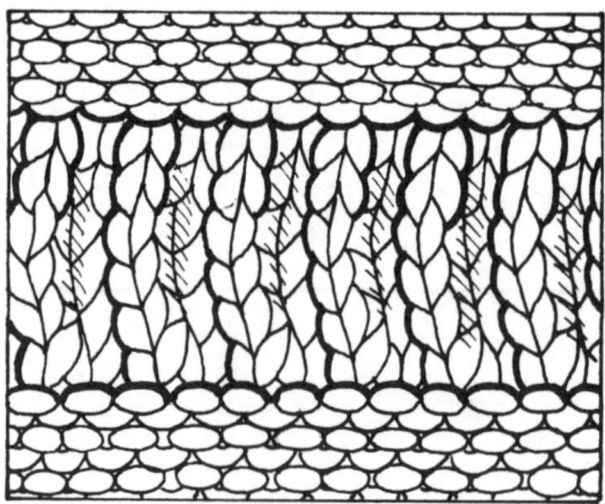

Working with knitting needles in 2 sizes creates rows of stitches with fullness.

For the **beginning row,** cast on the required number of stitches, using fine needles.

For the **first through sixth rows,** knit.

For the **seventh row,** change to larger needles. Knit twice into each stitch.

For the **eighth row,** purl.

For the **ninth row,** knit.

For the **tenth row,** purl.

For the **eleventh row,** knit.

For the **twelfth row,** purl, completing 6 rows of stockinette stitches.

For the **thirteenth row,** return to smaller needles. Knit 2 together across row.

Continue to knit 5 rows, completing 6 rows of garter stitches.

Alternate the rows of stockinette stitches made on the larger needles and garter stitches on the smaller ones as many times as required.

HOW TO MAKE A REVERSIBLE

When knitting an article that may be seen from both sides when worn, it is nice to have the sides appear the same. There are stitch patterns that produce this effect. Some of these are shown here.

Indian Cross Stitch

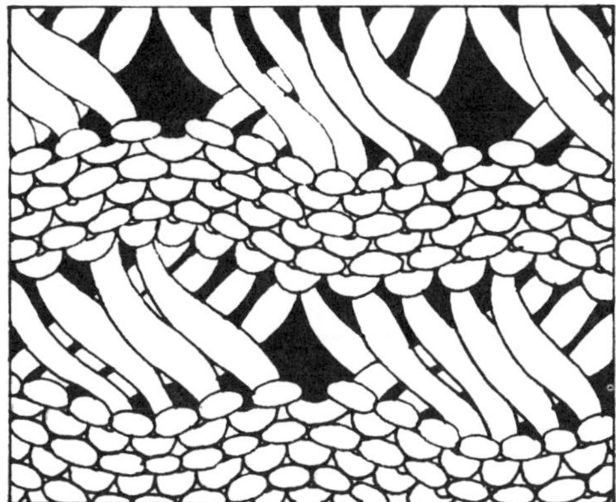

This arrangement of stitches produces a reversible fabric with many interesting lines.

For the **beginning row,** cast on a multiple of 8 stitches.

For the **first four rows,** knit.

For the **fifth row,** knit 1. Repeat the following procedure. * To start the cross stitches, insert needle into the next stitch. Wind yarn 4 times around tip of needle and knit the stitch, removing all of the wrapped stitches, as well as the needle. *

For the **sixth row,** repeat the following procedure. * To form 8 long stitches on the right-hand needle, slip 8 slip stitches with yarn in back, dropping the extra wrapped stitches. Insert left-hand needle into the first 4 long stitches and slip them over the second 4 stitches. Follow by returning all of the stitches to the left-hand needle in the crossed order. Knit in this order. Note that the first group of 4 stitches is knitted last. * Be careful not to twist stitches when crossing them, and to stretch them upward to keep the lengths the same.

For the **seventh through tenth rows,** knit, making the ridges of garter stitch.

For the **eleventh row,** repeat the fifth row.

For the **twelfth row,** slip 4 stitches, dropping the wrapped stitches. Insert left-hand needle into the first 2 long stitches and slip them over the second 2 stitches, as in sixth row. Knit these 4 stitches. Repeat the following procedure, as for sixth row. * Slip 8 stitches. Cross 4 stitches over 4 and knit as in the sixth row on each group of 8 stitches. * End row by crossing 2 stitches over 2.

Repeat the **first through twelfth rows** as many times as required.

Brioche Stitch

This stitch provides a dainty type of ribbing with a stretchy quality. It has an Eastern origin and is sometimes called Oriental Rib Stitch, Point D'Angleterre, Reverse Lace Stitch, or Shawl Stitch.

For the **beginning row,** cast on an even number of stitches.

For the **first row,** repeat the following procedure. * Put yarn over. Slip 1. Knit 1. *

For the **second row,** repeat the following procedure. * Put yarn over. Slip 1. Knit 2 together. *

Repeat the **second row** as many times as required.

Grand Eyelet Lace Pattern

Large eyelets dot this lacy stitch pattern, which is sometimes referred to as Reversible Grand Eyelet.

For the **beginning row,** cast on 4 stitches plus 4.

For the **first row,** purl 2. Repeat the following procedure. * Yarn over. Purl 4 together. * End with purl 2.

For the **second row,** knit 2. Repeat the following procedure. * Knit 1. Then, into the yarn-over of the previous row, knit 1, purl 1, and knit 1. * End with knit 2.

For the **third row,** knit.

Repeat the **first through third rows** as many times as required.

DOT WITH EYELETS

Just as in embroidery, eyelets in knitting produce an openwork effect in a solid material. The tiny holes give the fabric a dainty look. They can be arranged in innumerable ways, creating a variety of design patterns. A knitted article seems to assume a dressy feeling when an Eyelet Stitch pattern is used. A few of these designs are shown here.

Eyelet Check Pattern

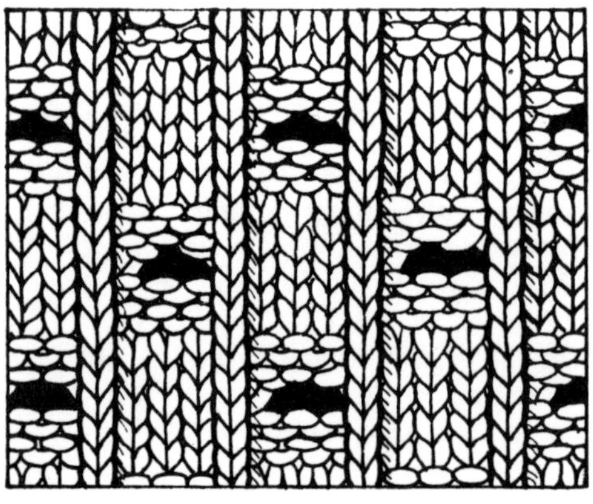

A checkered pattern is given added interest with an eyelet, dotting alternating squares.

For the **beginning row,** cast on a multiple of 8 stitches plus 5.

For the **first row,** repeat the following procedure. * Knit 5. Purl 3. * End with knit 5.

For the **second row,** purl 5. Repeat the following procedure. * Knit 3. Purl 5. *

For the **third row,** repeat the following procedure. * Knit 5. Purl 1. Wrap yarn around needle to make 1 stitch. Purl 2 together. * End with knit 5.

For the **fourth row,** repeat the second row.

For the **fifth row,** repeat the first row.

For the **sixth row,** purl.

For the **seventh row,** repeat the following procedure. * Knit 1. Purl 3. Knit 4. * End with knit 1. Purl 3. Knit 1.

For the **eighth row,** purl 1. Knit 3. Purl 1. Repeat the following procedure. * Purl 4. Knit 3. Purl 1. *

For the **ninth row,** repeat the following procedure. * Knit 1. Purl 1. Wrap yarn around needle to make 1 stitch. Purl 2 together. Knit 4. * End with knit 1. Purl 1. Wrap yarn around needle to make 1 stitch. Purl 2 together. Knit 1.

For the **tenth row,** repeat the eighth row.

For the **eleventh row,** repeat the seventh row.

For the **twelfth row,** purl.

Repeat the **first through the twelfth rows** as many times as required.

Eyelet Stitch

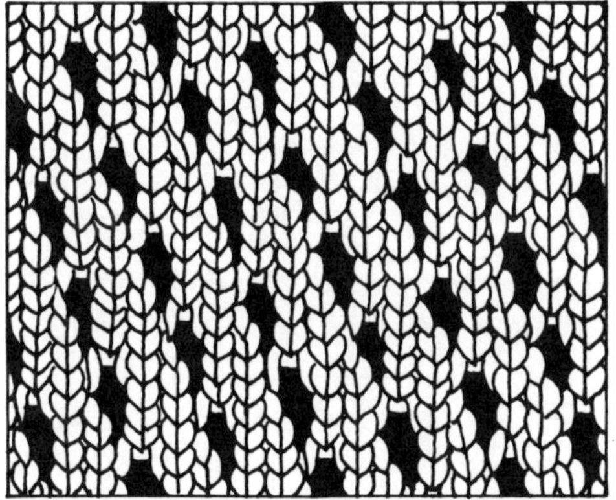

The eyelets seem to be imbedded in the fabric, creating a lovely 3-dimensional effect.

For the **beginning row,** cast on a multiple of 4 stitches.

For the **first row,** repeat the following procedure. * Knit 1. Wind yarn twice around needle, making a double stitch. Knit 2. *

For the **second row,** purl 2 together. Repeat the following procedure. * Knit 1. Purl 1 into the double stitch. Purl 2 together. *

For the **third row,** repeat the following procedure. * Wrap yarn around needle to make 1 stitch. Knit 4. Then wrap yarn around needle to make 1 more stitch. *

For the **fourth row,** repeat the following procedure. * Purl 1. Then purl 2 together twice. Knit 1. *

Repeat the **first through fourth rows** as many times as required.

Allover Cross Stitch

An unusual arrangement of stitches creates an eyelet effect and at the same time produces a soft, thick feeling.

For the **beginning row,** cast on a multiple of 4 stitches plus 3.

For the **first row,** purl.

For the **second row,** knit 2. In the row below, knit into the next stitch. Then slip that stitch onto the right-hand needle. Knit 2 together. Pass slip stitch over. Repeat the following procedure. * In the row below, knit into the next stitch. Knit that stitch. Knit again into the row below to the left of the stitch. Notice that 1 stitch has produced 3. Slip 1. Knit 2 stitches together. Pass slip stitch over. * At last 2 stitches on row, knit into the next stitch in the row below. Then knit the stitch itself. Finish by knitting 1.

For the **third row,** purl.

For the **fourth row,** knit 1. Knit 2 together. Repeat the following procedure. * Knit the next stitch 3 times by knitting into the next stitch in the row below, knitting the stitch itself, and knitting again into the row below to the left of the stitch. Then slip 1. Knit 2 together. Pass slip stitch over. * At the last 4 stitches, knit into the next stitch 3 times, by knitting into the row below, then the stitch itself, and then knitting again into the row below, as in row 2. Slip 1. Knit 1. Pass slip stitch over. Knit 1.

Repeat the **first through fourth rows,** until work is completed.

Eyelet Zigzag Pattern

A series of eyelets in the form of a V create a zigzag design.

For the **beginning row,** cast on a multiple of 11 stitches plus 2.

For the **first row,** purl.

For the **second row,** knit 6. Repeat the following procedure. * Yarn over. Then slip 1, knit 1, and pass slip stitch over. Knit 9. * End with knit 5.

For the **third row,** purl.

For the **fourth row,** knit 7. Repeat the following procedure. * Yarn over. Then slip 1, knit 1, and pass slip stitch over. Knit 9. * End with knit 4.

For the **fifth row,** purl.

For the **sixth row,** knit 3. Repeat the following procedure. * Knit 2 together. Yarn over. Knit 3. Yarn over. Then slip 1, knit 1, and pass slip stitch over. Knit 4. * End with knit 3.

For the **seventh row,** purl.

For the **eighth row,** repeat the following procedure. * Knit 2. Knit 2 together. Yarn over. Knit 5. Yarn over. Then slip 1, knit 1, and pass slip stitch over. * End with knit 2.

For the **ninth row,** purl.

For the **tenth row,** knit 1. Repeat the following procedure. * Knit 2 together. Yarn over. Knit 9. * End with knit 1.

For the **eleventh row,** purl.

For the **twelfth row,** repeat the following procedure. * Knit 2 together. Yarn over. Knit 9. * End with knit 2.

Repeat the **first through twelfth rows** as many times as required.

Bell Pattern

A dainty bell-shaped design gives a flowerlike quality to the knitting. Sometimes the pattern is referred to as Blue Bell or Hyacinth.

For the **beginning row,** cast on a multiple of 6 stitches plus 5.

For the **first row,** purl 2. Repeat the following procedure. * Knit 1. Purl 5. * End row with knit 1, purl 2.

For the **second row,** knit 2. Repeat the following procedure. * Purl 1. Knit 5. * End row with purl 1, knit 2.

For the **third row,** purl 5. Repeat the following procedure. * Put yarn over. Knit 1. Yarn over. Purl 5. *

For the **fourth row,** knit 5. Repeat the following procedure. * Purl 3. Knit 5. *

For the **fifth row,** purl 5. Repeat the following procedure. * Knit 3. Purl 5. *

For the **sixth row,** repeat the fourth row.

For the **seventh row,** repeat the fifth row.

For the **eighth row,** repeat the fourth row.

For the **ninth row,** purl 5. Repeat the following procedure. * Slip 1 stitch. Knit 2 together. Pass slip stitch over. Purl 5. *

For the **tenth row,** knit 5. Repeat the following procedure. * Purl 1. Knit 5. *

For the **eleventh row,** purl 5. Repeat the following procedure. * Knit 1. Purl 5. *

For the **twelfth row,** repeat the tenth row.

For the **thirteenth row,** purl 2. Repeat the following procedure. * Put yarn over. Knit 1. Yarn over. Purl 5. * End row with yarn over. Knit 1. Yarn over. Purl 2.

For the **fourteenth row,** knit 2. Repeat the following procedure. * Purl 3. Knit 5. * End row with purl 3, knit 2.
For the **fifteenth row,** purl 2. Repeat the following procedure. * Knit 3. Purl 5. * End row with knit 3, purl 2.
For the **sixteenth row,** repeat the fourteenth row.
For the **seventeenth row,** repeat the fifteenth row.
For the **eighteenth row,** repeat the fourteenth row.
For the **nineteenth row,** purl 2. Repeat the following procedure. * Slip 1. Knit 2 together. Pass slip stitch over. Purl 5. * End row with slip 1. Knit 2 together. Pass slip stitch over. Purl 2.
For the **twentieth row,** repeat the second row.
Repeat the **first through twentieth rows** as many times as required.

Chequered Florette Pattern

This eyelet design is one of the many lacy French patterns that give the look of an insertion.
For the **beginning row,** cast on a multiple of 12 stitches plus 5.
For the **first row,** knit 2. Repeat the following procedure. * Knit 4. Purl 2 together. Yarn over. Knit 1. Put yarn around needle. Purl 2 together. Knit 3. * End with knit 3.
For the **second row,** purl.
For the **third row,** knit 2. Repeat the following procedure. * Knit 4. Put yarn around needle. Purl 2 together. Knit 1. Purl 2 together. Yarn over. Knit 3. * End with knit 3.
For the **fourth row,** purl.
For the **fifth row,** repeat the third row.
For the **sixth row,** purl.
For the **seventh row,** repeat the first row.
For the **eighth row,** purl.
For the **ninth row,** knit 2. Repeat the following procedure. * Knit 1. Put yarn around needle. Purl 2 together. Knit 7. Purl 2 together. Put yarn over needle. * End with knit 3.
For the **tenth row,** purl.
For the **eleventh row,** knit 2. Repeat the following procedure. * Knit 1. Purl 2 together. Yarn over. Knit 7. Put yarn around needle. Purl 2 together. * End with knit 3.
For the **twelfth row,** purl.
For the **thirteenth row,** repeat the eleventh row.
For the **fourteenth row,** purl.
For the **fifteenth row,** repeat the ninth row.
For the **sixteenth row,** purl.
Repeat the **first through sixteenth rows** as many times as required.

Diamond Eyelet Pattern

This beautiful lacy pattern seems to develop a diagonal feeling that is most pleasing.

For the **beginning row,** cast on a multiple of 10 stitches plus 4.

For the **first row,** knit 2. Yarn over. Then slip 1, knit 1, and pass slip stitch over. Repeat the following procedure. * Knit 1. Knit 2 together. Put yarn over twice. Then slip 1 stitch, knit 1, and pass slip stitch over. * For the last 5 stitches, knit 1, knit 2 together, yarn over, and knit 2.

For the **second row,** purl. Do this in both the front and the back of each yarn-over.

For the **third row,** knit 2. Repeat the following procedure. * Knit 2 together. Yarn over. Knit 6. Yarn over. Then slip 1, knit 1, and pass slip stitch over. * End with knit 2.

For the **fourth row,** repeat the second row.

For the **fifth row,** knit 3. Repeat the following procedure. * Knit 2 together. Yarn over. Knit 4. Yarn over. Then slip 1, knit 1, and pass slip stitch over. Knit 2. * End with knit 1.

For the **sixth row,** repeat the second row.

For the **seventh row,** knit 4. Repeat the following procedure. * Knit 2 together. Yarn over. Knit 2. Yarn over. Then slip 1, knit 1, and pass slip stitch over. Knit 4. *

For the **eighth row,** repeat the second row.

For the **ninth row,** knit 2. Yarn over. Then slip 1, knit 1, and pass slip stitch over. Repeat the following procedure. * Knit 1. Knit 2 together. Put yarn over twice. Then slip 1, knit 1, and pass slip stitch over. * For the last 5 stitches, knit 1, knit 2 together, yarn over, knit 2.

For the **tenth row,** repeat the second row.

For the **eleventh row,** knit 5. Repeat the following procedure. * Yarn over. Then slip 1, knit 1, and pass slip stitch over. Knit 2 together. Yarn over. Knit 6. * End with knit 5.

For the **twelfth row,** repeat the second row.

For the **thirteenth row,** knit 4. Repeat the following procedure. * Yarn over. Then slip 1, knit 1, and pass slip stitch over. Knit 2. Knit 2 together. Yarn over. Knit 4. *

For the **fourteenth row,** repeat the second row.

For the **fifteenth row,** knit 3. Repeat the following procedure. * Yarn over. Then slip 1, knit 1, and pass slip stitch over. Knit 4. Knit 2 together. Yarn over. Knit 2. * End with knit 1.

For the **sixteenth row,** purl.

Repeat the **first through sixteenth rows** as many times as required.

Embroidery Eyelet Diamond Pattern

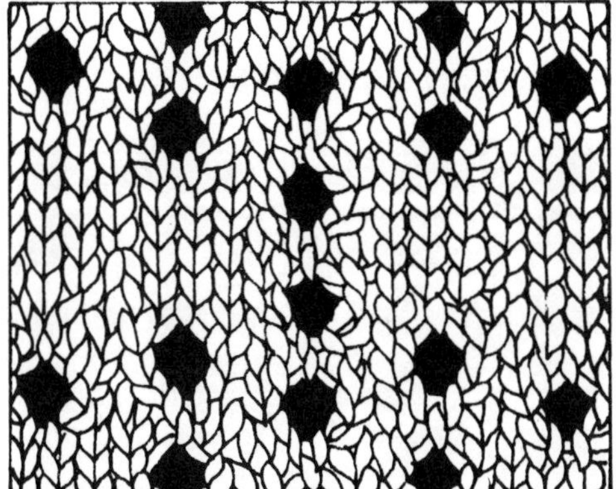

Eyelets are arranged in a diamond design, giving a striped effect to this openwork pattern.

For the **beginning row,** cast on a multiple of 21 stitches plus 3.

For the **first row,** purl.

For the **second row,** knit.

For the **third row,** purl.

For the **fourth row,** knit 10. Repeat the following procedure. * Knit 2 together. Yarn over. Then slip 1, knit 1, and pass slip stitch over. Knit 17. * End with knit 10.

For the **fifth row,** purl, but be sure to purl and knit into each yarn-over.

For the **sixth row,** knit 6. Repeat the following procedure. * Knit 2 together. Yarn over. Then slip 1, knit 1, and pass slip stitch over. Knit 4. Knit 2 together. Yarn over. Then slip 1, knit 1, and pass slip stitch over. Knit 9. * End with knit 6.

For the **seventh row,** repeat the fifth row.

For the **eighth row,** knit 3. Repeat the following procedure. * Knit 2 together. Yarn over. Then slip 1, knit 1, and pass slip stitch over. Knit 3. *

For the **ninth row,** repeat the fifth row.

For the **tenth row,** repeat the sixth row.

For the **eleventh row,** repeat the fifth row.

For the **twelfth row,** repeat the fourth row.

Repeat the **first through twelfth rows** as many times as required.

Laburnum Stitch

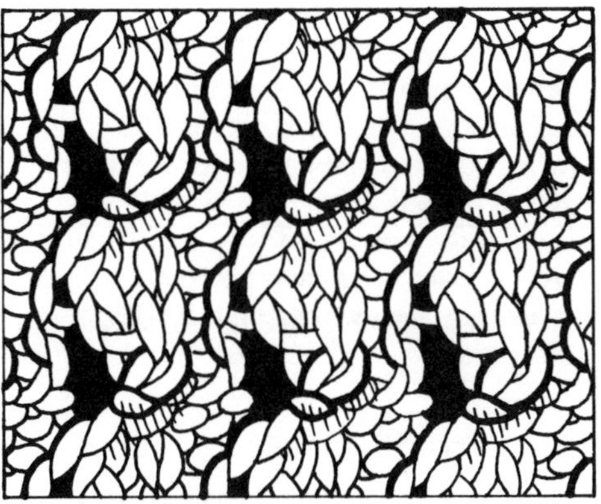

Eyelets form part of the ribbed effect of this openwork pattern.

For the **beginning row,** cast on a multiple of 5 stitches plus 2.

For the **first row,** purl 2. Repeat the following procedure. * With yarn in front, slip 1. Then, with yarn in back, knit 2 together and pass slip stitch over. Then wrap yarn over needle twice in reverse, bringing the yarn from the back over the needle and then under and over again. Purl 2. *

For the **second row,** knit 2. Repeat the following procedure. * Purl into the back of the first yarn-over and then into the front of the second yarn-over of the previous row. Purl 1. Knit 2. *

For the **third row,** purl 2. Repeat the following procedure. * Knit 3. Purl 2. *

For the **fourth row,** knit 2. Repeat the following procedure. * Purl 3. Knit 2. *

Repeat the **first through fourth rows** as many times as required.

LACY EFFECTS

Lace designs are often thought to be difficult to make. Some of them are; others, not. But one characteristic they all seem to have is a fragile, dainty look when made with a fine yarn and small needles. Working a lace-pattern stitch successfully seems to bring a feeling of satisfaction.

Garter Lace Stitch

Rows of stitches seem to create a lacy insertion.

For the **beginning row,** cast on a multiple of 2.

For the **first six rows,** knit.

For the **seventh row,** repeat the following procedure. * Wrap yarn around the needle to make 1 stitch. Knit 2 together.

For the **eighth row,** repeat the following procedure. * Wrap yarn around needle to make 1 stitch. Purl 2 together. *

For the **ninth row,** repeat the seventh row.

For the **tenth row,** repeat the eighth row.

Repeat the **first through tenth rows** as many times as required.

Lace Ladder Garter Stitch

Openwork stripes give this lacy design an interesting look.

For the **beginning row,** cast on a multiple of 4 stitches.

For the **first row,** repeat the following procedure. * Knit 2 together. Put yarn over twice. Then slip 1, knit 1, and pass slip stitch over. *

For the **second row,** repeat the following procedure. * Knit 1. Then, into the double yarn-over, knit 1 and purl 1. Knit 1. *

Repeat the **first and second rows** as many times as required.

Double Herringbone Faggot Pattern

A lovely lacy effect is created when the openwork stitches are defined with ribs moving vertically.

For the **beginning row,** cast on a multiple of 5 stitches.

For the **first row,** repeat the following procedure. * Knit 1. Yarn over. Knit 2 together. Yarn over. Knit 2 together. *

Repeat the **first row** as many times as required.

Veil Stitch

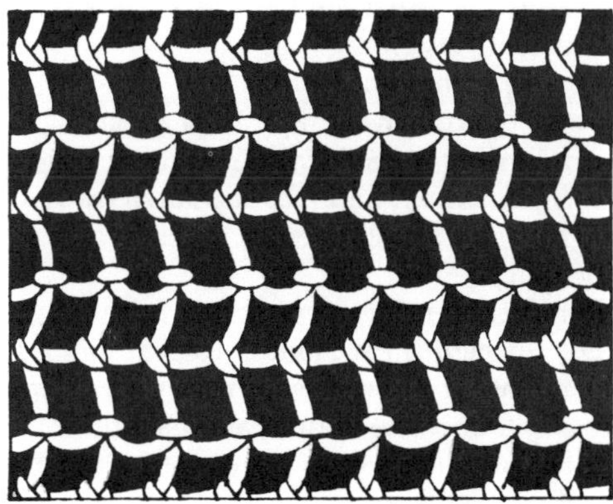

This stitch pattern is sometimes called Elongated Crossed Garter Stitch, which seems to explain how it is made.

For the **beginning row,** cast on the required number of stitches.

For the **first row,** insert the needle knitwise. Then bring the yarn over to the right-hand needle as for regular knitting, and continue to place it under and over the left-hand needle, and finally under and over the right-hand needle again. Spread the needles slightly. Then draw the last yarn-over through the first yarn-over and the stitch. This procedure makes 1 stitch on the right-hand needle. Slip the stitch off the left-hand needle together with the yarn-over. This results in a long crossed stitch. Repeat the procedure for each stitch as row is knitted.

Repeat the **first row** as many times as required.

Bramble Stitch

This well-known pattern, which has several names, creates an interesting directional and textural look. It is frequently used for panels in heavy sweaters, but it can also be used for a lacy effect.

For the **beginning row,** cast on a multiple of 4 stitches.

For the **first row,** purl.

For the **second row,** repeat the following procedure. * Working in the same stitch, knit 1, purl 1, knit 1. Then purl 3 stitches together. *

For the **third row,** purl.

For the **fourth row,** repeat the following procedure. * Purl 3 together. Then, working in the same stitch, knit 1, purl 1, and knit 1. *

Repeat the **first through fourth rows** as many times as required.

Crochet-knit Shell Pattern

By a careful arrangement of stitches, the effect of crocheted shells is produced.

For the **beginning row,** cast on a multiple of 6 stitches plus 3.

For the **first row,** knit 1. Repeat the following procedure. * Yarn over. Knit 1. * End with knit 1.

For the **second row,** knit, dropping off the needle all yarn-overs of previous row.

For the **third row,** knit 1. Knit 3 together. Repeat the following procedure. * Put the yarn over needle twice. Knit 1. Yarn over twice. Then slip 2, knit 3 together, and pass 2 slip stitches over. * End by putting yarn over twice. Knit 1. Yarn over twice. Knit 3 together. Knit 1.

For the **fourth row,** knit 1. Repeat the following procedure. * Knit 1. Knit into front and back of double yarn-over. * End with knit 2.

For the **fifth row,** repeat the first row.

For the **sixth row,** repeat the second row.

For the **seventh row,** knit 1. Repeat the following procedure. * Knit 1. Yarn over twice. Then do this twice: slip 2, knit 3 together, and pass 2 slip stitches over. * End with knit 2.

For the **eighth row,** repeat the fourth row.

Repeat the **first through eighth rows** as many times as required.

Miniature Leaf Pattern

This design pattern creates a tiny diamond motif outlined with eyelets.

For the **beginning row,** cast on a multiple of 6 stitches plus 1.

For the **first row,** purl.

For the **second row,** knit 1. Repeat the following procedure. * Knit 2 together. Yarn over. Knit 1. Yarn over. Then slip 1, knit 1, and pass slip stitch over. Knit 1. *

For the **third row,** purl.

For the **fourth row,** knit 2 together. Repeat the following procedure. * Yarn over. Knit 3. Yarn over. Slip 2 stitches knitwise, knit 1, and pass the 2 slip stitches over. *

For the **fifth row,** purl.

For the **sixth row,** knit 1. Repeat the following procedure. * Yarn over. Then slip 1, knit 1, and pass slip stitch over. Knit 1. Knit 2 together. Yarn over. Knit 1. *

For the **seventh row,** purl.

For the **eighth row,** knit 2. Repeat the following procedure. * Yarn over. Then slip 2 knitwise, knit 1, and pass the 2 slip stitches over. Yarn over. Knit 3. * End with knit 2.

Repeat the **first through eighth rows** as many times as required.

The knitters of the Shetland Islands are renowned for their lace knitting. Their skill results in knitting as delicate as a cobweb. Among their famous stitch patterns are Mrs. Hunter's, Cat's Paw, and Old Shale.

Mrs. Hunter's Pattern

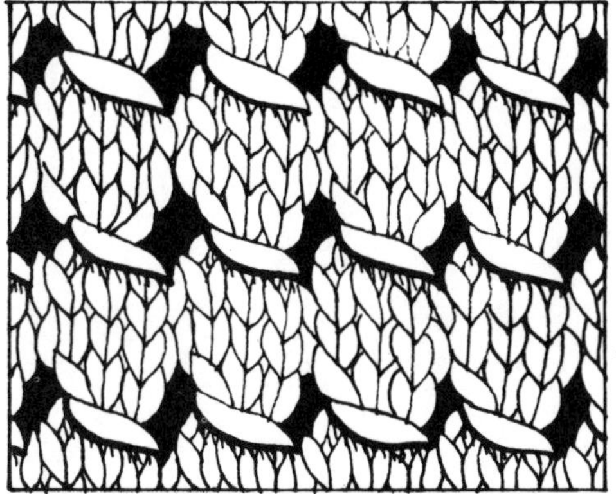

This stitch pattern is named for the woman who designed it, whose family is well known for its development of Shetland lace knitting.

For the **beginning row,** cast on a multiple of 4 stitches plus 2.

For the **first row,** knit.

For the **second row,** purl.

For the **third row,** knit 1. Repeat the following procedure. * Slip 1, knit 3, and pass slip stitch over the 3 knits. * End with knit 1.

For the **fourth row,** purl 1. Repeat the following procedure. * Purl 3. Wrap yarn around needle. * End with purl 1.

Repeat the **first through fourth rows** as many times as required.

Cat's Paw Pattern

This openwork pattern is another of the traditional Shetland designs.

For the **beginning row,** cast on 7 stitches.

For the **first row,** purl.

For the **second row,** knit 1. Knit 2 together. Yarn over. Knit 1. Yarn over. Then slip 1, knit 1, and pass slip stitch over. Knit 1.

For the **third row,** purl.

For the **fourth row,** knit 2 together. Yarn over. Knit 3. Yarn over. Then slip 1, knit 1, and pass slip stitch over.

For the **fifth row,** purl.

For the **sixth row,** knit 2. Yarn over. Then slip 1, knit 2 together, and pass slip stitch over. Yarn over. Knit 2.

Repeat the **first through sixth rows** as many times as required.

Bird's Eye Pattern

Although this pattern can be made in wools of different weights, it is most beautiful when worked in fine yarn as it would be in Shetland-type knitting for a lacy effect.

For the **beginning row,** cast on a multiple of 4 stitches.

For the **first row,** repeat the following procedure. * Knit 2 together. Put yarn over needle twice. Knit 2 together. *

For the **second row,** repeat the following procedure. * Knit 1. Then into the 2 yarn-overs in previous row knit 1 and purl 1. * End with knit 1.

For the **third row,** knit 2. Repeat the following procedure. * Knit 2 together. Put yarn over needle twice. Knit 2 together. * End with knit 2.

For the **fourth row,** knit 2. Repeat the following procedure. * Knit 1. Into the 2 yarn-overs of previous row knit 1 and purl 1. Knit 1. * End by knitting 2.

Repeat the **first through fourth rows** as many times as required.

Horseshoe Pattern

This stitch pattern is a basic one for lacy Shetland designs.

For the **beginning row,** cast on a multiple of 10 stitches plus 1.

For the **first row,** purl.

For the **second row,** knit 1. Repeat the following procedure. * Yarn over. Knit 3. Then slip 1, knit 2 together, and pass slip stitch over. Knit 3. Yarn over. Knit 1. *

For the **third row,** purl.

For the **fourth row,** purl 1. Repeat the following procedure. * Knit 1. Yarn over. Knit 2. Then slip 1, knit 2 together, and pass slip stitch over. Knit 2. Yarn over. Knit 1. Purl 1. *

For the **fifth row,** knit 1. Repeat the following procedure. * Purl 9. Knit 1. *

For the **sixth row,** purl 1. Repeat the following procedure. * Knit 2. Yarn over. Knit 1. Then slip 1, knit 2 together, and pass slip stitch over. Knit 1. Yarn over. Knit 2. Purl 1. *

For the **seventh row,** repeat the fifth row.

For the **eighth row,** purl 1. Repeat the following procedure. * Knit 3. Yarn over. Then slip 1, knit 2 together, and pass slip stitch over. Yarn over. Knit 3. Purl 1. *

Repeat the **first through eighth rows** as many times as required.

Fir Cone Pattern

This is another Shetland pattern; it creates a lovely, lacy effect.

For the **beginning row,** cast on a multiple of 10 stitches plus 1.

For the **first row,** purl.

For the **second row,** knit 1. Repeat the following procedure. * Yarn over. Knit 3. Then slip 1, knit 2 together, and pass slip stitch over. Knit 3. Yarn over. Knit 1. *

For the **third row,** purl.

For the **fourth row,** repeat the second row.

For the **fifth row,** purl.

For the **sixth row,** repeat the second row.

For the **seventh row,** purl.

For the **eighth row,** repeat the second row.

For the **ninth row,** purl.

For the **tenth row,** knit 2 together. Repeat the following procedure. * Knit 3. Yarn over. Knit 1. Yarn over. Knit 3. Then slip 1, knit 2 together, and pass slip stitch over. * End with knit 3. Yarn over. Knit 1. Yarn over. Knit 3. Then slip 1, knit 1, and pass slip stitch over.

For the **eleventh row,** purl.

For the **twelfth row,** repeat the tenth row.

For the **thirteenth row,** purl.

For the **fourteenth row,** repeat the tenth row.

For the **fifteenth row,** purl.

For the **sixteenth row,** repeat the tenth row.

Repeat the **first through sixteenth rows** as many times as required.

Lace Wings Pattern

This airy lace design is found in Dutch stitch patterns.

For the **beginning row,** cast on 7 stitches for a rib or panel of stitches.

For the **first row,** purl.

For the **second row,** knit 1. Knit 2 together. Yarn over. Knit 1. Yarn over. Then slip 1, knit 1, and pass slip stitch over. Knit 1.

For the **third row,** purl.

For the **fourth row,** knit 2 together. Yarn over. Knit 3. Yarn over. Then slip 1, knit 1, and pass slip stitch over.

Repeat the **first through fourth rows** as many times as required.

Madeira Mesh Pattern

This is another very old Spanish pattern. It creates a very sheer, lacy effect when worked in fine yarn.

For the **beginning row,** cast on a multiple of 6 stitches plus 7.

For the **first through sixth rows,** knit 2. Repeat the following procedure. * Wrap yarn around needle. Purl 3 together. Yarn over. Knit 3. * End row with wrap yarn around needle. Purl 3 together. Yarn over. Knit 2.

For the **seventh through twelfth rows,** knit 2. Repeat the following procedure. * Knit 3. Wrap yarn around needle. Purl 3 together. Yarn over. * End row with knit 5.

Repeat the **first through twelfth rows** as many times as required.

Traveling Vine Pattern

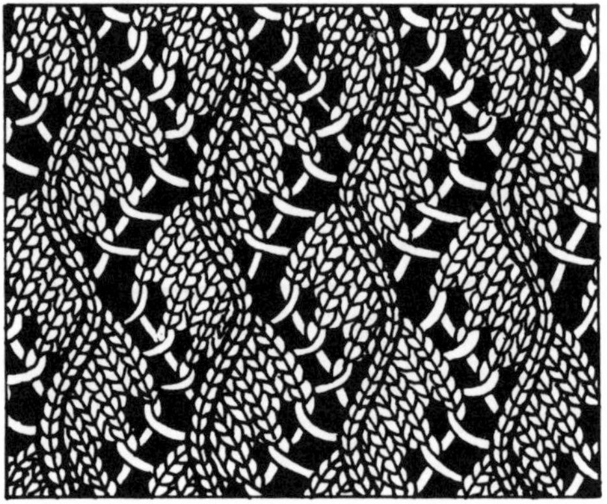

This is a lovely old French design that moves in graceful curves for a lacy effect.

For the **beginning row,** cast on a multiple of 8 stitches plus 4.

For the **first row,** knit 2. Repeat the following procedure. * Yarn over. Knit 1 in back. Yarn over. Then slip 1, knit 1, and pass slip stitch over. Knit 5. * End with knit 2.

For the **second row,** purl 6. Repeat the following procedure. * Purl 2 together in back. Purl 7. * End with purl 5.

For the **third row,** knit 2. Repeat the following procedure. * Yarn over. Knit 1 in back. Yarn over. Knit 2. Then slip 1, knit 1, and pass slip stitch over. Knit 3. * End with knit 2.

For the **fourth row,** purl 4. Repeat the following procedure. * Purl 2 together in back. Purl 7. *

For the **fifth row,** knit 2. Repeat the following procedure. * Knit 1 in back. Yarn over. Knit 4. Then slip 1, knit 1, and pass slip stitch over. Knit 1. Yarn over. * End with knit 2.

For the **sixth row,** purl 3. Repeat the following procedure. * Purl 2 together in back. Purl 7. * End with purl 1.

For the **seventh row,** knit 2. Repeat the following procedure. * Knit 5. Knit 2 together. Yarn over. Knit 1 in back. Yarn over. * End with knit 2.

For the **eighth row,** purl 5. Repeat the following procedure. * Purl 2 together. Purl 7. * End with purl 6.

For the **ninth row,** knit 2. Repeat the following procedure. * Knit 3. Knit 2 together. Knit 2. Yarn over. Knit 1 in back. Yarn over. * End with knit 2.

For the **tenth row,** repeat the following procedure. * Purl 7. Purl 2 together. * End with purl 4.

For the **eleventh row,** knit 2. Repeat the following procedure. * Yarn over. Knit 1. Knit 2 together. Knit 4. Yarn over. Knit 1 in back. * End with knit 2.

For the **twelfth row,** purl 1. Repeat the following procedure. * Purl 7. Purl 2 together. * End with purl 3.

Repeat **first through twelfth rows** as many times as required.

Florette Pattern

This is a beautiful old French pattern that creates a dainty, lacy effect.

For the **beginning row,** cast on a multiple of 6 stitches plus 5.

For the **first row,** purl.

For the **second row,** knit 2. Repeat the following procedure. * Purl 1. Yarn over. Then slip 1, knit 1, and pass slip stitch over. Knit 1. Knit 2 together. Yarn over. * End with knit 3.

For the **third row,** purl.

For the **fourth row,** knit 4. Repeat the following procedure. * Yarn over. Knit 3. * End with knit 1.

For the **fifth row,** purl.

For the **sixth row,** knit 2. Knit 2 together. Repeat the following procedure. * Yarn over. Then slip 1, knit 1, and pass slip stitch over. Knit 1. Knit 2 together. Yarn over. Then slip 2 knitwise, knit 1, and pass the 2 stitches over. * End with yarn over. Then slip 1, knit 1, and pass slip stitch over. Knit 1. Knit 2 together. Yarn over. Then slip 1, knit 1, and pass slip stitch over. Knit 2.

For the **seventh row,** purl.

For the **eighth row,** knit 2. Repeat the following procedure. * Knit 1. Knit 2 together. Yarn over. Knit 1. Yarn over. Then slip 1, knit 1, and pass slip stitch over. * End with knit 3.

For the **ninth row,** purl.

For the **tenth row,** repeat the fourth row.

For the **eleventh row,** purl.

For the **twelfth row,** knit 2. Repeat the following procedure. * Knit 1. Knit 2 together. Yarn over. Then slip 2 knitwise, knit 1, and pass the 2 slip stitches over. Yarn over. Then slip 1, knit 1, and pass slip stitch over. * End with knit 3.

Repeat the **first through twelfth rows** as many times as required.

Lace Butterfly Pattern

This is a traditional Italian pattern that can be adapted for an allover pattern or for lovely openwork panels.

For the **beginning row,** cast on a multiple of 14 stitches plus 4.

For the **first row**, repeat the following procedure. * Purl 1. Twist 2 by slipping the second stitch on the left-hand needle first, and then the first stitch, sliding both stitches off the needle together. Purl 1. Knit 3. Knit 2 together. Then put yarn over needle twice. Knit 2 together through back of stitch. Knit 3. * End with purl 1, twist 2, purl 1.

For the **second row,** repeat the following procedure. * Knit 1. Purl 2. Knit 1. Purl 4. Then, into the yarn-overs of the previous row, knit 1 in back and knit 1. Purl 4. * End with knit 1, purl 2, knit 1.

For the **third row,** repeat the first row.

For the **fourth row,** repeat the second row.

For the **fifth row,** repeat the following procedure. * Purl 1. Twist 2. Purl 1. Knit 1. Knit 2 together. Put yarn over needle twice. Knit 2 together through back of stitch. Knit 2 together. Put yarn around twice. Knit 2 together in back. Knit 1. * End with purl 1, twist 2, purl 1.

For the **sixth row,** repeat the following procedure. * Knit 1. Purl 2. Knit 1. Purl 2. Then, into the yarn-overs of the previous row, knit 1 in back and knit 1. Purl 2. Then knit 1 in back and knit 1 into the yarn-overs of the previous row. Purl 2. * End with knit 1, purl 2, knit 1.

For the **seventh row,** repeat the fifth row.

For the **eighth row,** repeat the sixth row.

Repeat the **first through eighth rows** as many times as required.

Herringbone Lace Pattern

Openwork outlines this stitch pattern, giving a zigzag movement to the design.

For the **beginning row,** cast on a multiple of 6 stitches plus 2.

For the **first row,** purl.

For the **second row,** repeat the following procedure. * Slip 1, knit 1, and pass slip stitch over. Knit 2. Yarn over. Knit 2. * End with knit 2.

For the **third row,** purl.

For the **fourth row,** repeat the second row.

For the **fifth row,** purl.

For the **sixth row,** repeat the second row.

For the **seventh row,** purl.

For the **eighth row,** knit 1. Repeat the following procedure. * Knit 2. Yarn over. Knit 2. Knit 2 together. * End with knit 1.

For the **ninth row,** purl.

For the **tenth row,** repeat the eighth row.

For the **eleventh row,** purl.

For the **twelfth row,** repeat the eighth row.

Repeat the **first through twelfth rows** as many times as required.

Zigzag Lace Trellis Pattern

This pattern creates the look of faggot stitches, moving first in one direction and then in the other.

For the **beginning row,** cast on a multiple of 2 stitches.

For the **first row,** purl.

For the **second row,** knit 1. Repeat the following procedure. * Yarn over. Knit 2 together. * End with knit 1.

For the **third row,** purl.

For the **fourth row,** repeat the second row.

For the **fifth row,** purl.

For the **sixth row,** repeat the second row.

For the **seventh row,** purl.

For the **eighth row,** knit 1. Repeat the following procedure. * Slip 1, knit 1, and pass slip stitch over. Yarn over. * End with knit 1.

For the **ninth row,** purl.

For the **tenth row,** repeat the eighth row.

For the **eleventh row,** purl.

For the **twelfth row,** repeat the eighth row.

Repeat the **first through twelfth rows** as many times as required.

Candle Pattern

A series of eyelets is the central point of each of the candlelike motifs that form this design pattern.

For the **beginning row,** cast on a multiple of 10 plus 1.

For the **first row,** knit 3. Repeat the following procedure. * Knit 2 together. Put yarn over. Knit 1. Yarn over. Then slip 1, knit 1, and pass slip stitch over knit stitch. Knit 5. * End by knitting 3.

For the **second row,** purl.

For the **third row,** knit 2. Repeat the following procedure. * Knit 2 together. Knit 1. Yarn over. Knit 1. Yarn over. Knit 1. Then slip 1, knit 1, and pass slip stitch over knit stitch. Knit 3. * End by knitting 2.

For the **fourth row,** purl.

For the **fifth row,** knit 1. Repeat the following procedure. * Knit 2 together. Knit 2. Yarn over. Knit 1. Yarn over. Knit 2. Then slip 1, knit 1, and pass slip stitch over. Knit 1. *

For the **sixth row,** purl.

For the **seventh row,** knit 2 together. Repeat the following procedure. * Knit 3. Yarn over. Knit 1. Yarn over. Knit 3. Slip 1. Knit 2 together. Pass slip stitch over the 2 stitches that are knit together. * End with slip 1, knit 1, and pass slip stitch over.

For the **eighth row,** purl.

For the **ninth row,** knit 1. Repeat the following procedure. * Yarn over. Then slip 1, knit 1, and pass slip stitch over. Knit 5. Knit 2 together. Yarn over. Knit 1. *

For the **tenth row,** purl.

For the **eleventh row,** knit 1. Repeat the following procedure. * Yarn over. Knit 1. Then slip 1, knit 1, and pass slip stitch over. Knit 3. Knit 2 together. Knit 1. Yarn over. Knit 1. *

For the **twelfth row,** purl.

For the **thirteenth row,** knit 1. Repeat the following procedure. * Yarn over. Knit 2. Then slip 1, knit 1, and pass slip stitch over. Knit 1. Knit 2 together. Knit 2. Yarn over. Knit 1. *

For the **fourteenth row,** purl.

For the **fifteenth row,** knit 1. Repeat the following procedure. * Yarn over. Knit 3. Slip 1. Knit 2 together. Pass slip stitch over the 2 stitches that are knit together. Knit 3. Yarn over. Knit 1. *

For the **sixteenth row,** purl.

Repeat the **first through sixteenth rows** as many times as required.

Lace Chevron Pattern

A series of eyelets seems to be defined in this stitch pattern, giving a zigzag effect.

For the **beginning row,** cast on 10 stitches plus 1.

For the **first row,** purl.

For the **second row,** repeat the following procedure. * Knit 5. Yarn over. Then slip 1, knit 1, and pass slip stitch over. Knit 3. * End with knit 1.

For the **third row,** purl.

For the **fourth row,** repeat the following procedure. * Knit 3. Knit 2 together. Yarn over. Knit 1. Yarn over. Then slip 1, knit 1, and pass slip stitch over. Knit 2. * End with knit 1.

For the **fifth row,** purl.

For the **sixth row,** repeat the following procedure. * Knit 2. Knit 2 together. Yarn over. Knit 3. Yarn over. Then slip 1, knit 1, and pass slip stitch over. Knit 1. * End with knit 1.

For the **seventh row,** purl.

For the **eighth row,** repeat the following procedure. * Knit 1. Knit 2 together. Yarn over. Knit 5. Yarn over. Then slip 1, knit 1, and pass slip stitch over. * End with knit 1.

For the **ninth row,** purl.

For the **tenth row,** knit 2 together. Yarn over. Knit 7. Repeat the following procedure. * Yarn over. Then slip 1, knit 2 together, and pass slip stitch over. Yarn over. Knit 7. * End with yarn over. Then slip 1, knit 1, and pass slip stitch over.

Repeat the **first through tenth rows** as many times as required.

Beech Leaf Lace Pattern

Solid leaves are outlined with openwork to create lacy columns.

For the **beginning row,** cast a multiple of 14 stitches plus 1.

For the **first row,** repeat the following procedure. * Knit 1. Put yarn over, knit 5. Yarn over, slip 1 stitch. Knit 2 together. Pass slip stitch over. Yarn over. Knit 5. Yarn over. * End with knit 1.

For the **second row,** purl.

For the **third row,** repeat the following procedure. * Knit 1. Put yarn over. Knit 1. Knit 2 together. Purl 1. Slip 1 stitch. Knit 1. Pass slip stitch over. Knit 1. Yarn over. Purl 1. Yarn over. Knit 1. Knit 2 together. Purl 1. Slip 1. Knit 1. Pass slip stitch over. Knit 1. Yarn over. * End with knit 1.

For the **fourth row,** purl 1. Repeat the following procedure. * Purl 3. Knit 1. Purl 3. Knit 1. Purl 3. Knit 1. Purl 4. *

For the **fifth row,** repeat the following procedure. * Knit 1. Put yarn over. Knit 1. Knit 2 together. Purl 1. Slip 1. Knit 1. Pass slip stitch over. Knit 1. Purl 1. Knit 1. Knit 2 together. Purl 1. Slip 1. Knit 1. Pass slip stitch over. Knit 1. Yarn over. * End with knit 1.

For the **sixth row,** purl 1. Repeat the following procedure. * Purl 3. Knit 1. Purl 2. Knit 1. Purl 2. Knit 1. Purl 4. *

For the **seventh row,** repeat the following procedure. * Knit 1. Put yarn over. Knit 1. Yarn over. Knit 2 together. Purl 1. Slip 1 stitch. Knit 1. Pass slip stitch over. Purl 1. Knit 2 together. Purl 1. Slip 1. Knit 1. Pass slip stitch over. Yarn over. Knit 1. Yarn over. * End with knit 1.

For the **eighth row,** purl 1. Repeat the following procedure. * Purl 4. Knit 1. Purl 1. Knit 1. Purl 1. Knit 1. Purl 5. *

For the **ninth row,** repeat the following procedure. * Knit 1. Yarn over. Knit 3. Yarn over. Slip 1 stitch. Knit 2 together. Pass slip stitch over. Purl 1. Knit 3 together. Yarn over. Knit 3. Yarn over. * End with knit 1.

For the **tenth row,** purl.

Repeat the **first through the tenth rows** until work is completed.

Drooping Elm Leaf Pattern

This stitch pattern is an adaptation of the Beech Leaf Lace Pattern, using a staggered arrangement of the leaves.

For the **beginning row,** cast on 15 stitches plus 1.

For the **first row,** repeat the following procedure. * Knit 1. Yarn over. Knit 1. Then slip 1, knit 1, and pass slip stitch over. Purl 1. Knit 2 together. Knit 1. Yarn over. Purl 1. Then slip 1, knit 1, and pass slip stitch over. Purl 1. Knit two together. Yarn over. Knit 1. Yarn over. Knit 1. Yarn over. * End with knit 1.

For the **second row,** purl 1. Repeat the following procedure. * Purl 4. Knit 1. Purl 1. Knit 1. Purl 3. Knit 1. Purl 4. *

For the **third row,** repeat the following procedure. * Knit 1. Yarn over. Knit 1. Then slip 1, knit 1, and pass slip stitch over. Purl 1. Knit 2 together. Knit 1. Purl 1. Then slip 1, knit 2 together, and pass slip stitch over. Yarn over. Knit 3. Yarn over. * End with knit 1.

For the **fourth row,** purl 1. Repeat the following procedure. * Purl 6. Knit 1. Purl 2. Knit 1. Purl 4. *

For the **fifth row,** repeat the following procedure. * Knit 1, and yarn over twice. Then slip 1, knit 1, and pass slip stitch over. Purl 1. Knit 2 together twice. Yarn over. Knit 5. Yarn over. * End with knit 1.

For the **sixth row,** purl 1. Repeat the following procedure. * Purl 7. Knit 1. Purl 1. Knit 1. Purl 5. *

For the **seventh row,** repeat the following procedure. * Knit 1. Yarn over. Knit 3. Yarn over. Then slip 1, knit 2 together, and pass slip stitch over. Purl 1. Yarn over. Knit 1. Then slip 1, knit 1, and pass slip stitch over. Purl 1. Knit 2 together. Knit 1. Yarn over. * End with knit 1.

For the **eighth row,** purl 1. Repeat the following procedure. * Purl 3 and knit 1 twice. Purl 7. *

For the **ninth row,** repeat the following procedure. * Knit 1. Yarn over. Knit 5. Yarn over. Then slip 1, knit 1, and pass slip stitch over. Knit 1. Then slip 1, knit 1, and pass slip stitch over. Purl 1. Knit 2 together. Knit 1. Yarn over. * End with knit 1.

For the **tenth row,** purl 1. Repeat the following procedure. * Purl 3. Knit 1. Purl 2. Knit 1. Purl 8. *

Repeat the **first through tenth rows** as many times as required.

Lace Medallion Pattern

This is one of the beautiful Italian patterns that create an interesting, lacy effect.

For the **beginning row,** cast on a multiple of 11 stitches plus 4.

For the **first row,** knit 2. Repeat the following procedure. * Knit 3. Knit 2 together. Yarn over. Knit 1. Yarn over. Knit 2 together through back. Knit 3. * End with knit 2.

For the **second row,** knit 2. Repeat the following procedure. * Knit 2. Purl 2 together through back of loop. Wrap yarn around needle. Purl 3. Wrap yarn around needle. Purl 2 together. Knit 2. * End with knit 2.

For the **third row,** knit 2. Repeat the following procedure. * Knit 1. Then knit two together and put yarn over twice. Knit 1. Follow with yarn over, and knit 2 together through back of loop twice. Knit 1. * End with knit 2.

For the **fourth row,** knit 2. Repeat the following procedure. * Purl 2 together through back of loop. Wrap yarn around needle. Purl 2 together through back of loop. Yarn over. Knit 3. Then wrap yarn around needle and purl 2 together twice. * End with knit 2.

For the **fifth row,** knit 2. Repeat the following procedure. * Knit 1. Then put yarn over and knit 2 together through back of loop twice. Knit 1. Follow with knit 2 together and yarn over twice. Knit 1. * End with knit 2.

For the **sixth row,** knit 2. Repeat the following procedure. * Knit 2. Wrap yarn around needle. Purl 2 together. Wrap yarn around needle. Purl 3 together. Wrap yarn around needle. Purl 2 together through back of loop. Yarn over. Knit 2. * End with knit 2.

For the **seventh row,** knit 2. Repeat the following procedure. * Knit 3. Yarn over. Knit 2 together through back of loop. Knit 1. Knit 2 together. Yarn over. Knit 3. * End with knit 2.

For the **eighth row,** knit 2. Repeat the following procedure. * Knit 4. Wrap yarn around needle. Purl 3 together. Yarn over. Knit 4. * End with knit 2.

Repeat the **first through eighth rows** as many times as required.

Baby Fern Pattern

When a delicate, lacy effect is needed for a ribbed effect, this is the pattern to use.

For the **beginning row,** cast on a multiple of 9 stitches plus 4.

For the **first row,** purl.

For the **second row,** knit 2. Repeat the following procedure. * Knit 2 together. Knit 2. Yarn over. Knit 1. Yarn over. Knit 2. Knit 2 together. * End with knit 2.

For the **third row,** knit 1. Then purl across row to last stitch, and knit this.

For the **fourth row,** knit 2. Repeat the following procedure. * Knit 2 together. Knit 1. Yarn over. Knit 3. Yarn over. Knit 1. Knit 2 together. * End with knit 2.

For the **fifth row,** repeat the third row.

For the **sixth row,** knit 2. Repeat the following procedure. * Knit 2 together.

Yarn over. Knit 5. Yarn over. Knit 2 together. * End with knit 2.

For the **seventh row,** repeat the third.

Repeat the **second through seventh rows** as many times as required.

Falling Leaves Pattern

Eyelets in a diamond pattern outline the design motif, giving a lightness to it.

For the **beginning row,** cast on a multiple of 10 stitches plus 6.

For the **first row,** knit 1. Wrap yarn around needle to make 1 stitch. Repeat the following procedure. * Knit 3. Then slip 1, knit 2 together, pass slip stitch over. Knit 3. Wrap yarn around needle to make a stitch. Knit 1. Make another stitch. * End with knit 3. Then slip 1, knit 1, and pass slip stitch over.

For the **second row,** purl.

For the **third row,** knit 2. Wrap yarn around needle to make 1 stitch. Repeat the following procedure. * Knit 2. Then slip 1, knit 2 together, and pass slip stitch over. Knit 2. Wrap yarn around needle to make 1 stitch. * End with knit 3. Wrap yarn around needle to make another stitch. Knit 2. Then slip 1, knit 1, and pass slip stitch over.

For the **fourth row,** purl.

For the **fifth row,** knit 3. Repeat the following procedure. * Wrap yarn around needle to make 1 stitch. Knit 1. Then slip 1, knit 2 together, and pass slip stitch over. Knit 1. Wrap yarn over to make 1 stitch. Knit 5. Wrap yarn over to make another stitch. * Knit 1. Then slip 1, knit 1, and pass slip stitch over.

For the **sixth row,** purl.

For the **seventh row,** knit 4. Wrap yarn around needle to make 1 stitch. Repeat the following procedure. * Slip 1, knit 2 together, and pass slip stitch over. Wrap yarn around needle to make 1 stitch. Knit 7. Wrap yarn around needle to make 1 stitch. * End with slip 1, knit 1, and pass slip stitch over.

For the **eighth row,** purl.

For the **ninth row,** slip 1, knit 1, and pass slip stitch over. Knit 3. Wrap yarn around needle to make 1 stitch. Repeat the following procedure. * Knit 1. Wrap yarn around needle to make 1 stitch. Knit 3. Then slip 1, knit 2 together, and pass slip stitch over. Wrap yarn around needle to make 1 stitch. * End with knit 1.

For the **tenth row,** purl.

For the **eleventh row,** slip 1, knit 1, and pass slip stitch over. Knit 2. Wrap yarn around needle to make 1 stitch. Knit 1. Repeat the following procedure. * Knit 2. Wrap yarn around needle to make 1 stitch. Knit 2. Then slip 1, knit 2 together, and pass slip stitch over. Knit 2. Wrap yarn around needle to make 1 stitch. Knit 1. * End with knit 1.

For the **twelfth row,** purl.

For the **thirteenth row,** slip 1, knit 1, and pass slip stitch over. Knit 1. Wrap yarn around needle to make 1 stitch. Knit 2. Repeat the following procedure. * Knit 3. Wrap yarn around needle to make 1 stitch. Knit 1. Then slip 1, knit 2 together, and pass slip stitch over. Knit 1. Wrap yarn around needle to make 1 stitch. Knit 2. * End with knit 1.

For the **fourteenth row,** purl.

For the **fifteenth row,** slip 1, knit 1, and pass slip stitch over. Wrap yarn around to make 1 stitch. Knit 3. Repeat the following procedure. * Knit 4. Wrap yarn around needle to make 1 stitch. Then slip 1, knit 2 together, and pass slip stitch over. Wrap yarn around needle to make 1 stitch. Knit 3. * End with knit 1.

For the **sixteenth row,** purl.

Repeat the **first through sixteenth rows** as many times as required.

CHANGING A BASIC DESIGN

One of the easiest ways to bring creativity to a knitted piece is to adjust a basic design. Just as a basic pattern in sewing can be given a new look by a change of fabric, color, and decorative details, so can one in knitting. Varying stitch patterns is one of the methods to use.

Substituting a Stitch Pattern

There are so many stitch patterns that your favorite basic sweater can be given innumerable new looks. However, you should always remember when selecting a substitute stitch pattern to choose one with the same "multiple of" or repeat as was noted in the directions. For instance, if the directions ask you to cast on 124 stitches, you know that the number must be divisible by a stated number of stitches—in this case, 2 or 4, not 6 or 8. Within this restriction, you will be able to find stitch patterns that will create different textural effects. Some will be solid and sturdy; others lacy and fragile. Some are easier to make than others, but each one allows you to produce a different look.

On the following pages you will find some suggestions you can use when you make a substitution. Consider the yarn to use and the gauge. Unless the correct ones are selected, the fit of the garment will not be maintained. Always knit a swatch in the new yarn and stitch pattern to check the gauge before starting your article.

Knotted Stitch

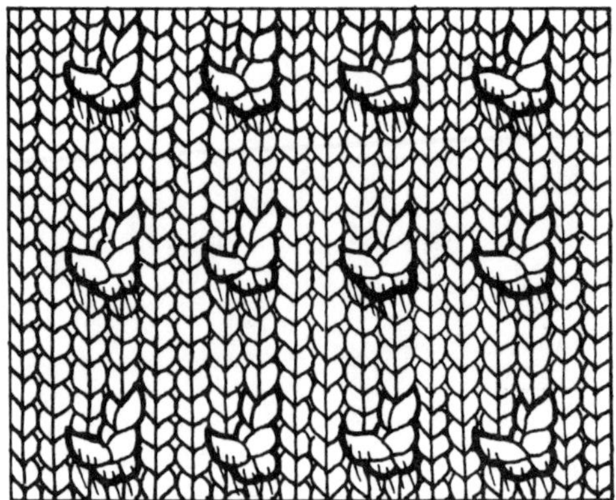

An interesting textural effect results when the surface is dotted with a small grouping of stitches.

For the **beginning row,** cast on a multiple of 4 stitches.
For the **first row,** knit.
For the **second row,** purl.
For the **third row,** knit.
For the **fourth row,** purl.
For the **fifth row,** repeat the following procedure. * Knit 2. To make the knot, wrap yarn around needle, making a stitch. Then pass the second stitch from the point of the right-hand needle over the first stitch and the made stitch. To complete the knot, wrap yarn around needle again and pass the second stitch over the 2 made stitches. *
Repeat the **first through fifth rows** as many times as required.

Syncopated Brioche Stitch

Broken ribs give a checked effect to this variation of the Brioche Stitch.

For the **beginning row,** cast on an even number of stitches.

For the **first row,** repeat the following procedure. * Put yarn over. Slip 1 stitch purlwise. Knit 1. *

For the **second row,** repeat the following procedure. * Put yarn over. Slip 1 stitch purlwise. Knit 2 together. *

For the **third through seventh rows,** repeat the second row.

For the **eighth row,** put yarn in front. Repeat the following procedure. * Slip 1 stitch purlwise. Put yarn over. Purl 2 together. *

For the **ninth through thirteenth rows,** repeat the eighth row.

Repeat the **second through thirteenth rows** as many times as required.

Coral Knot Stitch

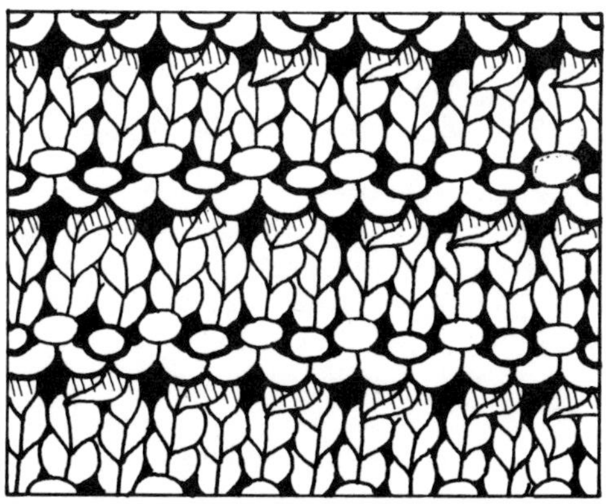

This pattern creates some interesting textural effects with stripes of eyelet and nubby stitches.

For the **beginning row,** cast on a multiple of 2 stitches.

For the **first row,** knit 1. Repeat the following procedure. * Knit 2 together. * End row with knit 1.

For the **second row,** knit 1. Repeat the following procedure. * Knit 1. Insert needle under yarn connecting the next stitch and the one just knitted, and knit a stitch. * End with knit 1.

For the **third row,** knit.

For the **fourth row,** purl.

Repeat the **first through fourth rows** as many times as required.

Slip Stitch Mesh

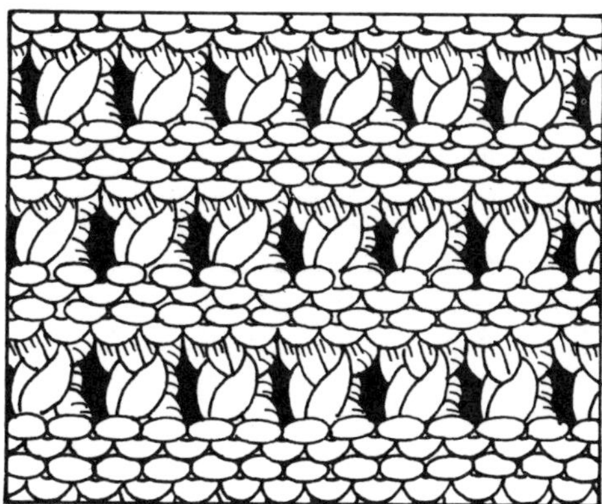

The openwork stripes and the 3-dimensional effect that the stitch creates make this an interesting stitch pattern.

For the **beginning row,** cast on a multiple of 2 stitches.

For the **first row,** purl.

For the **second row,** knit.

For the **third row,** knit 2. Repeat the following procedure. * Slip 1 with yarn in back. Knit 1. *

For the **fourth row,** repeat the following procedure. * Knit 1. Slip 1 with yarn in front. * End with knit 2.

For the **fifth row,** knit 1. Repeat the following procedure. * Yarn over. Knit 2 together. * End with knit 1.

For the **sixth row,** purl.

Repeat the **first through sixth rows** as many times as required.

Dimple Eyelet

Rows of eyelets give a dainty, striped look to this stitch pattern. Ribbons can be threaded through the eyelets.

For the **beginning row,** cast on a multiple of 2.

For the **first row,** knit.

For the **second row,** purl.

For the **third row,** purl 1. Repeat the following procedure. * Put yarn over needle in reverse by bringing it over the needle from back to front. Purl 2 together. * End by purling 1.

For the **fourth row,** purl. Purl all yarn-over stitches through back loops.

For the **fifth row,** knit.

For the **sixth row,** purl.

For the **seventh row,** purl 2. Repeat the following procedure. * Put yarn over needle in reverse by bringing it over the needle from back to front. Purl 2 together. *

For the **eighth row,** purl. Purl all yarn-over stitches through back loops.

Repeat the **first through eighth rows** as many times as required.

Faggot Stitch

This is a basic lace stitch that seems to give the feeling of crisscross faggoting stitches in embroidery.

For the **beginning row,** cast on a multiple of 2 stitches.

For the **first row,** knit 1. Repeat the following procedure. * Yarn over. Then slip 1, knit 1, and pass slip stitch over. * End with knit 1.

Repeat the **first row** as many times as required.

Purse Stitch

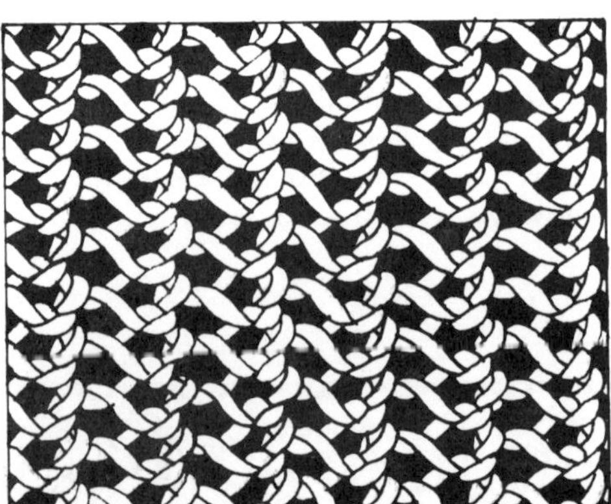

This easy-to-do stitch adds a yarn-over to the basic knit and purl stitches to create a slightly openwork pattern.

For the **beginning row,** cast on a multiple of 2 stitches.

For the **first row,** knit 1. Repeat the following procedure. * Yarn over. Purl 2 together. * End with knit 1.

Repeat the **first row** as many times as required.

Scroll Pattern

The lines of this stitch pattern seem to wander, with openwork emphasizing their direction.

For the **beginning row,** cast on a multiple of 2 stitches.

For the **first row,** knit 1. Repeat the following procedure. * Yarn over. Knit 8. Knit 2 together. * End with knit 1.

For the **second row,** purl 1. Repeat the following procedure. * Purl 2 together. Purl 7. Yarn over. Purl 1. * End with purl 1.

For the **third row,** knit 1. Repeat the following procedure. * Knit 2. Yarn over. Knit 6. Knit 2 together. * End with knit 1.

For the **fourth row,** purl 1. Repeat the following procedure. * Purl 2 together. Purl 5. Yarn over. Purl 3. * End with purl 1.

For the **fifth row,** knit 1. Repeat the following procedure. * Knit 4. Yarn over. Knit 4. Knit 2 together. * End with knit 1.

For the **sixth row,** purl 1. Repeat the following procedure. * Purl 2 together. Purl 3. Yarn over. Purl 5. * End with purl 1.

For the **seventh row,** knit 1. Repeat the following procedure. * Knit 6. Yarn over. Knit 2. Knit 2 together. * End with knit 1.

For the **eighth row,** purl 1. Repeat the following procedure. * Purl 2 together. Purl 1. Yarn over. Purl 7. * End with purl 1.

For the **ninth row,** knit 1. Repeat the following procedure. * Knit 8. Yarn over. Knit 2 together. * End with knit 1.

For the **tenth row,** purl 1. Repeat the following procedure. * Yarn over. Purl 8. Purl 2 together from back by inserting needle into back of stitches from left to right. * End with purl 1.

For the **eleventh row,** knit 1. Repeat the following procedure. * Slip 1, knit 1, and pass slip stitch over. Knit 7. Yarn over. Knit 1. * End with knit 1.

For the **twelfth row,** purl 1. Repeat the following procedure. * Purl 2. Yarn over. Purl 6. Purl 2 together from back by inserting needle into back of stitches from left to right. * End with purl 1.

For the **thirteenth row,** knit 1. Repeat the following procedure. * Slip 1, knit 1, and pass slip stitch over. Knit 5. Yarn over. Knit 3. * End with knit 1.

For the **fourteenth row,** purl 1. Repeat the following procedure. * Purl 4. Yarn over. Purl 4. Purl 2 together from back by inserting needle into back of stitches from left to right. * End with purl 1.

For the **fifteenth row,** knit 1. Repeat the following procedure. * Slip 1, knit 1, and pass slip stitch over. Knit 3. Yarn over. Knit 5. * End with knit 1.

For the **sixteenth row,** purl 1. Repeat the following procedure. * Purl 6. Yarn over. Purl 2. Purl 2 together from back, by inserting needle into back of stitches from left to right. * End with purl 1.

For the **seventeenth row,** knit 1. Repeat the following procedure. * Slip 1, knit 1, and pass slip stitch over. Knit 1. Yarn over. Knit 7. * End with knit 1.

For the **eighteenth row,** purl 1. Repeat the following procedure. * Purl 8. Yarn over. Purl 2 together from back, by inserting needle into back of stitches from left to right. * End with purl 1.

Repeat the **first through eighteenth rows** as many times as required.

COMBINING STITCH PATTERNS

Another effective way to use stitch patterns is to combine them to form stripes and panels. Alternating rows of garter and stockinette stitches can be pleasing. They can be worked in the same yarn or in contrasting ones such as fluffy with smooth. By varying the width of the stripes, a completely different look results. One of these combinations provides a puffy, indented texture in which the stockinette stitches seem to disappear. It can be made by knitting this arrangement of stitches.

Horizontal Welting

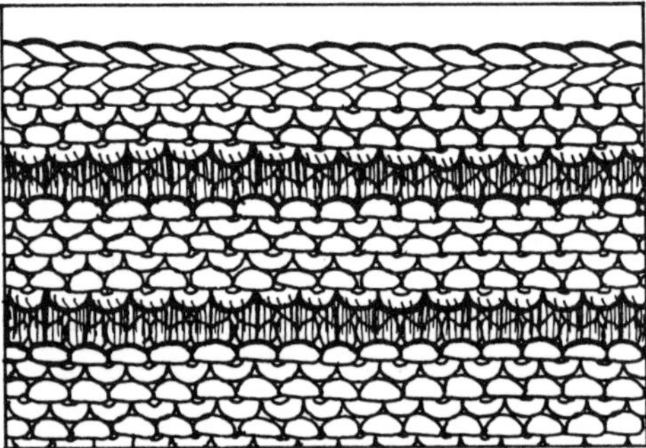

For the **beginning row,** cast on any number of stitches.
For the **first row,** knit all the stitches.
For the **second row,** purl.
For the **third row,** knit.
For the **fourth row,** knit.
For the **fifth row,** purl.
For the **sixth row,** knit.

Usually we think of these stitch combinations as being worked horizontally. However, it is possible to create a vertical direction in a design. In fact, some stitch patterns form vertical stripes, such as cables and the stitch patterns shown here.

Double Hourglass Pattern

This pattern is sometimes called Wavy Ribbing. It can serve as a panel or outline for decorative touches.

For the **beginning row,** cast on a multiple of 14 stitches plus 2.
For the **first row,** knit 1. Repeat the following procedure. * Purl 1. Knit 2. Purl 1. Knit 6. Purl 1. Knit 2. Purl 1. * End with knit 1.
For the **second row,** purl 1. Repeat the following procedure. * Slip 1 stitch onto a double-pointed needle and leave in front, purl 1, and knit the stitch on the double-pointed needle, making a front cross. Purl 1. Make another front cross. Purl 4. Then make a back cross by slipping 1 stitch onto a double-pointed needle and leave in back, purl 1, and knit the stitch on the double-pointed needle. Purl 1. Make another back cross. * End with purl 1.
For the **third row,** knit all the knit stitches and purl all the purl stitches.
For the **fourth row,** purl 1. Repeat the following procedure. * Purl 1. Then make a front cross by slipping 1 stitch onto a double-pointed needle and leave in front, purl 1, and knit the stitch on the double-pointed needle. Purl 1. Make another front cross. Purl 2. Then make a back cross by slipping 1 stitch onto a double-pointed needle and leave in back, purl 1, and knit the stitch on the double-pointed needle. Purl 2. Make another back cross. * End with purl 1.

For the **fifth row,** knit all the knit stitches and purl all the purl stitches.

For the **sixth row,** purl 1. Repeat the following procedure. * Purl 2. Make a front cross by slipping 1 stitch onto a double-pointed needle and leave in front, purl 1, and knit the stitch on the double-pointed needle. Purl 1. Make another front cross. Then make a back cross by slipping 1 stitch onto a double-pointed needle and leave in back, knit 1, and purl the stitch on the double-pointed needle. Purl 1. Then make another back cross. Purl 2. * End with purl 1.

For the **seventh row,** knit all the knit stitches and purl all the purl stitches.

For the **eighth row,** knit all the knit stitches and purl all the purl stitches.

For the **ninth row,** knit all the knit stitches and purl all the purl stitches.

For the **tenth row,** purl 1. Repeat the following procedure. * Purl 2. Make a back cross by slipping 1 stitch onto a double-pointed needle and leave in back, purl 1, and knit the stitch on the double-pointed needle. Purl 1. Make another back cross. Follow with a front cross by slipping 1 stitch onto a double-pointed needle and leave in front, purl 1, and knit the stitch on the double-pointed needle. Purl 1. Make another front cross. Purl 2. * End with purl 1.

For the **eleventh row,** knit all the knit stitches and purl all the purl stitches.

For the **twelfth row,** purl 1. Repeat the following procedure. * Purl 1. Make a back cross by slipping 1 stitch onto a double-pointed needle and leave in back, purl 1, and knit the stitch on the double-pointed needle. Purl 1. Make another back cross. Purl 2. Make a front cross by slipping 1 stitch onto a double-pointed needle and leave in front, purl 1, and knit the stitch on the double-pointed needle. Purl 1. Then make another front cross. Purl 1. * End with purl 1.

For the **thirteenth row,** knit all the knit stitches and purl all the purl stitches.

For the **fourteenth row,** purl 1. Repeat the following procedure. * Make a back cross by slipping 1 stitch onto a double-pointed needle and leave in back, purl 1, and knit the stitch on the double-pointed needle. Purl 1. Make another back cross. Purl 4. Then make a front cross by slipping 1 stitch onto a double-pointed needle and leave in front, purl 1, and knit the stitch on the double-pointed needle. Purl 1. Make another front cross. * End with purl 1.

For the **fifteenth row,** knit all the knit stitches and purl all the purl stitches.

For the **sixteenth row,** knit all the knit stitches and purl all the purl stitches.

Repeat the **first through sixteenth rows** as many times as required.

Marriage Lines Lace Pattern

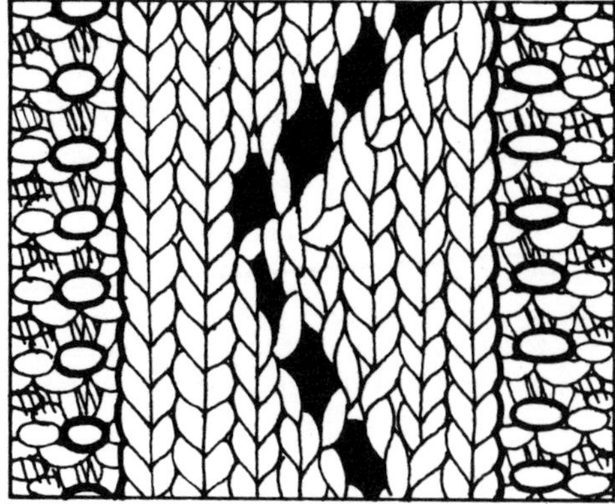

This is an unusual pattern in that it forms distinct panels, one dominated with a zigzag eyelet design and the other with moss or seed type stitches.

For the **beginning row,** cast on a multiple of 14 stitches plus 7.

For the **first row,** repeat the following procedure. * Purl 7. Knit 1. Yarn over. Knit 2 together. Knit 4. * End with purl 7.

For the **second row,** repeat the following procedure. * Knit 1 and purl 1 in back 3 times. Knit 1. Purl 7. * End with knit 1 and purl 1 in back 3 times. Knit 1.

For the **third row,** repeat the following procedure. * Purl 7. Knit 2. Yarn over. Knit 2 together. Knit 3. * End with purl 7.

For the **fourth row,** repeat the second row.

For the **fifth row,** repeat the following procedure. * Purl 7. Knit 3. Yarn over. Knit 2 together. Knit 2. * End with purl 7.

For the **sixth row,** repeat the second row.

For the **seventh row,** repeat the following procedure. * Purl 7. Knit 4. Yarn over. Knit 2 together. Knit 1. * End with purl 7.

For the **eighth row,** repeat the second row.

For the **ninth row,** repeat the following procedure. * Purl 7. Knit 3. Knit 2 together through back of loops. Yarn over. Knit 2. * End with purl 7.

For the **tenth row,** repeat the second row.

For the **eleventh row,** repeat the following procedure. * Purl 7. Knit 2. Knit 2 together through back of loops. Yarn over. Knit 3. * End with purl 7.

For the **twelfth row,** repeat the second row.

For the **thirteenth row,** repeat the following procedure. * Purl 7. Knit 1. Knit 2 together through back of loops. Yarn over. Knit 4. * End with purl 7.

For the **fourteenth row,** repeat the second row.

For the **fifteenth row,** repeat the following procedure. * Purl 7. Knit 2 together through back of loops. Yarn over. Knit 5. * End with purl 7.

For the **sixteenth row,** repeat the following procedure. * Knit 1 and purl 1 in back 3 times. Knit 1. Purl 7. * End with knit 1 and purl 1 in back 3 times. Knit 1.

Repeat the **first through sixteenth rows** as often as required.

Twisted Zigzag Pattern

Added interest can be given a zigzag design by using twisted stitches.

For the **beginning row,** cast on a multiple of 9 stitches plus 2.

For the **first row,** purl.

For the **second row,** knit 1. Repeat the following procedure. * Work this sequence of stitches 3 times: insert right-hand needle between first and second stitches on left-hand needle from back to front, and knit the second stitch before knitting the first. Then slip both stitches from needle. Follow by knitting 3 stitches. * End with knit 1.

For the **third row,** purl.

For the **fourth row,** knit 2. Repeat the following procedure. * Work this sequence of stitches 3 times: insert right-hand needle between first and second stitches on left-hand needle from back to front, and knit the second stitch before knitting the first. Then slip both stitches from needle. Follow by knitting 3 stitches. *

For the **fifth row,** purl.

For the **sixth row,** knit 3. Repeat the following procedure. * Work this sequence of stitches 3 times, inserting right-hand needle between first and second stitches on left-hand needle from back to front, and knitting the second stitch before knitting the first. Then slip both stitches from needle. Follow by knitting 3 stitches. * End last repeat by knitting 2 instead of 3.

For the **seventh row,** purl.

For the **eighth row,** knit 4. Repeat the following procedure. * Work this sequence of stitches 3 times: insert right-hand needle between first and second stitches on left-hand needle from back to front, and knit the second stitch before knitting the first. Then slip both stitches from needle. Follow by knitting 3 stitches. * End last repeat with knit 1 instead of knit 3.

For the **ninth row,** purl.

For the **tenth row,** knit 4. Repeat the following procedure. * Work this sequence of stitches 3 times: skip first stitch on left-hand needle and insert needle into second stitch from the front, knitting this stitch before knitting the skipped stitch, and slipping both stitches from needle. Follow by knitting 3. * End last repeat by knitting 1 instead of 3.

For the **eleventh row,** purl.

For the **twelfth row,** knit 3. Repeat the following procedure. * Work this sequence of stitches 3 times: skip first stitch on left-hand needle and insert needle into second stitch from the front, knitting this stitch before knitting the skipped stitch, and slipping both stitches from needle. Follow by knitting 3. * End last repeat by knitting 2 instead of 3.

For the **thirteenth row,** purl.

For the **fourteenth row,** knit 2. Repeat the following procedure. * Work this sequence of stitches 3 times: skip first stitch on left-hand needle and insert needle into second stitch from the front, knitting this stitch before knitting the skipped stitch, and slipping both stitches from needle. Follow by knitting 3. *

For the **fifteenth row,** purl.

For the **sixteenth row,** knit 1. Repeat the following procedure. * Work this sequence of stitches 3 times: skip first stitch on left-hand needle and insert needle into second stitch from the front, knitting this stitch before knitting the skipped stitch, and slipping both stitches from needle. Follow by knitting 3. * Knit last stitch.

Repeat the **first through sixteenth rows** as many times as required.

Frequently this type of stitch pattern is used singly to form a front panel or arranged in such a way as to produce an allover design as seen in Aran knitting. The Aran Isles in Ireland have lent their names to a specific type of knitting that is marked by vertical panels placed side by side. Combining various raised stitch patterns can offer an opportunity for originality. Some stitch patterns you may want to use are Plait Cable, Chain Cable, Cable, Basket Cable, Seed, Gull, Diamond, and Diamond Lattice, all shown elsewhere in this book.

Getting the Right Fit

The beauty of a knitted garment can be ruined if it does not fit the figure correctly. A fashion that is too loose or too tight, too long or too short will give you an out-of-proportion look. An ill-fitting garment seems to dwarf or exaggerate the figure in an unattractive way. Always consider sizing carefully before you select a knitting project.

There are several factors to think about, beginning with individual measurements and the manner of knitting. Too often one does not realize that the looseness or tightness of the stitches can make an article larger or smaller than the directions indicated.

NOTE THE SIZE

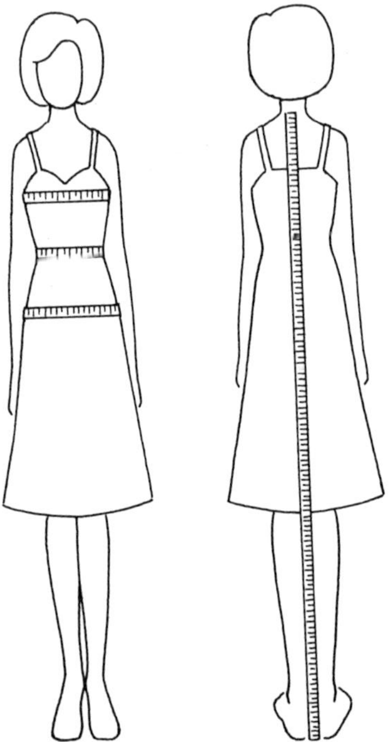

For selecting a knitting project, the bust or chest and hip measurements are the ones you will need. Take them carefully. Accuracy is important. Unless they are taken precisely, they will be of little value.

Check Body Measurements

It is best to take certain measurements before starting each project. This may surprise you, but measurements seem to fluctuate. Waistlines thicken, arms become flabby, hips bulge. Such changes can have disappointing results.

Misses', Women's, and Teens. Measurements should be taken when wearing the undergarments one expects to wear beneath the knitted garment. Measure around the fullest part of the bust, the natural waistline, and the fullest part of the hips when standing in a normal position.

It is best to have someone take the

measurements for you. Stand with your weight evenly distributed on both feet. A more accurate measure is made if the measurements are taken from the back.

Knowing your *height* will be helpful in determining the length of a sweater or garment. Stand in a natural position against a wall in stocking feet. Place a ruler on top of the head. Mark the point where the ruler touches the wall. Then measure the distance to the floor.

A handy measurement to have is the *back waist length*. Take this from the top of the prominent bone at base of the neck to the natural waistline and then to the floor or to the finished length. For a dress or sweater, the measurement is determined by measuring to the point where the hemline or lower edge will fall.

The *bust measurement* should be taken over the fullest part, well up under the arms, and straight across the back. Do not pull the tape measure too tight. Keep it parallel to the floor.

The *waist measurement* should be taken snugly at the smallest part of the figure between the ribs and hipline. This is the natural waistline.

The *hip measurement* should be taken over the fullest part of the figure, which is usually 7 to 9 inches (18–23 cm) below the natural waistline for an adult; about 4 to 6 inches (10–15 cm) for a child.

Men's and Boys'. The chest measurement is the important one. Hold the tape loosely and measure around the fullest part of the chest.

Children's. Again, the chest measurement is the significant one. Take it over the undergarments the child usually wears. Be careful not to hold the tape snugly or loosely. Children's garments are designed for an easy fit.

Consulting the Sizing Chart

In choosing the correct size, study the charts shown here. Select the size that represents the body measurements closest to those of the person for whom the article is being made. If none of the measurements match exactly, then choose the size by the bust measure. It is much easier to make adjustments to the waist

Type	Size	Bust	Waist	Hip	Height
Children's	6 mos.	19″	19″	20″	22″
	1	20	19½	21	25
	2	21	20	22	29
	3	22	20½	23	31
	4	23	21	24	33
Girls'	6	24	22	26	37
	8	27	23½	28	41
	10	28½	24½	30	45
	12	30	25½	32	49
	14	32	26½	34	53
Junior/	7/8	29	23	32	5′3″
Teens	9/10	30½	24	33½	
	11/12	32	25	35	
	13/14	33½	26	36½	
Misses'	6	30½	22	32½	5′6″
	8	31½	23	33½	
	10	32½	24	34½	
	12	34	25½	36	
	14	36	27	38	
	16	38	29	40	
	18	40	31	42	
Women's	38	42	34	44	5′7″
	40	44	36	46	
	42	46	38	48	
	44	48	40½	50	
	46	50	43	52	
	48	52	45½	54	
Boys'	1	20	19½	20	25″
	2	21	20	21	29
	3	22	20½	22	31
	4	23	21	23	33
	6	24	22	25	37
	8	26	23	27	41
	10	28	24	29	45
	12	30	25½	31	49
	14	32	27	33	53
	16	34	29	35½	55
Men's	34	34	30		5′9″
	36	36	32		
	38	38	34		
	40	40	36		
	42	42	38		
	44	44	40		

and hip area than to the shoulder and bust. Never choose children's sizing by age.

Sometimes when you select a design, you will notice that the sizing is listed as small, medium, or large. This type of marking encompasses two size ranges. The fit of the finished garment will not be quite so precise as when one size is indicated. Also the size designation is not always the same. For instance, small may be listed as a 6/8 or 8/10. You can see that the difference could make a variation in fit.

In studying the charts on the previous page, it should be remembered that the body measurements are given in inches.

Regard the Ease

You should remember that patterns do not duplicate body measurements exactly. A bit of ease is built into the design. It allows the body to move within the garment. Sometimes it is referred to as "wiggle room." The amount of ease depends on the type of garment and the look the designer is trying to achieve. For instance, a ski sweater would have more ease than a camisole top.

Knitting directions usually include the needed amount of ease for each size. Always study the picture of the item you are thinking of selecting. Generally it will indicate how the designer wants the garment to look. You can decide whether it reflects your personal taste.

Also think about how the garment is to be worn. If it is to be part of a layered look, you may need to select a size larger than you usually wear so it can be worn smartly over a blouse or sweater.

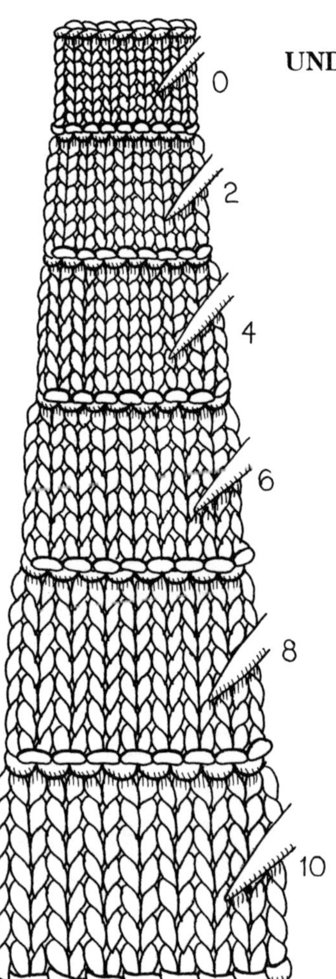

UNDERSTANDING GAUGE

The importance of gauge cannot be stressed too much. Unless the correct gauge is used, the size and fit of a garment will be less than perfect.

Gauge refers to the number of stitches and rows that are produced by knitting with a specific size needle and yarn. Perhaps you have noticed that at the beginning of directions there is a statement such as this: Gauge No. 6 needles; 6 sts = 1 inch (2.5 cm); 7 rows = 1 inch (2.5 cm). This means that if the article you are knitting is to be the same size as indicated by the directions, 6 stitches in your knitting should make 1 inch (2.5 cm) of horizontal stitches and that 7 rows should make 1 inch (2.5 cm) of vertical stitches on rows.

The number of stitches will vary according to the yarn and the size of the needle you use. You can see by studying the accompanying drawing how the size of the needle can change the look of the knitting when the same yarn is used. As the needles get smaller, so does the swatch. Also notice that the texture of the knitting seems to change. The smaller needles produce a firmness that seems stiff, having little elasticity, whereas the larger needles create a loose, stretchy fabric.

The gauge will also be affected by the way you knit. Some persons knit more tightly than others. Naturally it will be easier to duplicate the stated gauge if you knit with a moderate tension. This allows the stitches to be worked easily without leaving a visible space between the stitch loops and the needle. If you knit too tightly, you will find it difficult to insert the right-hand needle, but if you knit loosely, the stitches will slip off the left-hand needle when they should not. Also the knitted material will not hold its shape.

To knit with a moderate, even tension requires practice. Take some time to develop this skill. It will make your knitting more attractive.

Make a Swatch Gauge

Because of these variables, you should test your stitch gauge before starting a new project. This allows you to compare it with the required gauge.

To start your gauge, cast on 20 stitches using the specified yarn and needles. Work in the required pattern stitch for 3 inches (7.5 cm).

When the swatch is completed, smooth it out. Pin it to a firm surface. With a ruler, measure off 1 or 2 inches (2.5 or 5 cm) crosswise, and an equal distance lengthwise. Mark the ends of the measured space with pins. Some persons think that a 2-inch (5 cm) measure gives a more accurate gauge.

Count the stitches and rows between the pins. Stitches are easier to count on the knit side of the stockinette stitch, whereas the rows are easier to count on the purl side.

Even though the gauge varies by only a fraction of a stitch, do not ignore it. Your garment could be several inches too large or too tight. In analyzing the differences between the gauge you have knitted and the one the design requires, remember that if you knit more stitches to the inch than needed, then you are knitting too tightly. Try needles one size larger to correct the problem. But if you knit fewer stitches to the inch, you are knitting too loosely. Smaller needles may correct the situation.

Although the row gauge is not quite as important as the stitch gauge, it is better if it corresponds to the one mentioned in the directions. It makes for a better-fitting garment. However, if you wonder which gauge to follow when there is a variance in one, always select the stitch gauge.

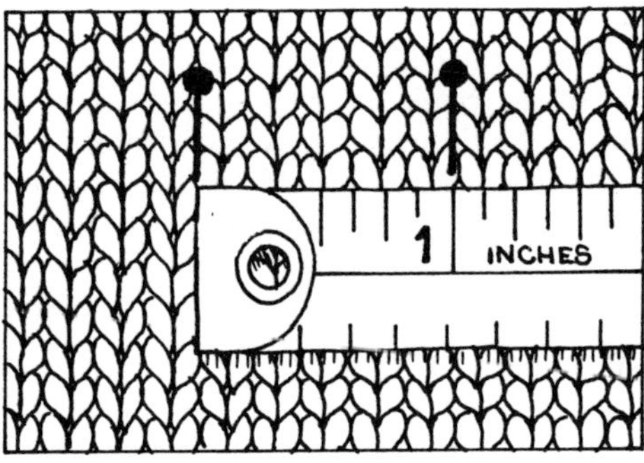

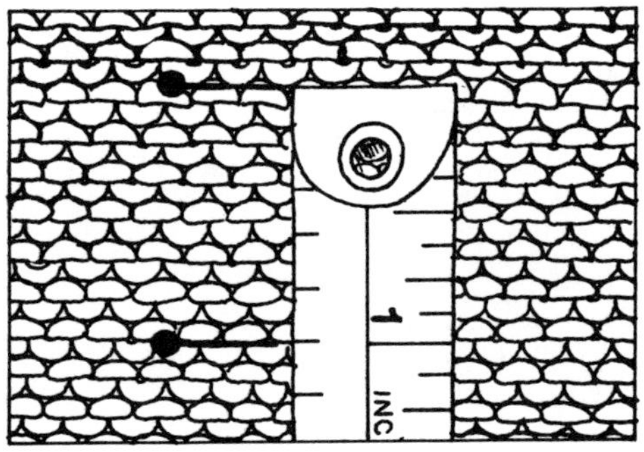

CONSIDER ADJUSTMENTS

Sometimes a slight adjustment to the design directions will produce a more attractive look and a better fit. Shortening or lengthening a garment is not difficult to do, whereas altering the width needs more skill. But in either case, both require some advance planning.

How to Shorten or Lengthen

Begin by considering the height of the person for whom the article is being made. Review the sizing chart. You will notice that the height of the figure is listed.

Patterns are designed for the average figure having the stated measurements. In case you are taller or shorter than the average, then it seems best to shorten or lengthen the garment as it is knitted. Using the height as a guide, consider how many inches may need to be added or subtracted.

Check the decision by interpreting the directions. Some instructions ask you to knit a certain number of inches before making a change in shaping. Others just ask you to knit a certain number of rows.

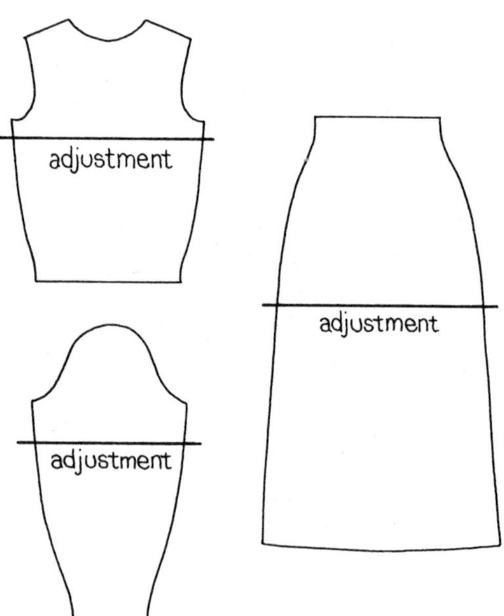

Whichever way is used, add the mentioned numbers for a total dimension. If the count is by rows, use the stated row gauge for determining the number of inches. When you have decided whether an adjustment is necessary, the next problem to solve is where.

Locate the Area. If you sew, you have observed the lines of the pattern pieces that indicate where adjustments should be made. Use these as guidelines for your knitting alterations. Notice they are placed where there is little or no shaping in the design. Keep in mind that the adjustments should be made to both the front and the back pieces as well as both sleeves. It is so easy to forget.

For a top or sweater, make the adjustment between the lower edge and the shaping for the armhole. Sometimes, if you are short-waisted, you may want to remove a small amount below the shoulder line in order to bring the neckline into its proper position. A gapping neckline is not attractive.

For sleeves, adjust above and below the elbow for long sleeves; above the lower edge of a short sleeve.

For a skirt, alter the directions between the lower edge and the point where the shaping for the hip line begins.

Determine the Amount. The row gauge should be your guide. If you decide that the garment should be 1 inch (2.5 cm) shorter, and the row gauge states that 6 rows equal 1 inch (2.5 cm), then you know that you need to remove 6 rows from the directions. If you need to add rows in order to lengthen the directions 1 inch, then add 6 rows to the directions.

Make the Adjustment. In knitting, this is not as easy to do as in sewing. There is no tissue pattern to tuck or spread and test before the project begins. Instead, the alterations are made as the knitting progresses. You have to depend on your ruler to tell you when the adjustment should be made. At the correct spot, make the adjustment by subtracting or adding rows for the desired effect. Some persons find it helpful to draw a sample pattern to use as a guide.

Note the Stitch Pattern. Not all stitch patterns lend themselves to lengthening and shortening. There is no problem with simple stitch patterns, but if a large repeat is required to create the stitch pattern, adjusting may not be possible. Using a complete repeat may be too much or not quite enough to make the correct adjustment. In making a decision, consult the gauge for the stitch pattern.

Think About Width

Usually an adjustment in the width is not necessary. The wide range of sizes solves this problem. However, it is a good idea to check the sizing just to be sure that the garment will fit properly.

Check the stitch gauge, which tells you how many stitches there are to the inch. Then notice how many stitches are to be cast on, remembering to add the number for back and front together. Divide this number by the number of stitches per inch and you have a number that should correspond to a personal measurement. For example, if your hips measure 36 inches (91.5 cm) and the stitch gauge is 6 stitches to the inch (2.5 cm), then you know that you will need to cast on 216 stitches, depending on the type of yarn. A few more stitches may be needed as an ease allowance. You do not want the knitting to look stretched over the bust and abdomen.

If you feel an adjustment is necessary, larger or smaller needles may correct the problem. A smaller needle will decrease the size; a larger one, increase it. Be sure to make a stitch gauge before starting the project.

Change Size. If you like a design and it is not available in your size, you can make it a size larger or smaller. Begin by studying the information at the beginning of the directions. For instance, you see this type of copy:

"**Sizes:** Directions for size 8. Changes for size 10, 12, and 14 are in parentheses."

Then you find these directions for knitting the back.

"Begin at lower edge, cast on 95 (99, 103, 107) sts."

Notice that there is an increase of 4 stitches between the sizing. So if you wanted to make a size 16, casting on 4 more stitches than size 14 requires should make this possible. Of course, if you make such an adjustment, you must remember to adjust the remaining directions accordingly.

Some persons find it helpful to make a simple drawing or diagram of each piece before starting to knit. On the diagram indicate specific directions such as the number of stitches to cast on, depth of ribbing, distance to knit before decreasing to shape armhole, the amount of decrease, width of shoulders, depth of armhole, shoulder shaping, and neckline. This visual aid is easy to follow.

Analyze the Yarn

Another factor that influences the fit of the knitted garment is the stretch of the yarn and the way it performs when worked into a garment. Just as knitted fabrics stretch more than woven ones, so do yarn and stitch patterns. You can analyze this property by checking the give in the gauge swatch you make. Too much or too little stretch will cause fitting problems.

CONSIDER CONSTRUCTION DETAILS

The placement of certain construction details, such as a buttonhole or a hem, influence not only the look of the garment but also the fit. Because of this, careful attention should be given the directions you are using. Be sure that the location of the detail is placed correctly before you begin to knit. Unless it is, the finished product will be a disappointment.

Think About Buttonholes

Buttons and buttonholes form the usual closing for knitted garments. It is best to plan the placement of the buttonholes before beginning your project in order that the spacing will be correct. Decide where the garment should fasten at the neckline, the fullest part of the bust, and at a point just above the border or hem. The other buttonholes should be evenly spaced between these points.

The placement of the buttonholes should be considered in connection with the buttons. A round buttonhole is aligned with the button exactly, whereas the upper edge of a vertical buttonhole falls one row above it. The end of a horizontal buttonhole, closest to the edge, should extend one stitch beyond it.

Although the directions you are following will indicate the buttonhole to use, there may be times when you would like to make a change. This can be done in various ways. However, the method you select should depend on the project and the look desired.

Buttonholes fall into three basic styles: the round or eyelet, the vertical, and the horizontal. The round one seems right for baby garments and fashions when a tiny button is needed. The vertical one creates an inconspicuous finish when used in a border of ribbing or garter stitches. The horizontal is most frequently employed on a cardigan, jacket, and coat.

Round Buttonhole. Work to the point where the buttonhole is to be made on a right-side row. Bring the yarn over the right-hand needle. Knit the next two stitches together. On the next row, work all stitches including the yarn-over in the pattern stitch you are using. If you wish, you can reinforce the edges with overcasting stitches.

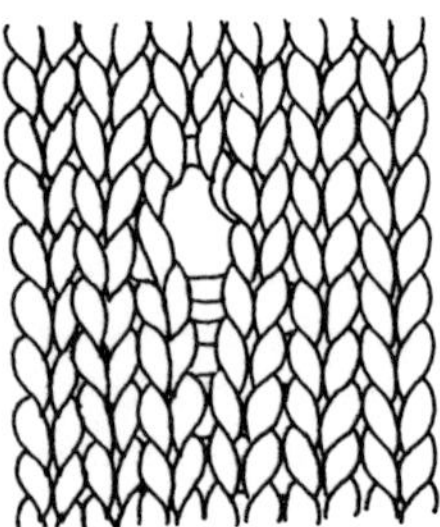

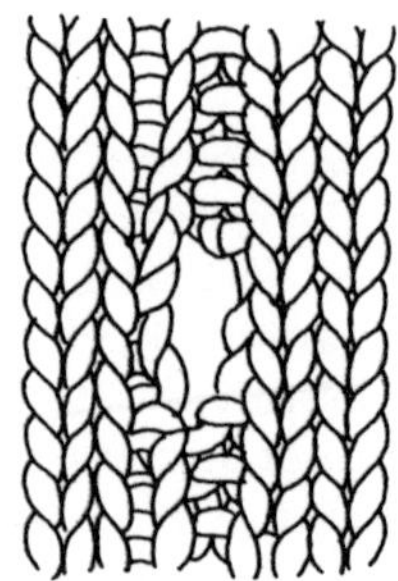

Vertical Buttonhole. Knit to the row where the buttonhole is to begin. Divide the number of stitches used for the band in half. Starting at the front edge, work the first half of the stitches.

At the base of the buttonhole, attach a second ball of yarn. Continue to knit all of the remaining stitches on the row.

For the next row, work to the opening. Lay aside the second ball of yarn. Pick up a strand from the original ball and complete knitting the row.

For the following row, turn and continue to knit to opening. Drop the original yarn and pick up the second ball in order to complete the row.

Continue working in this manner until the buttonhole is the desired size. By working in this manner both sides of the buttonhole are made as you knit a row.

On the joining row, work with the second ball to the opening and then continue to knit the stitches usually made with the original yarn. This closes the upper end of the buttonhole. Cut off the original ball of yarn, leaving an end to be worked into the stitches. After completing the row, continue to work as before starting the buttonhole.

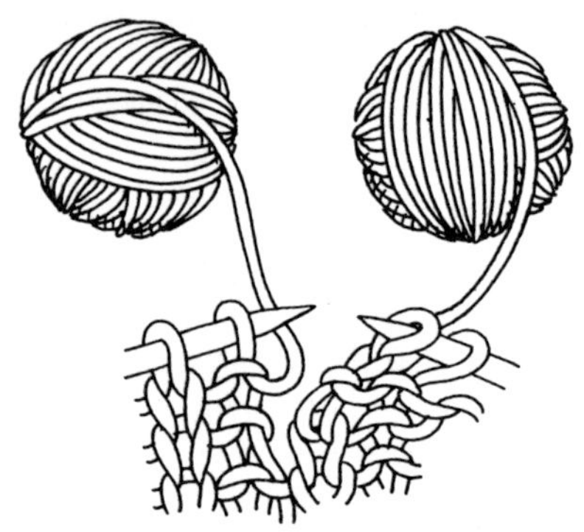

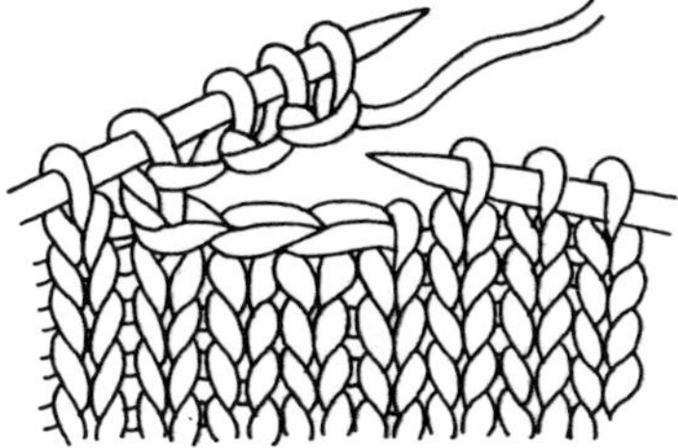

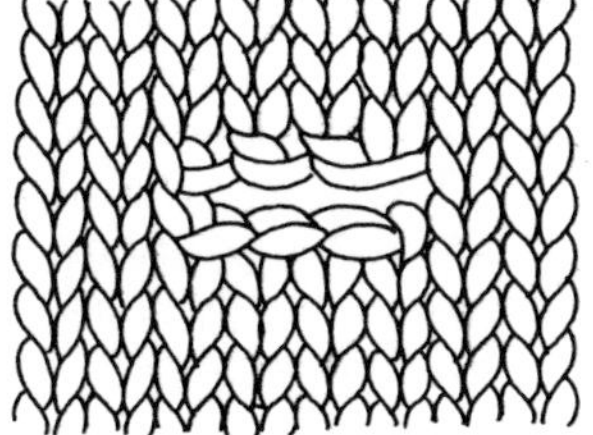

Horizontal Buttonhole. Knit to the point where the buttonhole begins. Bind off the required number of stitches, depending on the diameter of the button. This is done on a right-side row.

On the return or wrong-side row, knit to the stitch before bound-off stitches. Knit into the front and back of this stitch, increasing the number. Turn the knitting so you cast on stitches using method 1. Cast on one stitch less than you bound off. Turn the knitting to the wrong side and continue knitting. Working the buttonhole in this manner prevents an unattractive loop at the end of the buttonhole.

This type of buttonhole can be given a finishing touch. It strengthens the edge, keeping it in shape. Using a split strand of matching yarn, blanket-stitch around the opening. Keep the stitches evenly spaced with one stitch at each end of the buttonhole. Be sure the same number of stitches are made on each side. Finish by running the yarn through some stitches in the back.

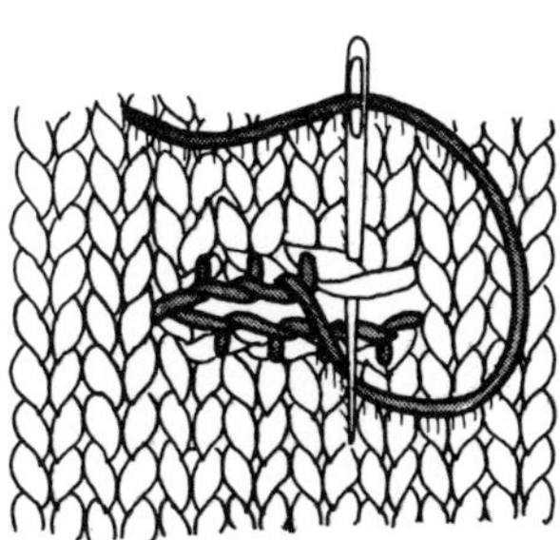

Turning a Hem

Sometimes a sweater or skirt is finished at the lower edge with a hem. This requires some preplanning in order for the fold line to allow for the correct length. This is especially so if the fold line is marked by a turning ridge.

The turning ridge produces a flat edge, which makes a more professional finish. Compare the needed measurements for length and those of the article you are making. It is so frustrating to find your garment is the wrong length when it is completed. Usually the width of the hem is about ½ to 1 inch (1.3 cm–2.5 cm) for an adult.

One important thing to remember is to use needles one or two sizes smaller than used for the garment when knitting the hem. This technique holds in the lower edge so it does not have a flared look.

Knit a Ridge. The ridge can be made in different ways. A purled ridge works nicely for a tailored garment made in a stockinette stitch, whereas a slip-stitch ridge seems more appropriate when using a bulky yarn or a textured-stitch pattern.

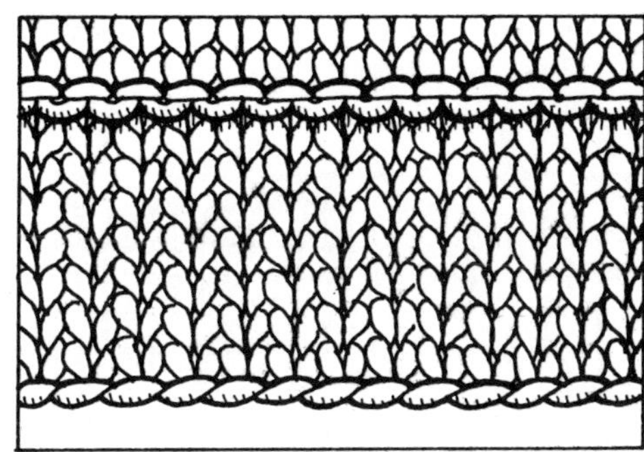

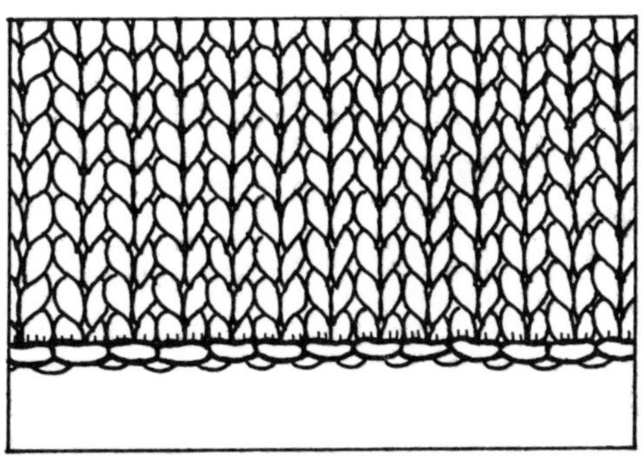

For a more decorative fold line, you can use a picot ridge, which creates a tiny scalloped edge. It makes an attractive finish for children's clothing and dressy items. Because of its supple nature, it can be used successfully for curved edges such as a collar.

To make a purl ridge, cast on the required number of stitches using smaller needles. Work in the stockinette stitch until the hem is the desired depth, ending with a wrong-side row. Turn the work, purling the next row on the right side. This forms the ridge. After completing the ridge row, change to the larger regular needles and continue to knit according to directions.

For a slip-stitch ridge, cast on the required number of stitches, using smaller needles. Work in the stockinette stitch until the hem is the desired depth, ending with a wrong-side row. Turn the work. On this row, repeat this procedure to the end of the right-side row. * Knit 1. With yarn forward, slip a stitch. Then with yarn in back, knit 1. * At the end of the row, change to the larger regular needle and continue knitting according to directions. The ridge marking is not as prominent as the one for the purl ridge.

For a decorative ridge, follow these directions. Tiny eyelets are made which, when folded, produce a dainty scalloped effect. It is sometimes known as a Picot or Cat's Tooth ridge.

Cast on an odd number of stitches using smaller needles. Work in the stockinette stitch until the hem is the desired depth. End with a wrong-side row. Turn the work. On the right-side row, repeat this procedure across the row. * Knit 2 stitches together with yarn over. * Then end with 1 knit stitch. Change to the larger regular needles and continue to knit according to directions.

To turn up the hem, fold along the middle of the eyelets. This produces the tiny scallops.

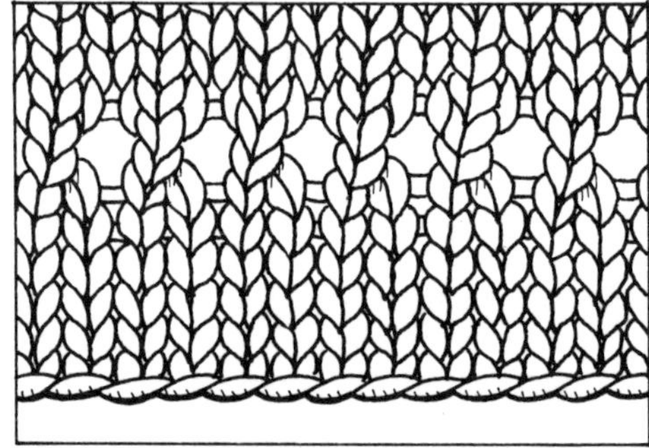

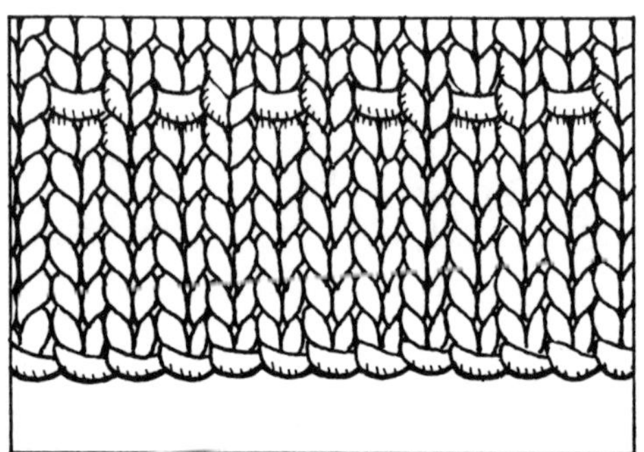

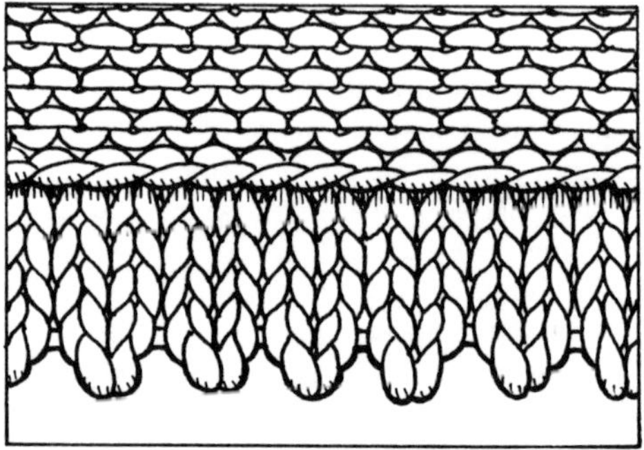

Sewing a Hem

A hem in knitting can be handled very much as it is in sewing. It can be sewn in place after the edge has been bound off. The stitches should be inconspicuous, so use matching yarn. If the yarn is too heavy, separate it using one or two plies. Also, do not pull the stitches too tight. You do not want the line to look puckered. Several different sewing stitches can be used. The one you choose depends on the knitting.

For medium- or lightweight knitting, a whip stitch can be used. Keeping the needle at a right angle to the hem edge, insert needle through the back of a garment stitch and a corresponding one in the hem. Pull yarn through. Proceed to the left and repeat the procedure.

For heavy or bulky knitting, use a slip stitch to sew between the garment and hem, concealing the stitches. Fold back the hem edge ¼ to ½ inch (6–12 mm). Take one stitch in the hem, using matching yarn. Proceeding slightly to the left, take a stitch in the garment. Follow the back-and-forth motions until the hem has been sewn in. Do not pull yarn too tight. This stitch is referred to as blind hemming.

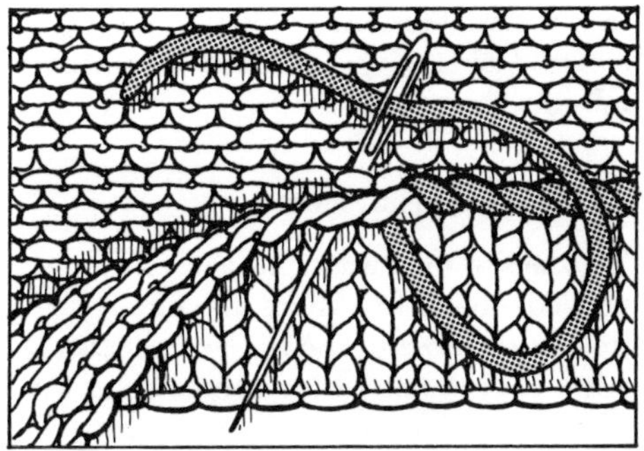

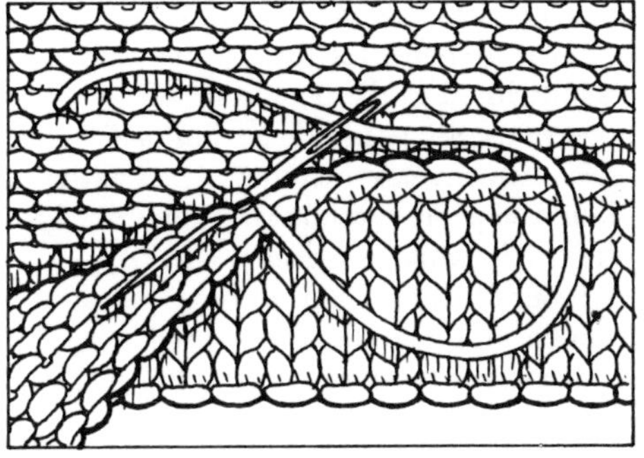

HOW TO BLOCK TO SIZE

Blocking is a procedure used to shape a piece of knitting to its correct size and shape. Just as pressing gives a professional finish to sewing, so does blocking to knitting. It changes uneven results into a smooth piece of knitting. At the same time, a nicely knitted article can appear amateurish if it is not blocked properly. In fact, the style and fit of a design can be adjusted by blocking. Good blocking helps to make a garment look smart and fit properly.

Each piece of a garment should be blocked separately before the sections are assembled. The method depends on the stitch pattern and yarn. Always read the label on the yarn for suggestions. But do remember that the yarn and stitch pattern should be tested for its reaction to the process before the actual blocking begins.

Reading Labels

Sometimes yarn manufacturers suggest the correct blocking method. Of course, if you read the words "do not block," you won't. Some types of yarn such as acrylics and some blends do not react well to blocking.

Each yarn and stitch pattern has certain characteristics that may be affected by blocking. Be sure to think about them before starting. For example, mohair yarn may lose its fluffiness if it is pressed flat. Also, mohair pieces seem to shrink in length, not in width. Because of this characteristic, it may require a little extra stretching in the length.

Some extra-heavy yarns and loosely knitted articles tend to stretch lengthwise. They measure more when held up than when lying on the blocking board. To compensate for this, block the pieces wider and shorter.

Some stitches that require an opening up of the design for the correct effect should be blocked 1 or 2 inches (2.5–5 cm) wider. This allows for the correct return. Cable, lacy, and rib stitch patterns fall into this group.

Checking Measurements

Two sets of measurements are needed—those for whom the item is being made and those of the finished article. Also study the picture accompanying the directions. Note where the seam lines fall and the fashion details that influence the fit, such as blousing.

Measurements for the garment are usually listed at the beginning of the directions. Sometimes blocking or finished measurements are included. In case they do not appear, compile your own list. Use the stitch gauge as a guide. List the number of stitches and in turn the number of inches for the needed measurements—lower edges, hip, waist, bust, shoulder, and underarm.

Compare these measurements with your own. For example, if you have knitted 84 rows before starting to shape the armhole, and if the gauge is 6 rows to the inch, then you know that the side seam should measure 16 inches (40.5 cm) when blocked. And if 30 stitches are cast off for the shoulder and the stitch gauge is 6 stitches to the inch (2.5 cm), then you know that the shoulder should be blocked to 5 inches (12.5 cm). After assembling this information, you can decide whether any adjustments are necessary.

Because damp yarn can be shaped, it is possible to make a slight adjustment in size. The actual amount will depend on the fiber content of the yarn and how tightly it is spun. You will find natural-fiber yarn easier to block than most synthetics. Also the type of stitch pattern influences the amount of adjustment that can be made. Open designs stretch more than closed ones do. Usually an adjustment is limited to making the garment one size larger. It is difficult to decrease the size.

Preparing the Knitted Piece

Dangling ends should be concealed. Weave each one into the edge for about 2 inches (5 cm). If you are using a bulky yarn, it may seem better to split it and run each end separately through the stitches. Use a blunt-pointed needle.

In case the knitting has become soiled, wash the piece according to the directions on the label. Handle carefully, squeezing out the water. Place flat on a Turkish towel. Smooth out, arranging each piece so it measures no more than the finished measurements suggest. Some knitting stretches excessively when wet. If this happens, keep the outline of the piece in position, but push the stitches together, creating a puckered look. The unevenness will disappear as the piece dries. The piece can be dried and then blocked or it can be blocked and allowed to dry. Sometimes this method works better for some synthetic yarns and highly textured pattern stitches.

Assembling the Equipment

The most important piece of equipment is a flat, padded surface. It should be large enough to allow the piece to be spread out completely. If you do a great deal of knitting, you may want to make a special board. Otherwise, a dressmaker's cutting board or a carpeted floor will prove adequate. Of course, you should protect the surface with a layer of plastic.

Whichever surface you choose, cover it with a piece of mattress covering or rug padding. Over this place a piece of muslin or sheet. For best results, the layers should be held tautly in place.

You will also need rust-proof pins, tape measure, firmly woven cheesecloth for pressing, and a steam iron.

Pinning the Piece

With the list of required measurements before you, begin to pin the smoothed-out piece to the board. Work with the wrong side up. Be sure to keep the stitches and rows straight as you would the grain of fabric when sewing. When the edges seem to be in the proper position, start to pin.

V-Neck Pullover
Page 228

Pullover with Two Necklines,
Crew or Turtle
Page 227

Poncho Shawl
Page 229

COURTESY OF COATS & CLARK, INC.

COURTESY OF COLUMBIA-MINERVA CORPORATION

Five-Color Gloves
Page 230

Tube Socks
Page 231

COURTESY OF C. J. BATES & SON

Afghan and Pillow
Page 232

COURTESY OF SUSAN BATES

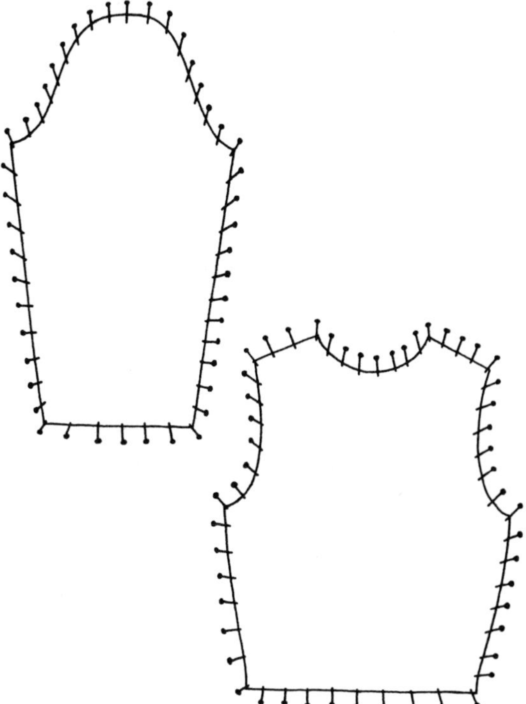

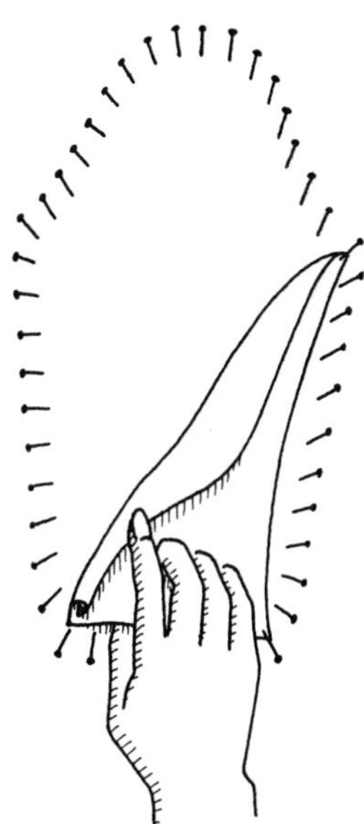

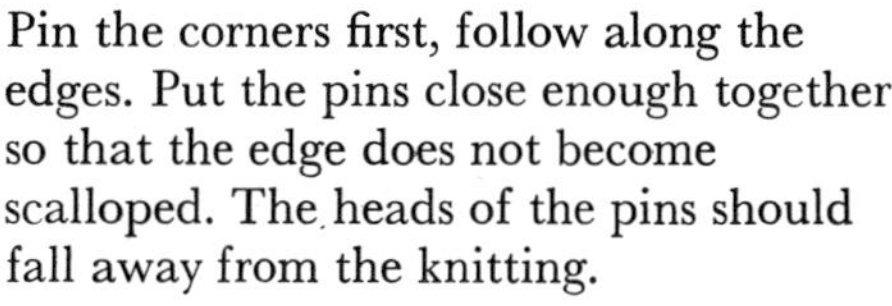

Pin the corners first, follow along the edges. Put the pins close enough together so that the edge does not become scalloped. The heads of the pins should fall away from the knitting.

Pressing

There are two ways that this can be done. One method places the iron on the knitting and is called flat press. The other does not allow the iron to touch the work and is called steam pressing. The method you use will depend on the yarn, the stitch pattern, and the look desired. For example, if you want to preserve a fluffy look, you should not press the knitting flat, just as you would not want to flatten the effect of a beautiful cable by pressing.

For flat pressing, place the press cloth on top of the pinned piece. Lower the steam iron so it comes in contact with the cloth. Use an up-and-down motion. Never push the iron back and forth in an ironing stroke. When the entire piece has been pressed, leave it until it is completely dry. Then remove the pins.

In case there is another piece to be blocked to the identical measurements, replace pins in original position. They will act as a guide so the duplicate piece will be the same size and shape.

For steam pressing, hold the iron as close to the knitting as possible without touching it. Move the iron slowly. You want the steam to penetrate the material. If the yarn is very heavy, you can use a damp press cloth to produce extra steam. Continue to press until the knit is uniformly damp. When the piece is thoroughly dry, remove the pins. It may need to be pressed very lightly.

Blocking Wet

This method can be used if the work needs to be washed or the pieces seem to be out of alignment. Wash the knitting, handling gently. Squeeze and roll in a Turkish towel. Place the piece on the blocking board. Pin in position. Allow it to dry thoroughly.

JOINING THE SECTIONS

After the pieces have been blocked, they are ready to be joined. There are several ways to do this. The two that seem best for joining pieces made with stockinette stitches are mentioned here. In order not to destroy the beauty of the knitting, the seam should be as invisible as possible. Also the correct width of the seam must be maintained so that the sizing remains correct.

Seaming the Edges

Place the two right sides of the pieces together. Thread a blunt needle with matching yarn. If the yarn is heavy, it may be best to split it. Working as you would in sewing, fasten the end without a knot at the edge.

Bring the needle up two stitches from the edge. Then carry the needle backward, inserting it at the edge. For the next stitch, move the needle forward four stitches. This time insert the needle close to the first stitch. Repeat this forward-and-backward process until the seam is completed.

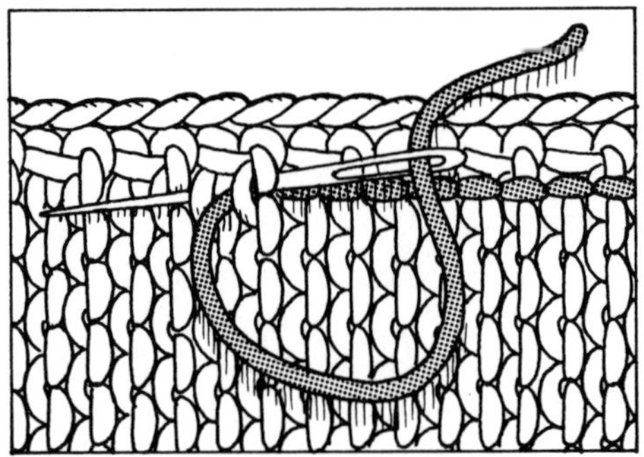

Be careful not to pull the stitches tight. Stretching out the seam after each stitch will help avoid this condition. Although the stitches should be placed close to the edge, you want to be sure that if there are decrease marks, they do not show on the right side. Fasten by taking a backstitch and running the thread through the knitted edge for a few stitches.

When the seam is completed, steam-press for a smooth effect. To do this, place the seam on a padded surface. Put a wet press cloth over the seam. Pass a hot iron over the cloth to create steam, but be careful not to let the weight of the iron rest on the cloth.

Weaving the Edges Together

This method works nicely on straight edges, producing a flat, almost invisible seam line. The edges seem to be woven together.

Before starting, look carefully at the knitting. Notice how the stitches are joined horizontally by a strand of yarn. It is this strand of yarn that you will use in making the seam.

To begin, place the pieces with the right sides up and the stitches and rows in perfect alignment. Be sure the ends match. Start at the right-hand end by attaching the yarn. Pass the needle under the horizontal bar first in one section and then in the other. Keep stitches parallel to the edge. Continue this way, weaving back and forth from one piece to the other. Do not pull the yarn tight. After taking a few stitches, stretch the seam to be sure this will not happen. Make certain that you work in the same groove so the width of the seam allowance will remain the same. It is not necessary to press the seam flat.

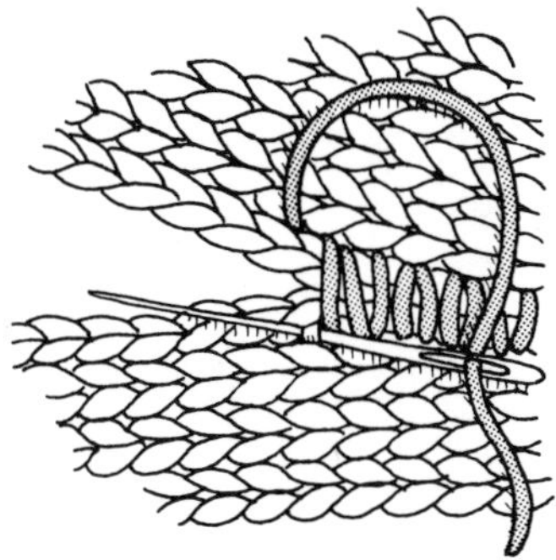

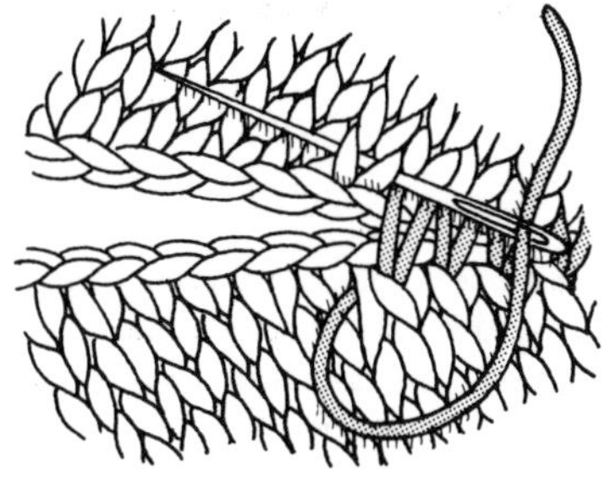

In case you would like to use this joining method for a straight slanting seam, the needle passes under the actual stitch, not the bar between the stitches. Use the stitches adjacent to the bound off edge.

For ribbing, try to blend the work so the ribbing matches exactly. Hold right sides of pieces together with stitches for each row in alignment. Fasten yarn at the right-hand end of the joining. Bring needle up through the center of two stitches and then down through the centers of the next two stitches that make up the edge. Continue in this way until the edges are joined.

Add a Decorative Touch

Sometimes an article may need a bit of decoration to make it more distinctive and interesting. Adding a binding, a bit of embroidery, a few beads can make a plain hand knit seem exciting. However, when planning these decorative details, it is most important that they seem to belong to the general design.

EDGING SMARTLY

Often the outer edge of knitting is not given too much attention. Stitches are cast on and cast off. Edges are formed in a routine manner. However, there are ways to add variety.

Finishing with Crochet

A row of single crochet creates a firm edge with a chain stitch finish. It works equally well on a straight or curved edge. *For a straight edge,* work one single crochet in each stitch or row of the knitting with two stitches taken at each corner for turning. *For a curved edge,* work a single crochet in each stitch of the knitting when working horizontally and one stitch in every other row when crocheting vertically.

Adding Binding

Finishing an edge with knitted binding is functional as well as decorative. It can be used on knitted and woven fabrics.

Before beginning, measure the edge you are binding. Decide on the width, remembering that the binding will be folded in half, also that the roll of the fold takes up part of the width. After

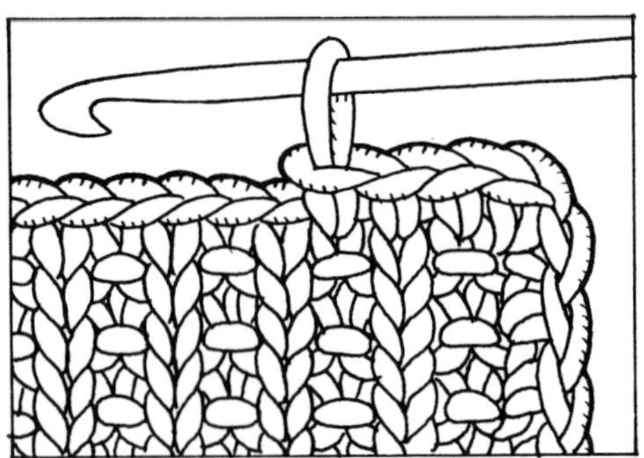

casting on an uneven number of stitches, knit the required number of rows, using a stockinette stitch, this way.

For the **first row,** which will be the right side, increase 1 stitch in the first stitch. Then knit across the row until 2 stitches remain on the needle. Knit these 2 stitches together.

For the **second row,** which will be the wrong side, purl each stitch.

Repeat the **first and second rows** as many times as required.

Other stitch patterns can be used for this type of trimming. A cable-stitch pattern is one you may want to try, using a 6-stitch cable for a binding made 10 stitches wide.

Fashion Loops

An attractive trimming can be made by using the loop stitch. One row creates a fringe effect; two or three, a looped banding. It adds a decorative touch to articles such as a jacket or a pillow. If you wish, you can repeat the rows many times to create a shaggy fabric. Coats, rugs, pillows are a few of the articles you can make with the loop stitch.

The loops can vary in length depending on the effect you wish. The number of times the yarn is wrapped around the fingers regulates the length. But whatever the length, it is important that the loops be kept even.

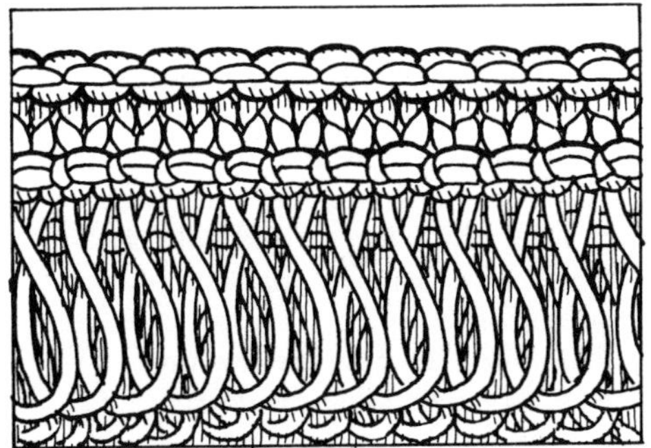

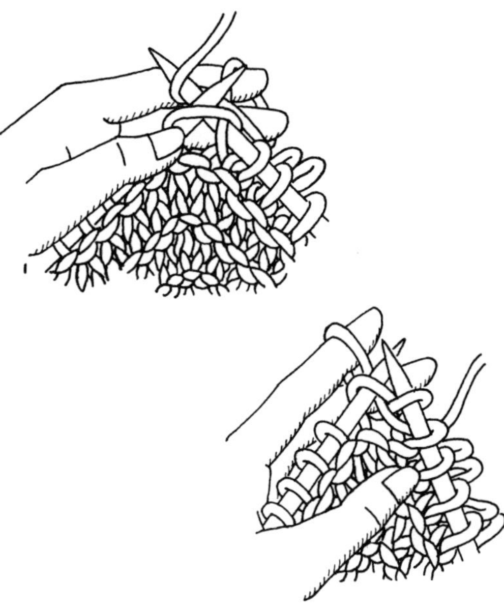

Loop Stitch

As you begin to make this stitch, you may find the procedure awkward. Wrapping the yarn around a needle and finger at the same time creates a problem. Keep trying until the loops fall in place easily.

Actually, there are several ways to knit the loop stitch. One of them is given here.

For the **beginning row,** cast on a multiple of 2 stitches plus 1.

For the **first row,** knit each stitch.

For the **second row,** knit 1. Repeat the following procedure to make each loop. * Insert the needle in the next stitch. Bring the yarn over the right-hand needle and then around a finger of the left hand before putting it over the right-hand needle again, as for knitting a stitch. Knit the stitch, drawing the two loops through the stitch. Insert the left-hand needle into the 2 loops and knit them together through the back. Tug at the loop gently so that it falls into place and the stitch is tightened. Knit 1. *

For the **third row,** knit.

For the **fourth row,** knit 2. Repeat the following procedure across the row. * Insert the needle in the next stitch and make a loop. Knit 1. *

Repeat the **first through fourth rows** as many times as required.

Try a Tassel, Fringe, Pompon

These dangling bits of decoration often add a finishing touch to a plainly knit fashion. No doubt you have seen a scarf or stole that seemed to need an edging of fringe or a pompon on a hat to give it dash.

Tassels and Fringe. On a knitted article, a series of tassels is used for a fringed effect. Each one is made separately and spaced along the edge for the desired look. The length and thickness can also vary depending on the fashion or suitability to the article you are decorating.

To make the tassel fringe, cut strands of yarn the desired length. When estimating the length, remember each strand will be folded in half and that a certain amount of length will be taken up in the knitting. It is wise to make a sample tassel before cutting all of the strands of yarn.

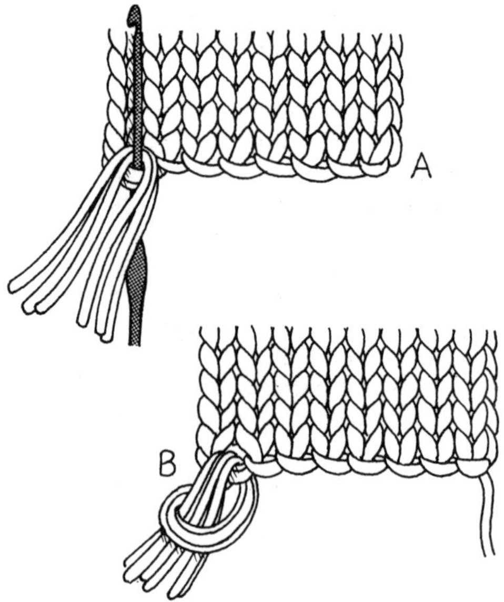

Pick up the required number of strands for a tassel. Fold in half. Insert a crochet hook in one of the knitted edge stitches (A). Draw the folded end of the strands through the stitch. Then draw the yarn ends through the loop (B). Pull ends to tighten, forming a knot. Repeat the process along the edge, using the desired spacing. If the fringe does not seem to be even in length when completed, cut the ends.

To make a tassel, cut two pieces of yarn about 7 inches (18 cm) long for tying. Using a 4-inch (10 cm) piece of cardboard, wrap yarn around it as many times as required. At one end, draw one of the short pieces of yarn under the wrapped yarn. Tie it securely, pulling the strands together. Cut the yarn at the other edge. Wrap the remaining short piece of yarn around the looped end twice and tie securely. If necessary, trim the ends evenly.

To make a pompon, follow the directions for winding the yarn as for a tassel. Remember the pompon is fuller than a tassel, so there will be many more wrappings of the yarn. Then slip a piece of yarn under the wrapped yarn and tie securely. Cut the yarn at the other end and you have a pompon. Shake it so that each strand stands up. Trim the ends for a rounded effect.

Scallop an Edge

Certain pattern stitches create a curved or pointed edge as they are being made. Some slope gently, whereas others offer a distinct shaping. They can provide a lovely finish for certain articles such as a shawl, a baby's jacket, or a skirt. Directions for making some of these stitch patterns are given here.

Lace Leaf Pattern

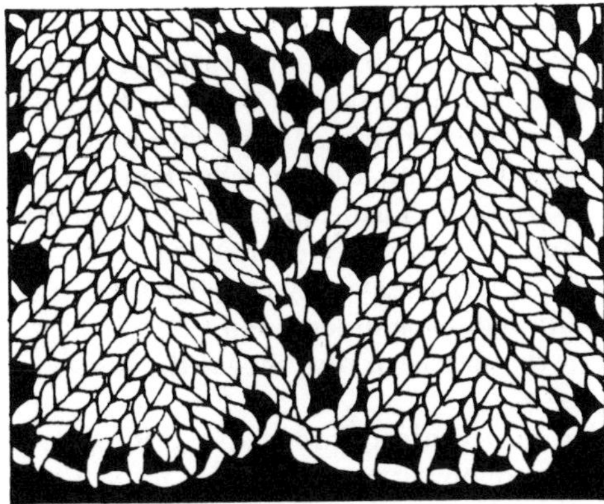

This graceful motif creates a lovely ribbed effect.

For the **beginning row,** cast on a multiple of 9 stitches plus 4.

For the **first row,** purl.

For the **second row,** knit 3. Repeat the following procedure. * Yarn over. Knit 2. Then slip 1, knit 1, and pass the slipped stitch over the knitted stitch. Knit 2 together. Knit 2. Yarn over. Knit 1. * End with knit 1.

For the **third row,** knit 2. Purl across row to the last 2 stitches. Knit these.

For the **fourth row,** knit 2. Repeat the following procedure. * Yarn over. Knit 2. Then slip 1, knit 1, and pass the slipped stitch over the knitted stitch. Knit 2 together. Knit 2. Yarn over. Knit 1. * End with knit 2.

For the **fifth row,** repeat the second row.

Repeat the **second through fifth rows** as many times as required.

Chevron Fantastic Pattern

This pattern forms vertical stripes with a rib of eyelets separating each pair of stripes.

For the **beginning row,** cast on a multiple of 8 stitches plus 10.

For the **first row,** knit 1. Then knit 1 stitch and leave it on needle. Insert the needle into the top of the stitch below the one that has just been knitted and make 1 knit stitch. Slip both stitches together from the needle. Knit 2. Repeat the following procedure. * Insert the needle into the back of the next 2 stitches and knit them together. Transfer the resulting stitch to the left-hand needle. Pass the next stitch over it and off the needle. Return the stitch to the right-hand needle. Knit 2. Knit into the top of the stitch below the next stitch. Then knit the next stitch through the back. Follow by knitting again into the top of the stitch already worked in. Knit 2. * End by inserting needle into the back of the next 2 stitches and knitting them together. Pass the next stitch over. Knit 2. Then knit into the stitch below the next stitch. Follow by knitting the next stitch in the regular manner.

For the **second row,** purl.

Repeat the **first and second rows** as many times as required.

Madeira Cascade Pattern

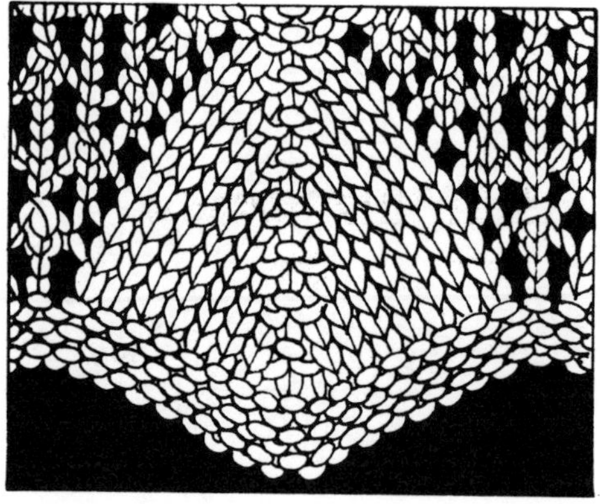

This is an old Spanish lace pattern that uses an interesting arrangement of shapes, both solid and lacy.

For the **beginning row,** cast on a multiple of 20 stitches plus 5.

For the **first row,** knit 2. Then purl across the row to the last 2 stitches. Knit 2.

For the **second row,** knit.

For the **third row,** knit 2. Repeat the following procedure. * Knit 1. Yarn over. Knit 8. Purl 3 together. Knit 8. Yarn over. * End with knit 3.

For the **fourth row,** repeat the first row.

For the **fifth row,** knit 2. Repeat the following procedure. * Knit 2. Yarn over. Knit 7. Purl 3 together. Knit 7. Yarn over. Knit 1. * End with knit 3.

For the **sixth row,** repeat the first row.

For the **seventh row,** knit 2. Knit 2 together. Repeat the following procedure. * Yarn over. Knit 1. Yarn over. Knit 6. Purl 3 together. Knit 6. Yarn over. Knit 1. * Yarn over. Knit 2 together in back of loop. End with knit 2.

For the **eighth row,** repeat the first row.

For the **ninth row,** knit 2. Repeat the following procedure. * Knit 4. Yarn over. Knit 5. Purl 3 together. Knit 5. Yarn over. Knit 3. * End with knit 3.

For the **tenth row,** repeat the first row.

For the **eleventh row,** knit 2. Repeat the following procedure. * Knit 1. Yarn over. Then slip 1, knit 2 together, and pass slip stitch over. Yarn over. Knit 1. Yarn over. Knit 4. Purl 3 together. Knit 4. Yarn over. Knit 1. Yarn over. Then slip 1, knit 2 together, and pass slip stitch over. Yarn over. * End with knit 3.

For the **twelfth row,** repeat the first row.

For the **thirteenth row,** knit 2. Repeat the following procedure. * Knit 6. Yarn over. Knit 3. Purl 3 together. Knit 3. Yarn over. Knit 5. * End with knit 3.

For the **fourteenth row,** repeat the first row.

For the **fifteenth row,** knit 2. Knit 2 together. Repeat the following procedure. * Yarn over. Knit 1. Yarn over. Then slip 1, knit 2 together, and pass slip stitch over. Yarn over. Knit 1. Yarn over. Knit 2. * End with purl 3 together. Knit 2. Yarn over. Knit 1. Yarn over. Then slip 1, knit 2 together, and pass slip stitch over. Yarn over. Knit 1. Yarn over. Knit 2 together through back of loop. Knit 2.

For the **sixteenth row,** repeat the first row.

For the **seventeenth row,** knit 2. Repeat the following procedure. * Knit 8. Yarn over. Knit 1. Purl 3 together. Knit 1. Yarn over. Knit 7. * End with knit 3.

For the **eighteenth row,** repeat the first row.

For the **nineteenth row,** knit 2. Repeat the following procedure. * Knit 1. Yarn over. Then slip 1, knit 2 together, and pass slip stitch over. Yarn over. Knit 1. Yarn over. Then slip 1, knit 2 together, and pass slip stitch over. Yarn over. Knit 1. Wrap yarn around needle. Purl 3 together. Yarn over. Knit 1. Yarn over. Then slip 1, knit 2 together, and pass slip stitch over. Yarn over. Knit 1. Yarn over. Then slip 1, knit 2 together, and pass slip stitch over. Yarn over. * Knit 3.

For the **twentieth row,** knit.

Repeat the **first through twentieth rows** as many times as required.

Pearl-barred Scallop Pattern

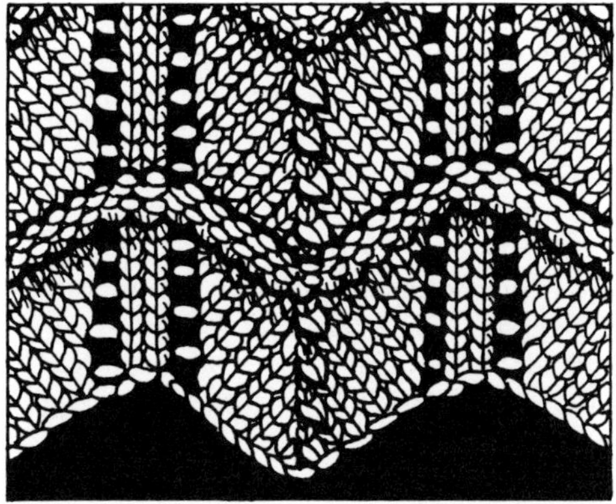

Although the stitch pattern may appear complicated, it is fairly easy to create. It was a favorite of Victorian knitting.

For the **beginning row,** cast on a multiple of 13 stitches plus 2.
For the **first row,** knit 2. Repeat the following procedure. * Yarn over. Knit 4. Then slip 1, knit 2 together, and pass slip stitch over the knit 2 together. Knit 4. Yarn over. Knit 2. *
For the **second row,** purl.
For the **third row,** repeat the first row.
For the **fourth row,** purl.
For the **fifth row,** repeat the first row.
For the **sixth row,** purl.
For the **seventh row,** repeat the first row.
For the **eighth row,** purl.
For the **ninth row,** repeat the first row.
For the **tenth row,** purl.
For the **eleventh row,** purl.
For the **twelfth row,** knit.
Repeat the **first through twelfth rows** as many times as required.

EMBELLISH WITH EMBROIDERY

It is surprising how a bit of embroidery or a few beads or sequins can change the appearance of plain knitting. An entirely new look can be created. Garter and stockinette stitches react beautifully to this simple technique.

Decorating with embroidery is a fun way to be creative. It adapts nicely to various articles and for a wide range of effects. Motifs, initials, and monograms can be worked in different embroidery stitches. Contrasting colors and yarns enhance the decorative effect. The fluffiness of mohair against a smooth background produces an interesting touch.

Before starting this embellishing, chart the design on graph paper. For ideas, you may want to check some cross-stitch designs, but remember the shape of the motif will be altered slightly. Knit stitches are not square, instead they are wider than they are high.

Working in Duplicate Stitch

As you might expect, the embroidery stitch repeats the knitted one, usually a stockinette stitch. Yarn is worked over a knitted stitch, tracing the outline. Swiss

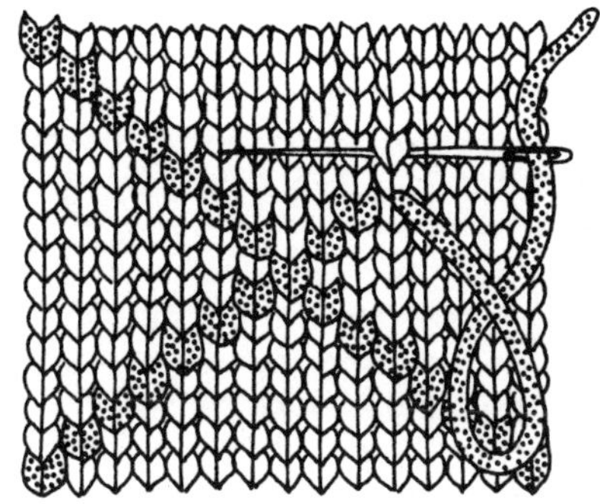

Darning is another name for the Duplicate Stitch.

Some persons find it easier to use this technique to add a colorful motif than it is to work one while knitting. The motif can be as simple or as elaborate as you wish, but it will be best to start simply.

Embroider with yarn that matches in type and thickness the one used for the article. This allows each stitch to be covered completely. Using a tapestry needle, bring it from the wrong to the right side of the knitting at the base of the stitch to be duplicated. Trace the outline of the stitch, slipping the needle under the stitch above at a point just above the

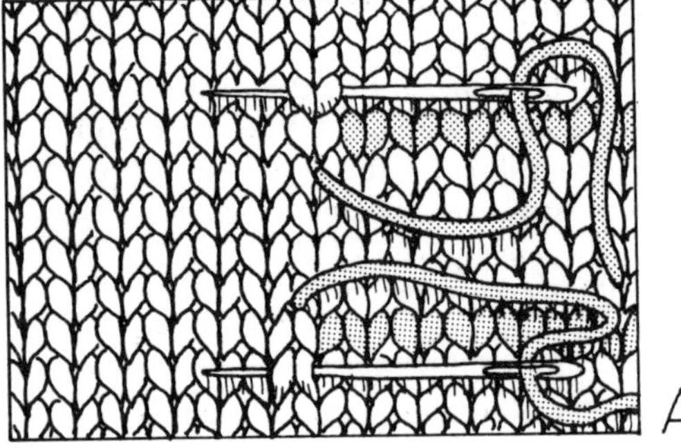

A

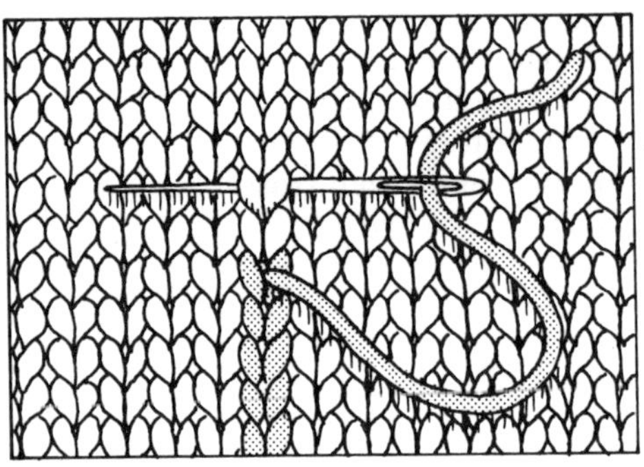

B

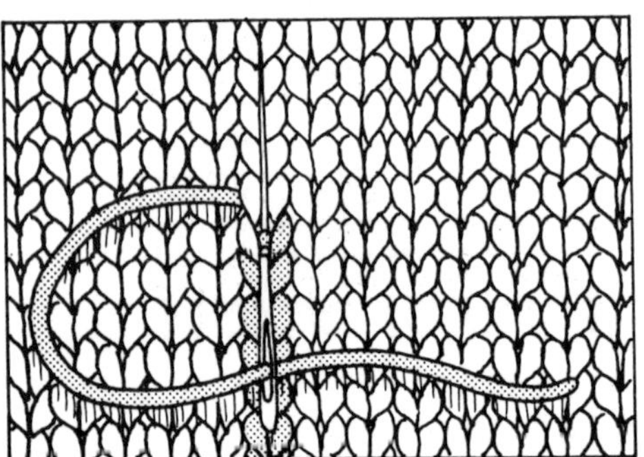

connecting strands before returning to the place where it first emerged. Insert the needle at this point, making a stitch.

Where the needle will emerge again depends on where the next stitch will be made. If working horizontally, bring it to the right side of the work in the stitch to the left (A). But if you are working vertically, let the needle emerge just above the connecting strands in the stitch above (B). For a diagonal direction, slip the needle through the base of the stitch above and to the left or right, depending on the design. As you make the stitches, be careful to keep the tension of the embroidery stitch the same as the knitted one. This eliminates any possibility of puckering.

Using Other Stitches

A knitted fabric can also be decorated by using various embroidery stitches. The cross stitch, which follows a counted-thread technique, works nicely, as does a chain stitch.

For a chain stitch, usually allow for one stitch per row. Work downward in a vertical direction. Bring the needle from back to front through center of first stitch. Hold the yarn with the left thumb so a loop can be formed as the needle is returned to the beginning point. Insert the needle and let it emerge through the center of stitch below. Draw the yarn through the loop. Repeat this process to make the second stitch. Be careful not to pull the yarn tightly. Allow for the same amount of give as in the knitting. To work horizontally, turn the piece so the chain stitch is made over stitches in the same row.

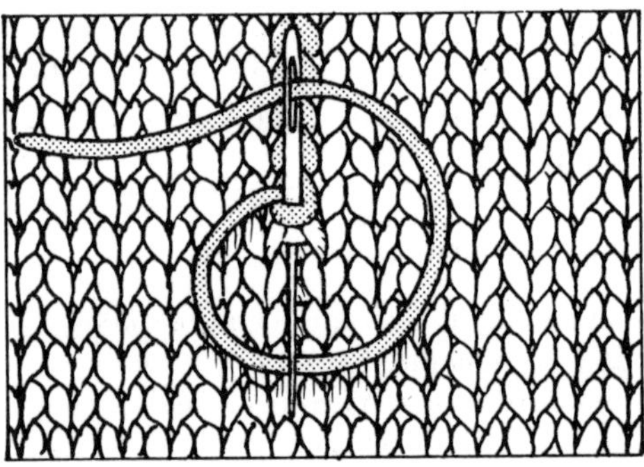

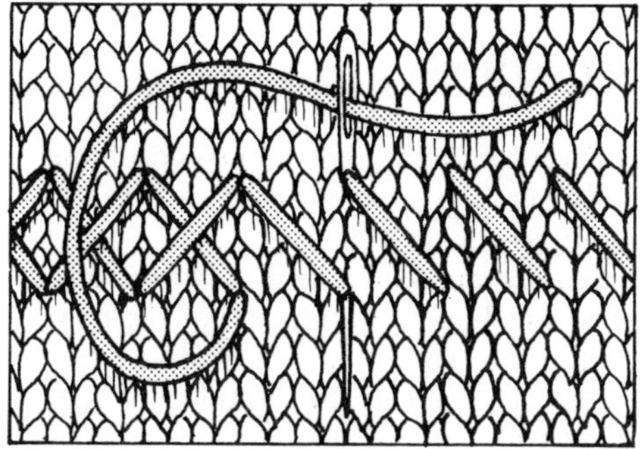

Chain stitches may be used effectively to create a check or plaid pattern, as well as for a motif. Also, this stitch can be employed as a Detached Chain or Lazy Daisy Stitch for a floral motif.

Cross Stitches (top) can also be used effectively on knitted material. The stitches can be made over various numbers of stitches and rows, depending on the look desired. Usually the stitches seem to look a bit more attractive if the stitches are taken over more rows than stitches. For instance, you might embroider in a proportion such as two stitches and three rows or three stitches and four rows.

Although each cross stitch can be made as a separate unit, it seems better to make a row of diagonal stitches slanting in one direction and then crossing each stitch in the opposite direction. By working in this manner, it is easier to control the tension of each stitch and you will be sure that all of the upper stitches cross in the same direction.

Smocking (top right) is another way to embroider knitted material. However, the fabric needs special preparation. The piece should be made twice as wide as the desired finished width. Various looks can be achieved, depending on whether you use a rib or stockinette stitch for the basic fabric.

Using a rib-patterned fabric, made by repeating this sequence of stitches: knit 1 and purl 3 for the first row, then purl 1 and knit 3 for the second row. The ribs are pulled together, forming a small diamond design. The size of the diamonds can vary.

To make the smocking stitches, work with tapestry needle and yarn in a matching or contrasting color. The stitches are constructed in a zigzag line across the material, as for Honeycomb or Seed Smocking. Use one or two small backstitches to hold two ribs together. Keep the distance between the horizontal smocking stitches evenly spaced by counting an equal number of stitches in each vertical row.

Using a stockinette stitch background, mark the material with basting stitches before starting to smock. Baste in even parallel lines, being sure to pick up the same vertical stitch on each row. Although the spacing can vary, basting 4, 5, or 6 stitches and 4, 5, or 6 rows apart can produce an attractive effect. After basting, pull the threads gathering the material to the desired width. The folds of material will then be treated as ribs and held together as in rib smocking by using a backstitch.

ADDING BEADS AND SEQUINS

For a very decorative type of knitting, you can add beads and sequins to a stitch pattern. Be sure to practice working with this type of ornamentation before beginning an actual project. It does require some skill.

Working with Beads

The beads can vary in size and shape, but they should be light in weight so that the knitting will not be dragged out of shape. In selecting the beads, be sure to choose ones with a hole large enough so the yarn can pass through it.

As for the design, you can create your own. Lining the beads in rows or scattering them in an irregular manner over the surface can prove effective. Plotting the design on a graph paper pattern will be helpful. Usually the stockinette and garter stitches provide the best background.

Begin by placing the beads on the yarn. To make it easier for the yarn to slide through the hole, try this. Cut a piece of thread about 12 inches (30.5 cm) long. Fold in half before threading the needle. Put the yarn through the thread loop. Then slip the needle through the bead, pushing it down the thread and onto the yarn (A). With beads on the ball of yarn, you are ready to start knitting.

When working in the stockinette stitch, the bead is brought into position when knitting a right-side row. With the yarn in back, push a bead close to the back of the work. Insert the right-hand needle into the back of the next stitch on the left-hand needle and knit the stitch (B). Push the bead through to the right side of the work as you bring the loop of the stitch into position (C). The bead should now lie flat against the material. Knit the next stitch in the usual manner.

Introducing Sequins

Working with sequins is very much like knitting with beads. However, it is more difficult to do and more time-consuming. But when it is done nicely, it can create a lovely effect.

Sequins are available in a variety of sizes and shapes, but remember the hole for the yarn should be at the top of the sequin. This allows the sequin to lie flat against the knitted surface.

In stringing the sequins on the yarn, place the cup part of the sequin so it faces the ball of yarn. This allows the cup to face outward on the surface of the material.

Plan the sequin design before beginning a project. Also practice until you develop a regularity in the placement of the sequin. After knitting a row with sequins, purl the next row. Then on the following right-side row, place a sequin over the stitch you knit in the back of the loop on the previous knit row, and not over the sequins. By knitting this way, the sequins are staggered, creating a prettier effect. It is best not to add a sequin to the first or last stitch on a row in order to make it easier to join the edges.

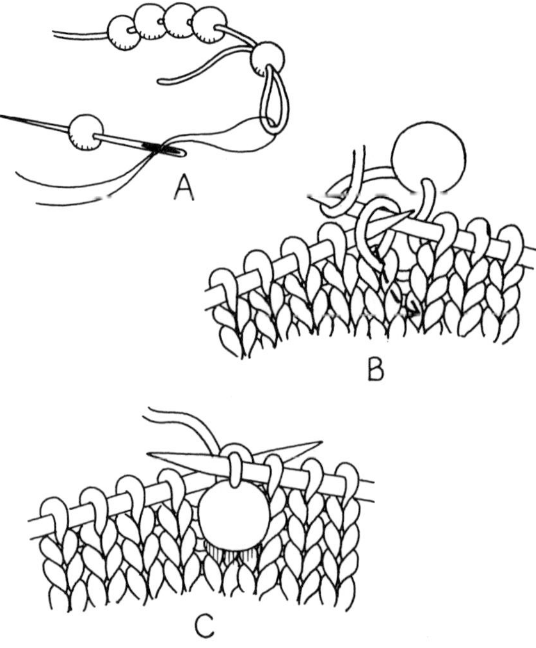

KNITTING A PLEATED EFFECT

Frequently, pleated skirts are a fashion item. At such a time, you may want to knit a pleated skirt. This can be done in different ways. You can select a stitch pattern that creates a pleated effect or you can use a sequence of stitches that allows the knitted fabric to be folded in a specific way.

Pennant Pleating and Mock Kilting are two of the stitch patterns that have a tendency to roll in such a way that a pleated effect results. It is also possible to create this type of knife pleating with ribbing.

Mock Kilting Pattern

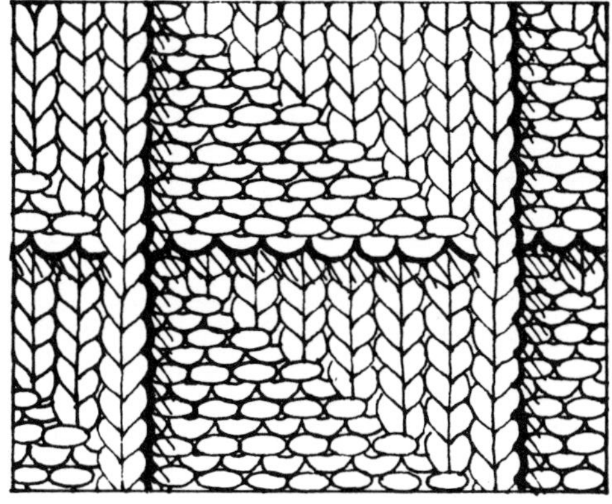

This is a Scottish pattern that uses an arrangement of triangles for an effective design. If left unpressed, it will roll up, giving a pleated effect.

For the **beginning row,** cast on a multiple of 9 stitches.

For the **first row,** repeat the following procedure. * Knit 8. Purl 1. *

For the **second row,** repeat the following procedure. * Knit 2. Purl 7. *

For the **third row,** repeat the following procedure. * Knit 6. Purl 3. *

For the **fourth row,** repeat the following procedure. * Knit 4. Purl 5. *

For the **fifth row,** repeat the following procedure. * Knit 4. Purl 5. *

For the **sixth row,** repeat the following procedure. * Knit 6. Purl 3. *

For the **seventh row,** repeat the following procedure. * Knit 2. Purl 7. *

For the **eighth row,** repeat the following procedure. * Knit 8. Purl 1. *

Repeat the **first through eighth rows** as many times as required.

Knife Pleating Rib

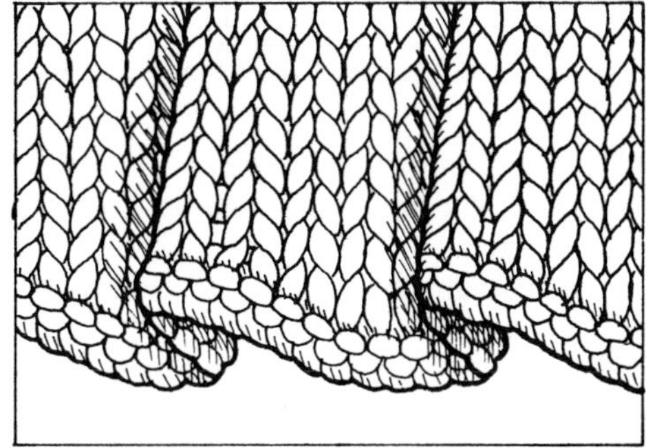

This easy-to-make arrangement of stitches produces soft folds. By placing a wider rib of knit next to a narrower rib of purl stitches, the wide rib rolls over the purled one. Because of the extra bulk that results, it is best to work in lighter-weight yarns.

For the **beginning row,** cast on a multiple of 13 stitches.

For the **first row,** repeat the following procedure. * Knit 4. Purl 1. Knit 1. Purl 1. Knit 1. Purl 1. Knit 1. Purl 3. *

For the **second row,** repeat the following procedure. * Knit 3. Purl 1. Knit 1. Purl 1. Knit 1. Purl 1. Knit 1. Purl 4. *

Repeat the **first and second rows** as many times as required.

Pennant Pleating

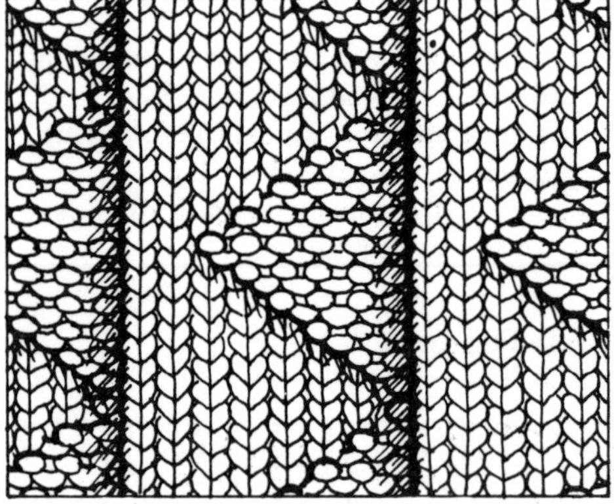

This is another of the triangular patterns that has a tendency to roll, giving a pleated effect.

For the **beginning row,** cast on a multiple of 10 stitches.

For the **first row,** repeat the following procedure. * Knit 2. Purl 2. Knit 6. *

For the **second row,** repeat the following procedure. * Purl 5. Knit 3. Purl 2. *

For the **third row,** repeat the following procedure. * Knit 2. Purl 4. Knit 4. *

For the **fourth row,** repeat the following procedure. * Purl 3. Knit 5. Purl 2. *

For the **fifth row,** repeat the following procedure. * Knit 2. Purl 6. Knit 2. *

For the **sixth row,** repeat the following procedure. * Purl 1. Knit 7. Purl 2. *

For the **seventh row,** repeat the following procedure. * Knit 2. Purl 8. *

For the **eighth row,** repeat the following procedure. * Purl 1. Knit 7. Purl 2. *

For the **ninth row,** repeat the following procedure. * Knit 2. Purl 6. Knit 2. *

For the **tenth row,** repeat the following procedure. * Purl 3. Knit 5. Purl 2. *

For the **eleventh row,** repeat the following procedure. * Knit 2. Purl 4. Knit 4. *

For the **twelfth row,** repeat the following procedure. * Purl 5. Knit 3. Purl 2. *

Repeat the **first through twelfth rows** as many times as required.

11

Knitting Projects for Everyone

Knitting is so versatile that it is possible to use it in innumerable ways. It may be employed to make articles for the baby as well as for grandfather. And of course household items should not be forgotten. A lovely afghan, a cozy pillow add a special touch. As for personal fashions, remember that knits can be worn for many occasions, no matter where you are or the time of the day. They look as right in the morning as in the evening; at school and office as at a party. A knitted fashion may be functional as well as pretty. It can prevent chilling or provide a luxurious bit to wrap around your shoulders for its decorative effect. But, however, if a knitted article is to be used, it is important that the design, the yarn, and the stitches be right for the wearer or the house in which it is to be shown. When the article achieves these characteristics, there will be a smartness about it.

On the following pages, you will find a variety of articles to knit. Some are easy to make; others, more difficult. Some can be made quickly; others take longer, although still may be classified as simple to knit. Whichever category they fall into, each one has been chosen to give you knitting pleasure.

When you decide to make one of the projects, be sure to read the preparatory information carefully, and then follow the directions exactly. The companies that devised the instructions for these items have made every effort to make them complete and accurate, but they caution that unless the directions are followed exactly, the results may not be perfect.

One aspect they emphasize especially is the importance of maintaining the stated stitch gauge. In case you knit more tightly or more loosely than was planned for the original design, there will be a deviation. Naturally, this will distort the look and the size of the finished article. Of course, this is something you want to avoid. If your gauge sample does not conform, try changing the size of the needle. Any size needle that creates the given stitch gauge can be substituted.

Sometimes it is impossible to obtain the suggested yarn. When this happens, read the labels on various yarns of the same type. When you find a label on which the gauge is the required one, the yarn will probably be one you can use.

EASY-TO-MAKE PULLOVER

This sweater couldn't be easier to make. The garter stitch is used to make the rectangles. No shaping is necessary. Although the general directions remain the same, it offers variations by changes in the weight of the yarn, the needle size, and color pattern. These characteristics make this pullover an interesting one to make.

Information to Study Before You Begin

Sizing: Instructions are written for Size 10. Changes for Sizes 12, 14, 16, and 18 are in parentheses.

• FINISHED CHEST MEASUREMENT: 34 (36, 38, 40, 42) inches.

Materials: For the *left-hand sweater,* these yarns were used: Brunswick Germantown Knitting Worsted, Group C (3.6 oz.—100 gr) pull skeins.

For the Main Color (MC), 6 (6, 7, 7, 8) skeins in Ecru.

For Stripes (CC), 1 skein of Golf Green (454); 1 skein of Primary Red (4241). If you wish, scraps of yarns can be used for the contrasting stripes.

Tools: For the left-hand sweater, use Knitting Needles, No. 8.

Gauge: 5 sts = 1 inch over garter stitch.

If you decide to knit the *right-hand sweater,* use this information.

Materials: Use Brunswick Vail or Innsbruck Homespun Bulky Yarn (3.6 oz.—100 gr) balls.

For the Main Color (MC), 7 (8, 8, 9, 9) balls in Light Grey Heather (1961).

For the Stripes, 1 ball Mediterranean Heather (1920); 1 ball Brick Heather (1974).

Tools: Knitting Needles, No. 10½.

Gauge: 3½ sts = 1 inch over garter stitch.

Directions to Follow

Front and Back. *For the left-hand sweater only,* cast on 85 (90, 95, 100, 105) stitches using Main Color.

For the right-hand sweater only, cast on 56 (59, 62, 65, 69) stitches using Main Color.

Then proceed in the same way for both sweaters. Work even in garter st for 10½ (10½, 10½, 11½, 11½) inches or 4 inches from desired length to underarm.

Stripe Pattern: * Next 6 rows: Change to CC 1 and stockinette st and work 6 rows.

Next 4 rows: Change to MC and garter st and work 4 rows.

Next 2 rows: Change to CC 2 and stockinette st and work 2 rows. *

Next row: Change to MC and garter st and work even until piece meas 22 (22, 22, 23, 23) inches from beg. Bind off.

Sleeves. *For the left-hand sweater only,* cast on 75 (78, 80, 83, 85) stitches using Main Color.

For the right-hand sweater only, cast on 49 (50, 52, 54, 55) stitches with Main Color.

Then proceed in the same way for both sweaters. Work even in garter st until piece meas 13½ (14, 14½, 15, 15½) inches or 4 inches from desired length to underarm. Work stripes as for front and back between *s. Change to MC and work even in garter st until sleeve meas 17½ (18, 18½, 19, 19½) inches or desired length to underarm. Bind off.

Finishing: Backstitch back to front at shoulders leaving 8½ (8½, 9, 9, 9) inches open at center for neck. Backstitch sleeves to armholes matching center of sleeve top to shoulder seam. Weave sleeve and side seams. Turn up bottom of sleeves for cuffs if desired.

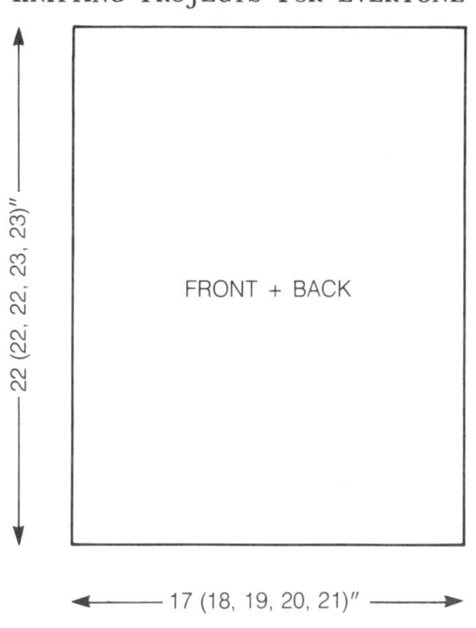
22 (22, 22, 23, 23)"
FRONT + BACK
17 (18, 19, 20, 21)"

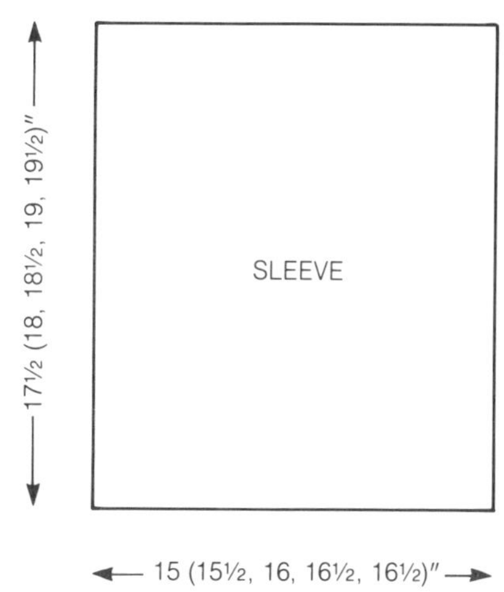
17½ (18, 18½, 19, 19½)"
SLEEVE
15 (15½, 16, 16½, 16½)"

TWIN SET

The Chanel-type styling of the cardigan and the textured look of the shell worn beneath produces an interesting fashion effect. Not only are they attractively worn together, but also separately. The cardigan makes an excellent jacket to wear over dresses.

Information to Study Before You Begin

Sizing: Directions are for Size 8. Changes for Sizes 10, 12, 14, and 16 are in parentheses.

• FINISHED MEASUREMENTS: Cardigan Bust: 34 (35, 37½, 39, 41) inches.
Width of Back at Underarm: 17 (17½, 18¾, 19½, 20½) inches.

Materials: The sweaters shown here are made of Caron Petite Dazzle-aire in 1½ oz. skeins.
7 (8, 9, 10, 11) skeins of Color A.
2 (2, 2, 3, 3) skeins of Color B.

Tools: Knitting Needles, Nos. 4, 5, and 6.

Gauge: Stockinette st made with No. 5 needles, 11 sts = 2 inches; 13 rows = 2 inches. Pattern st made with No. 6 needles, 11 sts = 2 inches; 8 rows = 1 inch.

Directions to Follow

CARDIGAN

Back: With Size 5 needles and A, cast on 93 (97, 103, 107, 113) sts.

Seed St—

Row 1: K 1, * P 1, K 1; rep from * across. Rep Row 1, 3 times more. Work in stockinette st (K 1 row, P 1 row) until 12 inches from beg or desired length to underarm, end with P row. Mark last row.

Shape Armholes: Bind off 5 sts at beg of next 2 rows. Dec 1 st each side edge every K row 5 (5, 6, 6, 7) times; 73 (77, 81, 85, 89) sts. Work even until 7 (7¼, 7½, 7¾, 8) inches above underarm marker, end with P row.

Shape Shoulders: Bind off 7 (8, 8, 9, 9) sts at beg of next 4 rows, then 8 (8, 9, 9, 10) sts at beg of next 2 rows; 29 (29, 31, 31, 33) sts. Sl sts to holder.

Left Front: With Size 5 needles and A, cast on 49 (51, 53, 55, 57) sts. Work 4 rows in seed st.

Next Row: K to within last 3 sts, work in seed st to end. Keeping 3 sts at front edge in seed st, work in stockinette st until same length as back to underarm, end with P row. Mark last row.

Shape Armhole: Bind off 5 sts at beg of next row. At armhole edge, dec 1 st every K row 5 (5, 6, 6, 7) times; 39 (41, 42, 44, 45) sts. Work even until 4¾ (5, 5¼, 5¼, 5½) inches above underarm marker, end P row.

Shape Neck and Shoulder:

Next Row: K to within last 8 sts, sl last 8 sts to holder. At neck edge, dec 1 st every row 4 times, then every other row 5 times, *at the same time,* when same length as back to shoulder, at armhole edge, bind off 7 (8, 8, 9, 9) sts twice, then 8 (8, 9, 9, 10) sts once.

Right Front: Work as for left front, reversing shapings.

Sleeves: With Size 5 needles and A, cast on 41 (41, 43, 43, 45) sts. Work 4 rows in seed st. Work in stockinette st until 2 inches from beg. Inc 1 st each side edge in next row, then every 8th row 10 (11, 12, 14, 14) times more; 63 (65, 69, 73, 75) sts. Work even until 17 inches from beg or desired length to underarm, end with P row.

Shape cap: Bind off 5 sts at beg of next 2 rows. Dec 1 st each side edge every K row 13 (14, 15, 16, 17) times, then every row 4 times. Bind off 4 (4, 4, 5, 5) sts at beg of next 2 rows; 11 (11, 13, 13, 13) sts. Bind off.

Finishing: Sew shoulder, side and sleeve seams. Sew in sleeves.

Neckband: Right side facing, with Size 5 needles and A, work in * st * seed across sts from right front holder, pick up 17 (17, 18, 18, 19) sts along side neck edge, K 29 (29, 31, 31, 33) sts from back holder, pick up 17 (17, 18,

18, 19) sts along side neck, work in seed st across sts from left front holder; 79 (79, 83, 83, 87) sts. Work 3 rows in seed st. Bind off loosely in seed st.

Pockets: With Size 5 needles and A, cast on 27 sts. Work 4 rows in seed st for top edge. Work in stockinette st until 4 inches from beg. Bind off. Position pocket 3 inches in from front edge with lower edge at top of seed st border of jacket. Sew in place with sl st so edges are blind.

SHELL

Pattern Stitch: Multiple of 4 sts plus 1.

Row 1: (wrong side) With A, P.

Row 2: With B, K 1, sl 1, * K 1, sl 3; rep from * across, end K 1, sl 1, K 1.

Row 3: With B, K 1, * P 3, sl 1; rep from * across, end P 3, K 1.

Row 4: With A, K 2, * sl 1, K 3; rep from * across, end sl 1, K 2.

Row 5: With A, P.

Row 6: With B, K 1, * sl 3, K 1; rep from * across.

Row 7: With B, K 1, P 1, * sl 1, P 3; rep from * across, end sl 1, P 1, K 1.

Row 8: K 4, * sl 1, K 3; rep from * across, end K 1.

Back: With Size 4 needles and A, cast on 83 (83, 87, 91, 95) sts. Work in K 1, P 1 ribbing until 1½ inches from beg. Change to Size 6 needles. Work Row 1 of pat st, inc 6 (10, 10, 10, 14) sts evenly spaced; 89 (93, 97, 101, 109) sts. Work in pat st until 11 inches from beg or desired length to underarm. Mark last row.

Shape Armholes: Bind off 5 sts at beg of next 2 rows. Dec 1 st each side edge every other row 3 times; 73 (77, 81, 85, 93) sts. Work even in pat until 6¾ (7, 7¼, 7½, 7¾) inches above underarm marker.

Shape Shoulders: Bind off 6 (6, 6, 7, 8) sts at beg of next 6 rows, then 5 (7, 8, 7, 7) sts at beg of next 2 rows; 27 (27, 29, 29, 31) sts. Sl sts to holder.

Front: Work same as back until 4¾ (5, 5, 5¼, 5½) inches above underarm marker; 73 (77, 81, 85, 93) sts.

Shape Neck:

Next Row: Work in pat across first 28 (30, 31, 33, 36) sts, sl next 17 (17, 19, 19, 21) sts to holder, join 2nd ball of yarn, work in pat to end. Working each side separately, at each neck edge, dec 1 st every row 3 times, then every other row twice; 23 (25, 26, 28, 31) sts each side. Work even until same length as back to shoulder.

Shape Shoulders: At each armhole edge, same as for back.

Finishing: Sew left shoulder seam.

Neck Edging: Right side facing, with Size 4 needles and A, K sts from back holder, pick up and K 19 (19, 21, 21, 23) sts along side neck edge, K 17 (17, 19, 19, 21) sts from front holder, pick up and K 19 (19, 21, 21, 23) sts along side edge.

Next Row: Bind off as to K. Sew right shoulder seam. Work armhole edging in same way, picking up 85 (87, 89, 91, 93) sts. Sew seams.

COWL-NECK PULLOVER

This classic sweater has been given dressmaker touches that add a certain softness to the design. The drape of the collar, the nipped in waistline, and ruffled effect at the wrist contribute to this feeling.

Information to Study Before You Begin

Sizing: Directions are for Size 8. Changes for Sizes 10, 12, 14, 16 are in parentheses.

• FINISHED MEASUREMENTS: Bust: 32 (34, 36, 38, 40) inches.
Width of back or front at underarm; 16½ (17, 18, 19, 20) inches.
Width of back or front at lower edge; 18¼ (18¾, 19¾, 20¾, 21¾) inches.
Width of sleeve at underarm; 11¼ (11¾, 12¼, 12¾, 13¼) inches.

Materials: This sweater is made of Columbia-Minerva Glimmerfluff in a 3 oz. ball. You need 4 (5, 6, 6, 7) balls. Or you may want to substitute other Columbia-Minerva yarns such as Nantuck 4-ply, Shannon, or Performer.

Tools: Knitting Needles, Nos. 7 and 9.

Gauge: Stockinette st using No. 9 Needle —4 sts = 1 inch; 11 rows = 2 inches.

Directions to Follow

Back: With Size 9 needles, cast on 73 (75, 79, 83, 87) sts.

Seed St—

Row 1: (wrong side) P 1, * K 1, P 1; rep from * across.

Row 2: Rep Row 1.

Row 3: P. Work in stockinette st (K 1 row, P 1 row) until 4½ inches from beg, end with K row. Change to Size 7 needles.

Ribbing—

Row 1: Rep seed st row, dec 18 (18, 18, 20, 20) sts evenly spaced; 55 (57, 61, 63, 67) sts.

Row 2: K 1, * P 1, K 1; rep from * across. Work in ribbing as established until 7½ inches from beg; end with wrong side row. Change to Size 9 needles.

Next Row: K, inc 12 (12, 12, 14, 14) sts evenly spaced; 67 (69, 73, 77, 81) sts. Work even in stockinette st until 8 inches above ribbing or desired length to underarm; end with P row. Mark last row.

Shape Armholes: Bind off 4 (4, 4, 4, 5) sts at beg of next 2 rows.

Dec Row: K 1, SKP, K to within last 3 sts, K 2 tog, K 1. Rep dec row every K row 2 (2, 3, 4, 4) times more; 53 (55, 57, 59, 61) sts. Work even until 6¼ (6½, 6¾, 7¼, 7½) inches above marker.

Shape Neck and Shoulders—

Next Row: Work across first 17 (18, 18, 19, 19) sts, sl next 19 (19, 21, 21, 23) sts to holder, join 2nd ball of yarn, work to end. Working each side separately, at each neck edge dec 1 st every row 3 times, *at the same time,* when 6¾ (7, 7¼, 7¾, 8) inches above marker, at each armhole edge, bind off 7 (8, 8, 8, 8) sts once. Work 1 row even. Bind off rem 7 (7, 7, 8, 8) sts.

Front: Work same as back until 4¼ (4½, 4¾, 4¾, 5) inches above underarm marker, end with K row.

Shape Neck and Shoulder—

Next Row: P 20 (21, 21, 22, 22) sts; sl next 13 (13, 15, 15, 17) sts to holder, join 2nd ball of yarn, P to end. Working each side separately, at each neck edge, dec 1 st every row 3 times, then every K row 3 times; 14 (15, 15, 16, 16) sts each side. Work even until 6¾ (7, 7¼, 7¾, 8) inches above marker. Shape shoulders same as for back.

Sleeves: Ruffle: With Size 9 needles, cast on 41 (43, 43, 47, 49) sts. Work 2 rows of seed st same as for back. P 1 row, K 1 row for 4 rows, dec 10 (10, 10, 12, 12) sts evenly spaced in last row; 31 (33, 33, 35, 37) sts. Change to Size 7 needles. Work ribbing same as back for 5 rows. Change to Size 9 needles. Work even in stockinette st for 8 rows. Inc 1 st at each side edge in next row, then every 8th row 6 (6, 7, 7, 7) times more; 45 (47, 49, 51, 53) sts. Work even until 16 inches from beg of ribbing or desired length to underarm, end with P row.

Shape Cap: Bind off 4 (4, 4, 4, 5) sts at beg of next 2 rows. Dec 1 st each side edge every K row 9 (10, 11, 12, 13) times, then every row 3 (3, 3, 3, 2) times. Bind off 2 sts at beg of next 2 rows. Bind off rem 9 sts.

Finishing: Sew left shoulder seam.

Cowl Neck: Right side facing, with Size 7 needles, beg at back neck, pick up 5 sts along side edge, K 19 (19, 21, 21, 23) sts from back holder, pick up 5 sts along side edge, 1 st in shoulder seam, 19 (19, 20, 21, 22) sts along front side edge, K 13 (13, 15, 15, 17) sts from holder, pick up 19 (19, 20, 21, 22) sts along side edge; 81 (81, 87, 87, 93) sts.

Ribbing—

Row 1: K 1, * P 1, K 1; rep from * across. Work in ribbing as established for 3 inches. Change to Size 9 needle. Work in ribbing until 8 inches from beg. Bind off loosely in ribbing pat. Sew right shoulder and cowl neck seam, having cowl seam invisible on turn down side. Sew side and sleeve seams. Sew in sleeves.

TURTLENECK SWEATER WITH EMBROIDERY

Color contrasts and embroidered details add interest to this classic design. The diamonds are embroidered onto the sweater in Duplicate stitch when pieces are completed.

Information to Study Before You Begin

Sizing: Directions are for Size 8. Changes for Sizes 10, 12, and 14 are in parentheses.
FINISHED MEASUREMENTS: At underarm, approximately 32½ (34½, 36½, 38½) inches.

Materials: Unger's Roly Sport yarn (1¾ oz. ball) was used for this sweater.
You need:
3 (3, 4, 4) balls of Camel (A); 4 (4, 5, 5) balls of Beige (B).

Tools: Knitting Needles, Nos. 4 and 5. Tapestry Needle.

Gauge: 6 sts = 1 inch; 8 rows = 1 inch.

Directions to Follow

Back: With smaller needles and A, cast on 99 (105, 111, 117) sts. Work in K 1, P 1 ribbing for 3 inches. Change to

larger needles and stockinette st. Work even 52 rows above ribbing. Join B. Work with both colors as follows:

Pat Row 1: K 1 A, * K 1 B, K 1 A; rep from * to end.

Row 2: P 1 A, * P 1 B, P 1 A; rep from * to end. Fasten off A. Work even with B in stockinette st until 16 inches from beg, ending with a P row.

Shape Armholes: Bind off 6 (6, 7, 7) sts beg next 2 rows. Dec 1 st each end every other row 5 (6, 6, 7) times—77 (81, 85, 89) sts. Work even until armhole meas 7 (7½, 8, 8½) inches, ending with a P row.

Shape Shoulders: Bind off 7 (7, 8, 8) sts beg next 4 (2, 6, 4) rows, then bind off 8 (8, 0, 9) sts beg next 2 (4, 0, 2) rows—33 (35, 37, 39) sts. Place rem sts on a holder.

Front: Work same as back until armhole meas 4¾ (5¼, 5¾, 6¼) inches, ending with a P row—77 (81, 85, 89) sts.

Shape Neck: K 30 (31, 32, 33) sts, sl center 17 (19, 21, 23) sts to a holder, attach a 2nd ball B, K 30 (31, 32, 33) sts. Work both sides at the same time. Dec 1 st at neck edge every row 4 times, every other row 4 times—22 (23, 24, 25) sts each side. Work even to shoulders as for back.

Shape Shoulders: At each arm edge, bind off 7 (7, 8, 8) sts every other row 2 (1, 3, 2) times, 8 (8, 0, 9) sts 1 (2, 0, 1) time.

Sleeves: With smaller needles and A, cast on 49 (53, 57, 61) sts. Work in K 1, P 1 ribbing for 3 inches, inc 8 sts evenly across last row—57 (61, 65, 69) sts. Change to larger needles and stockinette st. Inc 1 st each end of next row, then every 1½ inches for 6 (6, 7, 7) times more. *At the same time,* when 52 rows above ribbing, work pat Rows 1 and 2 as on back, then continue with B only in stockinette st—71 (75, 81, 85) sts. Work even until 17 inches from beg, or desired length to underarm, ending with a P row.

Shape Cap: Bind off 6 (6, 7, 7) sts beg next 2 rows. Dec 1 st each end every other row 16 (17, 18, 19) times. Bind off 2 sts beg next 4 rows. Bind off.

Finishing: Sew left shoulder seam.

Turtleneck: With smaller needles, B and right side facing, pick up 93 (97, 101, 105) sts around neck (this includes all sts on holders). Work in K 1, P 1 ribbing for 6 inches. Bind off in ribbing. Sew right shoulder and weave turtleneck seam. Mark center st of front, back and sleeves. Follow chart for diamonds working from center out to each side edge in duplicate st.

Note: Each duplicate st is worked over 2 rows. Sew side and sleeve seams. Sew in sleeves. *DO NOT BLOCK.* Wet block. (Wet with cold water. Lay on a towel to measurements. Dry away from heat and sun.)

COLOR KEY:

⊠ Knit A

Duplicate St A

⊡ Knit B

Duplicate St B

BOAT-NECK PULLOVER

The sleeveless sweater is an excellent design for summer wear. Making it in cotton yarn adds to its appropriateness.

COURTESY OF JOSEPH GALLER

Information to Study Before You Begin

Sizing: Small, Medium, and Large.
Materials: Joseph Galler's RBC Parisian Cotton is used for this sweater. You need:
For the Small Size, 12–13 balls.
For the Medium Size, 13–14 balls.
For the Large Size, 15–16 balls.
Tools—Knitting Needles:
For the Small Size, Nos. 4 and 6.
For the Medium Size, Nos. 5 and 8.
For the Large Size, Nos. 8 and 10.
Gauge: 6 sts = 1 inch.
Pattern Stitch—
Row 1: P 1, * K 1, yo, P 3 tog, yo, K 1, P 1, repeat from *.
Row 2: * K 1, P 1, K 3, P 1, repeat from *.
Row 3: P 1, * K 1, P 3, K 1, P 1, repeat from *.
Row 4: Same as Row 2.

Directions to Follow

Back: With 2 strands of cotton yarn and No. 4, 5, or 8 needles depending on the size you are making, cast on 84 sts.
K 1, P 1 for 2 inches. Increase 1 st on last row.
Change to No. 6, 8, or 10 needles and work pat for 12 inches or desired length to underarm.
Cast on 12 sts at beginning of next two rows.
Continue in pat for 6 inches from cast on sts.
Change to No. 4, 5, or 8 needles and work in K 1, P 1 (rib) on center 75 sts and keep pat on remaining sts for 1½ inches. Bind off all sts.

Front: Work same as for Back.

SWEATER WITH FASHION TOUCHES

Dressmaking details are featured in this sweater. Buttons and buttonholes add interest to the neckline opening. By working with two strands of yarn, a pleasing color effect can be created.

COURTESY OF BUCILLA

Information to Study Before You Begin

Sizes: Instructions are for Size 6–8; changes for Sizes 10–12 and 14–16 are in parentheses.

• FINISHED MEASUREMENTS:

Bustline, 32 (35, 38) inches.

Width of back at underarm, 16 (17½, 19) inches.

Materials: This sweater is made of Bucilla Tempo using 2 oz. skeins of Color A: 5 (6, 7) skeins; Color B: 5 (6, 7) skeins.

Tools: Knitting Needles, Size 8. Crochet Hook, Size G.

Gauge: 9 sts = 2 inches.

Note: Sweater is worked with 1 strand of A and 1 strand of B held together throughout.

Directions to Follow

Back—Cast on 65 (71, 77) sts.

Pat:

Row 1: Right side: K 1, * P 1, K 1; rep from * across.

Row 2: P. Rep these 2 rows for pat throughout.

Work until 14 inches from beg or desired length to underarm. Mark for underarms. Work until 6¾ (7¼, 7¾) inches from marker, end on wrong side.

Shape Shoulders: Bind off 18 (20, 22) sts at beg of next 2 rows. Bind off rem 29 (31, 33) sts in pat.

Front: Work as for back until 12½ inches from beg, end on wrong side.

Slit: Work across 30 (32, 34) sts and sl on holder for left side; work across rem 35 (39, 43) sts for right side.

Right side: Work for 5 rows, end at center edge.

Buttonhole: Work 2 (3, 3) sts, bind off next 3 (3, 3) sts, work to end.
Next Row: Cast on 3 sts over bound-off sts. Rep buttonhole every 8th row twice more. Work until armhole is 4½ (4¾, 5) inches from marker. End at center edge.

Shape Neck: Bind off 5 (6, 8) sts; then 3 sts every 2nd row twice. Dec 1 st at neck edge every row 6 (7, 7) times; 18 (20, 22) sts. Work until armhole is same length as back to shoulder, end at arm edge.

Shape Shoulder: Bind off all sts in pat.

Left Side: With free needle, cast on 5 (7, 9) sts; from wrong side, work across sts on holder; 35 (39, 43) sts. Work to correspond to right side, reversing shaping and omitting buttonholes.

Sleeves: Cast on 63 (67, 71) sts. Work in pat as for back. Work until 17 (17½, 17½) inches from beg or desired length to underarm. Bind off all sts in pat.

Finishing: Sew shoulder seams. Sew in sleeves between markers. Sew underarm and sleeve seams. Sew underlap and overlap in place. From right side, with 1 strand of A and 1 strand of B, beg at overlap, work 1 row of sc along slit, across neck and down other slit, working 3 sc in each corner to turn. Fasten off.

SWEATER SET

Although the classic lines of these matching sweaters are maintained, the pretty pattern stitch gives them a dressy feeling. The set will create an interesting addition to a wardrobe since you can wear them together or separately.

CARDIGAN

Information to Study Before You Begin

Sizing: Directions are for Size 6. Changes for Sizes 8, 10, 12, 14 are in parentheses.
• FINISHED MEASUREMENTS: At underarm (buttoned) approximately 34 (36, 38, 40, 42) inches.
Materials: You need 7 (7, 8, 9, 10) balls of Unger's Floretta (1¾ oz. ball). 11 bone rings or buttons.
Tools: Knitting Needles, Nos. 3 and 4. Crochet Hook, Size E.
Gauge: Pattern Stitch on Size 4 needles; 13 sts = 2 inches; 8 rows = 1 inch.
Pattern St—
Row 1: Wrong side. * K 2, P 2; rep from * , end K 2.
Row 2: * P 2, K 2; rep from *, end P 2.
Row 3: As Row 1.
Row 4: * P 2, K 1, yo, K 1; rep from *, end P 2.
Row 5: * K 2, P 3; rep from *, end K 2.
Row 6: * P 2, K 3, pull first K st over last 2 K and drop off needle; rep from *, end P 2. Rep these 6 rows for pat st.
Note: Make sure all extra sts in pat are worked off before binding off or decreasing.

COURTESY OF WILLIAM UNGER & CO., INC.

Directions to Follow

Back: With smaller needles, cast on 99 (103, 107, 111, 115) sts. Work in K 1, P 1 ribbing for 3 inches, inc evenly across last row to 106 (110, 114, 118, 122) sts. Change to larger needles and pat st. Work even until 15 inches from beg, or desired length to underarm.

Shape Armholes: Keeping continuity of pat, bind off 6 sts beg next 2 rows. Dec 1 st each end every other row 6 times—82 (86, 90, 94, 98) sts. Work even until armhole meas 7 (7½ 7¾, 8, 8¼) inches.

Shape Shoulders: Bind off 5 (9, 7, 6, 8) sts beg next 10 (6, 8, 10, 8) rows—32 (32, 34, 34, 34) sts. Place rem sts on a holder for back of neck.

Left Front: With smaller needles, cast on 53 (55, 57, 59, 61) sts. Work ribbing as for lower border of back, keeping 8 garter sts at front edge (garter st—K every row). On last row of border, K 8, work ribbing and inc 5 (7, 9, 11, 13) sts evenly spaced—58 (62, 66, 70, 74) sts. Change to larger needles and work 50 (54, 58, 62, 66) sts in pat st, place 8 garter sts on a holder (to be worked later on smaller needles). Work to underarm as for back.

Shape Armhole: At arm edge, bind off 6 sts once, dec 1 st every other row 6 times—38 (42, 46, 50, 54) sts. Work even until armhole meas 5 (5¼, 5½, 5½, 5¾) inches, ending at front edge.

Shape Neck: Work 8 (10, 12, 12, 14) sts and place on a holder, complete row. Dec 1 st at neck edge every row 2 (2, 2, 4, 4) times, then every other row 3 (3, 4, 4, 4) times—25 (27, 28, 30, 32) sts. Work even to shoulder as for back.

Shape Shoulder: At arm edge, bind off 5 (9, 7, 6, 8) sts every other row 5 (3, 4, 5, 4) times.

Right Front: Work to correspond to Left Front, reversing all shaping and working a buttonhole 1 inch from beg.

Buttonhole—

Row 1: K 3 at front edge, bind off 3, complete row.

Row 2: Cast on 3 sts above bound off sts of previous row.

Neckband: Sew shoulder seams. With smaller needles and right side facing, pick up 91 (95, 99, 103, 107) sts around neck (this includes all sts on holders). Work in K 1, P 1 ribbing for 1 inch. Bind off in ribbing.

Left Front Band: Place the 8 garter st border on smaller needles. Work in garter st to neck (this includes neckband) (stretch slightly when measuring). Bind off. Weave band to Left Front. Mark for 11 buttons evenly spaced, placing first opposite buttonhole on Right Front border and last in neckband.

Right Front Band: Work to correspond to Left Front, working in buttonholes opposite button markers.

Sleeves: With smaller needles, cast on 49 (51, 53, 53, 55) sts. Work in K 1, P 1 ribbing for 3 inches, inc evenly across last row to 74 (78, 82, 86, 90) sts. Change to larger needles and pat st. Work even until 16½ (17, 17, 17, 17) inches from beg, or desired length to underarm, ending with same pat row as at underarm of back.

Shape Cap: Bind off 6 sts beg next 2 rows. Dec 1 st each end every other row 6 times—50 (54, 58, 60, 66) sts. Work even until cap meas 5 (5½, 5¾, 6, 6¼) inches. Last row: * K 2 tog; rep from * across. Bind off.

Finishing: Sew side and sleeve seams. Sew in sleeves, easing in fullness.

Buttons: Sc over bone ring until completely covered. Fasten off, leaving a long strand. Turn outer edge to inside and weave center tog. Sew a small button in center. Sew on buttons. Crochet 1 row of sl st along each front edge, being careful not to draw in. *DO NOT BLOCK.* Wet block. (Wet with cold water. Lay on a towel to measurements. Dry away from heat and sun.)

SLEEVELESS SWEATER

Information to Study Before You Begin

Sizing: Directions are for Size 6. Changes for Sizes 8, 10, 12, 14 are in parentheses.

· FINISHED MEASUREMENTS: At underarm, approximately 33 (35, 37, 39, 41) inches.

Materials: You need 3 (4, 4, 5, 5) balls of Unger's Floretta (1¾ oz.).

Tools: Knitting Needles, Nos. 3 and 4.

Gauge: Size 4 Needles, 6 sts = 1 inch; 8 rows = 1 inch.

Panel Pattern: 22 sts.

Row 1: Wrong side. * K 2, P 2; rep from *, end K 2.

Row 2: * P 2, K 2; rep from *, end P 2.

Row 3: As Row 1.

Row 4: * P 2, K 1, yo, K 1; rep from *, end P 2.

Row 5: * K 2, P 3; rep from *, end K 2.

Row 6: * P 2, K 3, pull first K over last 2 K and drop off needle; rep from *, end P 2. Rep these 6 rows for center front panel.

Note: Whenever binding off, make sure that it is done on Rows 1, 2, or 3 of pat.

Directions to Follow

Back: With smaller needles, cast on 91 (95, 99, 103, 107) sts. Work in K 1, P 1 ribbing for 2½ inches, inc evenly across last row to 100 (106, 112, 118, 124) sts. Change to larger needles and stockinette st, starting with a P row. Work even until 14½ inches from beg, or desired length to underarm.

Shape Armholes: Bind off 6 sts beg next 2 rows. Dec 1 st each end every other row 6 (6, 7, 7, 7) times—76 (82, 86, 92, 98) sts. Work even until armhole meas 7 (7¼, 7½, 7¾, 8) inches.

Shape Shoulders: Bind off 6 (5, 9, 7, 6) sts beg next 8 (10, 6, 8, 10) rows—28 (32, 32, 36, 38) sts. Place rem sts on a holder.

Front: With smaller needles, cast on 91 (95, 99, 103, 107) sts. Work in K 1, P 1 ribbing for 2½ inches, inc evenly across last row to 100 (106, 112, 118, 124) sts. Change to larger needles and pat st.

Row 1: Wrong side. P 39 (42, 45, 48, 51) sts, work panel pat over next 22 sts, P 39 (42, 45, 48, 51) sts.

Row 2: K 39 (42, 45, 48, 51) sts, work panel pat over next 22 sts, K 39 (42, 45, 48, 51) sts. Work even as established, keeping the 39 (42, 45, 48, 51) sts on each side of center panel pat in stockinette st to meas same length as back to underarm.

Shape Armhole: Bind off and dec for armhole as for back—76 (82, 86, 92, 98) sts. Work even until armhole meas 4½ (4½, 5, 5, 5½) inches, ending with Row 2 of pat.

Shape Neck: Work 30 (31, 33, 35, 37) sts, place center 16 (20, 20, 22, 24) sts on a holder, attach another ball of yarn, work 30 (31, 33, 35, 37) sts. Work both sides at the same time. At each neck edge, dec 1 st every row 3 times, every other row 3 (3, 3, 4, 4) times—24 (25, 27, 28, 30) sts. Work to shoulder as for back.

Shape Shoulders: At each arm edge, bind off 6 (5, 9, 7, 6) sts every other row 4 (5, 3, 4, 5) times.

Neckband: Sew left shoulder seam. With smaller needles and right side facing, pick up 96 (100, 104, 108, 112) sts around neck (this includes sts on holders). Work in K 1, P 1 ribbing for 7 rows. Bind off in ribbing. Sew right shoulder and neckband seam.

Armband: With smaller needles and right side facing, pick up 92 (96, 100, 104, 108) sts around armhole. Work in K 1, P 1 ribbing for 5 rows. Bind off loosely in ribbing.

Finishing: Sew side seams. *DO NOT BLOCK.* Wet block. (Wet with cold water. Lay on a towel to measurements and dry away from heat and sun.)

FISHERFOLK CARDIGAN

The design of this sweater is based on the authentic patterning created by the fisherfolk of the Aran Isles. Classic stitches are combined in a pleasing arrangement. It is appropriate for both women and men.

Information to Study Before You Begin

Sizing: Directions are given for Misses' Size 10. Changes for Sizes 12 and 14 are in parentheses.

For Men's Sizes, directions for Sizes 38, 40, 42 are listed following the Misses' Size 14 in parentheses.

• FINISHED MEASUREMENTS: At underarm (buttoned), approximately 35½ (36½, 39, 42, 43, 45) inches.

Materials: Unger's Rygja (3.25 oz. skein) is used for this sweater. You need 8 (9, 10, 12, 13, 14) skeins. Rygja is an unscoured pure wool with properties that make it great for winter sportswear.

You also need buttons in an appropriate size and shape.

Tools: Double-pointed Needles, 6 (6, 6, 7, 7, 7).

Gauge: Pattern Stitches on Size 6 Needles. 5 sts = 1 inch.

Note: Use double strands of yarn throughout.

PATTERN STITCHES

Pattern 1—

Row 1: K 2nd st on left-hand needle, P first st on left-hand needle, slip both sts off needle (right twist made) purl into back of 2nd st on left-hand needle, K first st on left-hand needle, slip both sts off needle (left twist made); rep from * across.

Row 2: * P 1, K 2, P 1; rep from * across.

Row 3: * K 1, P 2, K 1; rep from * across.

Row 4: Rep Row 2.

Row 5: * Left twist, right twist; rep from * across.

Row 6: Rep Row 3.

Row 7: Rep Row 2.

Row 8: Rep Row 3. Rep these 8 rows for Pattern 1.

Pattern 2: 23 sts.

Row 1: P 2, K 3rd st on left-hand needle, then K the 1st and 2nd st on left-hand needle, slip all sts off needle (right cable twist), P 5, K 1, P 1, K 1, P 5, slip next st to dpn and hold in front of work, K next 2 sts, K the st from dpn (left cable twist). P 2.

Row 2: K 2, P 3, K 5, P 1, K 1, P 1, K 5, P 3, K 2.

Row 3: P 2, K 3, P 4, slip next st to dpn and hold in back of work, K 1, P the st from dpn (back cross), K 1, slip next st to dpn and hold in front of work, P next st, K the st from dpn (front cross), P 4, K 3, P 2.

Row 4: K 2, P 3, K 4, (P 1, K 1) twice, P 1, K 4, P 3, K 2.

Row 5: P 2, right cable twist, P 3, back cross, K 1, P 1, K 1, front cross, P 3, left cable twist, P 2.

Row 6: K 2, P 3, K 3, P 1, (K 1, P 1) 3 times, K 3, P 3, K 2.

Row 7: P 2, K 3, P 2, back cross, (K 1, P 1) twice, K 1, front cross, P 2, K 3, P 2.

Row 8: K 2, P 3, K 2, (P 1, K 1) 4 times, P 1, K 2, P 3, K 2.

Row 9: P 2, right cable twist, P 1, back cross, (K 1, P 1) 3 times, K 1, front cross, P 1, left cable twist, P 2.

Row 10: K 2, P 3, (K 1, P 1) 6 times, K 1, P 3, K 2.

Row 11: P 2, K 3, back cross, (K 1, P 1) 4 times, K 1, front cross, K 3, P 2.

Row 12: K 2, P 4, (K 1, P 1) 6 times, P 3, K 2.

Row 13: P 2, right cable twist, front cross, (P 1, K 1) 4 times, P 1, back cross, left cable twist, P 2.

Row 14: K 2, P 3, (K 1, P 1) 6 times, K 1, P 3, K 2.

Row 15: P 2, K 3, P 1, front cross (P 1, K 1) 3 times, P 1, back cross, P 1, K 3, P 2.

Row 16: K 2, P 3, K 2, (P 1, K 1) 4 times, P 1, K 2, P 3, K 2.

Row 17: P 2, right cable twist, P 2, front cross, (P 1, K 1) twice, P 1, back cross, P 2, left cable twist, P 2.

Row 18: K 2, P 3, K 3, (P 1, K 1) 3 times, P 1, K 3, P 3, K 2.
Row 19: P 2, K 3, P 3, front cross, P 1, K 1, P 1, back cross, P 3, K 3, P 2.
Row 20: K 2, P 3, K 4 (P 1, K 1) twice, P 1, K 4, P 3, K 2.
Row 21: P 2, right cable twist, P 4, front cross, P 1, back cross, P 4, left cable twist, P 2.
Row 22: K 2, P 3, K 5, P 1, K 1, P 1, K 5, P 3, K 2.
Row 23: P 2, K 3, P 5, slip next 2 sts to dpn and hold in front of work, K 1, K the first and P the 2nd st from dpn, P 5, K 3, P 2.
Row 24: K 2, P 3, K 6, P 2, K 5, P 3, K 2.
Row 25: P 2, right cable twist, P 5, K 1, front cross, P 5, left cable twist, P 2.
Row 26: K 2, P 3, K 5, P 1, K 1, P 1, K 5, P 3, K 2. Rep Rows 3 through 26 for Pat 2.

COURTESY OF WILLIAM UNGER & CO., INC.

Directions to Follow

Back: With double strand and No. 4 needles, cast on 86 (90, 98, 102, 106, 110) sts. Work in K 1, P 1 ribbing for 3 inches. Next row: wrong side. Purl across. Change to No. 6 needles and establish pat as follows:

Row 1: 12 (12, 16, 16, 20, 20) sts Pat 1; 23 sts Pat 2; 16 (20, 20, 24, 20, 24) sts Pat 1; 23 sts Pat 2 and 12 (12, 16, 16, 20, 20) sts Pat 1. Work even in pat as established until 14½ (14½, 15, 15½, 16, 16) inches from beg or desired length to underarm.

Shape Armholes: Bind off 5 (5, 6, 6, 6, 6) sts at beg of next 2 rows. Dec 1 st each end of every other row 3 times, 70 (74, 80, 84, 88, 92) sts. Work even until armholes are 7½, (7¾, 8, 8¾, 9, 9½) inches.

Shape Shoulders: Bind off 7 (7, 8, 8, 9, 9) sts at beg of next 4 rows; then 8 (9, 9, 10, 9, 10) sts at beg of next 2 rows, 26 (28, 30, 32, 34, 36) sts. Bind off remaining sts loosely.

Note: Buttonholes are worked on the right front for a woman and the left front for a man. Work the *button side* of the front first so that when completed you mark off for 6 (6, 6, 7, 7, 7) buttons evenly spaced, placing first ½ inch from lower edge and last ½ inch below start of neck shaping.

Buttonhole: Work 3 sts at front edge, bind off next 2 sts and complete the row.

Next row: Cast on 2 sts above those bound off on previous row.

Front: With double strand and No. 4 needles, cast on 51 (51, 55, 59, 63, 67) sts. Work ribbing border as back. Next row: Rib first 8 sts as established (front border), P across the rem sts. Change to No. 6 needles and establish pat as follows:

Row 1: On right side of work, starting at seam edge, 12 (12, 16, 16, 20, 20) sts Pat 1; 23 sts Pat 2; 8 (8, 8, 12, 12, 16) sts Pat 1; work the last 8 sts in ribbing as established. Work to underarm as for Back.

Shape Armhole and Neck: At arm edge, bind off 5 (5, 6, 6, 6, 6) sts, work in pat as established to within 10 sts from front edge, K 2 tog (neck dec), work 8 sts in ribbing as established. Dec 1 st at armhole edge every other row 3 times, *at the same time,* work neck dec as explained above every other row 12 (11, 12, 15, 18, 21) times more, 30 (31, 33, 34, 35, 36) sts. Work even to shoulder shaping as for Back.

Shape Shoulder: At arm edge, bind off 7 (7, 8, 8, 9, 9) sts every other row twice, 8 (9, 9, 10, 9, 10) sts once, 8 sts. Work even on remaining 8 sts in ribbing as established to meas to center back of neck. Bind off. Work other front to correspond, reversing shapings and working in the buttonholes opposite markers for buttons.

Sleeves: With double strand and No. 4 needles, cast on 47 (47, 55, 55, 55, 63) sts. Work in K 1, P 1 ribbing for 3 inches. P 1 row. Change to No. 6 needles and establish patterns as follows: 12 (12, 16, 16, 16, 20) sts Pat 1; 23 sts Pat 2; 12 (12, 16, 16, 16, 20) sts Pat 1. Work in pat as established increasing 1 st each end every 1¼ (1¼, 1½, 1¼, 1¼, 1½) inches 10 (11, 8, 10, 11, 8) times 67 (69, 71, 75, 77, 79) sts, working all increased sts in Pat 1. Work even until 16½ (17, 17, 19, 20, 20) inches from beg or desired length to underarm.

Shape Cap: Bind off 5 sts at beg of next 2 rows. Dec 1 st each end every other row until cap is 4 (4¼, 4½, 5, 5½, 6) inches. Bind off 2 sts at beg of next 6 rows. Bind off.

Finishing: Sew shoulder, side, and sleeve seams. Sew in sleeves. Sew short ends of back neckband tog and sew to back of neck. Buttonhole st around buttonholes with single strand. Sew on buttons. Block lightly.

JACKET SWEATER

For that extra jacket, this is a great design. Using a textured yarn gives it a fabric look.

Information to Study Before You Begin

Sizing: Directions are for Size 10. Changes for Sizes 12, 14, 16 are in parentheses. The bust measurement is 32½ (34, 36, 38).

Materials: Phildar yarns in Maritza and Pronostic were used for this jacket. You need:

17 (18, 19, 20) balls of Maritza in gray; 1 ball of Pronostic in blue for all sizes.

Shoulder Pads.

Tools: Knitting Needles, Nos. 3 and 9.

Gauge (Rev stockinette st in Maritza with No. 9 needles) : 12 sts = 4 inches; 18 rows = 4 inches.

Note: When garter st is needed: K every row.

When rev stockinette st is needed: P across Row 1, K across Row 2.

The P side is the right side of the work.

COURTESY OF PHILDAR

Directions to Follow

Sleeves: With larger needles cast on 36 (38, 40, 42) sts and work 4 rows in garter st, and then continue in rev stockinette st until work meas 1¼ inches (3 cm) from beg. Dec 1 st at beg and end of next row. 34 (36, 38, 40) sts remain.

Inc then 1 st at beg and end of * every 8th row once and of every foll 10th row once *, rep from * to * 4 times in all. There are 50 (52, 54, 56) sts on needle. Continue even until work meas 19 inches (48 cm) from beg. Shape Cap: Bind off 3 sts at beg of next 2 rows. Work 1 row even. Then dec 2 sts at beg and end of EVERY ROW 6 (7, 7, 7) times in all. 20 (18, 20, 22) sts remain. Then bind off 1 st at beg of next 8 (6, 8, 10) rows. 12 sts remain.

Continue even on these sts for 2¾ inches (7 cm).

Dec 1 st at beg and end of next row and on the row on foll 2¾ inches (7 cm). When tab measures 6¾ inches (17 cm) from beg, bind off at right edge ONLY on every other row: 3 sts once, then 2 sts twice and then 1 st once.

Work a second sleeve to correspond, reversing shapings.

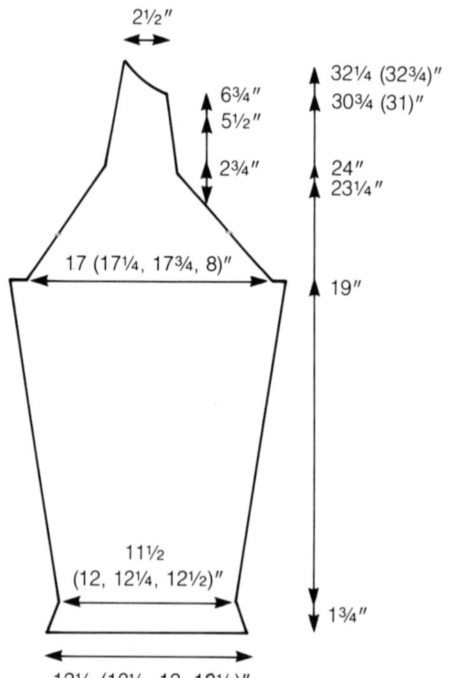

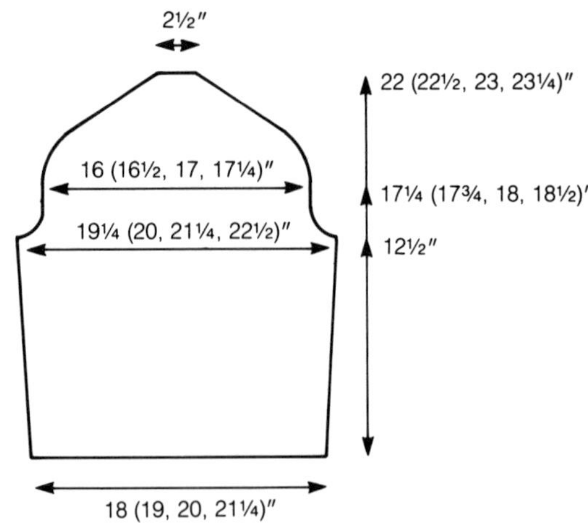

Back: With larger needles cast on 56 (58, 62, 66) sts and work 4 rows in garter st. Change to rev stockinette st inc 1 st at beg and end of row when work meas 4 inches (10 cm) AND 8 inches (20 cm) from beg. There are 60 (62, 66, 70) sts on needle.

Continue even until work measures 12½ inches (32 cm) from beg. Shape Armholes:

Size 10: Bind off 2 sts at beg of next 4 rows and then 1 st at beg of next 4 rows.

Size 12: Bind off 2 sts at beg of next 4 rows and then 1 st at beg of next 4 rows.

Size 14: Bind off 3 sts at beg of next 2 rows, then 2 sts at beg of next 2 rows and then 1 st at beg of next 4 rows.

Size 16: Bind off 3 sts at beg of next 2 rows, then 2 sts at beg of next 4 rows and then 1 st at beg of next 2 rows. 48 (50, 52, 54) sts remain.

Continue even until work meas 17¼ (17¾, 18, 18½) inches—44 (45, 46, 47) cm from beg.

Shape Shoulder—

Size 10: Bind off 1 st at beg of next 6 rows, then 2 sts at beg of next 14 rows, then 3 sts at beg of next 2 rows.

Size 12: Bind off 1 st at beg of next 6 rows, then 2 sts at beg of next 10 rows, then 3 sts at beg of next 2 rows, then 2 sts at beg of next 2 rows and then 3 sts at beg of next 2 rows.

Size 14: Bind off 1 st at beg of next 6 rows, then 2 sts at beg of next 6 rows, then 3 sts at beg of next 2 rows, then 2 sts at beg of next 2 rows, then 3 sts at beg of next 2 rows, then 2 sts at beg of next 2 rows, and then 3 sts at beg of next 2 rows.

Size 16: Bind off 1 st at beg of next 6 rows, then * 2 sts at beg of next 2 rows and then 3 sts at beg of next 2 rows *, rep from * to * 4 times in all.

All sizes: 8 sts remain. Bind off.

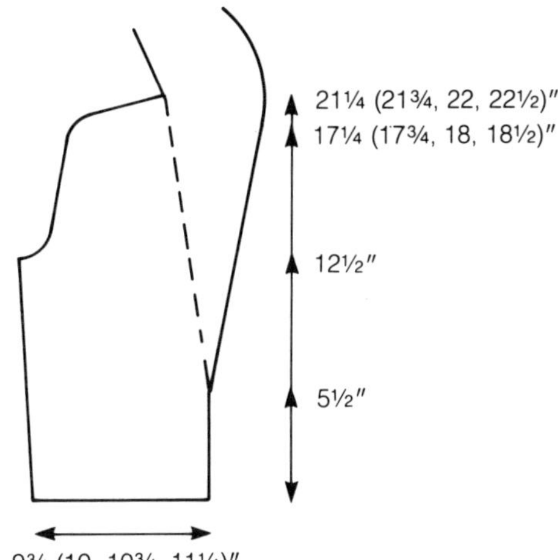

Front: With larger needles cast on 30 (32, 34, 36) sts and work 4 rows in garter st. Inc 1 st at beg of left edge ONLY when work measures 4 inches (10 cm) AND 8 inches (20 cm). There are 32 (34, 36, 38) sts on needle.

At the same time, when work meas 5½ inches (14 cm) from beg, shape collar: Inc 1 st at right edge ONLY on next row and then:

Size 10: on every 10th row 6 times more.

Sizes 12 and 14: on every 10th row 3 times and then on every foll 12th row 3 times more.

Size 16: on every 10th row twice and then on every foll 12th row 12 times more.

At the same time, when work meas 12½ inches (32 cm) from beg, shape Armhole at left edge ONLY: Bind off on every other row:

Sizes 10 and 12: 2 sts twice and then 1 st twice.

Size 14: 3 sts once, then 2 sts once and then 1 st twice.

Size 16: 3 sts once, then 2 sts twice and then 1 st once.

When work measures 17¼ (17¾, 18, 18½) inches—44 (45, 46, 47) cm from beg, shape Shoulder. Bind off at left edge ONLY on every other row:

Size 10: 1 st twice, then 2 sts 6 times and then 3 sts once.

Size 12: 1 st twice, then 2 sts twice, then 3 sts once, then 2 sts once, then 3 sts once, then 2 sts once and then 3 sts once.

Size 14: 1 st twice, then 3 sts once, then 2 sts once, then 3 sts once, then 2 sts once, then 3 sts once, then 2 sts once and then 3 sts once.

Size 16: 1 st twice, then 2 sts once, then 3 sts once, then 2 sts once and then 3 sts 4 times.

All sizes: 16 sts remain for collar.

Continue on these sts casting on 1 st at shoulder edge for seam.

There are 17 sts on needle. Continue in short rows as foll: Beg at outside edge, work 2 rows on all sts, then * on next row work 7 sts, TURN and work back, then work 4 rows on all sts *, rep from * to * 4 times in all. Work 4 more rows on all sts. Bind off.

Work the second **Front** to correspond, reversing all shapings.

Braid: With smaller needles cast on 12 sts in Pronostic and work in stockinette st for 98 (99¾, 102¾, 105¾) inches—249 (253, 261, 269) cm. Bind off. For sleeves: Cast on and work in the same manner for 12¼ (12½, 13, 13½) inches—31 (32, 33, 34) cm. Bind off. Work a second piece in the same manner.

Making Up: Sew the braid along lower edge of sleeves, wrong side of braid to right side of sleeve. Sew side, shoulder and sleeve seams. Sewing shoulder tabs between front and back. Sew the braid around garment in the same manner as sleeves.

ANGORA COZY

COURTESY OF JOSEPH GALLER

The fluffy softness of angora produces a lovely effect. An elegant look can be given a simple shape and basic stitches when this yarn is used. The yarn can be practical as well as pretty. Try it for a lovely shrug as well as a luxurious bed jacket.

Information to Study Before You Begin

Sizing: Sizes 8–10; For larger sizes use 2 more stitches for each size and make sweater 4 inches longer.
Materials: You need 15 balls Galler's 100 percent Angora "Belangor."
Tools: Knitting Needles, Nos. 6 and 9.
Gauge: 5 sts = 1 inch.

Directions to Follow

With No. 6 needles, cast on 46 sts. Work in ribbing—K 1, P 1—for 2 inches.
Change to No. 9 needles. Work in stockinette st as follows: K 1, inc 1, K 1, inc 1 to the end of the row (91 sts are now on the needle).
Continue work, making 1 inc at each end of every 4th row. Do this 8 times (107 sts are now on the needle).
When the piece meas 7 inches, work as follows; K 5, inc 1, K 97, inc 1, K 5.
For the next row: K 5, then P across row, K last 5 sts.
Work in this way, making 1 inc every 4th row after the first 5 sts and before the last 5 sts until there are 119 sts on needle.
Continue work until piece meas 16 inches. You have made the first half of the garment.
To knit the other half, work in reverse.

SWEATERS FOR THE FAMILY

This attractive cardigan and T-sweater have been designed for various family members. You can make them in a variety of sizes—children, women, and men.

CABLE T-SWEATER

A cable stitch pattern adds a decorative touch to this sweater made of garter stitches. To obtain this effect, the sweater is worked vertically in one piece.

Information to Study Before You Begin

Sizing: Children's: Small, Medium, and Large Sizes are enclosed by + signs.
Women's: Small, Medium, and Large Sizes are in parentheses ( ).
Men's: Small, Medium, and Large Sizes are in brackets [ ].
To make instructions easy to follow, circle number for size being made.
• FINISHED MEASUREMENTS (approx):
Bust/Chest: +26, 28, 30+ (32, 34, 36) [38, 40, 42] inches.
Upper Arm: +12, 13, 14+ (15, 16, 17) [19, 20, 21] inches.
Length to Underarm: +12+ (14) [16] inches.
Materials: Use Columbia-Minerva Nantuk 4-ply (4 oz. ball). You need: For Children: 3 balls; for Women: 4 balls; for Men: 5 balls.
Tools: Circular Knitting Needle No. 8—24 inch and 16 inch.
Cable Needle or Double-pointed Needle.
Gauge (garter st): 9 sts = 2 inches; 8 rows = 1 inch.

Directions to Follow

Sleeve: Beg at sleeve edge, cast on +54, 58, 62+ (68, 72, 76) [86, 90, 94] sts. Do not join. Work back and forth as with straight needles.
Rows 1–5 (border): Knit.
Row 6 (right side): Knit.
Row 7: K 9, P 6, Knit +9, 11, 13+ (16, 18, 20) [25, 27, 29], P 6, Knit +9, 11, 13+ (16, 18, 20) [25, 27, 29], P 6, K 9. Rep Rows 6 and 7 twice more.
Next—Cable Row (right side): K 9, * sl next 3 sts to cable needle, hold at **back** of work, K next 3 sts, K 3 from cable needle, K +9, 11, 13+ (16, 18, 20) [25, 27, 29]; rep from * once, work cable, end K 9 (3 cables made). * * Rep **Row 7.** Rep Rows 6 and 7 4 times. Work cable row * *. Rep between * * for pat (working cable row every 10th row) until +5+ (6) [8] inches from beg or desired length of sleeve.

Body—Front and Back: Cast on +54+ (63) [72] sts at beg of next 2 rows—+162, 166, 170+ (194, 198, 202) [230, 234, 238] sts. Work cast-on sts in garter st (K every row) and rem sts in pat as established until +3½, 4, 4½+ (4½, 5, 5½) [5½, 6, 6½] inches from beg of front and back, end with wrong-side row.

Divide for Neck: Work +72, 74, 76+ (86, 88, 90) [102, 104, 106] sts in pat, sl next +18+ (22) [26] sts to a holder for neck, join a second skein and work rem sts in pat. Working front and back at same time, work until neck opening measures +6+ (7) [8] inches, end with wrong-side row. Work +72, 74, 76+ (86, 88, 90) [102, 104, 106] sts in pat, cast on +18+ (22) [26] sts for other side of neck, continue across rem sts with same yarn. Cut 2nd skein. Continuing in pat as established (with 3 cables) on +162, 166, 170+ (194, 198, 202) [230, 234, 238] sts for +3½, 4, 4½+ (4½, 5, 5½) [5½, 6, 6½] inches. Bind off +54+ (63) [72] sts at beg of next 2 rows (front and back completed). Work in pat on rem +54, 58, 62+ (68, 72, 76) [86, 90, 94] sleeve sts until there are same number of rows as on first sleeve to border, end with right-side row. K 5 rows for border. Bind off.

Finishing—Neckband: With right side facing and 16 inch circular needle, K sts from holder, pick up and K 1 st in every 2nd row (each ridge) and 1 st in each cast-on st around neck edge. Join, work in rnds.

Rnds 1, 3, and 5: Knit.

Rnds 2, 4, and 6: Purl. Bind off. Sew side and sleeve seams.

CABLE CARDIGAN

An interesting combination of seed and cable stitches are used for this sweater.

Sizes: Children's: Small, Medium, and Large are enclosed by + signs.

Women's: Small, Medium, and Large are listed in parentheses ( ).

Men's: Small, Medium, and Large are in brackets [ ].

To make instructions easy to follow, read them carefully. Then circle the numbers to be used for the size you are making.

• FINISHED MEASUREMENTS:

Bust/Chest: +26, 28, 30+ (32, 34, 36) [38, 40, 42] inches buttoned.

Materials: Use Columbia-Minerva Nantuk 4-ply yarn (4 oz. ball).

For Children: 3 balls for each size.

For Women: 4 balls (Small); 4 balls (Medium); 5 balls (Large).

For Men: 5 balls (Small); 6 balls (Medium); 6 balls (Large).

Buttons: Number depends on length of cardigan. The size and shape should be appropriate for the sweater.

Tools: Knitting Needles No. 8—23-inch Circular Needle.

Cable Needle.

Gauge (seed st): 9 sts = 2 inches; 6 rows = 1 inch.

Directions to Follow

Body: Cast on +121, 133, 141+ (151, 161, 167) [177, 187, 195] sts for fronts and back. Do not join, work back and forth as with straight needles.

Lower Border—

Row 1 (right side): K 1, * P 1, K 1; rep from * to end. Rep Row 1 for seed st. Work even until there are +4+ (6) [8] rows from beg, end on wrong side.

For Girls and Women Only—Next (Buttonhole) Row: Beg at right front edge, work seed st over 3 sts, bind off next 2 sts, continue seed st to end. On next row, cast on 2 sts over the bound-off sts.

For Boys and Men Only—Next (Buttonhole) Row: Work seed st to last 5 sts, bind off next 2 sts, work last sts. On next row cast on 2 sts over the bound-off sts.

All sizes—Work seed st for +4+ (6) [8] rows. This completes lower border. Rep buttonhole in front borders every 2½ inches, dec at center back +1, 1, 0+ (1, 1, 1) [0, 1, 1] st to give correct number of sts for next pat.

Cable Pattern for All Sizes—

Row 1 (right side): [K 1, P 1] 3 times for seed st border, P +3, 2, 3+ (4, 4, 4) [3, 4, 3]; * K +4, 4, 4+ (4, 4, 6) [6, 6, 6], P +3, 4, 3+ (5, 4, 4) [3, 2, 4]; rep from *, +13, 13, 16+ (13, 16, 13) [16, 19, 16] times; K +4, 4, 4+ (4, 4, 6) [6, 6, 6], P +3, 2, 3+ (4, 4, 4) [3, 4, 3] ** P 1, K 1; rep from ** twice for seed st border.

Row 2: Work 6 sts in seed st, continue across row, knitting the K sts and purling the P sts to last 6 sts, work 6 sts in seed st border.

Rows 3 and 4: Rep Rows 1 and 2.

Row 5 (Cable Row): Work border, P +3, 2, 3+ (4, 4, 4) [3, 4, 3], * sl next +2, 2, 2+ (2, 2, 3) [3, 3, 3] sts to cable needle, hold at *back* of work, K next +2, 2, 2+ (2, 2, 3) [3, 3, 3] sts, K sts from cable needle for cable twist, P +3, 4, 3+ (5, 4, 4) [3, 2, 4]; rep from * +13, 13, 16+ (13, 16, 13) [16, 19, 16] times, twist cable, P +3, 2, 3+ (4, 4, 4) [3, 4, 3], work border.

Row 6: Rep Row 2. Rep these 6 rows for cable pat to +10, 11, 12+ (14, 14, 14) [15, 15, 15] inches from beg or 1 inch less than desired length to armhole.

Next Row: Work seed st, inc at center back +1, 1, 0+ (1, 1, 1) [0, 1, 1] st to give correct number of sts for pat. Continue in seed st until desired length to armhole, end with right-side row.

Divide for fronts and back: Keep pat as established.

Next Row (wrong side): Work +32, 34, 36+ (38, 40, 42) [44, 46, 48] sts and place on holder for left front, bind off 1 st, work until there are +55, 63, 67+ (73, 79, 81) [87, 93, 97] sts from bind-off and place on holder for back, bind off 1 st, work to end.

Right Front: Continue pat until armhole meas +4, 4½, 5+ (5½, 6, 6½) [7½, 8, 8½] inches, end on wrong side.

Neck: Work +16, 16, 16+ (16, 18, 20) [18, 20, 20] sts and place on holder. Continue pat on +16, 18, 20+ (22, 22, 22) [26, 26, 28] sts until armhold meas +5½, 6, 6½+ (7, 7½, 8) [9, 9½, 10] inches from beg, end on right side. Bind off all sts for shoulder.

COURTESY OF COLUMBIA-MINERVA CORPORATION

Left Front: Place sts on needle and working first row from right side, complete to correspond to right front, reversing neck shaping.

Back: Place sts on needle and working first row from right side, work to same number of rows as on right front. Bind off.

Sleeves: Cast on +53, 58, 61+ (71, 74, 78) [87, 88, 94] sts for top edge.

Row 1: K 1, * P 1, K 1; rep from * +4, 4, 6+ (6, 8, 7) [6, 8, 6] times, place marker on needle, ** P +3, 4, 3+ (5, 4, 4) [3, 2, 4], K +4, 4, 4+ (4, 4, 6) [6, 6, 6]; rep from ** +3+ (3) [5] times, P +3, 4, 3+ (5, 4, 4) [3, 2, 4], place marker on needle, K 1, * P 1, K 1; rep from last * to end. Slip markers every row. Keeping sts before first marker and after last marker in seed st and rem sts in cable pat as on body, dec 1 st each side every 6th row +8, 9, 9+ (12, 10, 8) [13, 11, 11] times, every 4th row +0, 0, 0+ (1, 4, 7) [5, 6, 8] times. Work even on +37, 40, 43+ (45, 46, 48) [51, 54, 56] sts until sleeve meas +9½, 10½, 12+ (15½, 15½, 15½) [16½, 16½, 16½] inches from beg or 1½ inches less than desired length of sleeve.

Next Row: Work seed st on all sts, dec at center of sleeve +0, 1, 0+ (0, 1, 1) [0, 1, 1] st. Continue in seed st to desired length. Bind off in pat.

Neckband: Sew shoulder seams. Working buttonhole on right front band for Girls and Women, left front band for Boys and Men, K across sts on holder, pick up 1 st in each row on shaped neck edge, pick up 1 st in each bound-off st at back of neck and 1 st in each row on shaped edge. K across sts on holder. Work in K 1, P 1 rib for 1 inch. Bind off in rib.

Finishing: Sew sleeve seams. With center of cast-on row of sleeves at shoulder seams, sew sleeves to armholes. Sew buttons opposite buttonholes.

COLLARED PULLOVER

This design with its bulky look seems so right for a future athlete. It has grown-up detailing which a small child will love.

Information to Study Before You Begin

Sizing: These directions are for Toddler's Size 1. Changes for Sizes 2, 3, 4 are in parentheses.

Materials: You need 1 (1, 2, 2) balls of Bernat Berella "4" (4 oz.).

Tools: Knitting Needles, Nos. 6 and 10 (Bernat U.S.).

Gauge: 9 sts = 2 inches; 6 rows = 1 inch.

Directions to Follow

Front: Using smaller needles, cast on 46 (46, 50, 50) sts.

Row 1: K 2, * P 2, K 2, repeat from * across row.

Row 2: P 2, * K 2, P 2, repeat from * across row. Repeat these 2 rows for 1 inch, inc 0 (1, 0, 1) st each end of last row—46 (48, 50, 52) sts. Change to larger needles and work even in stockinette st until piece meas 5 (5½, 6, 7) inches, ending with a P row.

Shape Yoke—

Row 1: K 20 (21, 22, 23) sts, put a marker on needle, P 2, K 2, P 2, put a marker on needle, K last 20 (21, 22, 23) sts.

Row 2: P to first marker, K 2, P 2, K 2, P to end of row.

Row 3: K to 4 sts before first marker, P 2, (K 2, P 2) 3 times, K to end of row.

Row 4: P to 4 sts before marker, K 2, (P 2, K 2) 3 times, P to end of row. Keeping 6 sts between markers in ribbing pattern as established, continue in this manner to work 4 sts more at side of each marker in K 2, P 2 ribbing every other row until 46 sts have been worked and remaining 0 (1, 2, 3) sts at each end have been worked in stockinette st, ending with a wrong-side row. Piece should meas approximately 7 (7½, 8, 9) inches.

Shape Sleeves: At the beg of each of the next 2 rows cast on 34 (36, 38, 40) sts.

Divide Front: K 34 (37, 40, 43) sts, put a marker on needle, P 2, (K 2, P 2) 5 times, K 1, join another ball of yarn, K 1, (P 2, K 2) 5 times, P 2, put a marker on needle, K last 34 (37, 40, 43) sts.

Row 2: K 5, P to marker, work in ribbing on next 22 sts, K 1; K 1, work to marker, P to last 5 sts, K 5. Working on both sides at once and keeping 5 sts at each sleeve edge and 1 st at each front edge in garter st, work even in pattern as established until sleeves meas 3¾ (4, 4¼, 4½) inches above cast-on sts.

Shape Neck: At each front edge sl 11 sts onto a holder, work to end of row.

Shape Back Neck: Starting at left arm edge, work in pat as established to front edge, cast on 22 sts for back neck, break off extra ball of yarn and work across sts of right side in pat as established. Keeping 46 sts at center in ribbing as established, work 5 sts at each sleeve edge in garter st and remaining sts in stockinette st until sleeves meas 7½ (8, 8½, 9) inches above cast-on sts. At the beg of each of the next 2 rows bind off 34 (36, 38, 40) sts. Work remaining 46 (48, 50, 52) sts in stockinette st until piece measures 6 (6½, 7, 8) inches above last group of bound-off sts, ending with a P row, dec 0 (1, 0, 1) st each end of needle on the last row—46 (46, 50, 50) sts. Change to smaller needles and rep Rows 1 and 2 of front ribbing for 1 inch. Bind off.

Finishing: Sew underarm and sleeve seams.

Collar: With right side facing you, sl 11 sts for right front from holder onto larger needles, join yarn and work in pattern as established across these 11 sts, pick up and K 22 (22, 26, 26) sts across cast-on sts of back neck, sl 11 sts for left front from holder onto needle and work in pattern as established across these 11 sts—44 (44, 48, 48) sts. Keeping 1 st at each front edge in garter st, work remaining sts in K 2, P 2 ribbing for 2 inches. K 2 rows in garter st. Bind off as if to K.

DECORATED SWEATER

Embroidery adds a pretty touch to this sweater. Of course it can be made without the decorative stitches. You may decide to knit it plain for a more boyish look.

Information to Study Before You Begin

Sizing: These directions are for Toddler's Size 1. Changes for Sizes 2, 3, 4 are in parentheses.

Materials: You need 1 (1, 2, 2) balls for Main Color (MC) of Bernat Berella "4" (4 oz.).
For Embroidery: 2 Blue (Color A) and 1 Pink (Color B) skeins of Bernat 1-2-3 ply Persian Type Yarn (12½ yd skeins).

Tools: Knitting Needles, Nos. 6 and 10 (Bernat U.S.); 1 set No. 6 Double-pointed Needles.
Quickpoint Needle.

Gauge: 9 sts = 2 inches; 6 rows = 1 inch.

Directions to Follow

Pattern Stitch for Front

Row 1: K to first marker, P 1, K to end of row.

Row 2 and all even rows: P.

Row 3: K to 1 st before first marker, P 1, K 1, P 1, K to end of row.

Row 5: K to 2 sts before first marker, P 1, K 3, P 1, K to end of row.

Row 7: K to 3 sts before first marker, P 1, K 5, P 1, K to end of row.

Row 9: K to 4 sts before first marker, P 1, K 7, P 1, K to end of row.

Row 11: K to 5 sts before first marker, P 1, K 9, P 1, K to end of row.

Row 13: K to 6 sts before first marker, P 1, K 5, P 1, K 5, P 1, K to end of row.

Row 15: K to 7 sts before first marker, P 1, K 5, P 1, K 1, P 1, K 5, P 1, K to end of row.

Row 17: K to 8 sts before first marker, P 1, K 5, P 1, K 3, P 1, K 5, P 1, K to end of row.

Row 19: K to 9 sts before first marker, P 1, K 5, P 1, K 5, P 1, K 5, P 1, K to end of row.

Continue in this manner to move the P sts to 1 st nearer each arm edge every other row, being sure to keep 5 sts between the 1st and 2nd V-P st rows.

Front: Using smaller needles, cast on 46 (48, 50, 52) sts. K 1, P 1 in ribbing for 1 inch, inc 1 st at end of last row—47 (49, 51, 53) sts. Change to larger needles and work even in stockinette st until piece meas 3 inches, ending with a K row. On the next row P 23 (24, 25, 26) sts, put a marker on needle, P 1, put a marker on needle, P to end of row. Work even in pattern st for front until piece meas 7 (7½, 8, 9) inches. Put a marker in each side of work to mark start of armholes and continue in pattern as established for 2 rows, ending with a P row.

Shape V-Neck: Continuing in pattern as established, work 23 (24, 25, 26) sts, sl center st onto a holder, join another ball of yarn and work to end of row. Working on both sides at once, dec 1 st at each neck edge every other row 10 times. Work even on 13 (14, 15, 16) sts each side, if necessary, until armholes meas 3¾ (4, 4¼, 4½) inches above markers in work.

Shape Shoulders: At each arm edge bind off 6 (7, 8, 9) sts once and 7 sts once.

Back: Work to correspond to front, omitting pattern st and V-neck shaping until armholes meas 3¾ (4, 4¼, 4½) inches above markers in work.

Shape Shoulders: At the beg of each of the next 2 rows bind off 6 (7, 8, 9) sts. At the beg of each of the next 2 rows bind off 7 sts. Sl remaining 21 sts onto a holder.

Sleeves: Using smaller straight needles, cast on 24 (26, 28, 30) sts. K 1, P 1 in ribbing for 1 inch. Change to larger needles and K the next row, inc at even intervals to 34 (36, 38, 40) sts. Continue in stockinette st for 7 rows more, ending with a P row. P the next row to form a ridge. Starting with a P row, work in stockinette st for 8 rows, ending with a K row. K the next row to form a ridge. Starting with a K row, continue in stockinette st until piece meas 7½ (8½, 9½, 10½) inches. Bind off.

Finishing: Sew underarm and shoulder seams. Sew bound-off edge of sleeves to armholes between markers.

Neckband: With right side facing you, using dpn pick up 21 sts along left front neck edge, put a marker on needle, K st from holder, put a marker on needle, pick up 21 sts along right front neck edge, K across sts of back holder.

Round 1: K 1, * P 1, K 1, rep from * to 2 sts before first marker, K 2 sts tog, K center st, sl 1, K 1, psso, P 1, * K 1, P 1 in ribbing to end of rnd.

Round 2: Work even in ribbing, being sure to K the center st. Repeat the last 2 rounds until piece meas 1 inch. Bind off in ribbing.

Embroidery: Sleeves: Using Color A, work in duplicate st on each garter st row of sleeves as follows: With right side facing you and starting at sleeve seam, holding yarn in back of work, bring yarn to right side of work through space between two stockinette sts 1 row above garter st ridge, draw yarn under upper loop of garter st ridge one st to the right and then under upper loop of garter st ridge one st to the left, now bring yarn to wrong side of work through same space where yarn was brought to front of work. *Do not pull tightly.* Continue in this manner across both garter st ridges of each sleeve.

V Patterns of Front: With right side facing you and using Color A make a cross st under each P st loop of each V pattern, as shown in photograph.

Flowers: Using Color B and starting at center st between 2 V patterns, embroider 3 flower petals in straight st. Work 2 leaves at base of flower in straight st. Work 2 more flowers evenly spaced on each side between V patterns as shown in photograph.

STRIPED T-SWEATER

Although this sweater is shown on a youthful model, it has been sized for the entire family. The sweater is made in one piece in stockinette stitch. You start working at a sleeve edge, introducing stripes as you knit. In case you have leftover yarns that you would like to use, here is a place to do just that.

Information to Study Before You Begin

Sizing: Instructions are given for Children's, Women's, and Men's Sizes.
Children's: Small, Medium, and Large Sizes. The changes are listed between + marks.
Women's: Small, Medium, and Large. The changes are enclosed in parentheses ( ).
Men's: Small, Medium, and Large Sizes are in brackets [ ].
• FINISHED MEASUREMENTS (approx):
Bust / Chest +26, 28, 30+ (32, 34, 36) [38, 40, 42] inches.
Upper Arm: +12, 13, 14+ (15, 16, 17) [19, 20, 21] inches.
Materials: You need: 1 ball each of 5 colors—Green (A), Yellow (B), Red (C), Purple (D), Turquoise (E) in Columbia-Minerva Performer (3 oz. ball) and
For Children's sweater—1 ball white (MC).
For Women's sweater—2 balls white (MC).
For Men's sweater 3 balls white (MC).
Tools: No. 8 Circular Knitting Needles in 24- and 16-inch lengths.
Gauge: 9 sts = 2 inches. 6 rows = 1 inch.
Note: Striped pattern is worked with yarns carried at side edge. Cut color when no longer needed.

Directions to Follow

Sleeve: With A, cast on +54, 58, 62+ (68, 72, 76) [86, 90, 94] sts. Do not join. Work back and forth as with straight needles. K 3 rows (2 ridges for border). Beg striped pat.
Row 4 (right side): With MC Knit.
Row 5: With MC, Purl. Join A. Continue stripe pat of 2 rows MC, 2 rows A, until there are a total of +32, 44, 48+ (48, 52, 56) [64, 64, 68] rows, end with 2 rows A. Cut A.
Next 2 Rows: With MC, K 1 row, P 1 row. Join B. Continue stripe pat of 2 rows MC, 2 rows B until there are +16, 24, 24+ (24, 24, 24) [32, 32, 32] rows from last A stripe, end with 2 rows B. Sleeve should measure approx +8, 11, 12+ (12, 13, 13½) [16, 16, 17] inches. If longer sleeve is desired, continue with MC and B stripes to desired length. Join MC at end of last row.

Body (Back and Front): With MC, cast on +54+ (63) [72] sts, K to end. Cast on +54+ (63) [72] sts. There are +162, 166, 170+ (194, 198, 202) [230, 234, 238] sts. Keeping 2 sts at lower edges in garter st (K every row) continue stripe pat of MC and B until there are a total of +32, 44, 48+ (48, 52, 56) [64, 64, 68] rows in MC and B section, end with 2 rows B. Cut B, join C. With MC, work 2 rows, with C, work 2 rows.
Divide for Neck: With MC, Knit +72, 74, 76+ (86, 88, 90) [102, 104, 106] sts, drop MC, slip next +18+ (22) [26] sts to holder for neck, join 2nd skein MC, K to end. Work back and front with separate yarn in MC and C stripes until there are +38+ (42) [50] rows in this section. End with 2 rows MC.
Next Row: With C, Knit, cast on +18+ (22) [26] sts for other side of neck, with same skein of yarn, K rem sts. Cut extra skein, P 1 row on +162, 166,

170+ (194, 198, 202) [230, 234, 238] sts. With MC and D, work +16, 20, 22+ (22, 26, 30) [30, 34, 34] rows stripe pat (2 rows less than number of MC and B rows on body). Bind off +54+ (63) [72] sts at beg of next 2 rows. Continue MC and D stripe pat on +54, 58, 62+ (68, 72, 76) [86, 90, 94] sts to same number of rows as MC and B section. With MC and E, complete to correspond to MC and A section. K 4 rows A. Bind off.

Finishing—Neckband: With A and right side facing and 16-inch circular needle, K across sts on holder, pick up 1 st in every 2nd ridge and 1 st in each cast-on st around neck edge. Join and work in rnds.

Rnds 1 and 3: Knit.

Rnds 2 and 4: Purl. Bind off. Sew side and sleeve seams, matching stripes.

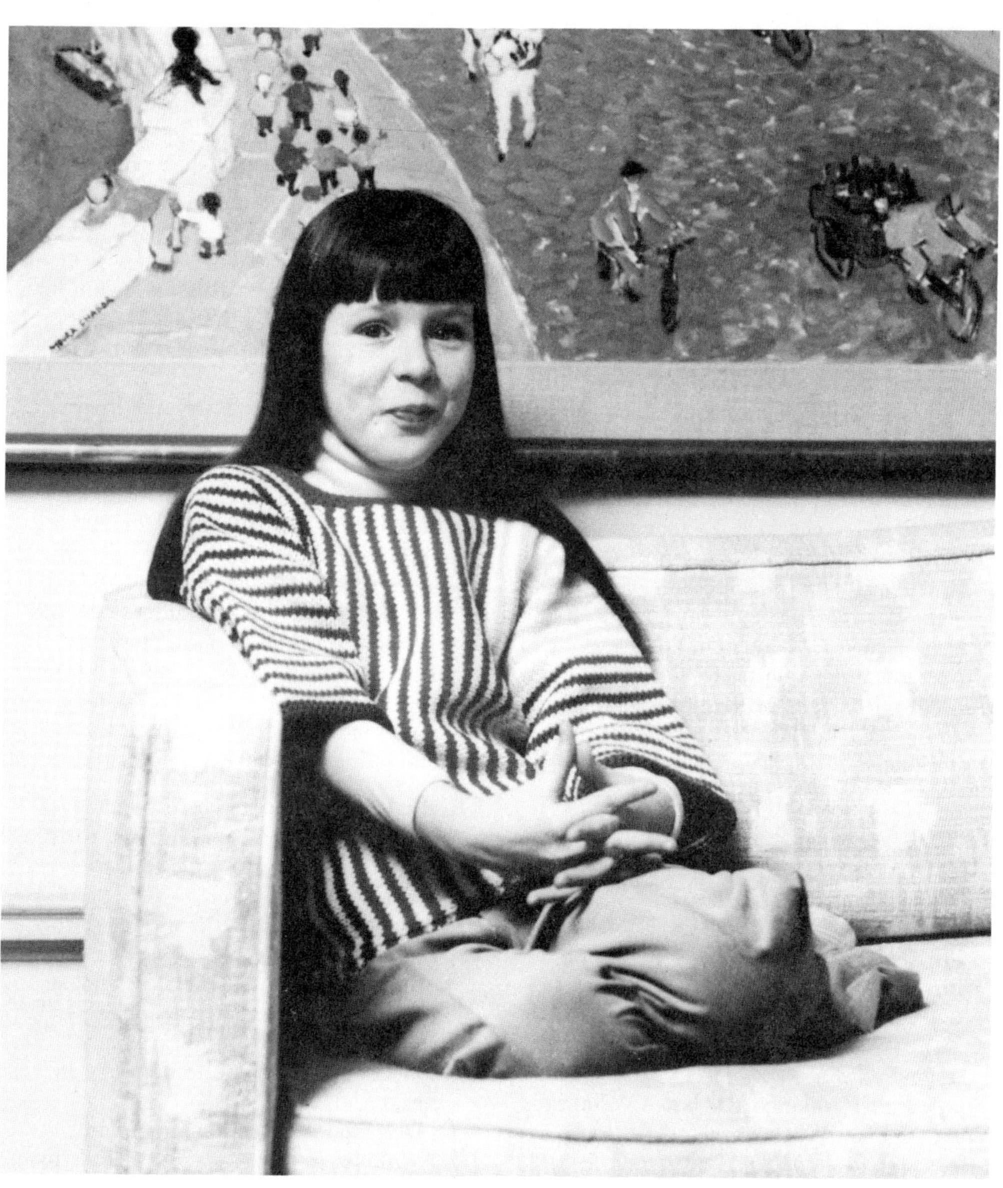

CLASSIC CARDIGAN

Fashions in sweaters change, but the classic always seems to be in style for both boys and girls. By varying the weight of the yarn and the needle size, a sweater acquires a different look.

Information to Study Before You Begin

Sizing: Directions are written for Sizes 4, 6, 8, 10, 12, 14.

Materials: In reading the directions, you will notice two sets of numbers in parentheses. The first set is given for sports-weight yarn; those in the second set, for worsted-weight yarn.

For sports-weight yarn, such as Berella Sportspun (2 oz.), you need (4, 4, 4, 5, 5, 5) balls.

For worsted-weight yarn, such as Berella "4" (4 oz.), you need (3, 3, 3, 4, 4, 4) balls or Bernat Sesame "4" (3½ oz.), you need (3, 3, 3, 4, 4, 4) balls.

Buttons.

1 yard of 1-inch grosgrain ribbon.

Tools: *For sports-weight yarn,* Knitting Needles (straight), Nos. 3 and 5. Crochet Hook, Size 2:00 mm (B).

For worsted-weight yarn, Knitting Needles (straight), Nos. 5 and 8. Crochet Hook, Size 4:00 mm (F).

Gauge: *For sports-weight yarn,* 6 sts = 1 inch; 8 rows = 1 inch on No. 5 Needles in stockinette st.

For worsted-weight yarn, 5 sts = 1 inch; 7 rows = 1 inch on No. 8 Needles in stockinette st.

Directions to Follow

Back: Using smaller needles, cast on (76, 80, 84, 90, 96, 102) (64, 68, 70, 76, 80, 86) sts. K 2, P 2 in ribbing for 1½ inches. Change to larger needles and work even in stockinette st until piece meas (9, 10, 11, 11½, 12, 12½) inches, ending with a P row.

Shape Full-Fashioned Raglan Armholes: At the beg of each of the next 2 rows bind off (4, 4, 5, 5, 7, 7) (2, 2, 2, 2, 2, 3) sts.

Row 3: K 2, K 2 tog, K to last 4 sts, sl 1, K 1, psso, K 2.

Row 4: Purl. Rep the last 2 rows (20, 22, 23, 25, 26, 27) (19, 20, 21, 23, 25, 26) times more. Sl remaining (26, 26, 26, 28, 28, 32) (20, 22, 22, 24, 24, 26) sts onto a holder.

Note: For girl's cardigan, make left front first and work buttonholes on right front: for boy's cardigan make right front first, omitting buttonholes and work buttonholes on left front.

Left Front: Using smaller needles, cast on (42, 44, 46, 50, 52, 56) (34, 36, 38, 40, 42, 44) sts. K 2, P 2 in ribbing for 1½ inches. Change to larger needles and work even in stockinette st until piece meas (9, 10, 11, 11½, 12, 12½) inches, ending with a P row.

Shape Full-Fashioned Raglan Armhole: At arm edge bind off (4, 4, 5, 5, 7, 7) (2, 2, 2, 2, 2, 3) sts, K to end of row.

Row 2: Purl.

Row 3: K 2, K 2 tog, K to end of row. Repeat the last 2 rows (15, 17, 18, 20, 21, 22) (13, 14, 15, 17, 19, 20) times more, ending with **Row 3**—(22, 22, 22, 24, 23, 26) (18, 19, 20, 20, 20, 20) sts.

Shape Neck: At the beg of the next row P (6, 6, 6, 8, 7, 10) (4, 5, 6, 6, 6, 6) sts and sl these sts onto a holder, P to end of row. Continue to dec 1 st at arm edge in same manner as before 6 times more, and *at the same time,* at neck edge bind off 2 sts (4) (3) times. Sl remaining 2 sts onto a holder.

Right Front: Work to correspond to left front, reversing all shaping and forming first buttonhole when piece meas 1 inch.

Buttonhole: Starting at front edge, work 2 sts, bind off the next 2 sts, work to end of row. On the next row cast on 2 sts over those bound off previous row. Make 5 more buttonholes, evenly spaced—the last one to be made in neckband.

To Dec for Full-Fashioned Raglan Armhole: K to last 4 sts, sl 1, K 1, psso, K 2.

Sleeves: Using smaller needles, cast on (36, 40, 40, 44, 44, 44) (28, 28, 32, 32, 36, 36) sts. K 2, P 2 in ribbing for 2 inches. Change to larger needles and work in stockinette st, inc 1 st each end of needle every ¾ inch (9, 9, 11, 11, 14, 15) (10, 11, 10, 12, 12, 14) times. Work even on (54, 58, 62, 66, 72, 74) (48, 50, 52, 56, 60, 64) sts until piece meas (10, 11, 12, 12½, 13, 13½) inches, ending with a P row.

Shape Full-Fashioned Raglan Cap: At the beg of each of the next 2 rows bind off (4, 4, 5, 5, 7, 7) (2, 2, 2, 2, 2, 3) sts. Dec in same manner as on back. Sl remaining 4 sts onto a holder.

Finishing: Sew sleeves to back and front armholes. Sew underarm seams.

Neckband: Using smaller needles, with right side facing you pick up (90, 90, 94, 94, 98, 98) (82, 82, 86, 86, 90, 90) sts around neck, including sts from holders. K 2, P 2 in ribbing, forming another buttonhole in same manner as before when band meas ½ inch. Continue in ribbing as established until band meas 1 inch. Bind off in ribbing. Work 1 row sc on each front edge. Shrinking ribbon first, face fronts. Finish buttonholes. Steam. Sew on buttons.

YOKED PULLOVER

The yoked effect and embroidered detail give a new look to this boyish sweater. It is a design for the young set to admire.

Information to Study Before You Begin

Sizing: Directions are for Size 4. Changes for Sizes 6, 8, 10, 12 are in parentheses. Made to fit chest measurement of 23 (25, 27, 28, 30) inches.

Materials: Phildar Kadischa was used for this sweater. You need:
6 (7, 8, 9, 10) balls ecru; 2 (2, 3, 3, 3) balls col Gris Moyen (gray);
1 ball of col Brasero (red) for all sizes; a small amount of col Noir (black).

Tools: Knitting Needles, Nos. 8 and 10. Stitch Holders.

Gauge (stockinette st with No. 10 needles):
13 sts = 4 inches; 19 rows = 4 inches.

Stitch Pattern
K 1, P 1 ribbing—Stockinette st
Embroidery in Duplicate st, Back st, and Straight st—see Chart.
Single increases 2 sts from edges.

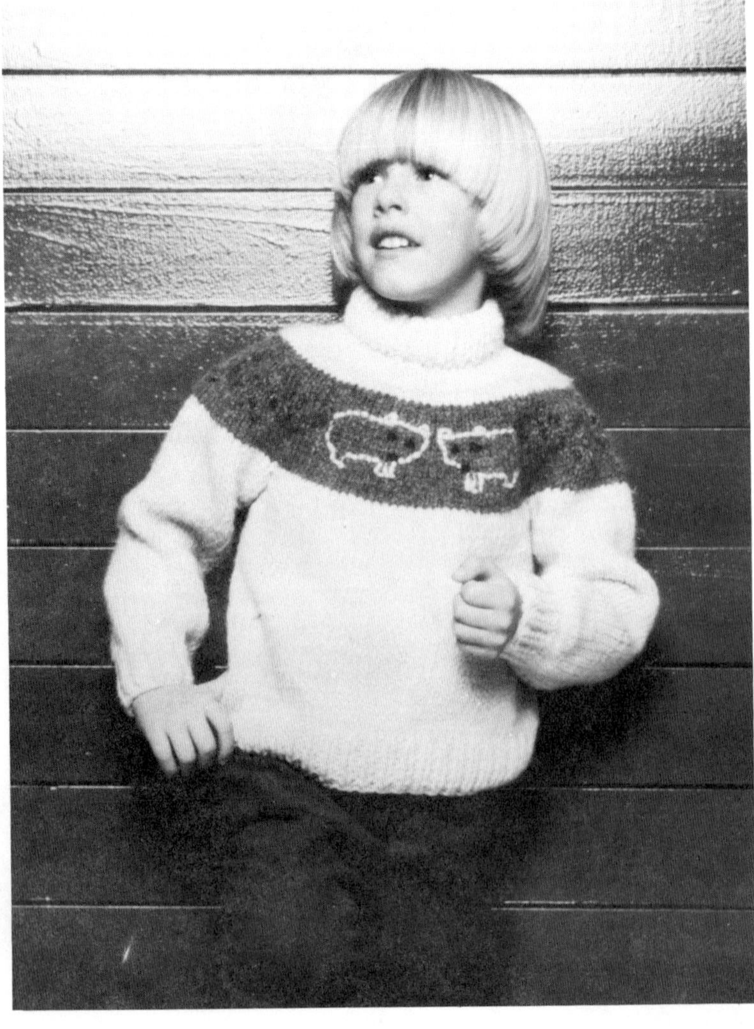

COURTESY OF PHILDAR

Directions to Follow

Sleeves: With smaller needles cast on 22 (24, 28, 30, 32) sts col Ecru and work in K 1, P 1 ribbing for 2 inches (5 cm). Change to larger needles and stockinette st inc 5 (6, 5, 5, 6) sts evenly spaced of first row. There are 27 (30, 33, 35, 38) sts on needle.
Inc then 1 st at beg and end of—

Size 4: foll 4th row once, then on every foll 6th row 5 times more—

Size 6: foll 6th row once and then on every foll 8th row 4 times more—

Size 8: every 10th row 4 times—

Size 10: on foll 10th row once and then on every foll 12th row 3 times more—

Size 12: on foll 12th row once and then on every foll 14th row 3 times more. There are 39 (40, 41, 43, 46) sts on needle.
When work meas 21 (24, 27, 30, 34) sts from beg of stockinette st—

Shape beg of Armholes. All sizes: Bind off 3 sts at beg of next 2 rows. 33 (34, 35, 37, 40) sts rem. Slip sts to a stitch holder.

Back: With smaller needles cast on 48 (50, 52, 56, 62) sts and work in K 1, P 1 ribbing for 2 inches (5 cm). Change to larger needles and stockinette st even until work measures 6¾ (7½, 8¼, 9, 10¼) inches—17 (19, 21, 23, 26) cm from beg of stockinette st.

Shape beg of Armholes. All sizes: Bind off 3 sts at beg of next 2 rows. 42 (44, 46, 50, 56) sts remain. Slip sts to a stitch holder.

Front: Cast on and work in the same manner as back until work measures 5½ (6¼, 7, 8, 9) inches—14 (16, 18, 20, 23) cm from beg of stockinette st. Continue in short rows as foll.

Size 4: Beg at right edge, work on 19 sts, *turn* and work back.

Next row: work on 9 sts, *turn* and work back.

Sizes 6 and 8: Beg at right edge, work on 20 sts, *turn* and work back.

Next row: work on 10 sts, *turn* and work back.

Size 10: Beg at right edge, work on 22 sts, *turn* and work back.

Next row: work on 11 sts, *turn* and work back.

Size 12: Beg at right edge, work on 25 sts, *turn* and work back.

Next row: work on 12 sts, *turn* and work back.

All sizes: Beg at *left edge,* work to correspond.

Next row: Work 1 row on *all* sts, then shape beg of armholes:

All sizes: Bind off 3 sts at beg of next 2 rows. Slip sts to a stitch holder.

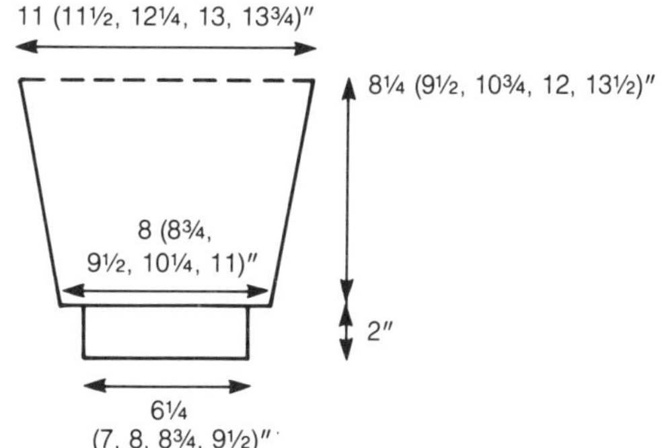

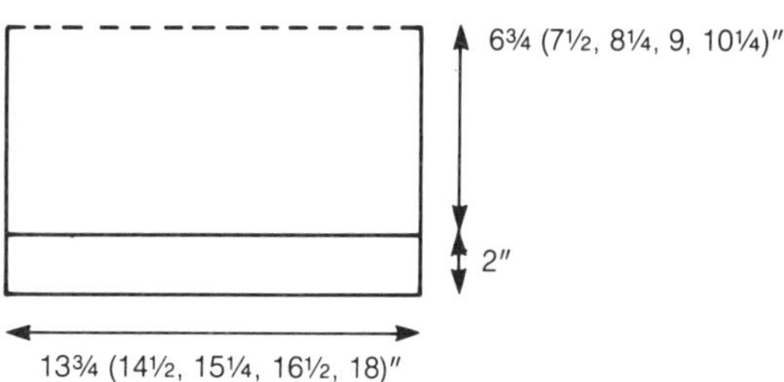

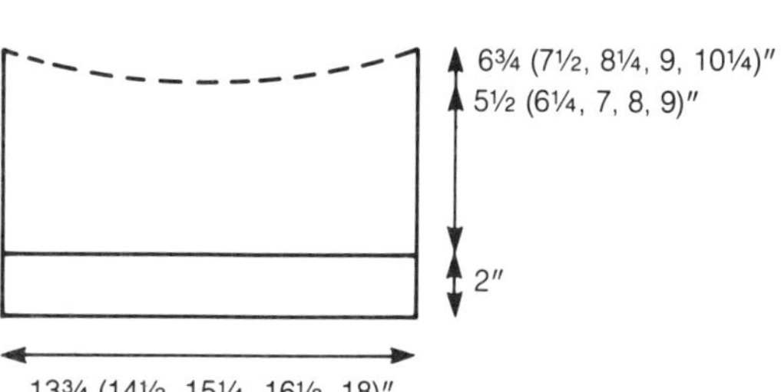

Yoke: col Gris Moyen. Cast on 1 st, then work on the 33 (34, 35, 37, 40) sts from one sleeve, then on the 42 (44, 46, 50, 56) sts from front, then on the 33 (34, 35, 37, 40) sts from the second sleeve, and then on the 42 (44, 46, 50, 56) sts from back, cast on 1 st.

Note: The 2 cast-on sts will be the edge sts for seam. There are 152 (158, 164, 176, 194) sts on needle. Work 6 (6, 6, 6, 8) rows even and then dec on next row as foll: 3 sts, * * 2 sts tog, 4 sts * * rep from * * to * * end with 2 sts tog and 3 sts instead of 4. 127 (132, 137, 147, 162) sts rem.

Work 5 (5, 7, 7, 7) rows even and then dec as foll on next row: 3 sts, * * 2 sts tog, 3 sts * *, rep from * * to * * end with 2 sts tog and 2 sts. 102 (106, 110, 118, 130) sts rem.

Work 5 (5, 5, 7, 7) rows even, then dec on next row as foll: 2 sts, * * 2 sts tog, 2 sts * *, rep from * * to * *. 77 (80, 83, 89, 98) sts rem.

Work 5 (5, 7, 7, 7) rows even and then dec on next row as foll: 1 st, * * 2 sts tog, 1 st * *, rep from * * to * * end with 2 sts tog and 2 sts. 52 (54, 56, 60, 66) sts rem.

At the same time. When you have knitted 18 rows from the yoke in Gris Moyen, continue then in Ecru to end.

Note: After the last row of dec work 6 (6, 6, 8, 8) rows even.

Change to smaller needles and K 1, P 1 ribbing for 3¼ inches (8 cm).

Making up: Sew side, sleeve and yoke seams including collar. Fold collar in half to wrong side and sl st.

Embroider around yoke, except for front, in the Gris Moyen stripe, foll #1 Chart, in duplicate st col Brasero, and then embroider on front, with back stitch, col Ecru #2 Chart, embroidering eyes and muzzle in straight stitch col Noir.

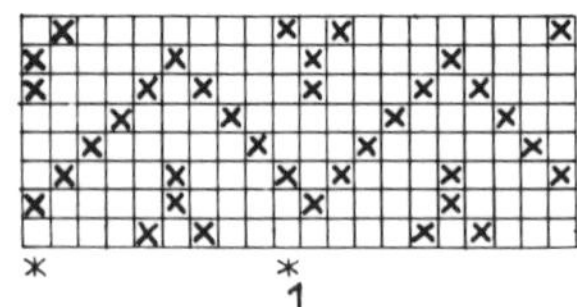

Repeat from * to *

□ Col GRIS MOYEN

⊠ Embroidery in duplicate st col BRASERO

⊟ Embroidery in back stitch col ECRU

■ EMBROIDERY in straight stitch col NOIR

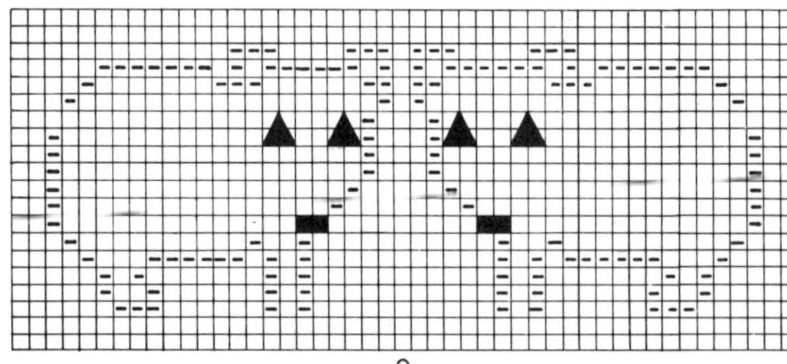

ZIPPERED JACKET

This design is sure to please the young girl who likes to be outdoors. It provides an attractive way to keep warm.

Information to Study Before You Begin

Sizing: Directions are for 7 years. Changes for 9, 11, and 13 are in parentheses. Made to fit chest of 26 (30, 32, 33) inches.

Materials: Phildar Sagitaire yarn was used for the jacket. You need:
9 (10, 11, 12) balls in Rouge (red).
Zippers: 1 for front closing.
2 for pockets in lengths 4 (4, 4, 5) inches.
Lining material for pockets.

Tools: Knitting Needles, Nos. 3 (3 mm) and 6 (4 mm).

Gauge (meas over stitch pattern on No. 6 needles) : 25 sts = 4 inches; 46 rows = 4 inches.

Stitch Pattern

St 1: K 1 P 1 rib.

St 2: Fancy Rib (worked over an odd No. of sts).

1st row: K.

2nd row: K 1, * K 1B, P 1, rep from * to last 2 sts. K 1B. K 1.

These 2 rows form pat.

COURTESY OF PHILDAR

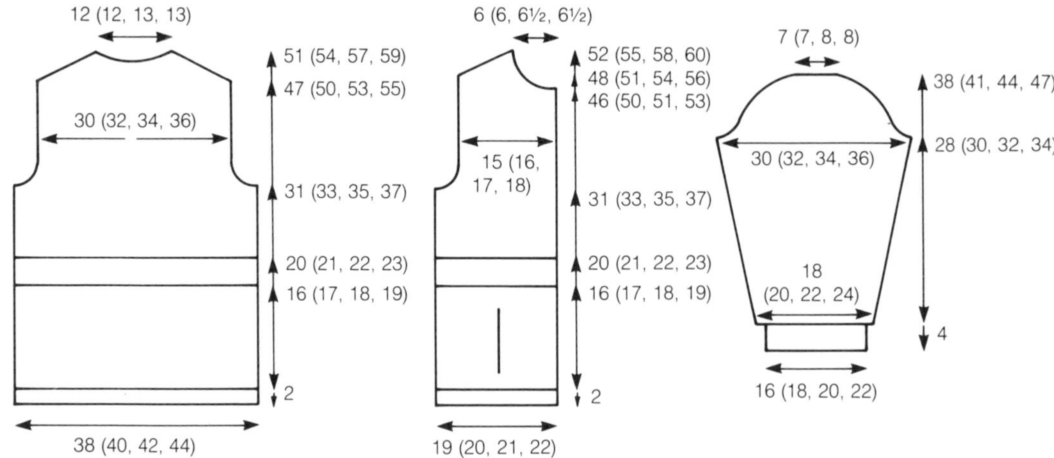

Note: Measurements are in centimeters.

Directions to Follow

Back: With No. 3 needles, cast on 97 (101, 107, 111) sts, work ¾ inch (2 cm) in K 1 P 1 rib. *Change to* No. 6 Needles and pat as given and work straight until Back meas 7 (7½, 8, 8¼) inches—18 (19, 20, 21) cm from cast-on edge, ending with a 2nd pat row.

Change to No. 3 Needles and work 1¾ inches (4 cm) in rib as for welt. *Change to* No. 6 Needles and cont in pat until Back meas 13 (13¾, 14½, 15¼) inches—33 (35, 37, 39) cm from cast on edge.

Shape Armholes: Cont in pat cast off 3 sts at beg of next 2 rows, and 2 sts and beg of next 4 rows. Dec 1 st at beg of next 6 rows; 77 (81, 87, 91) sts. Cont straight until Back meas 19¼ (20½, 21¾, 22½) inches—49 (52, 55, 57) cm from cast-on edge, ending with a 2nd pat row.

Shape Shoulders: Cast off 2 (2, 3, 3) sts at beg of next 8 (4, 12, 12) rows.

For 1st and 2nd Sizes only: Cast off 3 sts at beg of next 4 (8) rows.

All Sizes: Shape Back Neck and Shoulders.

1st row: Cast off 3 sts. K 16 (16, 17, 19) incl st on needle after cast-off, cast off 11 sts K to end. Cont on last set of sts only.

2nd row: Cast off 3 sts pat to end.

3rd row: Cast off 5 (5, 6, 6) sts K to end.

4th row: Cast off 3 (3, 3, 4) sts pat to end.

5th row: Cast off 5 sts K to end.

Cast off rem 3 (3, 3, 4) sts. Rejoin yarn to neck edge or rem sts.

1st row: Cast off 5 (5, 6, 6) sts pat to end.

2nd row: Cast off 3 (3, 3, 4) sts K to end.

3rd row: Cast off 5 sts pat to end.

Cast off rem 3 (3, 3, 4) sts.

Left Front: With No. 3 Needles, cast on 49 (51, 55, 57) sts. Work ¾ inch (2 cm) in rib as for Back.

Change to No. 6 needles and pat as for Back. Work until Front meas 2 (2, 2¼, 2¼) inches—5 (5, 6, 6) cm, ending with a 2nd pat row * *.

Divide for Pocket—

Next row: K 24, turn and cont on these sts only, leave rem sts on a spare needle.

Cont straight until work meas 6 (6, 6¼, 7¼) inches—15 (15, 16, 18) cm from cast-on edge, ending with a 2nd pat row. Leave sts on a spare needle. Rejoin yarn to inner edge of rem 25 (27, 31, 33) sts and cont straight in pat until work meas same as other side, ending with a 2nd pat row. Break yarn. Now join work thus:

Next row: K across 24 sts from spare needle, then K across rem sts 49 (51, 55, 57) sts.

Cont in pat until Front meas 7 (7½, 8, 8¾) inches—18 (19, 20, 21) cm from cast-on edge, ending with a 2nd pat row.

Change to No. 3. needles and work 1¾ inches (4 cm) in rib as for Back.

Change to No. 6 needles and cont in pat until Front meas 13 (13¾, 14½, 15¼) inches—33 (35, 37, 39) cm from cast-on edge, ending at side edge.

Shape Armhole: Cont in pat cast off 3 sts at beg of next row, then cast off 2 sts at beg of next 2 alt rows and 1st at beg of next 3 alt rows. 39 (41, 45, 47) sts. Cont straight until Front meas 18½ (19¾, 20½, 21¼) inches—47, (50, 52, 54) cm from cast-on edge, ending at Front edge.

Shape Neck: Cast off 4 sts at beg of next row, then cast off 3 sts at beg of next alt row, 2 sts at beg of next 3 (3, 4, 4) alt rows, and 1 st at beg of next 3 alt rows: 23 (25, 27, 29) sts. Cont straight until Front meas 19¾ (20¾, 22, 22¾) inches—50 (53, 56, 58) cm from cast-on edge, ending at armhole edge.

Shape Shoulder: For 1st Size Only:
Cast off 2 sts at beg of next and foll 3 alt rows, then cast off 3 sts at beg of next 5 alt rows.

For 2nd Size Only:
Cast off 2 sts at beg of next and foll alt row, then cast off 3 sts at beg of next 7 alt rows.

For 3rd Size Only:
Cast off 3 sts at beg of next and foll 8 alt rows.

For 4th Size Only:
Cast off 3 sts at beg of next and foll 6 alt rows, then cast off 4 sts at beg of next 2 alt rows.

Right Front: Work as for Left Front to * *.

Divide for Pocket: Next row: K 25 (27, 31, 33) turn and cont on these sts only, leave rem sts on spare needle.

Cont straight until work meas 6 (6, 6¼, 7¼) inches—15 (15, 16, 18) cm from cast-on edge, ending with a 2nd pat row. Leave sts on spare needle.

Rejoin yarn to inner edge of rem 24 sts and cont straight until work meas same as other side, ending with a 2nd pat row.

Now join thus:

Next row: K across sts from spare needle, then K rem 24 sts 49 (51, 55, 57) sts. Now work as for Left Front, rev shapings.

Sleeves: With No. 3 needles, cast on 42 (46, 52, 56) sts and work in K 1 P 1 rib for 1½ inches (4 cm), inc 5 sts evenly across last row. 47 (51, 57, 61) sts. *Change to* No. 6 needles and pat inc 1 st at each end of every 7th (8th, 8th, 9th) row until there are 77 (81, 87, 91) sts, work straight in pat until sleeve meas 12½ (13½, 14½, 15) inches—32 (34, 36, 38) cm.

Shape Top: Cast off 3 sts at beg of next 2 rows.

For 1st and 2nd Sizes Only:
Cast off 2 sts at beg of next 4 rows.

All Sizes: Dec 1 st at beg of every row until 27 (27, 30, 31) sts rem. Cast off 2 sts at beg of next 2 rows, and 3 sts at beg of foll 2 rows. Cast on rem 17 (17, 21, 21) sts.

Collar: With No. 3 needles, cast on 87 (87, 91, 97) sts. Work 5½ (6¼, 7, 8) inches—14 (16, 18, 20) cm in rib as for Back. Cast off in rib.

To Complete: Join shoulder, side and sleeve seams. Set in sleeves. Sew zips into pocket openings. Sew in open-ended zip fastener. Sew cast-on edge of collar to neck edge. Fold collar in half and sew cast-off edge along inside of neck edge. Join side edges of collar. Make linings for pockets and sew them on wrong side of work.

BABY LAYETTE SET

Each part of this layette shows how garter and stockinette stitches can be combined for a pretty effect. A white and red color combination is suggested, which may seem unusual for the newborn baby.

Information to Study Before You Begin

Sizing: Instructions are for Sizes 6 to 12 Months.
Approximate size of blanket 24 × 34 inches.

Materials: Columbia-Minerva Nantuk 4-ply yarn in 4 oz. balls is used. You need:
2 balls in white for blanket; 1 ball in white for jacket, cap, and booties; 1 ball in red for the pants.

Tools: Knitting Needles, No. 8.
Crochet Hook, Size 1.

Gauge (stockinette st): 9 sts = 2 inches; 6 rows = 1 inch.

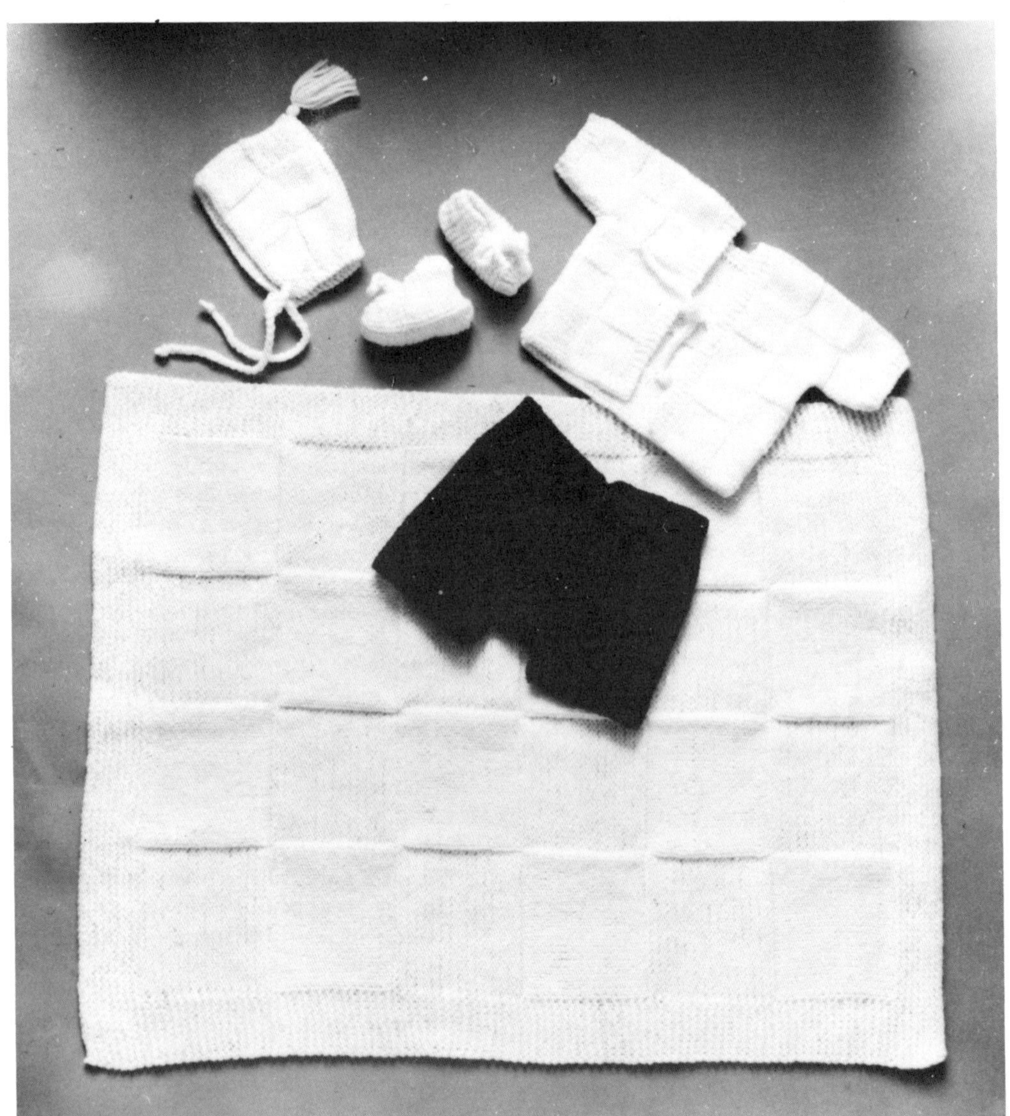

COURTESY OF COLUMBIA-MINERVA CORPORATION

Directions to Follow

JACKET

Finished Chest Measurement: 20 inches.
Note: Jacket is worked in one piece. Beg at lower edge of back, cast on 45 sts.
Row 1 (wrong side): K. K 2 rows more.

First Section—
Row 1 (right side): K 9, [P 9, K 9] twice.
Row 2: P 9, [K 9, P 9] twice. Rep these 2 rows for pat for a total of 12 rows.
Second Block Pat Section—
Row 1 (right side): P 9, [K 9, P 9] twice.
Row 2: K 9, [P 9, K 9] twice. Continue to work block pat alternating K and P squares every 12 rows, following photograph, until 3 sections are complete.

Cast on for Sleeve: Cast on 12 sts at end of last row. K 3, work pat to end, cast on 12 sts at end of row. K 3, work pat to last 3 sts, K 3—69 sts. Continue in pat on all sts until a total of 4 sections are complete. Place marker at each side of center 9 st block pat—work these 9 sts in garter st and rem sts in established pat for 4 rows.

Divide for Neck (5th row of 5th section —right side): K 3, P 9, K 9, K 3, bind off center 3 sts for back of neck; join a second skein, K 3, P 9, K 9, P 9, K 3. Keeping first and last 3 sts of each side in garter st border, continue to work each side with a separate skein. At beg of 11th and 12th rows of 7th block pat section, bind off 12 sts (sleeves completed—21 sts rem). Work 8th, 9th, and 10th sections in pat. K across all 21 sts on each side for 3 rows (2 ridges) for garter st border. Bind off.

Finishing: Sew side and sleeve seams. With crochet hook and double strand, chain two 6-inch ties and sew to front edges as shown in photograph.

BOOTIES

Beg at center back edge, cast on 29 sts.
Row 1 (right side): Knit.
Row 2: K 10, P 1, K 7, P 1, K 10. Rep these 2 rows for 1¾ inches end on wrong side.
Dec Row: K 2 tog (dec), K to last 2 sts, K 2 tog. Work 1 row even. Rep dec row—25 sts. Work even in pat until 3½ inches from beg, end on wrong side.
Toe Ribbing—
Row 1: K 1, * P 1, K 1; rep from * to end.
Row 2: P 1, * K 1, P 1; rep from * to end. Rep these 2 rows once.
Next Row: K 1, [K 2 tog] 4 times, work 7 sts in ribbing, [sl 1, K 1, psso] 4 times, K 1—17 sts. Cut yarn leaving an end for sewing. Thread into yarn needle and draw through sts. Pull tog tightly, secure end.
Finishing: Fold cast-on row in half and sew for back seam. Beg at toe, sew top tog for 1½ inches. Draw needle through the 7 sts between K ribs and draw up tightly for heel.
Drawstring Tie: With crochet hook and double strand, chain for 15 inches, weave through top edge.

CAP

Cast on 60 sts for face edge.
Knit 3 rows for garter st border.
First Block Pat Section—
Row 1 (right side): K 3 (border), [K 9, P 9] 3 times; K 3 (border). Rep this row for pat for a total of 12 rows.
Second Block Pat Section—
Row 1 (right side): K 3, [P 9, K 9] 3 times, K 3. Rep this row for pat for a total of 12 rows. K 3 rows for garter st border. Bind off.
Finishing: Fold piece in half and sew bound-off edge tog for back seam. With crochet hook and double strand, chain 25 inches for tie. Weave tie through sts at lower edge as shown. Make a tassel and attach to top.

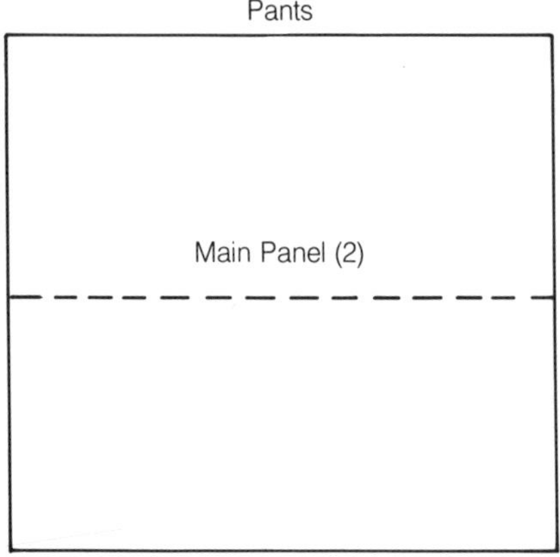

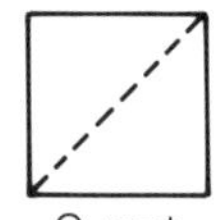

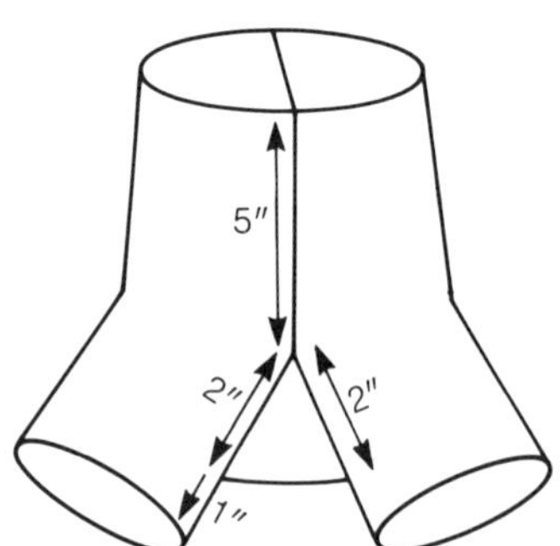

PANTS

Main Panel (Make 2): Cast on 36 sts. Knit every row for garter st for 10 inches. Bind off.

Gusset: Cast on 10 sts. Work in garter st for 2 inches. Bind off.

Finishing: Following diagram, beg at waist sew front and back seams for 5 inches. Sew points of gusset and 2 inches each side. Sew 1 inch tog on each leg.

Drawstring Tie: With crochet hook and double strand, chain for 30 inches. Thread through pants at waist 1 inch from top edge.

BLANKET

Approximate size 24 × 34 inches. Cast on 108 sts loosely.

Garter St Border—

Row 1 (wrong side): Knit.

Rows 2–13: K, ending on wrong side work should meas approx 2 inches (7 ridges).

*** First Block Pat Section—**

Row 1 (right side): K 10 (border), [P 22, K 22] twice, K 10 (border). Rep this row for pat for 5 inches (30 rows total). End on wrong side.

Second Block Pat Section—

Row 1 (right side): K 10, [K 22, P 22] twice, K 10. Rep this row for pat for 5 inches (30 rows total). End on wrong side *. Rep between *'s twice.

Garter St Border: Knit all sts for 13 rows (7 ridges or 2 inches). Bind off.

SOFT DOLL FOR A SMALL BABY

Finding a gift for a baby that has a new look is often a problem. This little doll may solve the problem. Babies will enjoy watching them as they lay in their cribs.

Information to Study Before You Begin

Size: 11¾ inches high.
Materials: Phildar Anouchka Yarn was used for this doll. You need:
1 ball White (A);
1 ball Blue (B);
1 ball Gray (C).
Lining Fabric—10 × 11¾ inches.
Stuffing.
Tools: Knitting Needles, No. 7.
Note: Yarn is used double throughout.
Stitches used: St 1—Stockinette st.
St 2—Garter st.

Directions to Follow

Body: Cast on 46 sts with col B. Work in garter st as folls:
16 rows col B.
8 rows col C.
6 rows col B.
4 rows col C.
4 rows col B.
2 rows col C.
2 rows col B.
2 rows col C.
* * 2 rows col A, 2 rows col B, 2 rows col A, 2 rows col C * *. Rep from * * to * * once more and finish with 2 rows col A, 2 rows col C, 8 rows col B. Cast off.

Head: Cast on 37 sts with col A. Work in stockinette st for 30 rows. Cast off.

Hood: Cast on 37 sts with col C. Work in stockinette st for 22 rows. Cast off.

To Make Up: Cut a rectangle of lining fabric 9½ × 8 inches (24 × 20 cm) for the body, and 8 × 4 inches (20 × 10 cm) for the head.
Fold in half short sides together and join. Gather bottom and draw up to close. Turn right side out, stuff, gather and draw up top.
Fold knitted body in half, join side seam, gather bottom to close and insert stuffed lining.

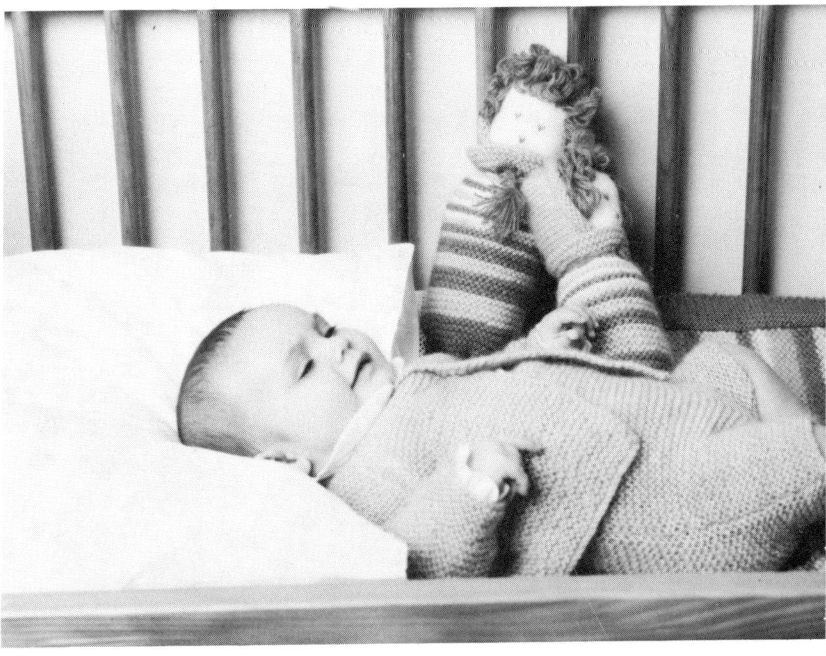

HAIRBANDS

If you like to wear something to keep your hair in place when the wind is blowing or you are playing tennis, then here is something for you to make. It can be made in different widths, and if you wish you can add a bow.

HEADBAND

Information to Study Before You Begin

Size: 1½ inches (3.8 cm) wide. Check gauge so you will knit the band the correct length.

Materials: 1 ball in desired color of Phildar's Relais yarn.

Tools: Knitting Needles, No. 0.

Directions to Follow

Cast on 170 sts.
Work in K 1, P 1 rib for 1½ inches.
Cast off.
Join edge firmly with a fine seam.

BANDEAU WITH BOW

Information to Study Before You Begin

Size: 2½ inches (6.5 cm) wide. Check gauge so you will knit the band the correct length.

Material: 1 ball in desired color of Phildar's Brousse Yarn.
Knitting Needles, No. 0.

Directions to Follow

Cast on 170 sts.
Work in K 1, P 1 rib for 2½ inches.
Cast off loosely in rib.
For the Bow, cast on 39 sts.
Then for—

Row 1: K 2, * P 1, K 1, rep from * to last st. K 1.

Row 2: K 1, * P 1, K 1, rep from * to end.

Rep these 2 rows until strip measures 2½ inches.
Cast off.

To Make Up Bandeau, do not press band. Using a flat seam, join ends. Join sides of bow in same way. Use running stitches through center stitches to gather band. Sew bow in place.

CHECK TIE

Knitted ties can be expensive. This one provides a smart way to be thrifty and in fashion.

Information to Study Before You Begin

Materials: 1 oz. Red (No. 905); 1 oz. Camel (No. 328); 2 oz. Navy (No. 858) of 3-ply Coats and Clark's Red Heart® Sock and Sweater Yarn, Art. E253.
Tools: Knitting Needles, No. 3.
Gauge: 9 sts = 1 inch; 14 rows = 1 inch.

Directions to Follow

Starting at front point, with Camel cast on 4 sts. Drop Camel, attach Navy.

Row 1 (right side): With yarn in front sl 1 as to P, K 1, sl 1 as before; K in front and in back and in front of next st—2 sts inc . . . 6 sts. Drop Navy, attach Red.

Row 2: With yarn in back sl 1 as to P, * P 1, sl 1 as before. Rep from * to last st; P in front and in back and in front of next st—2 sts inc. Drop Red, pick up Camel and twist strands.

Row 3: With yarn in front sl 1 as to P, * K 1, sl 1 as before. Rep from * to last st, inc 2 sts in last st—2 sts more than on previous row. Drop Camel, pick up Navy and twist strands. Working 1 row with each color as established until otherwise stated, rep Rows 2 and 3 alternately until 76 sts are on needle, end on wrong side.

Next Row: * With yarn in front sl 1 as to P, K 1. Rep from * across.

Following Row: * With yarn in back sl 1 as to P, P 1. Rep from * across. Rep last 2 rows alternately until total length from point is 3 inches, end on wrong side.

Next Row: Dec one st at each end, work in pattern across.

Following 13 Rows: Work even. Rep last 14 rows 23 more times—28 sts remain on needle. Fasten off all colors. Slip first 7 sts on a stitch holder, slip next 14 sts on a dpn, slip last 7 sts on another stitch holder; then slip the 14 sts from dpn back onto long needle. Sts on holders will be secured later. Attach Navy and work in K 1, P 1 ribbing over the 14 sts on needle for 29 inches. Continuing in ribbing, dec one st at each end of next 6 rows; then K 2 tog.

Having wrong sides tog, fold side edges on lower end of tie to center back. With Navy and a tapestry needle, weave sts on holders to corresponding sts of ribbing. Sew tie seam. Press.

LEG WARMERS

Following the lead of the ballet dancer, adds a cozy warmth on chilly days. Two-color combinations are suggested here. Of course, you can change them if you wish.

Information to Study Before You Begin

Materials: *For Right-hand Warmers* you need:
5 oz. Bright Pink (No. 741) for Color A.
For striped trim, 2 oz. Yellow (No. 230) for Color B.
Add 1 oz. Skipper Blue (No. 848) for Color C.
For Left-hand Warmers, you need:
5 oz. Orange (245) for Color A.
For striped trim, 2 oz. Amethyst (No. 588) for Color B.
And 1 oz. Mint Julep (No. 669) for Color C.
The suggested yarn is Coats and Clark's Red Heart®, 4-ply Hand-knitting Yarn made in ready-to-use pull-out skeins.
Tools: Knitting Needles, No. 8.
Gauge: 4 sts = 1 inch; 8 rows = 1 inch.

Directions To Follow

Starting at cuff with Color A, cast on 60 sts. Work in garter st (K each row) for 9 rows. Break off Color A, attach Color B. Always change colors in this way. Continuing in garter st, work in following stripe pat: (4 rows Color B, 2 rows Color C, 4 rows Color B, 6 rows Color A) 3 times.

Next Row: With Color A, * P 1, K 2 tog. Rep from * across—40 sts. Continuing with Color A only, work in P 1, K 1 ribbing for 12 inches.

Following Row: Bind off 7 sts, continue in rib pat until there are 6 sts on right-hand needle for strap section; place rem sts on a stitch holder to be worked later. Work in pat over the 6 sts until strap meas 3 inches. Bind off. Slip sts from holder onto needle, attach yarn and bind off next 14 sts, continue in rib pat as established until there are 6 sts on right-hand needle for other strap section; place rem sts on holder to be worked later. Work over the 6 sts to correspond with other strap section. Slip sts from holder onto needle, attach yarn, and bind off these sts.

Sew center back seam of leg warmer. Sew ends of strap sections together. Make another Leg Warmer.

COURTESY OF COLUMBIA-MINERVA CORPORATION

IMPORTANT ACCESSORIES

Shown here is a collection of small items that many persons find most useful. They make excellent gifts as well as articles to sell at the bazaar. They also offer you a way to use up bits of yarn that have been left from other projects.

FAMILY SLIPPERS

Nothing could be nicer than these easy fitting ribbed slippers to provide warmth with a pretty touch. They can be made for the various members of the family using their favorite colors.

Information to Study Before You Begin

Sizing: Instructions are for Children's Size. Changes for Women's and Men's Sizes are in parentheses.
Materials: You need 1 ball of Columbia-Minerva Nantuk 4-ply yarn in 4 oz. balls.
Tools: Knitting Needles, No. 8. Crochet Hook, Size 1.
Gauge: 9 sts = 2 inches; 6 rows = 1 inch.

Directions to Follow

Cast on 37 (43, 49) sts for back edge.
Row 1 (right side): K 4, P 1, K 27 (33, 39), P 1, K 4.
Row 2: K 14 (16, 18), P 1, K 7 (9, 11), P 1, K 14 (16, 18). Rep these 2 rows for 3 (3½, 4) inches, end with Row 2.
Next Row: Bind off 6 sts, K 26 (32, 38), P 1, K 4.
Next Row: Bind off 6 sts, K next 7 (9, 11), P 1, K 7 (9, 11), P 1, K 8 (10, 12).
Foot—
Row 1: K 2, [K 1, P 1] 3 (4, 5) times, K 9 (11, 13), [P 1, K 1] 3 (4, 5) times, K 2.
Row 2: K 2, [P 1, K 1] 3 (4, 5) times, P 1, K 7 (9, 11), P 1 [K 1, P 1] 3 (4, 5) times, K 2. Rep Rows 1 and 2 until foot meas 4 (5, 6) inches or desired length from heel to toe. Break yarn leaving end. Thread end into yarn needle and draw through sts on needle. Pull tog tightly and secure. Sew seam at top of foot. Beg at top sew back seam. With crochet hook and double strand of yarn make a 36-inch ch. Tie into bow and sew to front of slipper as shown.

FAMILY MITTENS

Three different looks are shown here. Each one seems appropriate for the person for whom it has been planned. Adding touches of bright color to the tips of the thumb and hand seem right for a child. Ridges of garter stitch gives a prettier look to the women's version, whereas the chain stitch ribs create a sturdier design for the men.

Information to Study Before You Begin

Sizing: Instructions are for Children's style. Changes for Women's and Men's styles are in parentheses.
Materials: You need Columbia-Minerva Nantuk 4-ply (4 oz.) balls.
For Children: 1 ball of the Main Color (MC) and small amounts of yarn for color contrasts (A and B).
For Women: 1 ball of Tea Rose (MC).
For Men: 1 ball of Camel (MC).
Tools: Knitting Needles, No. 8.
Gauge: 9 sts = 2 inches; 6 rows = 1 inch.

Directions to Follow

Beg at cuff edge, with MC, cast on 24 (28, 32) sts.
Row 1: * K 1, P 1, rep from * to end. Rep Row 1 for K 1, P 1 rib to 2 (4, 3) inches from beg.

For Children's (Women's) Styles Only—Next Row (right side): * K 5 (6), inc 1 st in next st; rep from * 3 times—28 (32) sts. P 1 row.

Thumb—Next Row: K 13 (15), place marker on needle, inc 1 st in each of next 2 sts, place marker on needle (4 sts between markers). K to end of row. Sl markers every row. P 1 row. Continue in stockinette st (K 1 row, P 1 row), inc 1 st after first marker and 1 st before 2nd marker every K row until there are 12 (14) sts between markers, end with K row.

Next Row: P 14 (16) and sl these sts to a holder, P 10 (12) for thumb, sl rem 14 (16) sts to a 2nd holder. Work in stockinette st on thumb sts for 2 (10) rows more.

Children's Style Only: Cut MC, join A and work in stockinette st for 5 rows more.

Children's (Women's) Styles Only: Cut yarn leaving 6-inch end, thread into yarn needle, draw through sts of thumb, pull tog tightly, and secure. On wrong side, sew thumb seam. Rejoin yarn at beg of 2nd holder with P side facing you, P to end of row.

Next Row: K 14 (16), K 14 (16) from first holder—28 (32) sts.

Children's Style Only: Continue in stockinette st for 14 rows more. Cut MC, join B. Work in stockinette st for 3 rows.

Women's Style Only— * Next Row (wrong side): Knit (forms ridge on right side). [K 1 row, P 1 row] 4 times. K 1 row *. Rep between * once, K 1 row (3 ridges). [K 1 row, P 1 row] twice.

Top Decreases, Children's (Women's) Styles Only—

Row 1: * K 2 tog, K 2; rep from * to end.

Row 2: Purl.

Row 3: * K 2 tog, K 1; rep from * to end.

Row 4: P 2 tog across row—7 (8) sts. Cut yarn leaving 12-inch end, draw through sts, pull tog tightly, secure end. On wrong side, sew side seam.

For Men's Style Only—Next Row (right side): P 4, * [K 1, P in front then in back of next st for 1 st inc] twice, K 1 *; P 13, rep between * once, P 5—36 sts.

Next Row: K 5, [P 1, K 2] twice, P 1, K 13, [P 1, K 2] twice, P 1, K 4. Continue to work in reverse stockinette st (purl side is right side) keeping 7 rib sts in pat as established.

Thumb—Next Row: Work 17 sts in pat, place marker on needle, inc 1 st in each of next 2 sts, place marker on needle (4 sts between markers) work in pat to end of row. Sl markers every row. Continue in pat, inc 1 st after first marker and 1 st before 2nd marker on every right-side (P) row until there are 14 sts between markers. End with K row.

Next Row: Work 18 sts in pat and sl to a holder, work 12 sts for thumb, sl rem 18 sts to a 2nd holder. Work on thumb sts in reverse stockinette st for 10 rows more. Cut yarn leaving 6-inch end, draw through sts of thumb, pull tog tightly. Secure end. Sew thumb seam. Rejoin yarn at beg of 2nd holder with K side facing you, work in pat to end of row.

Next Row: Work 18 sts in pat, work sts from first holder—36 sts. Continue in pat for 20 rows more. Work in reverse stockinette st on all sts for 5 rows. Work top decreases and finishing same as top decreases and finishing of children's mittens.

FLOOR PILLOW

For a different decorative touch, try this interesting design. The contrast in textures seems to create an elegant look.

Information to Study Before You Begin

Size: 20 × 20 inches.
Materials: This pillow is made of Columbia-Minerva Nantuk 4-ply yarn in 4 oz. balls. You need:
4 balls.
1 pillow form 20 inches square, or polyester filling.
Tools: Knitting Needles, No. 8.
Crochet Hook, Size G.
Gauge (stockinette st):
9 sts = 2 inches; 6 rows = 1 inch.

Directions to Follow

Square (Make 2): Beg at lower edge, cast on 91 sts.
Row 1 (wrong side): Knit.
Rows 2–15: Rep Row 1. Work should meas approx 2 inches.
Row 16 (right side): Knit.
Row 17: K 9, P to last 9 sts, K 9.
Rows 18, 20, 22, 24, and 26: Knit.
Rows 19, 21, 23, 25, and 27: Rep Row 17 (approx 4 inches from beg).
Beg Seed St Pat—
Row 28: K 18, P 1, * K 1, P 1; rep from * to last 18 sts, K 18.
Row 29: K 9, P 9; P 1, * K 1, P 1; rep from * to last 18 sts; P 9, K 9. Rep Rows 28 and 29 until 16 inches from beg, end with a right-side row. Rep Rows 17 and 16 six times (12 rows). Knit 15 rows. Bind off.

Finishing: From right side, holding 2 pieces tog, matching ridge for ridge and st for st, work sc through double thickness of each ridge and st, work 3 sc at corners. Join 3 sides this way, insert form or filling, join 4th side. Make 4 large tassels and attach to corners of pillow.

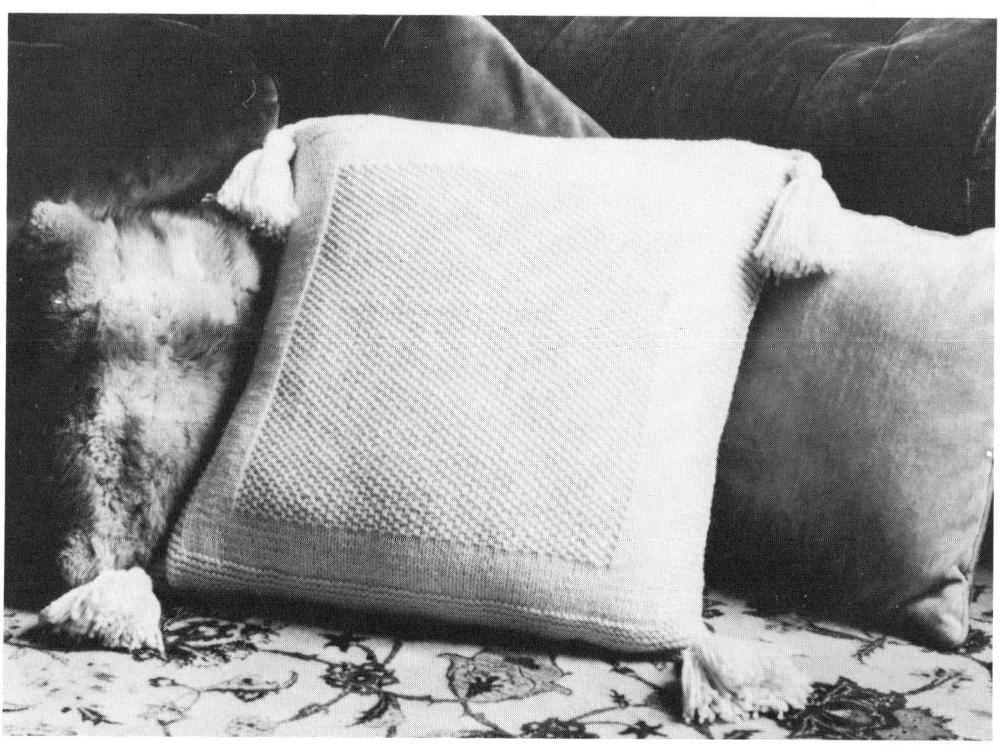

INSTRUCTIONS FOR ILLUSTRATIONS IN THE COLOR SECTION

PRETTY SEPARATES

A smart two-piece dress can be fashioned by combining a skirt with a decorative sweater top. The parts can be worn separately to expand your wardrobe in an interesting way.

Information to Study Before You Begin

SKIRT

Sizing: These directions are for Small Size (8–10). Changes for Medium Size (12–14) and Large Size (16–18) are in parentheses.

Materials: Bernat Carioca yarn (1 oz. tube) was used for this skirt. You need: 10 (11, 12) tubes.
1 yard of 1-inch elastic.

Tools: Circular Knitting Needles, Nos. 4 and 6 (Bernat-Aero), or any size needle that will give the stitch gauge given below.

Gauge: 6 sts = 1 inch; 8 rows = 1 inch.

Note 1: This skirt has been planned for 27-inch finished length. If you wish your skirt to be longer or shorter, work more or less inches before lower hemline.

Note 2: All increases are made by knitting in *back loop* of next stitch in row below.

Knit in one piece on a circular needle. Waistline down.

Note 3: Knit in one piece on a circular needle working from the waistline down.

Directions to Follow

Using smaller needle, cast on 168 (180, 210) sts. Join, being careful not to twist sts and put a marker on needle to mark beg of round. K around and around in stockinette st until piece meas 1 inch. P the next round in *back loops* to form upper hemline. K around and around until piece meas 1 inch above hemline. Change to larger needle and K 1 round. On the next round, starting at marker on needle, * K 28 (30, 35) sts, put a marker on needle, repeat from * 4 times more, K last 28 (30, 35) sts. INC ROUND: Starting at beg of round, * K 1, inc 1 st, K to 1 st before next marker, inc 1 st, K 1, rep from * 5 times more—12 sts inc. Continuing to work in stockinette st, repeat inc round every 1 inch 4 times more. Work even on 228 (240, 270) sts until piece meas 27 inches above hemline or desired finished length. P the next round in *back loops* to form lower hemline. Change to smaller needle and work in stockinette st for 1 inch. Bind off.

Finishing: Hem lower and upper edges. Draw elastic, cut to waist measurement through upper hem and sew ends.

SWEATER TOP

Sizing: These directions are for Small Size (8–10). Changes for Medium Size (12–14) and Large Size (16–18) are in parentheses.

Materials: Bernat Carioca yarn (1 oz. tube) was used for this top. You need: 24 (25, 27) tubes.

Tools: Straight Knitting Needles, Nos. 4 and 6 (Bernat-Aero) or any size needles that will give the stitch gauge given below.
Circular Needle No. 4.

Gauge: 6 sts = 1 inch; 8 rows = 1 inch.

Pattern Stitch A

Rows 1 and 3: K 14 (17, 20), * K 2 tog, yo, K 1, yo, sl 1, K 1, psso, K 17 (19, 21) *, rep between *'s, ending K 14 (17, 20) instead of K 17 (19, 21).

Row 2 and all even rows: P.

Rows 5, 7, 9, 11 and 13: K.

Rows 15 and 17: K 3 (5, 7), rep between *'s of Row 1, ending K 3 (5, 7) instead of K 17 (19, 21).

Rows 19, 21, 23, 25, and 27: K.

Row 28: P.

Repeat these 28 rows for pat st A.

Directions to Follow

Back: Using smaller straight needles, cast on 98 (110, 122) sts. K 1, P 1 in ribbing for 3 inches, inc 1 st at end of last row—99 (111, 123) sts. Change to larger needles and work even in pat st A until piece meas 13½ inches, ending with a P row.

Shape Armholes: At the beg of each of the next 2 rows bind off 7 (7, 8) sts. Dec 1 st each end of needle every other row 5 (6, 7) times. Work even on 75 (85, 93) sts until armholes meas 5 (5½, 6) inches, ending with a right side row.

Shape Neck: P 30 (35, 37) sts, join another ball of yarn and bind off center 15 (15, 19) sts, P to end of row. Working on both sides at once in pat as established, at each neck edge bind off 4 (5, 5) sts 4 times. Work even in pat as established on rem 14 (15, 17) sts of each side until armholes meas 7¼ (7¾, 8¼) inches.

Shape Shoulders: At each arm edge bind off 7 (7, 8) sts once and 7 (8, 9) sts once.

Front: Work to correspond to back until piece meas 10 inches, ending with a P row.

Shape Neck: Work 46 (52, 58) sts, K 2 tog, K 1, sl center st onto a holder, join another ball of yarn and K 1, sl 1, K 1, psso, work to end of row. Working on both sides at once and working in pat as established, at each neck edge dec 1 st in same manner as before every other row 2 (8, 10) times more and then

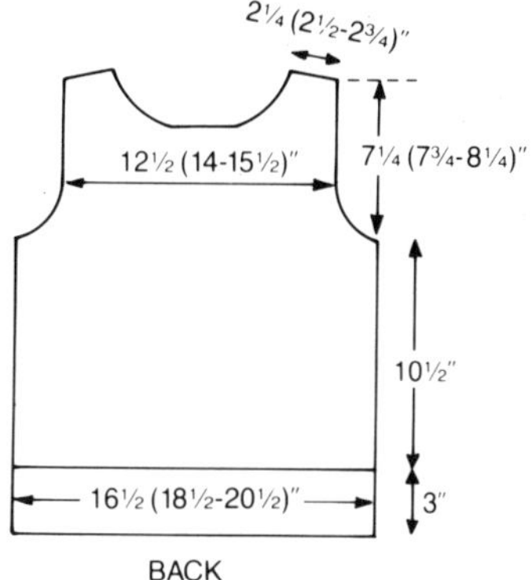

BACK

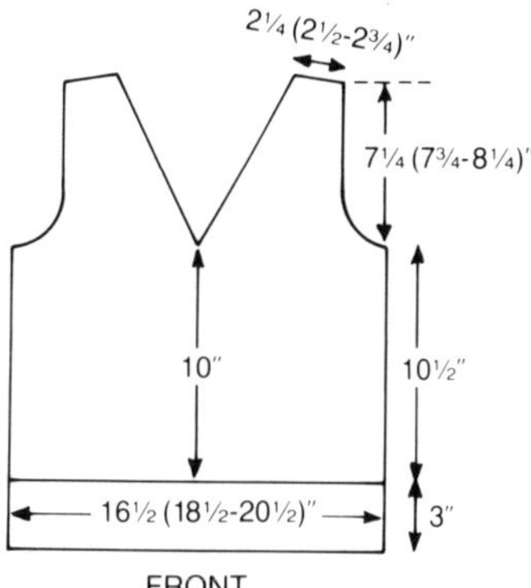

FRONT

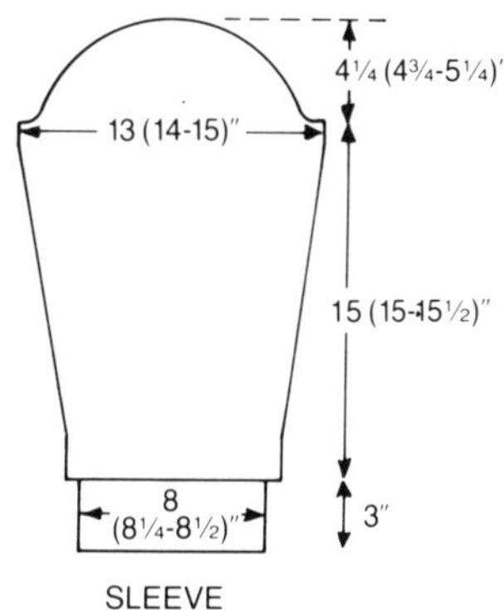

SLEEVE

every 4th row 19 (17, 17) times, and *at the same time,* when piece meas 13½ inches, ending with the same row of pat st as on back at underarm.

Shape Armholes: At each arm edge bind off 7 (7, 8) sts. Dec 1 st at same edges every other row 6 (7, 8) times. When all neck decs have been completed, work even, if necessary, on 14 (15, 17) sts until armholes meas 7¼ (7¾, 8¼) inches.

Shape Shoulders: At each arm edge bind off 7 (7, 8) sts once and 7 (8, 9) sts once.

Pattern Stitch B

Row 1: K 2, * sl 1, K 1, psso, yo, K 2 tog, rep from * across row.

Row 2: P 1, * K, P in yo, P 2, rep from *, ending last rep P 3 instead of P 2.

Row 3: * Sl 1, K 1, psso, yo, K 2 tog, rep from *, ending K 2.

Row 4: P 1, * P 2, K, P in yo, rep from *, ending P 1.

Rep these 4 rows for lower part of sleeve.

Sleeves: Using smaller straight needles, cast on 48 (50, 52) sts. K 1, P 1 in ribbing for 3 inches, inc to 54 (62, 70) sts, evenly spaced across last row. Change to larger needles. Work even in pat st B for lower part of sleeve for 14 rows, inc 1 st at end of last row—55 (63, 71) sts. Working in pat st A and starting with Row 5, inc 1 st each end of needle every 1 inch 12 (11, 10) times, forming new patterns as sts are inc. Work even in pat as established on 79 (85, 91) sts until piece meas 18 (18, 18½) inches, ending with same row of pat st as on back at underarm.

Shape Cap: At the beg of each of the next 2 rows bind off 7 (7, 8) sts. Dec 1 st each end of needle every other row for 4¼ (4¾, 5¼) inches. At the beg of each of the next 6 rows bind off 3 sts. Bind off rem sts.

Finishing: Sew underarm, shoulder, and sleeve seams. Set in sleeves.

Neckband: With right side facing you, using circular needle and starting at right front neck edge, pick up and K 77 (79, 81) sts, 58 (62, 66) sts at back neck, 77 (79, 81) sts at left front neck edge, put a marker on needle, sl st from holder for center front onto needle and K this st, put a marker on needle—213 (221, 229) sts.

Round 1: K 2 tog (neck dec), K 2, * sl 1, K 1, psso, yo, wrapping yarn around needle twice, K 2 tog, rep from *, ending K 2, sl 1, K 1, psso (neck dec), K 1 (center st).

Round 2: K 2 tog (neck dec), K 2, * dropping extra wrap, K 1, P 1 in yo, K 2, rep from *, ending K 2, sl 1, K 1, psso (neck dec), K 1.

Round 3: K 2 tog (neck dec), yo, * K 2 tog, sl 1, K 1, psso, yo, wrapping yarn around needle twice, rep from *, ending K 2 tog, K 2, sl 1, K 1, psso (neck dec), K 1.

Round 4: K 2 tog (neck dec), * K 2, dropping extra wrap, K 1, P 1 in yo, rep from *, ending K 2, sl 1, K 1, psso (neck dec), K 1.

Round 5: Rep Round 3, ending K 2 tog, K 2, sl 1, K 1, psso, K 1.

Rounds 6, 8, 10, 12, and 14: Rep Round 4.

Rounds 7, 9, 11, and 13: Rep Round 5. Continuing to dec 1 st each side of center st, K 1, P 1 in ribbing for 5 rounds. Bind off in ribbing.

SHAWL AND SACQUE

This adorable set is made by using the same combinations of stitches. Adding a lovely border of fan stitches to center of easy-to-make garter stitches produces the dainty look. The contrast in stitch patterns is most effective.

FAN STITCH SHAWL

Information to Study Before You Begin

Size: Measures 41 inches square.
Materials: 12 oz. of White (No. 1) in Coats and Clark's Red Heart "Baby Wintuk" Pompadour, 3-ply ("Tangleproof" pull-out skeins).
Tools: Knitting Needles, No. 8.
Gauge: 5 sts = 1 inch; 10 rows = 1 inch.

Directions to Follow

Starting at one side of center square, cast on 100 sts.
Rows 1–200: Sl 1, K across.
Border—
Row 1 (right side): K 4, * inc 1 st in next st, K 9. Rep from * across, end with inc 1 st in next st, K 5, place a marker to indicate right side of work—110 sts.
Row 2: K 2, yo, K 9, * (yo, K 1) 8 times; (K 2 tog) twice; K 4, (K 2 tog) twice. Rep from * to within last 11 sts, K 9, yo, K 2—136 sts.
Rows 3–7: K across.
Row 8: K 2, (yo, K 1) twice; K 4, (K 2 tog) 4 times; * (yo, K 1) 8 times; (K 2 tog) 8 times. Rep from * to within last 24 sts, (yo, K 1) 8 times; (K 2 tog) 4 times; K 4, (yo, K 1) twice; K 2—140 sts.
Rows 9–13: K across.
Note: **Between each of the following rows, rep Rows 9–13.**
Row 14: K 2, (yo, K 1) 3 times; K 3, (K 2 tog) 5 times; * (yo, K 1) 8 times; (K 2 tog) 8 times. Rep from * to within last 26 sts, (yo, K 1) 8 times; (K 2 tog) 5 times; K 3, (yo, K 1) 3 times; K 2—144 sts.
Row 20: K 2, (yo, K 1) 4 times; K 2, (K 2 tog) 6 times; * (yo, K 1) 8 times; (K 2 tog) 8 times. Rep from * to within last 28 sts, (yo, K 1) 8 times; (K 2 tog) 6 times; K 2, (yo, K 1) 4 times; K 2—148 sts.
Row 26: K 2, (yo, K 1) 5 times; K 1, (K 2 tog) 7 times; * (yo, K 1) 8 times; (K 2 tog) 8 times. Rep from * to within last 30 sts, (yo, K 1) 8 times; (K 2 tog) 7 times; K 1, (yo, K 1) 5 times; K 2—152 sts.
Row 32: K 3, (yo, K 1) 5 times; * (K 2 tog) 8 times; (yo, K 1) 8 times. Rep from * to within last 24 sts, (K 2 tog) 8 times; (yo, K 1) 5 times; K 3—154 sts.
Row 38: K 1, K 2 tog, (yo, K 1) 6 times; * (K 2 tog) 8 times; (yo, K 1) 8 times. Rep from * to within last 25 sts. (K 2 tog) 8 times; (yo, K 1) 6 times; K 2 tog, K 1—156 sts.
Row 44: K 2, K 2 tog, (yo, K 1) 6 times; * (K 2 tog) 8 times; (yo, K 1) 8 times. Rep from * to within last 26 sts, (K 2 tog) 8 times; (yo, K 1) 6 times; K 2 tog, K 2—158 sts.
Row 50: K 2, K 2 tog, (yo, K 1) 7 times; * (K 2 tog) 8 times; (yo, K 1) 8 times. Rep from * to within last 27 sts, (K 2 tog) 8 times; (yo, K 1) 7 times; K 2 tog, K 2—162 sts.
Row 56: K 2, (K 2 tog) twice; (yo, K 1) 7 times; * (K 2 tog) 8 times; (yo, K 1) 8 times. Rep from * to within last 29 sts, (K 2 tog) 8 times; (yo, K 1) 7 times; (K 2 tog) twice; K 2—164 sts.
Row 62: K 2, (K 2 tog) twice; * (yo, K 1) 8 times; (K 2 tog) 8 times. Rep from * to within last 14 sts, (yo, K 1) 8 times; (K 2 tog) twice; K 2—168 sts.
Row 68: K 4, (K 2 tog) twice; * (yo, K 1) 8 times; (K 2 tog) 8 times. Rep from * to within last 16 sts, (yo, K 1) 8 times; (K 2 tog) twice; K 4—172 sts.
Row 74: K 3, (K 2 tog) 3 times; (yo, K 1) 9 times; * (K 2 tog) 8 times; (yo, K 1) 8 times. Rep from * to within last

34 sts, (K 2 tog) 8 times; (yo, K 1) 9 times; (K 2 tog) 3 times; K 3—176 sts.

Rows 75–79: K across. Bind off very loosely.

Working along opposite side of cast-on sts, pick up and K 110 sts.

Rep **Rows 2–79.** Bind off as before.

Work border on rem 2 sides in same way. Sew corners together.

GARTER STITCH SACQUE

Information to Study Before You Begin

Sizing: Directions are given for 6 Months Size. Changes for 1 Year and 18 Months Sizes are shown in brackets.

Materials: 4 [5, 5] ounces of White (No. 1) in Coats and Clark's Red Heart "Baby Wintuk" + Pompadour, 3-ply ("Tangleproof" pull-out skeins).

1 yard of ribbon, ½ inch wide.

Tools: Knitting Needles,

No. 3 for Size 6 Months.

No. 4 for Size 1 Year.

No. 6 for Size 18 Months.

Crochet Hook, Size F.

Gauge: Garter Stitch:

No. 3 Needles, 13 sts = 2 inches; 14 rows = 1 inch.

No. 4 Needles, 12 sts = 2 inches; 13 rows =1 inch.

No. 6 Needles, 11 sts = 2 inches; 11 rows = 1 inch.

BLOCKING MEASUREMENTS

Sizes	6 Mos.	1 Year	18 Mos.
Body Chest Size *(In Inches)*			
	19	20	21
Actual Knitting Measurements: Chest			
	20	21	22
Length from back of neck to lower edge			
	9	10	11
Length from underarm to lower edge			
	5½	6¼	6½
Length of sleeve seam			
	6	6½	7
Width across sleeve at upper arm			
	8	8¾	9½

Directions to Follow

Sacque is worked in one piece from lower edge to underarm.

Starting at lower edge with No. 3 [No. 4, No. 6] needles, cast on 193 sts.

Rows 1–3: Knit.

Row 4: K 1, (yo, K 1) 4 times; * (K 2 tog) 8 times; (yo, K 1) 8 times. Rep from * across, end last rep with (yo, K 1) 4 times instead of 8 times. Rep Rows 1–4 for pattern until piece meas 5½ [6¼, 6½] inches, end with Row 3. Now divide sts as follows: **Next Row (right side):** (K 1, K 2 tog) 16 times; place these 32 sts on a stitch holder to be worked later for right front yoke; (K 2 tog) twice; K 1, (K 2 tog, K 2) 22 times; (K 2 tog) twice; place these 71 sts on another stitch holder for back yoke; (K 2 tog, K 1) 16 times. Leave the last 32 sts on needle for left front yoke.

Left Front Yoke: Row 1: K to within last 2 sts, K 2 tog—**one st decreased at armhole edge.** Work in garter st (K each row), decreasing one st at armhole edge every 4th row until 28 sts rem. End at armhole edge. Place these sts on a holder to be used later. Break off.

Back Yoke: Slip sts from back stitch holder onto needle. With wrong side facing, attach yarn to first st. Working in garter st, dec one st at both ends of next and every 4th row until 63 sts rem. Place these sts on another holder. Break off.

Right Front Yoke: Slip sts from right front holder onto needle. With wrong side facing, attach yarn to first st. Working in garter st, dec one st at armhole edge on next and every 4th row until 28 sts rem, end at front edge. Place these stitches on another holder. Do not break off yarn.

Sleeve (make 2): Starting at lower edge, cast on 40 sts. Work in K 1, P 1 ribbing for ¾ inch.

Next Row: Increasing 13 sts evenly spaced, K across—53 sts. Work even in garter st until total length is 6 [6½, 7] inches. Mark each end st of last row to indicate beg of armhole. Continuing in garter st, dec one st at both ends of next and every 4th row until 45 sts rem. Place sts on a holder. Break off.

Now place sts from all holders onto needle in the following order: Left front yoke, one sleeve, back yoke, other sleeve, and right front yoke—209 sts on needle. Pick up dropped yarn at right front edge and work across all sts on needle as follows:

Row 1: K 27, K 2 tog, K 43, K 2 tog, K 61, K 2 tog, K 43, K 2 tog, K 27—205 sts.

Row 2: K across.

Row 3: K 7, * K 2 tog, K 7. Repeat from * across.

Rows 4–6: K across.

Row 7: K 7, * K 2 tog, K 6. Rep from * across. Continue in this manner, decreasing 22 sts every 4th row and having one st less between decreases until 51 sts rem.

Neck Shaping: Bind off 10 sts at beg of next 2 rows. Bind off 5 sts at beg of following 2 rows. Bind off rem sts. Pin out to measurements, dampen, and leave to dry. Sew sleeve and underarm seams.

Front-and-Neckband: With right side facing, using crochet hook, attach yarn to lower corner of right front.

Row 1: Ch 1, sc evenly along front edge to corner at neck, ch 5, skip ¼ inch of neck edge, dc in neck edge, * ch 2, skip ¼ inch of neck edge, dc in neck edge. Rep from * to within ¼ inch of opposite corner, ch 5, sc in corner st, sc evenly to lower corner of left front. Break off and fasten.

Row 2: Attach yarn to first sc of right front, ch 1, sc in same place, * ch 1, skip next sc, sc in next sc. Rep from * to first sp at neck; ch 1, in each sp along neck edge make sc, ch 1, and dc. Work along left front edge to correspond with opposite edge. Break off and fasten.

Draw ribbon through sps of neckband.

LACY BABY SET

This lovely blanket, sacque, and bonnet set is the perfect gift for the new baby. The pattern stitch creates an interesting textured contrast to the garter stitch border.

Information to Study Before You Begin

Sizing: Directions are for Infant Size. Changes for 6 Months and 1 Year Sizes are in parentheses.

• FINISHED MEASUREMENTS—

Sacque: Chest, 20 (21, 22) inches.

Width of back at underarm, 10 (10½, 11) inches.

Width of each front at underarm, 5 (5¼, 5½) inches.

Bonnet: Width across back, 3 (3¼, 3½) inches.

Depth from front edge to back, 3½ (3¾, 4) inches.

Length around front, 11½ (12, 12½) inches.

Blanket: Approximately 26 × 32 inches.

Materials: To make the set, you need 8 (9, 10) balls (1 oz.) of Columbia-Minerva Monique.

Tools: Knitting Needles, Nos. 6 and 8. Crochet Hook, Size E.

Gauge: Pattern Stitch, No. 8 Needle 9 sts = 2 inches; 6 rows = 1 inch.

Pattern Stitch: Multiple of 3 sts.

Row 1 (wrong side): K 2, * yo, K 3, pass first of last 3 sts over last 2 sts; rep from * across, end K 1.

Rows 2 and 4: K across.

Row 3: K 1, * K 3, pass first st over last 2 sts, yo; rep from * across, end K 2. Rep Rows 1 through 4 for pat.

Directions to Follow

BLANKET

With No. 8 needles, cast on 117 sts. Work 9 rows in garter st (K each row).

Pat—Row 1: K 6 for border, work in pat st to within last 6 sts, K 6 for border. Keeping 6 sts at each side edge in garter st, work pat st over rem 105 sts until 31 inches from beg, end with row 2 or 4. K 8 rows. Bind off.

SACQUE

Back: With No. 8 needles, cast on 47 (53, 59) sts. Work 3 rows in garter st (K each row).

Pat—Row 1: K 1 for edge st, work in pat to within last st, K 1 for edge st. K first and last st of every row and working rem sts in pat st, work even until 6 (7, 8) inches from beg, end with pat row 1 or 3.

Shape Sleeves: Cast on 23 (26, 29) sts at beg of next row, K 3, place marker on needle, work across in pat, drop yarn; with separate strand of yarn cast 23 (26, 29) sts on free needle for 2nd sleeve, with dropped yarn, join and work across in pat to within last 3 sts, place marker on needle, K 3; 93 (105, 117) sts. Carry markers. Keeping 3 sts each end in garter st, work rem sts in pat until 3½ (4, 4½) inches above cast-on edge of sleeve, end with pat Row 1 or 3. Mark last row for shoulder.

Divide for Neck and Fronts—

Next Row: Work in pat across first 36 (42, 45) sts, join 2nd ball of yarn, work across next 21 (21, 27) sts and sl to holder for neck, work to end. Working each side separately, at each neck edge inc 1 st every right-side row 9 (9, 12) times, (work inc sts in garter st until there are 3 sts for a pat rep), then cast on 3 sts once; 48 (54, 60) sts each side. Working 3 sts at front edges in garter st, work even until sleeves are 7 (8, 9) inches from cast on edge. At each sleeve edge, bind off 23 (26, 29) sts once; 25 (28, 31) sts each side. Working 1 each side edge and 3 sts at front edge in garter st, work even until 3 rows less than back to lower edge, end with pat row 2 or 4. K 2 rows. Bind off.

Finishing: Sew side and sleeve seams.

Neckband: Right side facing, with No. 6 needles, beg at right front edge, pick up 3 sts in cast-on sts, 18 (19, 20) sts along side edge, K 21 (21, 27) sts from back holder, pick up 18 (19, 20) sts along side edge, 3 sts in cast-on sts; 63 (65, 73) sts. K 2 rows.

Beading Row: K 1, * yo, K 2 tog; rep from * across. K 1 row. Bind off.

Tie: With Size E hook and 2 strands of yarn, make a ch 28 inches long. Fasten off. Weave ch through beading row on neckband. Make 2 1-inch pompons and attach one to each tie.

BONNET

Front Section: With No. 8 needles, cast on 48 (54, 60) sts for front edge. K 3 rows for border.

Pat—Row 1: K 3, place marker on needle, work in pat st to within last 3 sts, place marker on needle, K 3. Working 3 sts at each side edge in garter st and rem sts in pat st, work even until 4 (4½, 5) inches from beg, end with pat row 1 or 3.

Back: Next Row: Bind off first 16 (18, 20) sts, K next 15 (18, 20) sts for back section, join 2nd ball of yarn, bind off last 16 (18, 20) sts. Work back section in garter st until 3 (4, 4½) inches above side bind-off, or until back piece is same length as bound-off edges of front section.

Finishing: Sew side back edges to bound-off edges of front section.

Neckband: Right side facing, with No. 6 needles, pick up 23 (23, 25) sts along side neck edge, 16 (18, 20) sts along back edge, 23 (23, 25) sts along side edge; 62 (64, 70) sts. Work same as neckband of sacque. Make tie and pompons same as for sacque.

STRIPED CABLE SWEATER

Three pattern stitches and colors are used to create this roomy pullover from France. The "Big Brother" look seems right for both women and men.

Information to Study Before You Begin

Sizing: Directions are written for the Petite Size. Changes for Small, Medium, and Large Sizes are in parentheses.

• GARMENT MEASUREMENTS:

At underarm around sweater about 37½ (41, 44½, 48) inches.

Width across dropped shoulders about 18¾ (20½, 22¼, 24) inches.

Width of sleeve at underarm about 16 (16¾, 17½, 18½) inches.

Length from shoulder to lower edge about 25 (26, 27, 28) inches.

Materials: Laine Plassard Musarde yarn in 50 gr skeins was used for this sweater. Musarde is a homespun type of wool/alpaca blend. The texture is irregular and the color variegated. Be sure to read the suggestions on the back of the label for knitting with Musarde. You need:

For Petite and Small Sizes, 7 skeins of Gres 89 (A) for the Main Color (MC).

For Medium Size, 8 skeins for the Main Color (MC).

For Large Size, 9 skeins for the Main Color (MC).

For the color contrasts in all sizes: 4 skeins of Blue 90 (B); 3 skeins of Ecru 91 (C).

Tools: Knitting Needles, Nos. 4 and 7. Tapestry Needle.

Gauge (Stockinette st on No. 7) 19 sts = 4 inches.

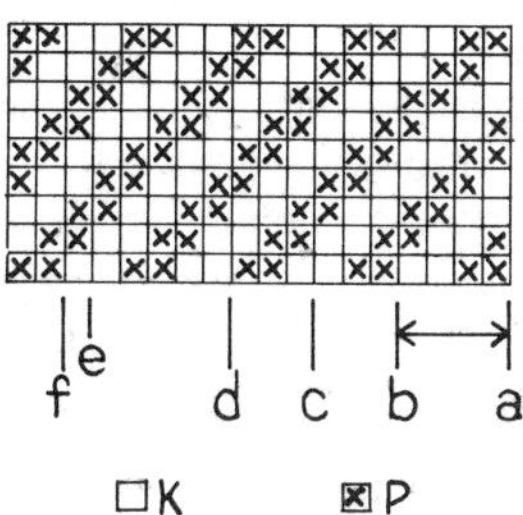

Directions to Follow

Back: With No. 4 needles and A, loosely cast on 95 (104, 113, 122) sts.

Petite and Medium Sizes Only:

Row 1 (wrong side): K 1, * P 1, K 1; rep from * across row.

Row 2: P 1, * K 1, P 1; rep from *. Rep Rows 1 and 2 until ribbing meas 2½ inches ending with Row 2.

Small and Large Sizes Only: Beg on wrong side, work in K 1, P 1, ribbing for 2½ inches ending on right side of work.

All Sizes: Change to No. 7 needles and beg on wrong side, work in cable pat:

Row 1, 3, 5: K 5, * P 4, K 5; rep from * across.

Row 2: P 5, * sl next 2 sts onto cable needle and hold in front of work, K next 2 sts on left-hand needle, K 2 sts from cable needle, P 5; rep from * across row.

Rows 4, 6: P 5, * K 4, P 5; rep from *. Rep Rows 1 through 6 for pat for 23 rows in all. Change to B and wheat st:

Petite and Medium Sizes Only:

Rows 1, 4: K 1, * P 1, K 1; rep from *.

Rows 2, 3: P 1, * K 1, P 1; rep from *. Rep Rows 1 through 4 for pat until it meas 2 inches; end on wrong side.

Small and Large Sizes Only:

Rows 1, 4: K 1, P 1, across row.

Rows 2, 3: P 1, K 1, across row. Rep Rows 1 through 4 until pat meas 2 inches ending on wrong side.

All Sizes: Change to C and diagonal pat following 9 rows of chart. Rep from "a" to "b" across row ending at "c" ("d," "e," "f").

Continue in this manner, working each pat in this order until back meas 25 (26, 27, 28) inches from beg. Bind off marking center 33 (36, 39, 42) sts for back of neck.

Front: Work as for back until it meas 21½ (22½, 23½, 24¾) inches from beg; end on wrong side of work.

Shape Neck: Mark center 13 (16, 19, 22) sts. On next row work over to then bind off marked sts, complete row. Working on right-hand side only and continuing pat, at neck edge bind off on every other row 4 sts, 3 sts, 2 sts; dec 1 st at neck edge on next row. Work even over 31 (34, 37, 40) sts until same length as back. Bind off.
Join wool at first bound-off neck st and complete left-hand side of neck to correspond, reversing shaping.

Sleeves: With No. 4 needles and A, loosely cast on 38 (40, 44, 48) sts. Beg on wrong side, work in K 1, P 1, ribbing for 2½ inches; end on right side of work, inc 16 sts at even intervals across last row—54 (56, 60, 64) sts. Change to No. 7 needles and cable pat. First row will be: P 2, K 5 (P 3, K 5/K 1/K 3), P 4, K 5; rep from * across row ending with P 2 (P 3/P 4, K 1/P 4, K 3). In same manner as for body, continue in pat and stripe sequence. Inc 1 st at each end of needle on every 4th and 6th rows alternately until there are 82 (86, 90, 94) sts in all, working added sts in to pat as possible. When sleeve meas 18 (19¾, 20½, 21¼) inches or desired length of sleeve to dropped shoulder, bind off loosely marking center of row.

Finishing: On wrong side, sew front to back at right shoulder. On right side, with No. 4 needles and A, pick up sts around neck front and across back between marks—about 80 (86, 94, 102) sts in all. Work in K 1, P 1, ribbing for about 1¼ inches. Bind off loosely in ribbing.
On wrong side, sew left shoulder and ends of ribbing tog. Holding right sides tog and matching center mark of sleeve with shoulder seam, pin sleeves against body top. Sew in place. On wrong side, sew side and underarm sleeve seams, neatly overcasting sleeve ribbing.

STRIPED SWEATER

Stripes add a fashion touch to this sweater for a young girl. Its loose fit makes it easy to wear.

Information to Study Before You Begin

Sizing: Directions are for Size 26. Changes for other sizes are in parentheses. Designed to fit chest measurements: 26 (28, 30/32) inches.
Materials: Phildar yarn Relais 5 was used for this sweater. You need:
4 (5, 6) balls white (Blanc); 1 ball straw (Paille) or yellow; 1 ball blue (Gauloise).
Tools: Knitting Needles, Nos. 3 and 1.
Gauge (Stockinette st using No. 3 needle):
30 sts = 4 inches; 40 rows = 4 inches.
Stitches:
St 1: K 1, P 1 rib.
St 2: Stockinette st.

Stripe Pattern
Work 2 rows in Paille, 2 rows in Gauloise, and 26 rows in Blanc. Rep last 30 rows for Stripe Pattern.

Directions to Follow

Back: Using No. 1 needles and Blanc cast on 115 (121, 127) sts.
1st Row: K 1, * P 1, K 1; rep from * to end.
2nd Row: P 1, * K 1, P 1; rep from * to end. Rep last 2 rows until rib meas 2½ inches (6 cm).
Change to No. 3 needles and work 4 rows in stockinette st. Continue in stockinette st and following stripe pat as given at beg (starting with the 2 rows in Paille), work straight until Back measures 10 (11, 12) inches—26 (28, 30) cm ending with a P row.
Shape Armholes: Keeping stripe pat correct, cast off 9 sts at beg of next 2 rows. 97 (103, 109) sts remain * *. Work straight until armholes meas 5½ (6, 6¼) inches—14 (15, 16) cm ending with a P row.

Shape Back Neck: 1st Row: K 39 (42, 44), turn and complete this side first. Cast off 4 sts at beg of next and every alt row until 27 (30, 32) sts remain. Work 1 row straight. Cast off.
Slip next 19 (19, 21) sts at center onto a holder for neckband.
With right side of work facing, rejoin yarn to neck edge of rem sts and K to end. P 1 row. Cast off 4 sts at beg of next and every alt row until 27 (30, 32) sts rem. Cast off.

Front: Work as given for back to * *. Work straight until armholes meas 3½ (4, 4) inches—9 (10, 10) cm ending with a P row.

Shape Neck: 1st Row: K 38 (41, 43), turn and complete this side first * *. Dec 1 st at neck edge on next 6 rows, then every alt row until 27 (30, 32) sts remain. Work straight until front meas same as back to shoulder. Cast off.
Slip next 21 (21, 23) sts at center onto a holder for neckband.
With right side of work facing you, rejoin yarn to neck edge of rem sts and K to end. Complete as given for first side from * * to end.

Sleeves: Using No. 1 needles and Blanc, cast on 85 (91, 97) sts and work 10 rows in K 1, P 1 rib as given for back. Change to No. 3 needles and work 10 rows in stockinette st.
Continuing in stockinette st and foll stripe pat as given at beg (starting with the 2 rows in Paille), inc 1 st at each end of next and every foll 6th (8th, 10th) row until there are 97 (103, 109) sts. Work straight until sleeve meas 6 (6¾, 7½) inches—15 (17, 19) cm or required seam length. Tie a marker at each end of last row. Work 12 more rows. Cast off.

Finishing: Press pieces on wrong side, using a hot iron over a damp cloth. Join left shoulder seam.

Neckband: With right side of work facing you and using No. 1 needles and Blanc, pick up and K 12 sts down right back neck. K across sts on holder at back neck decreasing 1 st at center, pick up and K 12 sts up left back neck, 27 (27, 31) sts down left front slope. K across sts on holder at front and pick up and K 27 (27, 31) sts up right front slope.

1st Row: P 1, * K 1, P 1; rep from * to end. Keeping rib correct, work 9 more rows. Cast off loosely in rib.
Join right shoulder seam and ends of neckband. Join side seams. Join sleeve seams to markers. Insert sleeves. Press seams.

Note: Measurements are in centimeters.

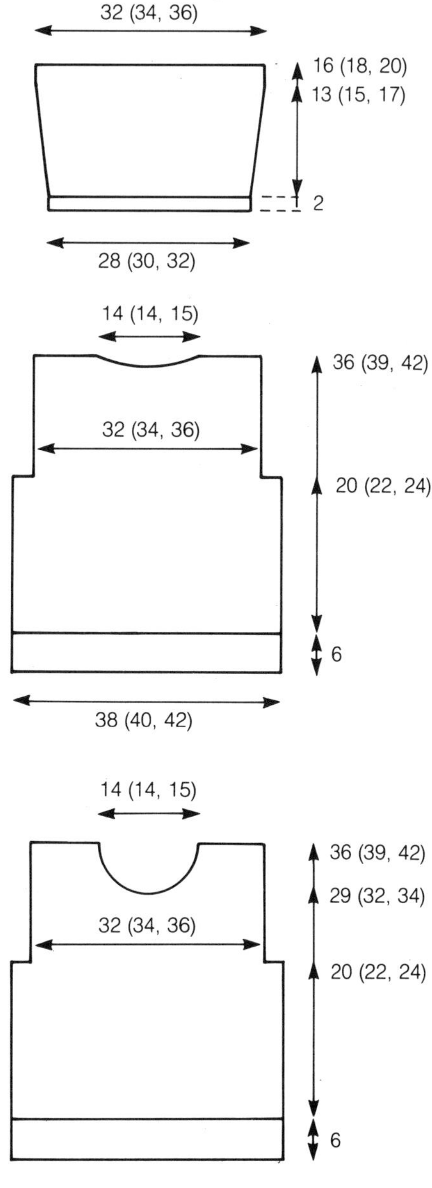

HIS AND HER SWEATER

Although this sweater is shown on a man, it is just as appropriate for a woman. The raglan sleeves and textured yarn give the design a smart, casual look.

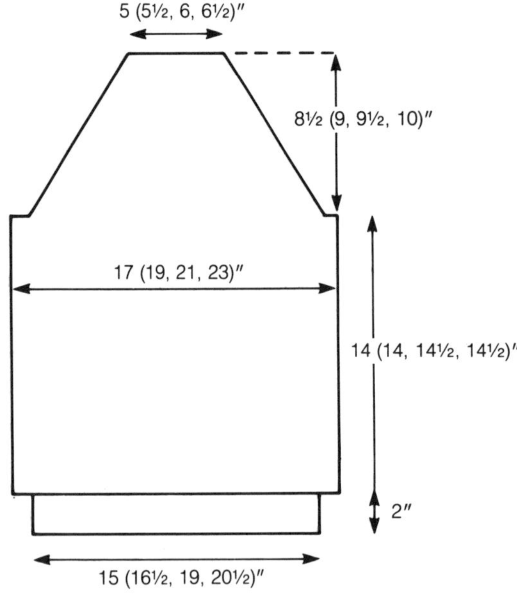

BACK AND FRONT

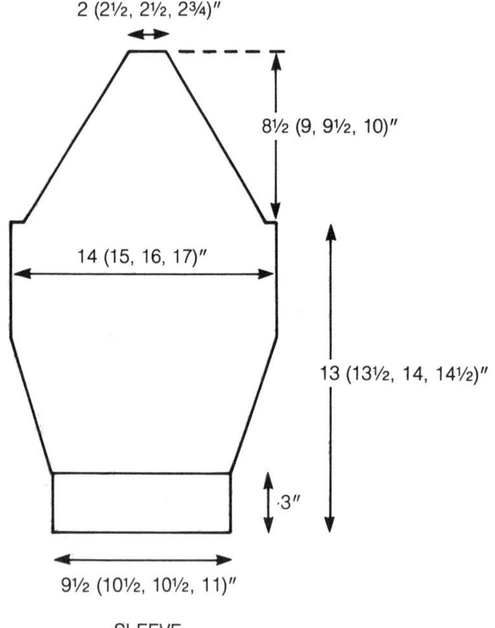

SLEEVE

Information to Study Before You Begin

Sizing: *For Women,* Small (32–34), Medium (36–38), Large (40–42), Extra Large (44–46).
For Men, Small is Women's Medium Size (36–38), Medium (40–42), Large (44–46).
The directions given here are for Women's Small Size. Changes for other sizes are in parentheses.
Materials: *For the Main Color* (MC), you need 7 (7, 8, 8) balls of Bernat Calico (50 gr).
For the Contrasting Color (CC), you need 5 (5, 6, 6) balls of Bernat Saluki™ (50 gr).
Tools: Knitting Needles, Nos. 11 and 13 (Bernat U.S.).
Crochet Hook, Size 4.50 mm (G).
Gauge: 5 sts = 2 inches.
Note 1: When working K 1, P 1 in ribbing, always K in *back* of each K st.
Note 2: CC is used double for ribbing at lower edges, cuffs, and neckband.

Directions to Follow

Back: Using smaller needles and CC double, cast on 38 (42, 48, 52) sts. K 1, P 1 in ribbing for 2 inches, inc 5 (6, 5, 6) sts evenly spaced on last row. Drop 1 strand CC; join 1 strand MC. Change to larger needles and using 1 strand each of MC and CC, work even in stockinette st on 43 (48, 53, 58) sts until piece meas 16 (16, 16½, 16½) inches or desired length to underarm, ending with a P row.
Shape Full-fashioned Raglan Armholes: At the beg of each of the next 2 rows bind off 1 st.
Row 3: K 1, sl 1, K 1, psso, K to last 3 sts, K 2 tog, K 1.
Rows 4 and 6: Purl.
Row 5: Knit. Rep Rows 3 through 6 two (1, 0, 0) times more, then repeat Row 3 and 4 *only* 11 (14, 17, 19) times more. Sl rem 13 (14, 15, 16) sts onto a holder.

Front: Work to correspond to back.

Sleeves: Using smaller needles and CC double, cast on 24 (26, 26, 28) sts. K 1, P 1 in ribbing for 3 inches, inc 1 (0, 0, 1) st at end of last row. Drop 1 strand CC; join 1 strand MC. Change to larger needles and using 1 strand each of MC and CC, work in stockinette st, inc 1 st each end of needle every 1¾ inches 5 (6, 7, 7) times. Work even on 35 (38, 40, 43) sts until piece meas 16 (16½, 17, 17½) inches or desired length, ending with a P row.

Shape Full-fashioned Raglan Cap: At the beg of each of the next 2 rows bind off 1 st. Rep Rows 3 through 6 of back shaping 3 (3, 3, 4) times, then rep Rows 3 and 4 *only* of back shaping 11 (12, 13, 13) times. Sl remaining 5 (6, 6, 7) sts onto a holder.

Finishing: Using crochet hook and CC double, with right side facing you and working in sc, join right sleeve to back and front armholes and left sleeve to front armhole.

Neckband: Using smaller needles and CC double with right side facing you, pick up and K 64 (68, 72, 76) sts around neck edge, including sts from holders. K 1, P 1 in ribbing for 1 inch. Bind off in ribbing. Sew neckband. Join left sleeve to back armhole. Sew underarm and sleeve seams.

PULLOVER WITH THREE NECKLINES

This classic sweater has been designed with versatility in mind. Not only can you change the neckline, but also you can knit it in different types of yarn. Some prefer the lighter sports-weight yarn to the worsted weight.

CREW AND TURTLE NECK

Information to Study Before You Begin

Sizing: Directions are written for sizes 10, 12, 14, 16, 18.

Materials: In reading the directions, you will notice two sets of numbers in parentheses. The first set is given for sports-weight yarn; those in the second set, for worsted-weight yarn.

For sports-weight yarn, such as Berella Sportspun (2 oz.), you need 6, 7, 7, 8, 8 balls.

For worsted-weight yarn, such as Bernat Sesame 4 (4 oz.), you need 4, 4, 4, 5, 5 balls or skeins.

Tools: *For sports-weight yarn,* Knitting Needles, Nos. 3 and 5 (Bernat-Aero). Double-pointed needles, No. 3.

For worsted-weight yarn, Knitting Needles, Nos. 5 and 8. Double-pointed needles, No. 5.

Gauge: *For sports-weight yarn,* 6 sts = 1 inch; 8 rows = 1 inch on No. 5 Needles in stockinette st.

For worsted-weight yarn, 5 sts = 1 inch; 7 rows = 1 inch on No. 8 Needles in stockinette st.

Directions To Follow

Back: Using smaller straight needles, cast on (102, 108, 114, 120, 126) (86, 90, 96, 100, 106) sts. K 1, P 1 in ribbing for 2 inches. Change to larger needles and work even in stockinette st until piece meas 14 inches, ending with a P row. **Shape Full-fashioned Raglan Armholes:** At the beg of each of the next 2 rows bind off (7, 8, 9, 10, 11) (4, 4, 5, 5, 6) sts. **Row 3:** K 2, K 2 tog, K to last 4 sts, sl 1, K 1, psso, K 2. **Row 4:** Purl. Rep the last 2 rows (29, 30, 31, 32, 33) (25, 26, 27, 28, 29) times more. Sl rem (28, 30, 32, 34, 36) (26, 28, 30, 32, 34) sts onto a holder.

Front: Work to correspond to back until there are (44, 46, 48, 50, 52) (42, 44, 46, 48, 50) sts on needle, ending with a K row. **Shape Neck:** P 13, sl center (18, 20, 22, 24, 26) (16, 18, 20, 22, 24) sts onto a holder, join another ball of yarn and P last 13 sts. Working on both sides at once, continue to dec 1 st at each arm edge in same manner as before every other row 8 times more, and *at the same time,* at each neck edge dec 1 st every other row 3 times. Sl rem 2 sts of each side onto a holder.

Sleeves: Using smaller straight needles, cast on (42, 44, 46, 48, 50) (40, 42, 44, 44, 46) sts. K 1, P 1 in ribbing for 2½ inches. Change to larger needles and work in stockinette st, inc 1 st each end of needle every (¾, ¾, ¾, ½, ½) (1) inch (18, 19, 20, 21, 22) (12, 12, 13, 14, 15) times. Work even on (78, 82, 86, 90, 94) (64, 66, 70, 72, 76) sts until piece meas 18 inches, ending with a P row. **Shape Full-fashioned Raglan Cap:** At the beg of each of the next 2 rows bind off (7, 8, 9, 10, 11) (4, 4, 5, 5, 6) sts. Dec in same manner as on back. Sl rem 4 sts onto a holder.

Finishing: Sew sleeves to back and front armholes. Sew underarm seams.

Neckband: Using dpn, with right side facing you pick up (90, 94, 98, 102, 106) (86, 92, 96, 100, 104) sts around neck including sts from holders. K 1, P 1 in ribbing for 1 inch for Crew Neck and for 5 inches for Turtle Neck. Bind off in ribbing. Steam seams.

BERNAT YARN & CRAFT CORP. © 1966

V-NECK

Many persons prefer the V-neck version of this classic design because of its slenderizing effect. It can be very flattering.

Information to Study Before You Begin

Sizing: Directions are written for sizes 10, 12, 14, 16, 18.

Materials: In reading the directions, you will notice two sets of numbers in parentheses. The first set is given for sports-weight yarn; those in the second set, for worsted-weight yarn.

For sports-weight yarn, such as Berella® Sportspun (2 oz.), you need 6, 7, 7, 8, 8 balls.

For worsted-weight yarn, such as Bernat Sesame 4 (4 oz.), you need 4, 4, 4, 5, 5 balls or skeins.

Tools: *For sports-weight yarn,* Knitting Needles, Nos. 3 and 5. (Bernat-Aero) Double-pointed needles, No. 3.

For worsted-weight yarn, Knitting Needles, Nos. 5 and 8. Double-pointed needles, No. 5.

Gauge: *For sports-weight yarn,* 6 sts = 1 inch; 8 rows = 1 inch on No. 5 Needles in Stockinette st.

For worsted-weight yarn, 5 sts = 1 inch; 7 rows = 1 inch on No. 8 Needles in Stockinette st.

Directions to Follow

Back: Work in same manner as back of Crew Neck Pullover until (28, 30, 32, 34, 36) (26, 28, 30, 32, 34) sts rem, ending with a K row. On the next row P (13, 14, 15, 16, 17) (12, 13, 14, 15, 16) sts, P 2 tog, P to end of row. Sl rem (27, 29, 31, 33, 35) (25, 27, 29, 31, 33) sts onto a holder.

Front: Work in same manner as back until piece meas 13 inches, ending with a P row—(102, 108, 114, 120, 126) (86, 90, 96, 100, 106) sts. **Shape V Neck:** On the next row K (49, 52, 55, 58, 61) (41, 43, 46, 48, 51) sts, K 2 tog (neck dec) and sl these (50, 53, 56, 59, 62) (42, 44, 47, 49, 52) sts onto a holder for left front. **Right Front:** K 2 tog (neck dec), K to end of row. Continue to dec 1 st at neck edge every 4th row (11, 12, 13, 14, 15) (10, 11, 12, 13, 14) times more, and *at the same time,* when piece meas 14 inches, ending with a K row. **Shape Full-fashioned Raglan Armhole: Row 1:** At arm edge bind off (7, 8, 9, 10, 11) (4, 4, 5, 5, 6) sts, P to end of row. **Row 2:** K to last 4 sts, sl 1, K 1, psso, K 2. **Row 3:** Purl. Repeat the last 2 rows (29, 30, 31, 32, 33) (25, 26, 27, 28, 29) times more. Sl rem 2 sts onto a holder. **Left Front:** Sl (50, 53, 56, 59, 62) (42, 44, 47, 49, 52) sts from holder onto larger needle, join yarn at neck edge, and finish to correspond to right front, reversing all shaping. **To Dec at Arm Edge:** K 2, K 2 tog, K to end of row.

Sleeves: Work in same manner as sleeves for Crew Neck Pullover.

Finishing: Sew sleeves to back and front armholes. Sew underarm seams.

Neckband: Using dpn, with right side facing you and starting at center front, pick up (58, 60, 62, 64, 66) (52, 54, 56, 58, 60) sts along right front neck edge, including sts from holders; on 2nd needle pick up (27, 29, 31, 33, 35) (25, 27, 29, 31, 33) sts from back holder; on 3rd needle pick up (58, 60, 62, 64, 66) (52, 54, 56, 58, 60) sts along left front neck edge, including sts from holders. Work back and forth as follows: **Row 1:** P 1, * K 1, P 1, rep from * across row. **Row 2:** K 2 tog, work in ribbing as established to last 2 sts on 3rd needle, K 2 tog. **Row 3:** Work in ribbing as established. Repeat the last 2 rows until piece meas 1 inch, ending with Row 3. Then work as follows: **Row 1:** Inc 1 st, work in ribbing to last st on 3rd needle, inc 1 st in last st. **Row 2:** Work in ribbing as established. Rep the last 2 rows until entire piece meas 2 inches. Bind off loosely in ribbing. Sew center front of band and fold in half. Hem. Steam seams.

PONCHO SHAWL

Combining two panels in an unusual fashion creates an interesting wrap. A short and a long panel are sewn together to form a right angle. Although the shawl could be made in a solid color, the striped effect adds a special note. If you are in a creative mood, plan a color scheme of your own.

Information to Study Before You Begin

Size: The short panel is 18 × 28 inches. The long panel is 18 × 48 inches.

Materials: Coats and Clark's suggest their Red Heart®, 4-ply Hand Knitting Art. E267 in 4 oz. "Tangleproof" pull-out skeins. You need: 3 skeins of No. 111 Eggshell; 1 skein of No. 283 Pantile Brown; 1 skein of No. 603 Light Gold. Or if you wish, Knitting Worsted, 4-ply, Art. E234 can be used.

Tools: Knitting Needles, No. 15.

Gauge: 3 sts = 1 inch; 5 rows = 1 inch.

Note: When changing colors, always drop color not in use to wrong side of work and twist the unused color around the other to prevent making holes.

Directions to Follow

Long Panel: Starting at narrow edge, with Eggshell cast on 6 sts, drop Eggshell; with Brown cast on 8 sts, drop Brown; with another skein of Eggshell cast on 18 sts, drop Eggshell; with Gold cast on 10 sts, drop Gold; with another skein of Eggshell cast on 12 sts—54 sts.

Row 1: With Eggshell (K 1, P 1) 6 times, drop Eggshell; pick up Gold and (K 1, P 1) 5 times, drop Gold; with Eggshell (K 1, P 1) 9 times, drop Eggshell; with Brown (K 1, P 1) 4 times, drop Brown; with Eggshell (K 1, P 1) 3 times. Mark side of work facing you for right side of panel. Turn.

Row 2: With Eggshell (P 1, K 1) 3 times; with Brown (P 1, K 1) 4 times; with Eggshell (P 1, K 1) 9 times; with Gold (P 1, K 1) 5 times; with Eggshell (P 1, K 1) 6 times. Rep these 2 rows until total length is 48 inches. Bind off loosely in corresponding colors.

Short Panel: Work as for Long Panel until total length is 28 inches. Bind off as before.

Pin pieces out to measurements, dampen and leave to dry. Sew one narrow edge of short panel to a long edge of long panel to form a right angle (see Diagram).

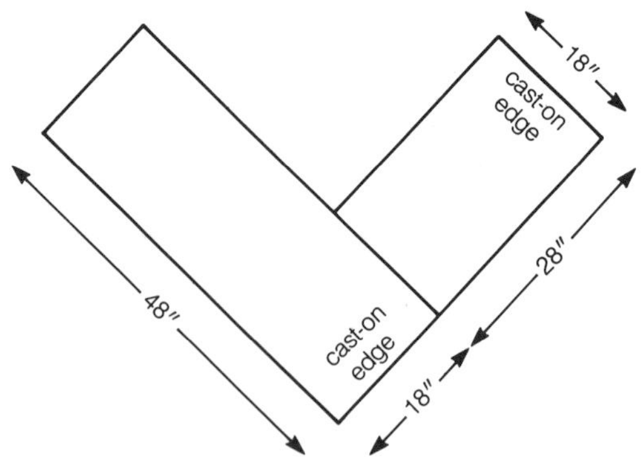

Fringe: Cut 2 strands of Eggshell each 9 inches long. Double these strands to form a loop. Insert hook in first st of one narrow edge and draw loop through. Draw loose ends through loop and pull up tightly to form a knot. Matching colors of fringes to stripes, knot 2 strands as before in each st around entire outside edge of shawl. Trim evenly.

ONE-PIECE GLOVES

If you have always thought gloves were difficult to make, you will be glad to know that they aren't when knitted in one piece in garter stitch. Although they can be made in a solid color, it is much more fun to use a crayon color for each finger.

FIVE-COLOR GLOVES

Information to Study Before You Begin

Sizing: Directions are for 1 size.
Materials: You need small amounts of Yellow (A), Red (B), Violet (C), Blue (D), Green (E) of Columbia-Minerva Nantuk 4-ply yarn in 4 oz. balls.
Tools: Knitting Needles, No. 8.
Gauge: 9 sts = 2 inches; 8 rows = 1 inch.

Directions to Follow

Beg at seam edge of little finger with A, cast on 35 sts. Work in garter st (K every row) as follows:
Little Finger—Row 1 (right side): Knit. Knit 4 rows more.
Next Row: Bind off 8 sts. Sl last st from bind-off to needle with rem sts. Cut A, leave a 4-inch end for sewing.
Ring Finger: With B, cast on 13 sts on needle with sts. K 6 rows on 40 sts.
Next Row: Bind off 10 sts. Cut B.
Middle Finger: With C, cast on 13 sts on needle with sts. K 6 rows on 43 sts.
Next Row: Bind off 13 sts.
Index Finger: With D, cast on 11 sts. K 6 rows on 41 sts. Bind off 19 sts.
Thumb: With E, cast on 8 sts. K 12 rows on 30 sts.
Next Row: Bind off 8 sts.
Index Finger: With D, cast on 19 sts. K 6 rows on 41 sts.
Next Row: Bind off 11 sts.
Middle Finger: With C, cast on 13 sts. K 6 rows on 43 sts.
Next Row: Bind off 13 sts.
Ring Finger: With B, cast on 10 sts. K 6 rows on 40 sts.
Next Row: Bind off 13 sts.
Little Finger: With A, cast on 8 sts. K 5 rows on 35 sts. Bind off all sts. Make 2nd glove in same way. Fold glove in half at thumb. Matching colors, sew seam at side and around fingers.

SOLID GLOVES

These gloves are made in the same way as the Five-Color Gloves, except that the color changes are omitted.

Information to Study Before You Begin

Sizing: Directions are for 1 size.
Materials: You need 1 ball of Winter White in Columbia-Minerva Nantuk 4-ply (4 oz. ball).
Tools: Knitting Needles, No. 8.
Gauge: 9 sts = 2 inches; 8 rows = 1 inch.

Directions to Follow

Work and finish gloves same as Five-Color Gloves, omitting color changes.

TUBE SOCKS

For those persons who want to make socks easily and quickly, this is the pattern. Although color patterns are suggested, it is possible for you to create your own design once you have learned to knit the socks. In fact, you may decide to make your first pair in a solid color.

Information to Study Before You Begin

Sizing: Directions are for Children's sizing. Changes for Women and Men are in parentheses.
Materials: Sport yarn in 2 oz. skeins is suggested.
For double-striped sock, you need 2 skeins Navy, 1 skein Yellow.
For candy-striped sock, you need 1 skein Red, 1 skein White.
For multi-striped sock, you need 1 skein each of Black, Red, Yellow, Blue, Green, Gold, Purple, Orange, Navy.
For confetti sock, you need 2 skeins Ombre.
Tools: Double-pointed Knitting Needles, Nos. 5 and 7 (Susan Bates® or Marcia Lynn®).
Gauge: 10 sts = 1 inch; 8 rows = 1 inch.

Directions to Follow

Double-Striped Sock: Make 2. Beg at top with small needles and Yellow, cast on 52 (60, 68) sts. Divide sts onto 3 needles. Work around in (K 2, P 2) ribbing for 1½ (2, 3) inches. Change to larger needles. Work with Navy for 1 (1, 1½) inches. Work 4 rows ea Yellow, Navy, and Yellow. Work with Navy until piece meas 14 (20, 24) inches, or desired length.
Shape Toe: K 2 tog all around. K 1 rnd. Rep last 2 rnds once more. Pull end through all sts and gather tog.

Multi-Striped Sock: Make 2. With Black cast on 52 (60, 68) sts. Divide sts onto 3 needles. Work around in (K 2, P 2) ribbing for 2 rnds. With Red, keeping in ribbing, work 19 (25, 29) rnds, changing to larger needles when work meas 1½ (2, 3) inches. When Red is completed, work 2 rnds Black. Work rem stripes same as Red in sequence above, working 2 rnds Black between. Finish same as Double-Striped Sock.

Candy-Striped Sock: Beg with Red make same as Double-Striped Sock, but alternate 1 inch Red, then 1 inch White stripes.

Confetti Sock: Make same as Double-Striped Sock, but all in Ombre yarn.

AFGHAN AND PILLOW

A beautiful textured effect makes this cover and pillow outstanding. Worked on large needles, it can be considered a jiffy knit.

Information to Study Before You Begin

Size: Afghan—48 × 66 inches plus fringe.
Pillow—14 × 14 inches.
Materials: Select a bulky yarn in 2 oz. skeins (75 yds. each) that will produce the gauge listed below.
For afghan, 29 skeins, Ecru.
For pillow, 5 skeins, Ecru.
Pillow form, 14 × 14 inches.
Tools: Knitting Needles, No. 35 (Susan Bates®).
Cable Stitch Holder.
To make fringe and tassels, a Susan Bates® Adjustable Trim-Tool™ can be used.
Gauge: 2 sts = 1 inch (stockinette st).
Note: Two strands of yarn are held together throughout.
K into the back of all K sts and P into the back of all P sts throughout, *except on* center 40 sts. Specific directions for some abbreviations found within the pat st follow:
C 7: Sl next 2 sts to cable holder and hold in back of work, K 1, K 2 from cable holder, K 1, sl next st to cable holder and hold in front of work, K 2, K 1 from cable holder.
RT: K 2nd st on left needle from front, then K 1st st and drop both off needle at same time.
LT: K 2nd st on left needle from back, then K 1st st from back and drop both sts off needle at same time.
Pattern Stitch—
Row 1: K 3, P 7, K 1, P 8, K 1, P 4, (K 1, P 1) twice, * (K 1, P 1, K 1) in next st, P 3 tog; rep from * 8 times, (P 1, K 1) twice, P 4, K 1, P 8, K 1, P 7, K 3.
Row 2: K 2, P 1, C 7, P 10, RT, LT, (P 1, K 1) twice, P 36, (K 1, P 1) twice, RT, LT, P 10, C 7, P 1, K 2.
Row 3: K 3, P 7, K 1, P 8, K 1, P 4, (K 1, P 1) twice, * P 3 tog, (K 1, P 1, K 1) in next st; rep from * 8 times, (P 1, K 1) twice, P 4, K 1, P 8, K 1, P 7, K 3.
Row 4: K 2, P 1, K 7, P 1, K 8, P 1, RT, LT, (P 1, K 1) twice, P 36, (K 1, P 1) twice, RT, LT, P 1, K 7, P 1, K 2.
Rep Rows 1–4 for pat st.

AFGHAN

Body: With 2 strands Ecru cast on 92 sts. Work in pat st until piece meas 66 inches. Bind off.

Fringe: With Trim-Tool™ set for 6-inch fringe. Cut fringe lengths. Using 2 strands at once, knot fringe in ea st along both short ends.

PILLOW

Pattern Stitch—
Row 1, 3: Purl.
Row 2: K 1, * P 3 tog, (K 1, P 1, K 1) in next st; rep from * across, end K 1.
Row 4: K 1, * (K 1, P 1, K 1) in next st, P 3 tog; rep from * across, end K 1.
Rep Rows 1–4 for pat st.

Front: With 2 strands Ecru cast on 30 sts. Work in pat st until piece meas 14 inches. Bind off. Make back in same manner. Sew 3 sides of both pieces tog. Insert form and sew 4th side.

Tassels: Make four 4-inch tassels. Attach tassels at ea corner.

Bibliography

Researching a book requires one to browse through the works of other authors. I found the books and booklets mentioned here, as well as the instruction leaflets of yarn manufacturers, informative and inspiring. I think you will also.

ABBEY, BARBARA. *The Complete Book of Knitting.* The Viking Press, 1974.

COATS & CLARK. *Learn to Knit—No. 190-A.* Coats & Clark Inc., 1975.

MON TRICOT. *Knit and Crochet.* Crown Publishers.

———. *Knitting Dictionary Patterns.* Crown Publishers.

NORBURY, JAMES. *Traditional Knitting Patterns.* Dover Publications, 1973.

THOMAS, MARY. *Book of Knitting Patterns.* Dover Publications, 1972. (This Dover edition is an unabridged republication of the work originally published in 1943 by Hodder and Stoughton, London.)

———. *Knitting Book.* Dover Publications, 1972. (This Dover edition is an unabridged republication of the work originally published in 1938 by Hodder and Stoughton, London.)

READ, SUSANNAH, General Editor. *The Needleworker's Constant Companion.* The Viking Press, 1979.

Reader's Digest Complete Guide to Needlework. The Reader's Digest Association, Inc., 1979.

TAYLOR, GERTRUDE. *America's Knitting Book.* Charles Scribner's Sons, 1974.

Index